3~

THE NORTHEAST

Jerry E. Jennings, Editor

CONTRIBUTORS

BENJAMIN CHINITZ
Deputy Assistant Secretary
for Economic Development
U.S. Department of Commerce
Washington, D.C.

WALTER E. HAVIGHURST
Research Professor of English
Miami University
Oxford, Ohio

CHARLES P. LOOMIS
Professor of Sociology
Michigan State University
East Lansing, Michigan

VINCENT H. MALMSTRÖM
Associate Professor of Geography
Middlebury College
Middlebury, Vermont

PENROD MOSS
Professor of Education
California State College
Dominguez Hills, California

G. ETZEL PEARCY
Chairman, Department of Geography
California State College at Los Angeles
Los Angeles, California

BERNARD A. WEISBERGER
Professor of History
The University of Rochester
Rochester, New York

ANNLEE DECENT
Manuscript Editor

LYNNE A. DEUR
Staff Writer

JAMES G. EKWALL
Staff Writer

RAYMOND E. FIDELER
Editor and President

DONALD GOOD
Staff Writer

JERRY E. JENNINGS
Senior Staff Writer

JOYCE KORTES
Manuscript Editor

RUTH MATHEWS
Manuscript Editor

MARY MITUS
Map Editor

RUTH A. MOEN
Picture Editor

CONNIE J. NEGARAN
Manuscript Editor

BETTY O'CONNOR
Staff Writer

T. J. O'CONNOR
Staff Writer

CAROL S. PRESCOTT
Senior Manuscript Editor

DOROTHY M. ROGERS
Manuscript Editor

BARB M. ROYS
Design Editor

MARION H. SMITH
Staff Writer

JANE VANDERVEER
Manuscript Editor

SONIA W. WARRINER
Manuscript Editor

AUDREY J. WITHAM
Index Editor

In the Green Mountains of New England. The Northeast is a region of mountains and valleys, cities and towns, large factories and prosperous farms.

THE NORTHEAST

Jerry E. Jennings, Editor

THE FIDELER COMPANY

GRAND RAPIDS   TORONTO

CONTENTS

Maps, Charts, and Special Studies

EDITORIAL AND MAP ACKNOWLEDGMENTS

Grateful acknowledgment is made to Scott, Foresman and Company for the pronunciation system used in this book, which is taken from the Thorndike-Barnhart Dictionary Series.

Grateful acknowledgment is made to the following for permission to use cartographic data in this book: Creative Arts: Pages 42 and 43, and top maps on page 359; Base maps courtesy of the Nystrom Raised Relief Map Company, Chicago 60618: Pages 21 and 27, and bottom map on page 359; Panoramic Studios: Page 16; Rand McNally and Company: Pages 18 and 19; United States Department of Commerce: Bureau of the Census: Pages 167 and 190.

"The Pasture," page 231: From *Complete Poems of Robert Frost*. Copyright, 1939, © 1967 by Holt, Rinehart and Winston, Inc. Reprinted by permission of Holt, Rinehart and Winston, Inc.

PICTURE ACKNOWLEDGMENTS

Grateful acknowledgment is made to the following for permission to use the illustrations found in this book:

A. Devaney, Inc.: Pages 24, 54, 114, 183 (lower), 211, 305, 313, and 319
Aero Service Corporation: Pages 204, 242, and 261
Alpha Photo Associates: Pages 45, 244, and 291
American Airlines: Pages 207, 271, and 323
Armsden: Pages 41, 276, 284, 285, and 286
Association of American Railroads: Page 102
Authenticated News International: Pages 89, 111 (right), 119, 308, and 332
Baltimore Area Convention and Visitors Council: Page 269
Beerhorst: Page 106
Bethlehem Steel Corporation: Page 266
Black Star: Pages 53, 128, 148, 177, 206, 213, 214, 217, 220, and 253

Boston Chamber of Commerce: Page 279
Bowdoin College Museum of Fine Arts: Page 84 (lower right)
Bristol Museum and Art Gallery—Bristol, England: Page 59
Brown Brothers: Page 231
Buffalo Chamber of Commerce: Page 309
Bureau of Mines: Pages 340 and 341
Bureau of Public Roads: Pages 98 and 99
Chase Manhattan Bank: Page 171 by Arthur Lavine
Connecticut Development Commission: Pages 234 and 240
Consolidated Edison Company: Page 131
Culver Pictures, Inc.: Pages 86 and 122
Cushing: Page 84 (upper right)
Delaware River Port Authority: Page 322

TO THE STUDENT

Why the social studies are important to you. During the next few years, you will make an important choice. You will choose whether or not you will direct your own life. Many people are never aware of making this choice. They drift through life, never really trying to understand what is going on around them or why things turn out the way they do. Without knowing it, these people have chosen not to direct their own lives. As a result, they miss many enriching experiences. Other people make a serious effort to choose a way of life that will bring them satisfaction. If you decide to live by choice instead of by chance, you will be able to live a more satisfying life.

You will need three types of knowledge to live by choice successfully. Living by choice will demand a great deal from you. You will have to keep growing in three different types of learnings — understandings, values and attitudes, and skills. As the chart on the opposite page shows, the type of learnings we call understandings includes the kinds of information you need in order to understand yourself, your country, and your world. The type of learnings we call values and attitudes deals with the way you feel toward yourself and your world. The third type of learnings includes the skills you need to use in gaining understandings and developing constructive values and attitudes. Among these skills are those you need for obtaining and using knowledge, and for working effectively with other people.

The social studies can help you grow in the three types of learnings. Your social studies class is one of the best places in which you can explore the three types of learnings. Here you can obtain much of the information you need for understanding yourself and your world. You can practice many important skills. Through many experiences, you can begin to evaluate what in life is worthwhile to you.

The problem-solving method will help you achieve success in social studies. Since the social studies are of such great importance, you want to use the best possible study method. You could just read a textbook and memorize answers for a test. If you did so, however, you would forget much of the information soon after the test was over. Your thinking ability would not improve, and you would not gain new, constructive values and attitudes. You would not have the opportunity to use many important skills, either. We suggest that you use a special way of studying called the problem-solving method. To use this method in learning about the Northeast, you will need to follow these steps:

1. Do some general background reading about the Northeast or about one of the states of the Northeast in which you are most interested.

2. Choose an important, interesting problem that you would like to solve. Write it down so that you will have clearly in mind what it is you want to find out. (Look at the sample problem on page 10.) If there are small problems that need to be solved in order to solve your big problem, list them, too.

3. Consider all possible solutions to your problem and list the ones that seem most likely to be true. These possible solutions are called "educated guesses," or hypotheses. You will try to solve your problem by finding facts to support or disprove your hypotheses.

4. Test your hypotheses by doing research. This book provides you with four main sources of information about the Northeast. These are the pictures, the text, the maps, and the Glossary. To locate the information you need, you may

Thinking and the Three Types of Learnings

THINKING

One of the main reasons you are attending school is to develop your ability to think clearly. Thinking includes seven different thought processes. (See definitions below.) If you learn to use your higher thought processes, rather than simply repeat information you have memorized, you will achieve greater success in school and in life. In fact, your ability to fulfill your obligations as a citizen will depend largely on how well you learn to think. Your ability to think clearly will also help you make progress in the three types of learnings included in the social studies. (See chart below.)

Seven Thought Processes

1. **Remembering** is recalling or recognizing information.
2. **Translation** is changing information from one form into another, such as words into pictures.
3. **Interpretation** is discovering relationships among facts, concepts,* and generalizations.*
4. **Application** is applying the appropriate knowledge and skills to the solution of a new problem.
5. **Analysis** is separating complicated material into its basic parts to see how those parts were put together, how they are related to each other, and how the parts are related to the whole.
6. **Synthesis** is putting ideas together in a form that is not only meaningful but also new and original.
7. **Evaluation** is judging whether something is acceptable or unacceptable, according to definite standards.

THREE TYPES OF LEARNINGS

Understandings	Values and Attitudes	Skills
Concepts	Beliefs	Obtaining knowledge
Generalizations	Appreciations	Using knowledge
Facts	Ideals	Working with others

Understandings

You will truly gain an understanding of important concepts and generalizations when you use your thought processes to organize information in meaningful ways. In turn, the concepts and generalizations you develop will help you learn to think critically about new situations you meet.

Values and Attitudes

You will develop many constructive values and attitudes as you improve your thinking ability. Success in the higher levels of thinking will bring you faith that you can solve problems and make wise decisions. In turn, positive values and attitudes will help you to develop your thinking ability.

Skills

You will be more successful in developing the social studies skills when you use your higher thought processes described above. In turn, you will find that the social studies skills will help you do the critical thinking needed for solving the many difficult problems you will face during your lifetime.

*See *Four Words To Understand*, page 10.

use the Table of Contents and the Index. The suggestions on pages 347-350 will help you to locate and evaluate other sources of information.

As you do research, make notes of all the information you find that will either support your hypotheses or disprove them. You may discover that information from one source disagrees with information from another. If this should happen, check still further and try to decide which facts are correct.

5. Summarize what you have learned. Have you been able to support one or more of your hypotheses with facts? Have you been able to disprove one or more of your hypotheses? What new facts have you learned? Do you need to do further research?

You may want to write a report about the problem. To help other people share the ideas that you have come to understand, you may decide to illustrate your research project with maps, pictures, or your own drawings. You will find helpful suggestions for writing a good report on pages 345-347.

You can use the problem-solving method throughout your life. In addition to helping you to achieve success in the social studies, the problem-solving method can help you in another way. By using it, you will learn a way of dealing with problems that will be valuable to you throughout your life. Many successful scientists, businessmen, and government leaders use this method to solve problems.

A sample problem to solve. As you study the Northeast, you may wish to investigate problems about the Northeast as a whole or about one state in this region. The following sample problem is about the Northeast as a whole:

Although the Northeast covers only about 6 percent of the total area of the United States, it is a very important part of our country. **Why is the Northeast such an important part of the United States?** In order to solve this problem, you will need to make several hypotheses. In forming your hypotheses, you will need to consider the part the Northeast has played in:

a. industry   d. education
b. trade and finance   e. government
c. the arts   f. transportation

Four Words To Understand

1. **A concept** is a big, general idea that includes many smaller, more specific ideas. An example of a concept is the idea of "trade." Many kinds of exchange are included in this idea. Two boys who exchange marbles on the playground are carrying on trade. A woman who pays money to the grocer for a loaf of bread is also carrying on trade; so is a factory that buys raw materials from other countries and sells its manufactured products overseas. Only as you come to see the various things that the word "trade" includes do you grow to understand this concept. Another example of a concept is the idea of "climate."

2. **A generalization** is a general rule or principle that expresses a meaningful relationship among two or more concepts. It is formed by drawing a conclusion from a group of facts. For example, "Through trade, all people on the earth can have a better living," is a generalization drawn from facts about trade and the way people live in various parts of the world. It includes the concepts: "trade," "all people,"

"the earth," and "a better living." These have been put together to give a significant understanding about the world. The many facts you read about, hear about, or experience will make more sense if you think of them as statements that can be combined to form meaningful generalizations. Remember, however, that if a generalization is based on wrong or insufficient facts, or is carelessly thought out, it may be false. Make certain that you understand the concepts in a generalization, and judge carefully whether or not you think it is true.

3. **Values** are the things in life that a person considers right, desirable, or worthwhile. For instance, if you believe that every individual is important, we may say that one of your values is the worth of the individual.

4. **Attitudes** are the outward expression of a person's values. For example, a person who truly values the worth of every individual will express this value by treating everyone he meets with consideration.

Part 1
Land and Climate

Autumn is a beautiful time of year in the highlands of Vermont.

1 Where Is the Northeast?

A Study Guide

1. What would you see if you could travel around the earth in a space-craft?
2. What are stars? How many stars are there in the universe?
3. What are the names of the nine main planets in the solar system?
4. On which continent is most of our country located?
5. What is the conterminous United States?
6. Which states of our country are in the Northeast? What is the District of Columbia?

A space flight begins at Cape Kennedy. It is early morning at Cape Kennedy, the United States government's huge space center on the eastern coast of Florida. Ground crews are busy making final preparations for the launching of a spacecraft that will carry astronauts into orbit around the earth.

At exactly 9:30 a.m., a huge rocket lifts off from its launching pad in a cloud of smoke and flame. Perched at the very tip of the rocket is the space-craft carrying the astronauts. At first the rocket rises slowly. Then it begins to gain speed and soars upward into the sky, heading toward the east. Soon the first section, or stage, of the rocket sep-arates from the rest and drops into the Atlantic Ocean.

A rocket lifts off from its launching pad at Cape Kennedy, Florida.

The spacecraft goes into orbit. About five minutes after lift-off, the rocket and the spacecraft are more than one hundred miles above the surface of the earth. As the second stage of the rocket drops away, the spacecraft goes into orbit. The astronauts are now launched on their journey around the earth. Their spacecraft is traveling more than seventeen thousand miles an hour. At this speed, it will circle the earth once in every ninety-six minutes.

What the astronauts can see from their spacecraft. When the astronauts look out the windows of their spacecraft, they can view a scene much like the one in the picture on this page. Below them is the curving surface of the earth. Much of it is covered with a layer of white, fleecy clouds. In places, the astronauts can catch a glimpse of the blue Atlantic Ocean.

Here in outer space, the sky appears black instead of blue. However, the

The earth and the moon photographed from a spacecraft. At high altitudes, the curve of the earth can be seen plainly. The dark object at the lower left is the nose of the spacecraft.

13

sun is still shining brightly. In the distance is the moon, which looks like a silver coin hanging in space. The moon is really a large ball of rock that travels in orbit around the earth about once every month. It is about 240,000 miles away from the earth. This may seem like a great distance to us, but it is only a short distance in outer space.

About forty-five minutes after lift-off, the spacecraft has reached the other side of the earth. Now the sun is out of sight, but the astronauts can see many tiny lights shining in the blackness of space. These are stars.

The sun is one of countless stars in the universe. The stars that the astronauts can see in the night sky are huge,

whirling balls of burning gases. Some of them are many times larger than our sun, which is also a star. However, all of them appear to be much smaller than the sun because they are such a long distance away. Even the nearest of these stars is so far from the earth that it would take a spacecraft traveling one million miles an hour almost three thousand years to reach it.

There are so many stars in space that no one could ever count them all. The stars are grouped into huge systems called galaxies. The galaxy in which our sun is located — the Milky Way — contains about 100 billion stars. Scientists believe there are billions of galaxies in the universe.

A starry night. Most of the lights shining out in space are balls of burning gases, like our sun. Others are balls of fairly solid material, like our earth. These are called planets.

Our solar system includes nine main planets. Some of these main planets, such as our earth, have one or more moons. The solar system also includes many smaller planets, called asteroids.

The earth is a planet that travels around the sun. A few of the lights that the astronauts can see from their spacecraft are balls of fairly solid material, like our earth. These are called planets. They do not give off light of their own, as the stars do. Instead, they reflect the light of the sun.

The earth on which we live is one of nine main planets that travel in orbit around the sun. These planets differ greatly in size. Some planets are much larger than the earth, and some are smaller. The planets also differ in their average distance from the sun. Several planets have one or more moons. There are also many smaller planets, called asteroids, which revolve around the sun. Together, our sun and its family of planets and smaller bodies are called the solar system. (See illustration above.)

There are oceans and continents on the earth. From their spacecraft, the astronauts can see that the earth's surface is made up partly of water and partly of land. The largest bodies of water are called oceans. They cover about three fourths of the earth's surface. The largest masses of land are called continents.

A global view. The surface of the earth is made up partly of land and partly of water. The largest masses of land are called continents, and the largest bodies of water are called oceans. North America and South America are two of the continents on our earth. They are bordered by the Atlantic and the Pacific oceans. On the map above, the dotted line outlines the Northeast.

Most of the United States is located on the continent of North America. The land area of the earth is divided into about 140 independent countries, as well as a number of territories that are not independent. Some countries, such as the United States and Canada, are very large. Others are very small. On maps, boundary lines may be drawn to show where different countries are located. These lines are only imaginary, however. If you were to fly over the earth in a spacecraft, you would not see any boundary lines. You would not be able to tell where one country ends and another begins.

Most of our country, the United States, is located on the continent of

ALASKA U.S.A.

C A N A D A

U N I T E D   S T A T E S

MEXICO

North America. Most of our country, the United States, is on this continent. The countries of Canada and Mexico are our neighbors.

CANAL ZONE (U.S.A.)

17

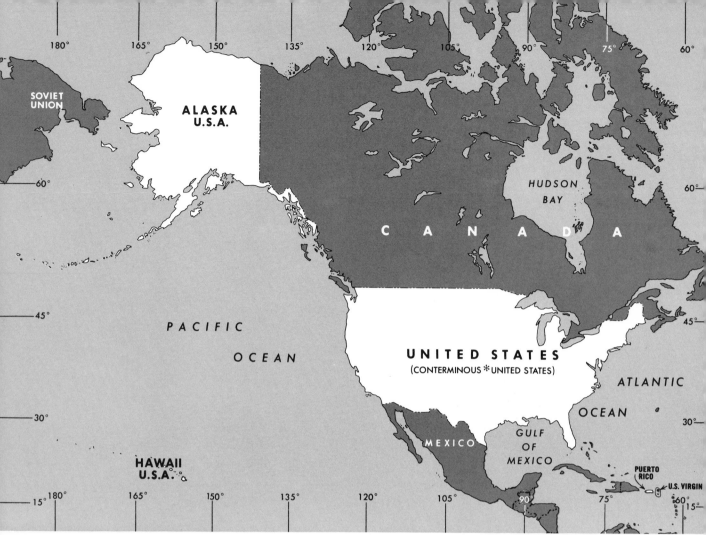

The United States. Alaska and Hawaii are separated from our other forty-eight states. The part of our country where the forty-eight states are located is called the conterminous United States.

North America. The map above shows that the countries of Canada and Mexico are our closest neighbors on this continent.

The Northeast is part of the conterminous United States. Our country is made up of fifty states. Two of these, Alaska and Hawaii, are separated from the others. Alaska, like most of our country, is located on the North American continent. Hawaii, however, is an island state in the Pacific Ocean. The part of our country that is made up of the other forty-eight states is called the conterminous United States. (Compare map above with map on pages 18 and 19.)

The Northeast is a group of twelve states located in the northeastern part of the conterminous United States. It

*See Glossary

Build Your Vocabulary

the conterminous United States   orbit   planet   lift-off   astronaut

solar system   universe   spacecraft   the Northeast   continent

United States

(CONTERMINOUS UNITED STATES)

The states in the conterminous United States may be divided into groups. The following table lists the states in each of these groups. The District of Columbia is included in the North- east. (Compare the map on this page with the map on pages 18 and 19.) Not all geography books group the states in this way. Can you think of any other ways of grouping them?

The West	The Midwest and Great Plains		The South	The Northeast	
	The Midwest	Great Plains States			
Arizona	Illinois	Kansas	Alabama	Connecticut	New Jersey
California	Indiana	Nebraska	Arkansas	Delaware	New York
Colorado	Iowa	North Dakota	Florida	District of	Pennsylvania
Idaho	Michigan	Oklahoma	Georgia	Columbia	Rhode Island
Montana	Minnesota	South Dakota	Kentucky	Maine	Vermont
Nevada	Missouri	Texas	Louisiana	Maryland	West Virginia
New Mexico	Ohio		Mississippi	Massachusetts	
Oregon	Wisconsin		North Carolina	New Hampshire	
Utah			South Carolina		
Washington			Tennessee		
Wyoming			Virginia		

21

also includes a small area called the District of Columbia, which is the home of our national government. (See map and table on page 21.)

The states of the Northeast may be divided into two groups, New England and the Middle Atlantic states. New England is made up of Maine, New Hampshire, Vermont, Massachusetts, Connecticut, and Rhode Island. The Middle Atlantic states are New York, Pennsylvania, New Jersey, Delaware, Maryland, and West Virginia.

The Northeast is a very important part of our country. Although the Northeast covers only about 6 percent of the area of the United States, it contains about 25 percent of our country's population.

More than 55 million people make their homes in the Northeast. New York, the largest city in the United States, lies in this region. Several other great cities are also located in the Northeast. Among them is our nation's capital city, Washington, D.C.

The Northeast was one of the first sections of our country to be settled by people from Europe. There were busy cities here when most of America was still a wilderness. Many great events in our nation's history took place in the Northeast. As the United States expanded westward, the Northeast continued to grow in population and wealth.

Today the Northeast is a great manufacturing and trading region. There are

New York, the largest city in our country, is one of several great cities in the Northeast. Although the Northeast covers only a small area of the United States, it contains about one fourth of our country's population. It is an important manufacturing and trading region.

thousands of factories here, producing a wide variety of goods. The Northeast provides other regions of our country with many items they need. In return, it buys many things that other regions have to sell. It also carries on much trade with foreign countries.

There are other reasons, too, why the Northeast is an important part of the United States. Many of our country's largest business firms have their main offices here. In the Northeast, there are a number of large banks and other financial agencies. Many of the television programs watched by people throughout the United States are broadcast from studios located in the Northeast. Here, too, are companies that publish most of our country's books and magazines. The cities of the Northeast are noted for their fine museums, libraries, theaters, and concert halls. Some of our country's best-known colleges and universities are located in the Northeast. This region is also the home of a world organization called the United Nations.

In the following chapters of this book, you will learn about the land features, the climate, and the history of the Northeast. You will also learn about the people of this region and the ways in which they earn their living. In addition, you will come to understand some of the great problems and opportunities facing the people of the Northeast today.

Explore the Solar System

Read about the earth and its neighbors in space, and then write a report about the solar system to share with your class. Answer these questions in your report:
1. What is the solar system?
2. Name the nine main planets in the solar system.
3. In what galaxy is the solar system located?
4. What are two differences between a star and a planet?
5. What is our moon made of? How often does it orbit the earth?

In writing your report, follow the suggestions on pages 345-347.

Get Acquainted With the Northeast
1. What two groups of states make up the Northeast? Name the states in each group.
2. What area that is not a state is also included in the Northeast?
3. List four reasons why the Northeast is an important part of our country.

Learn To Read Maps

Maps will help you gain much information throughout your study of the Northeast. To make the best use of maps, there are certain things you must know. Study the special feature on pages 353-360 and then answer the following questions:
1. What is the "scale" of a map?
2. What does each of the following terms mean?
   latitude
   longitude
   parallel
3. Why is a flat map of the world less accurate than a globe?
4. What does a map legend, or key, show?
5. What is a topographic map?

Practice Your Map Skills

Use the maps on pages 18, 19, 20, and 21 to answer the following questions:
1. What two countries are the closest neighbors of the United States?
2. Which states of the Northeast border on the Atlantic Ocean?
3. Which state of the Northeast lies farthest north? Which state extends farthest west?
4. Approximately how far is it from Washington, D.C., to Boston, Massachusetts?

Rolling hills, high ridges, and rounded mountains make up much of the Northeast. Only a small part of this region is low and level. However, the lowlands of the Northeast are very important, because many of the people in the region live and work in these areas.

2 Land

A Problem To Solve

How do land features affect the lives of people in the Northeast? The following questions suggest some hypotheses you may need to make to solve this problem:

a. How do the land features of the Northeast affect transportation?

b. How do the land features of this region affect farming?

c. How do the land features of this region affect industry?

d. How has the Fall Line affected the location of cities?

See TO THE STUDENT, pages 8-10.

If you were to travel through the Northeast, you would notice that the land differs greatly from one place to another. In some parts of this region, there are forest-covered mountains. In other areas, the land consists of plateaus and rolling hills. Only a small part of the Northeast is low and level. The lowlands are very important, however, since many of the people in the Northeast live and work in these areas. To find out more about the Northeast, we will take a trip by helicopter over this important region. The route we will follow on our trip is shown on the map on page 25.

The Lowlands

Our trip will first take us over lowland areas of the Northeast. Some of the lowlands we will see stretch along the Atlantic coast. Others border rivers that cut far inland through the highland regions. We will also learn about an important lowland area that extends along Lake Ontario and Lake Erie.

Lowlands of New England. The sun is rising as we board our helicopter at Cutler, a small fishing village in eastern Maine. (See map below.) As our helicopter rises high in the air, we see the blue-green waters of the Atlantic Ocean. Below us, the white surf crashes against the rocky shore.

Our trip will take us southward. We will fly over the coastal lowlands of Maine, New Hampshire, Massachusetts, Rhode Island, and Connecticut. Most of the people in New England live on these coastal lowlands.

As we fly southwestward along the coast of Maine, we notice hundreds of little bays and inlets. In sheltered inlets, we see small fishing villages. Some fishermen wave to us from fishing boats that are chugging out to sea. Our guide tells us that these are lobster fishermen.

Looking inland from the coast, we notice large forests of evergreen trees. Forests cover more than three fourths of the land in New England. From time to time we see neat white farmhouses surrounded by green pastures and fields of crops. As we fly farther along the coast, we see more towns and villages. Soon a large seaport comes into view. This is Portland. Although it is the largest city in Maine, fewer than eighty thousand people live here.

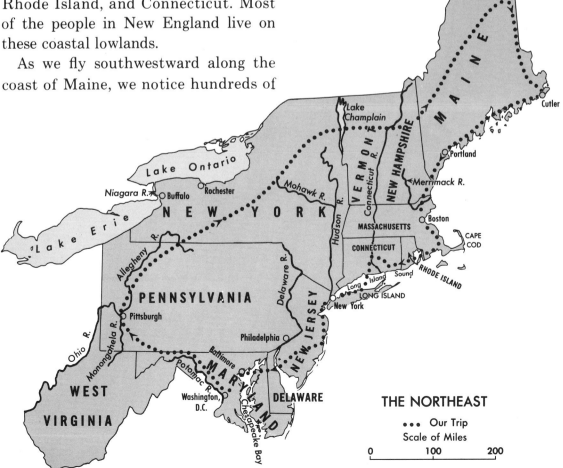

THE NORTHEAST

••• Our Trip

Scale of Miles

0   100   200

Boston Harbor. Hundreds of bays and inlets indent the lowlands that extend along the Atlantic coast of New England. Some of them provide excellent natural harbors. Vessels of many kinds steam in and out of the great port of Boston. Fishing boats sail from many harbors along the coast.

Now we are flying over northeastern Massachusetts. Below us is the winding Merrimack River. Along its banks are the manufacturing cities of Lowell, Lawrence, and Haverhill. Our guide tells us that the Merrimack contributed to the growth of these cities. In the 1800's, when waterpower was used to run factory machinery, textile mills and other industries were built near falls in the river. Today, waterpower is used by hydroelectric plants along the banks of the Merrimack to produce electricity for factories and homes.

Farther south, we come to the great city of Boston, the capital of Massa-

chusetts. Docks and warehouses extend along the harbor of the city. In the water below us, we notice ocean liners, freighters, and fishing vessels. Inland from the harbor, the city seems to stretch out as far as we can see. Our guide tells us that this is not just one city, but about seventy-five separate cities and towns. Boston and its neighboring communities are so close together that they appear to be one great city. Together they are called Greater Boston. More than two and a half million people live in this metropolitan* area.

Flying southeastward from Boston, we see Cape Cod, a peninsula that

*See Glossary

26

Land Regions

CANADA

SUPERIOR
UPLAND

INTERIOR

PLAINS

INTERIOR
HIGHLANDS

APPALACHIAN HIGHLANDS

4

3

4

1

2

3

2

4

1

8

7

5

6

6

COASTAL PLAIN

ATLANTIC OCEAN

GULF OF MEXICO

Scale of Miles

0 50 100 150 200

COASTAL PLAIN
APPALACHIAN HIGHLANDS

1 Piedmont Plateau
2 Blue Ridge
3 Appalachian Ridges and Valleys
4 Appalachian Plateau
5 New England Lowlands

6 New England Highlands
7 Adirondack Mountains
8 St. Lawrence Valley

INTERIOR PLAINS

INTERIOR HIGHLANDS

SUPERIOR UPLAND

|||||||||| The Northeast

27

Tobacco fields along the Connecticut River. The Connecticut Valley contains some of the most fertile farmland in the Northeast. Farmers here grow excellent tobacco. Some of the fields are covered with white cheesecloth to protect the growing tobacco plants.

reaches far out into the Atlantic Ocean. (See map on page 25.) Many visitors come to Cape Cod each year to spend their summer vacations on its sandy beaches.

Our helicopter turns westward toward the tiny state of Rhode Island. Soon we pass over Narragansett Bay. This narrow inlet almost divides the state into two parts. Rhode Island is the smallest state in our country. It takes less than thirty minutes for our helicopter to cross Rhode Island.

West of Rhode Island, we come to the sandy beaches and gently rolling hills of Connecticut's coastal lowland. We turn northwestward and fly to the central part of the state. Soon we are over the Connecticut River. This is the longest river in New England. It begins far to the north, in the mountains of New Hampshire.

The valley of the Connecticut River contains some of the most fertile farmland in the Northeast. From the air, it looks as if some of the fields here are

New York City lies along the Atlantic coast. On Manhattan Island, many skyscrapers reach high into the sky.

Harvesting tomatoes on the Coastal Plain of New Jersey. Much of the land along the Northeast's Atlantic coast lies in the Coastal Plain region of our country. The land here is level or gently rolling. Farmlands and huge urban areas cover most of the Northeast's Coastal Plain.

covered with snow. We are surprised to learn that these are tobacco fields. The farmers have covered them with white cheesecloth to protect the growing tobacco plants. (See picture on page 28.) Farmers in the Connecticut Valley grow some of our country's finest tobacco. They also grow fruits and vegetables in the fertile soil here.

Now we turn southward and fly back to the coast of Connecticut. Ahead of us is Long Island Sound, which is an arm of the Atlantic Ocean. (See map on page 25.) After crossing the sound, we fly over the western end of Long Island. This island is a part of New York State. In the distance, we can see the tall buildings of New York City. Our guide

tells us that part of this great city is located on Long Island. In a short while, our helicopter lands at New York's busy La Guardia airport for refueling.

Middle Atlantic lowlands. As we wait, our guide tells us that we will next visit the Middle Atlantic lowlands. These important lowlands stretch along the Atlantic coast between Connecticut and Virginia. They are part of a vast region called the Coastal Plain. The land in this region is level or gently rolling, and the soil is generally sandy. Only a small part of the Northeast lies in the Coastal Plain. (See map on page 27.)

Now we are ready to continue our flight. As our helicopter rises, we have a magnificent view of New York City.

On Manhattan Island, skyscrapers reach high into the sky. In the harbor are huge ocean liners, tugboats, freighters, and ferryboats. More ships load and unload cargo at New York than at any other seaport in the United States.

Flying southward over the lowlands of New Jersey, we notice long, sandy beaches along the coast. People are swimming in the surf below us, and we see many large hotels. New Jersey is noted for its seashore resorts.

When our helicopter turns inland over New Jersey, we begin to see fields of green beans, tomatoes, and other vegetables. Vegetables raised here are shipped to nearby cities, where they are sold to supermarkets and restaurants. Raising vegetables for sale is called truck farming. This type of farming is usually very profitable in the Northeast, for there are millions of city people in this region to buy and eat the vegetables raised here.

In the distance to our right, we can see the buildings of several cities. Our guide tells us that these are the cities of Trenton and Camden in New Jersey and Philadelphia in Pennsylvania. All of these cities are located along the Delaware River.

Soon we leave New Jersey and cross Delaware Bay. Now we are flying over a large peninsula that stretches far southward into the Atlantic Ocean. Most of Delaware and part of Maryland are located on this peninsula. The land here is very low and level. We see few large towns, but there are a great number of farms. Many of these are truck farms, but there are also poultry farms. Farmers in Delaware and Maryland raise millions of chickens each year to ship to the great cities of the Northeast.

Now we are flying over Chesapeake Bay. (See map on page 25.) The water below us is crowded with fishing boats and ocean freighters. To our right, we see tall buildings and the smoke from many factories. Our guide tells us that this is the great port city of Baltimore.

We are approaching our nation's capital, Washington, D.C., where we will spend the night before continuing our trip. As we come in for a landing at Washington National Airport, we can see the Washington Monument and the United States Capitol across the Potomac River. In Chapter 18, you will learn more about the beautiful city of Washington.

Other lowlands of the Northeast. In our trip along the Atlantic coast, we could not see all the lowland areas of the Northeast. Some important lowlands lie far inland. One of these is a broad, fertile plain in the western part of New York and the northwestern part of Pennsylvania. This plain lies along Lake Ontario and Lake Erie.

If you could visit the Erie-Ontario Lowland, you would see people working in vineyards and orchards and on dairy farms. In large cities like Buffalo and Rochester, you would see many factories and mills.

One of the most interesting sights in this part of the Northeast is beautiful Niagara Falls. These falls are located on the Niagara River, which forms part of the border between the United States and Canada. The Niagara River flows northward from Lake Erie to Lake Ontario. Lake Erie is much higher than

The New York State Barge Canal extends through the Erie-Ontario Lowland and the valley of the Mohawk River. The Mohawk and Hudson valleys form a natural pathway through the highlands of New York. Good roads and railroads help to make this an important trade route.

Lake Ontario. About midway between these two lakes, the river plunges over a steep cliff, forming Niagara Falls. Each year, thousands of tourists come to see these famous falls. Waterpower from the falls is used to produce electricity for factories and homes in both the United States and Canada.

East of the plain along Lake Erie and Lake Ontario is another important lowland area. Here, the valleys of the Hudson and Mohawk rivers form a natural pathway through the highlands of New York. Large boats carry goods up the Hudson River from New York City as far north as Albany. From a point near here goods are transported westward on the New York State Barge Canal, which extends through the Mohawk Valley and the Erie-Ontario Lowland to Buffalo, on Lake Erie. Good roads and railroads in the Hudson and Mohawk valleys also help to make this lowland an important trade route.

The Highlands

More than three fourths of the Northeast lies in a vast region called the Appalachian Highlands. (See map on page 27.) These highlands extend for more than 1,600 miles from central Alabama northeastward into Canada. In this region are mountain ranges, high ridges, and deep valleys. Plateaus and hilly land also make up a large part of the Appalachian Highlands. During the remainder of our trip, we will be flying over these highlands.

The Piedmont Plateau. Our helicopter rises high over Washington, D.C., and we follow the winding Potomac River northwestward. The land below us is

The Ridges and Valleys section of West Virginia is part of the Appalachian Highlands region of our country. This region of mountain ranges, ridges, plateaus, valleys, and hills extends from Alabama northeastward into Canada. It covers more than three fourths of the Northeast.

Farmlands on the Piedmont, in Pennsylvania. The land in the Piedmont Plateau section of the Appalachian Highlands is gently rolling.

gently rolling. We are flying over a plateau that slopes gradually upward from the Coastal Plain to the mountainous land that lies farther west. This part of the Appalachian Highlands is called the Piedmont Plateau. (See map on page 27.) The word piedmont means "foot of the mountain."

Many fast-flowing rivers cross the Piedmont on their way to the Atlantic Ocean. As these rivers drop from the plateau onto the Coastal Plain, they form swift rapids and waterfalls. For this reason, the dividing line between the Piedmont and the Coastal Plain is called the Fall Line. (See page 35.)

Some of the Northeast's largest cities lie along the Fall Line. In the early days of our country, settlers traveling upstream by boat were stopped at the Fall Line by the falls and rapids. Here they had to unload their goods, and many of them settled nearby. Water-

power from the falls was used to run machines in small mills and factories. Gradually, many settlements along the Fall Line became important cities.

The Blue Ridge. Soon we leave the Piedmont and fly over a broad, forest-covered ridge. This is part of the Blue Ridge, a chain of mountain ranges that extends from Pennsylvania southwestward into Georgia. It is called the Blue Ridge because its slopes often appear blue from a distance.

The Appalachian Ridges and Valleys. Beyond the Blue Ridge, we come to a broad valley. We learn that this is the easternmost part of the Appalachian Ridges and Valleys section of the Appalachian Highlands. The valley below us is part of a long chain of valleys, called the Great Valley. On the valley floor, we see herds of dairy cattle grazing in green meadows.

Northwestward from the Great Valley, we cross a series of heavily wooded ridges separated by narrow valleys. Occasionally we fly over a small town, but we have not seen a large city since leaving Washington. One reason why this area has not been heavily settled is lack of transportation. It has been difficult to build roads and railroads through this mountainous area.

The Appalachian Plateau. Our guide tells us that we have crossed into southern Pennsylvania and are now flying over the Appalachian Plateau. In the Northeast, this section of the Appalachian Highlands extends over large areas of Pennsylvania, New York, and West Virginia. (See map on page 27.)

The land below us is hilly and rugged. Usually we think of a plateau as an area of high, flat land. We learn that

The Fall Line

What is the Fall Line? If you compare the map above with the map on page 27, you will see that the Fall Line is the border between the Coastal Plain and the Piedmont Plateau. This line extends from northeastern New Jersey to central Alabama. As the diagram below shows, the land slopes gently upward from the ocean to the Piedmont Plateau. In most places along the Fall Line, there is not much difference in elevation between the Piedmont and the Coastal Plain. In places where rivers flow from the plateau to the plain, however, the elevation drops sharply. Here there are rapids and waterfalls, which have given the Fall Line its name.

How were the waterfalls formed? The diagram below helps to explain how the waterfalls along the Fall Line were formed. As you will note, the Piedmont is hard rock under the surface soil, but the Coastal Plain is made up of soft sand and clay. As a result, rivers flowing to the sea carry away much more soil from the plain than from the plateau. Through the centuries, these rivers have cut across the plain, carving valleys almost down to the level of the sea. Near the ocean, where the land is low, the valleys are shallow. Farther inland, however, where the land slopes upward, the valleys are deeper. At the points where the rivers drop from the rocky Piedmont Plateau into the valleys of the Coastal Plain, they form rapids and waterfalls.

How has the Fall Line been important? During the early days of our country, settlers traveling upstream from the coast by boat were stopped by the falls and rapids at the Fall Line. Here the settlers had to unload their goods. As a result, many of them settled nearby. Later, people in settlements along the Fall Line found that they could use the power of the falling water to run machines in mills and factories. Many of the early settlements that started on rivers along the Fall Line have grown into large cities. (See map on this page.) Today, some waterfalls along the Fall Line are used to produce hydroelectricity. (See page 131.)

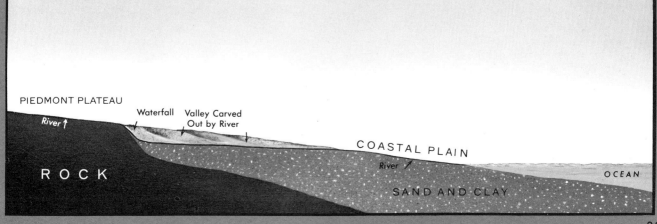

at one time the surface of the Appalachian Plateau was smooth and unbroken. Through the centuries, however, rivers and streams have cut thousands of valleys into the plateau, leaving rugged hills and mountains. We see few farms in this region.

In some of the valleys below us, there are small mining communities. The hills of the Appalachian Plateau contain large deposits of bituminous* coal. West Virginia and Pennsylvania lead the nation in coal production.

Ahead of us we see the tall buildings of a large city. This is Pittsburgh, one of the greatest steelmaking cities in the world. It is situated at the point where the Allegheny and Monongahela rivers meet to form the Ohio River. (See map on page 25.) Tall furnaces of steel mills rise near the riverbanks. Towboats are pushing barges loaded with coal and other raw materials needed to make steel. Nearby raw materials and cheap transportation have helped Pittsburgh become a great manufacturing city.

The Adirondack Mountains. From Pittsburgh, our trip takes us far northeastward to the Adirondack Mountains of New York. (Compare maps on pages 25 and 27.) These are the oldest mountains in the Appalachian Highlands. They were formed hundreds of millions of years ago.

The Adirondack Mountains are located in the northern part of New York State. They are the oldest mountains in the Appalachian Highlands. Through countless centuries, wind, rain, and frost have worn down their slopes and rounded their peaks.

The Green Mountains of Vermont. These beautiful mountains owe their name to the evergreen forests that cover their slopes. The highlands of New England attract many tourists each year.

As we fly over the Adirondacks, we notice that the mountain peaks are not very high or rugged. Through countless centuries, wind, rain, and frost have worn down the slopes and rounded the peaks of the mountains. In the forested valleys below us, hundreds of lakes glisten like jewels. Our guide points out hotels and hunting lodges along many of the lakes. The beautiful scenery and the wildlife of the Adirondacks attract thousands of tourists each year.

Highlands of New England. Flying eastward, we cross Lake Champlain and are soon over the gently rounded Green Mountains of Vermont. The Green Mountains owe their name to the forests of evergreen trees that cover

their slopes. As in the Adirondacks, we notice many resort hotels. Tourists come to the cool mountains in the summertime to escape the heat of the cities. Many vacationers also come to the Green Mountains in the winter to ski and enjoy other sports.

Now we are flying over the White Mountains of New Hampshire. These mountains seem to rise higher than any others we have seen on our trip. Our guide tells us that one of these peaks, Mt. Washington, rises to nearly 6,300 feet above sea level. This is the highest point in the Northeast.

The highlands of New England are very old. Many thousands of years ago, the land here was covered with huge

The Story of Glaciers

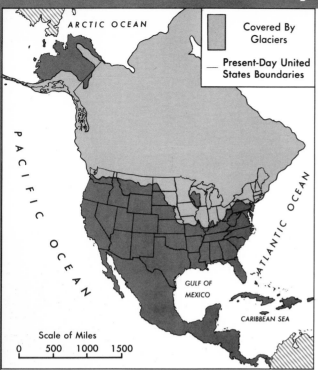

North America. The map above shows the part of North America that was covered by glaciers at one time or another during the Great Ice Age.

The Great Ice Age. About one million years ago, the climate of the earth was colder than it is today. Great quantities of snow fell in and near Arctic regions of the world. In some places more snow fell in winter than melted in summer. The snow piled higher and higher each year, and the bottom layers gradually turned to ice. Finally, the enormous weight of the snow on top caused the ice below to spread out in all directions. A mass of moving ice formed in this way is called a glacier.

As the centuries passed, glaciers spread over large areas in Europe, Asia, and North America. In some places, they were almost two miles thick. As glaciers moved across the land, they carried away soil and rocks, scooped out deep hollows, and rounded off the jagged tops of mountains.

Gradually, the climate of the earth became warmer. The glaciers began to melt. As they melted, they left behind the soil, rocks, and other material they had carried. Some of the hollows that had been made by the glaciers were filled with water from the melting ice. In this way, many lakes and ponds were formed.

Three more times during the Great Ice Age the earth's climate cooled and then became warmer again. Each time, glaciers spread over large areas of the earth's surface and then melted. The last of these ice sheets retreated only about 18,000 years ago. Scientists are not completely certain why these great changes in climate took place.

How glaciers affected the Northeast. During the Great Ice Age, glaciers moved over much of the Northeast. They made great changes in the land features of this region. Many mountains and hills were worn down and rounded off by the glaciers. In New England, glaciers scraped away much of the soil. As the glaciers melted, they left behind stones and gravel. This explains why much of the soil in New England today is thin and stony. Boulders and rocks left in riverbeds by melting glaciers caused falls and rapids to form in many of the Northeast's rivers. The melting glaciers also formed thousands of lakes, including the Great Lakes and the Finger Lakes.

Present-day glaciers. Today, glaciers are still being formed in some parts of the world. They are found mainly in cold, mountainous areas that receive abundant snowfall. For example, there are many small glaciers in the Cascade Mountains in the state of Washington. The island of Greenland and the continent of Antarctica are almost completely covered by huge glaciers. There are no glaciers in the Northeast, however.

A rocky field in New England. During the Great Ice Age, glaciers scraped away much of the soil in New England and left behind stones and gravel.

masses of ice called glaciers. The glaciers moved slowly down the mountains and valleys. As they moved across New England, they scraped away the soil in many places. When the glaciers melted, they left large amounts of stones and gravel behind. As a result, much of the soil in New England is thin and stony. Farmers find it difficult to raise crops here.

Soon we cross the border between New Hampshire and Maine and fly northeastward. As far as the horizon, we see forested mountains and hills. Forests cover more than four fifths of the land in Maine. Very seldom do we see an open patch of farmland or a town.

When our helicopter reaches northeastern Maine, we see many farms below us. Our guide tells us that this is Aroostook County, which contains the only large area of fertile land in Maine. This county is famous for its fine potatoes. Maine is one of the leading potato-producing states in our country.

Now our trip is almost over. Our flight over the Northeast has helped us to understand how land features affect the ways in which people live and work.

Develop Important Understandings
1. Name three important lowland areas in the Northeast.
2. What is the Fall Line?
3. Why are many of the Northeast's large cities located along the Fall Line?
4. Why are the valleys of the Hudson and Mohawk rivers important?
5. What are some of the things you would see on a trip through the Erie-Ontario Lowland?

Describe the Highlands of the Northeast
Most of the Northeast is made up of highlands. Listed below are the names of five highland areas in the Northeast.

Piedmont Plateau
Appalachian Ridges and Valleys
Appalachian Plateau
Adirondack Mountains
Highlands of New England

Write a brief paragraph about each of these highland areas, describing what you might see on a visit there. You will find the suggestions on page 347 helpful in writing your paragraphs.

Make a Chart of the Northeast's Waterways
Waterways have been important to the people of the Northeast since the early days of our country. Listed below are the names of some of the waterways used by people of the Northeast.

Hudson River	Mohawk River
Chesapeake Bay	Lake Erie
Lake Ontario	Ohio River
Merrimack River	Delaware River

Do research to learn how these waterways have been important to the people of the Northeast. Then show your findings on a chart similar to the one below.

Waterway	Importance
Ohio River	This river is an important route for transporting coal and other raw materials.

Use the Index of this book to find the information needed to complete this project.

Explore an Interesting Topic
Select one of the topics below and write a report about it to share with your class.

How Glaciers Affected the Land of New England
A Visit to Niagara Falls
A Trip up the Hudson River

You will find the suggestions on pages 345-349 helpful in locating the information you need and in preparing your report.

Walking down a country road in autumn. In the Northeast, each season brings great changes in the weather. Temperatures differ not only from season to season but also from place to place.

3 Climate

A Problem To Solve

In the Northeast, temperatures differ considerably from place to place. Why is this true? In order to solve this problem, you will need to find out what the climate is like in different parts of the Northeast. Then you will need to make a number of "educated guesses," or hypotheses, that you think explain these differences. In forming your hypotheses, you may find it helpful to consider each of the following questions:

a. How are temperatures in different places affected by distance from the equator?

b. How does altitude affect temperature?

c. How are temperatures in different places affected by distance from large bodies of water?

See TO THE STUDENT, pages 8-10.

In the Northeast, each season brings great changes in the weather. Summer days in most parts of this region are often hot and humid. Winter days are usually cold. In some places, snow covers the ground for weeks at a time. During the spring and fall, the weather is seldom very hot or very cold.

The weather in the Northeast differs not only from season to season but also from place to place. In the northern part of this region, temperatures are usually different from those in the southern part. The weather in the highlands is not the same as that in the lowlands. There are also differences between the weather along the seacoast and the weather farther inland.

To learn more about the climate of the Northeast, let us imagine that we are spending a year in this region. We will begin our visit in the winter.

Winter

Winters are cold and snowy in much of the Northeast. We are visiting a ski resort in the White Mountains of New Hampshire. The temperature on this January afternoon is twenty degrees. The mountain slopes and the valleys are covered with a blanket of fresh, white snow. In many places, strong winds have piled the snow into deep drifts. We notice that a pond nearby is covered with ice. All around us, skiers dressed in bright winter clothing are gliding down the snowy mountain slopes.

Skiing in the mountains of New Hampshire. Winters are cold and snowy in most highland areas of the Northeast. In the lowlands along the Atlantic coast, winters are generally milder.

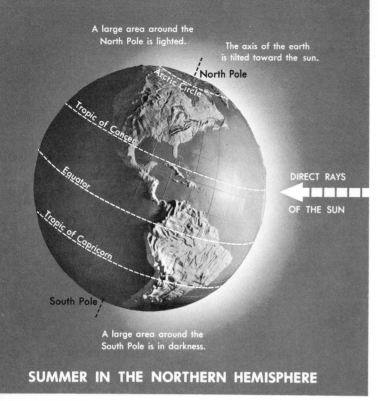

A large area around the
North Pole is lighted.

The axis of the earth
is tilted toward the sun.

North Pole

Arctic Circle

Tropic of Cancer

Equator

DIRECT RAYS

Tropic of Capricorn

OF THE SUN

South Pole

A large area around the
South Pole is in darkness.

SUMMER IN THE NORTHERN HEMISPHERE

The chart above shows how the earth is lighted by the sun at noon on June 21, the first day of summer in the Northern Hemisphere.

THE SEASONS

The year is divided into four natural periods, or seasons, which we call summer, autumn, winter, and spring. Each season is marked by changes in the length of day and night and by changes in temperature.

The seasons are caused by the tilt of the earth's axis and the revolution of the earth around the sun. It takes one year for the earth to revolve around the sun. On this trip, the earth remains tilted at the same angle to the path along which it travels. The chart below shows how this causes the Northern Hemisphere to be tilted toward the sun on June 21 and away from the sun on December 22. On March 21 and September 22, the Northern Hemisphere is tilted neither toward the sun nor away from it.

The chart on the left shows that on June 21 the sun shines directly on the Tropic of Cancer.* This is the northernmost point ever reached by the sun's direct rays. In the Northern Hemisphere, June 21 is the first day of summer and the longest day of the year.

The chart on the right shows that on December 22 the sun shines directly on the Tropic of Capricorn.* This is the southernmost point ever reached by the sun's direct

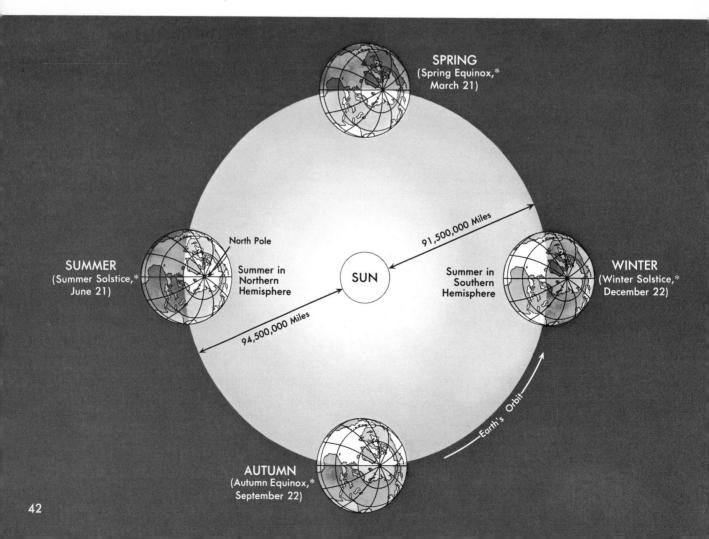

SPRING
(Spring Equinox,*
March 21)

SUMMER
(Summer Solstice,*
June 21)

North Pole

Summer in
Northern
Hemisphere

91,500,000 Miles

SUN

Summer in
Southern
Hemisphere

WINTER
(Winter Solstice,*
December 22)

94,500,000 Miles

Earth's Orbit

AUTUMN
(Autumn Equinox,*
September 22)

OF THE YEAR

rays. In the Northern Hemisphere, December 22 is the first day of winter and the shortest day of the year.

When one hemisphere is tilted toward the sun, the other is tilted away from the sun. For this reason, the seasons in the Southern Hemisphere are just the opposite of those in the Northern Hemisphere. Summer in the Southern Hemisphere begins on December 22, and winter begins on June 21.

Temperatures are affected by the slant of the sun's rays as they strike the surface of the earth. Study the chart below, and the picture of Washington, D.C., to help you understand why this is true.

Near the equator, the sun is almost directly overhead throughout the year. For this reason, the weather near the equator is always hot, except in the mountains. In areas farther away from the equator, the sun's rays are more slanted. Therefore, the weather is usually cooler.

The northern part of the United States is farther from the equator than the southern part of our country. This explains why the weather is generally cooler in the north than it is in the south.

*See Glossary

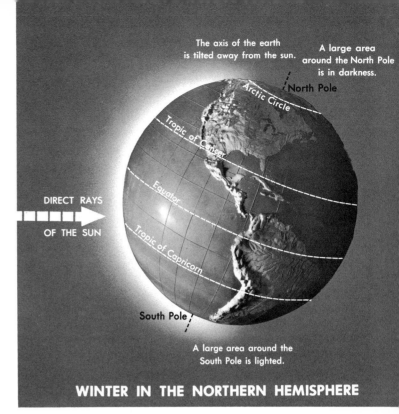

WINTER IN THE NORTHERN HEMISPHERE

The chart above shows how the earth is lighted by the sun at noon on December 22, the first day of winter in the Northern Hemisphere.

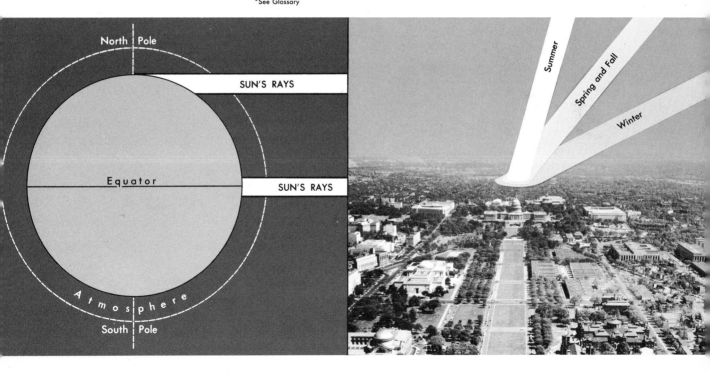

The chart above shows that when the sun's rays strike the earth at a slant, they must travel through more atmosphere than when they strike it directly. This affects temperatures because the atmosphere absorbs heat from the sun's rays. The more atmosphere the rays must pass through, the less heat they retain to warm the earth. This is one reason why temperatures are higher if the sun is directly overhead than they are if the sun is low in the sky.

This picture also helps to explain how changes in temperature are caused by the different angles at which the sun's rays strike the surface of the earth. During the summer, the noonday sun is high in the sky. The rays of the sun are concentrated into narrow areas. As a result, they produce much heat. During the winter, the noonday sun is low in the sky. The slanting rays of the sun are spread over much wider areas, so they produce less heat.

43

Shortly after four o'clock, the sun disappears behind a mountain peak to the west. Here in New Hampshire, January days are short. The time between sunrise and sunset is less than ten hours long. As the sky grows darker, the cold evening air makes us shiver. Tonight the temperature will probably drop to near zero. Weather like this is common in the highlands of New England during the wintertime.

Winters are also cold and snowy in the highlands of New York and Pennsylvania. Temperatures often stay below freezing for weeks at a time, and snowstorms are frequent. In the Adirondack Mountains of northern New York, more than twelve feet of snow may fall during the winter. Many people come to the Adirondacks in winter to enjoy skiing, skating, and other sports.

One reason why winters are so cold in the Northeast is that this region lies in the northern part of the United States. The weather in the northern part of our country is generally cooler than the weather in the southern part. (See the feature on pages 42 and 43.)

There is also another reason why the Northeast has such cold winters. During the winter months, the winds that pass over this region are often from the northwest. These winds, which come from the frigid areas of northern Canada, are cold and dry. They help to bring bitterly cold weather to the Northeast.

Not all of the winds that blow across the Northeast during the winter come from Canada. Often, a mass of warm, moist air drifts northward from the Gulf of Mexico. When this air meets the cold air from the north, it rises and becomes cooler. (See the description of cyclonic rainfall on page 51.) As it becomes cooler, it drops some of its moisture in the form of snow. This helps to explain why many areas in the Northeast receive heavy snowfall.

There are many ways in which cold, snowy winters affect the lives of people in the Northeast. The houses in this region are solidly built to keep out the cold. They are usually heated by furnaces that burn gas, oil, or coal. People in the Northeast usually need to wear warm clothing in the winter. Although a snowy landscape is a beautiful sight, snowstorms can cause much trouble and inconvenience. After a snowstorm, people must shovel the snow off their walks and driveways. Cities must use snowplows to clear the streets. Cars often become stuck in snowdrifts, and icy roads make driving dangerous. Buses and trains are sometimes delayed by heavy snow.

Winters are milder in some parts of the Northeast. In the lowlands along the Atlantic coast, winter weather is not as cold as it is in the highlands. Large bodies of water lose their heat more slowly than land does. For this reason, the Atlantic Ocean is warmer during

Build Your Vocabulary

growing season   cyclonic rainfall   hemisphere

convectional rainfall   atmosphere   climate   orographic rainfall

the winter than the land nearby. Breezes from the ocean bring mild weather to the lowlands along the coast. In the lowlands of Maryland and Delaware, winters are so mild that snow seldom stays on the ground for more than a day or two at a time.

On the plain along Lake Erie and Lake Ontario, winters are slightly milder than they are in the highlands. Winds from the north and west are warmed as they blow across the Great Lakes. They help to prevent extremely cold weather along the eastern and southern shores of the lakes. As these winds pass over the lakes, they take up much moisture. Some of this moisture later returns to the earth in the form of snow. Buffalo and other cities in western New York often receive heavy snowfall in winter.

Spring

Spring comes early in some lowland areas. It is April, and we are visiting the city of Washington, D.C. (See map on page 25.) The air is pleasantly warm, and a soft breeze is blowing. Cherry trees are pink with blossoms. After a while, the sky grows dark and a gentle rain begins to fall. The gardens and

Spring in Washington, D. C. Spring comes early in some lowland areas of the Northeast. In Washington, cherry trees blossom in April. The growing season here is six months long.

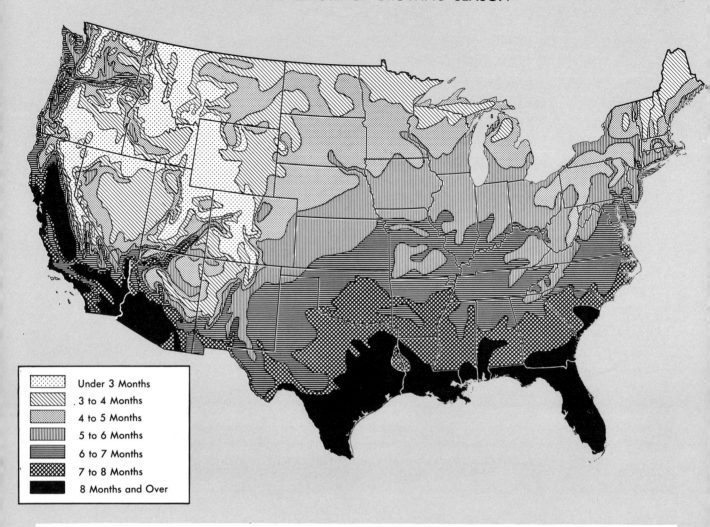

Under 3 Months
. 3 to 4 Months
4 to 5 Months
5 to 6 Months
6 to 7 Months
7 to 8 Months
8 Months and Over

The growing season is the period of time during which crops can be grown outdoors without being killed by frost.

The growing season in the Northeast lasts from three to seven months. It is shortest in the Adirondack Mountains and in the highlands of northern New England. In other mountain areas, it lasts from four to five months. The growing season is longest near the coast and in the southern states of the Northeast.

parks that we see as we tour the city are fresh and green.

If we were to drive through the countryside near Washington, we would see farmers plowing their fields. In this part of the Northeast, the last severe frost of spring comes in early April. The first severe frost of autumn usually comes in October. Therefore, crops can be grown outdoors for six months of the year without danger of being killed by frost. This frost-free period is known as the growing season.

The map above shows the length of the growing season in various parts of the Northeast. You can see that the growing season is especially long in the lowlands along the Atlantic coast. In some places, farmers can grow crops outdoors for more than six months.

The long growing season along the Atlantic coast is helpful to farmers. There are many truck farms on Long Island, and in New Jersey, Delaware, and Maryland. These farms produce vegetables for sale to people in the large cities of the Northeast. Because the farmers can plant their crops early in the spring, they can get their vegetables to market sooner than farmers in other parts of the Northeast.

The plain along Lake Ontario and Lake Erie also has a fairly long growing season. The climate of this area is very well suited to growing fruit. In the spring, the Great Lakes do not become warm as quickly as the land nearby. Winds from the north and west are cooled as they blow across the lakes. The cool winds keep fruit trees and grapevines from budding while there is danger of frost. In the fall, the Great Lakes are warmer than the land. Warm winds from the lakes help to protect ripening fruit from early frosts. Large quantities of apples, peaches, grapes, and other fruit are grown on the plain along Lake Erie and Lake Ontario.

The growing season is shorter in the highlands. At the same time that flowers are blooming in the coastal lowlands, snow still covers many hillsides and

Harvesting potatoes in northern Maine. In some highland areas of the Northeast, the growing season is less than four months long. Farmers in these areas cannot raise crops which need a long growing season. They must grow crops such as potatoes and hay, which ripen in a short time.

mountain slopes in the Northeast. As you can see by comparing the map on page 46 with the map on page 27, highland areas in the Northeast generally have a shorter growing season than nearby lowlands.

The growing season is especially short in the Adirondack Mountains and in the highlands of northern New England.

In some places, farmers cannot plant their crops until late in May. The first killing frost may come in September. Therefore, the growing season is less than four months long. Farmers here cannot raise crops that need a long growing season. They must grow crops such as hay and potatoes, which do not take a long time to ripen.

Summer

In most parts of the Northeast, summers are hot and humid. We are strolling along Fifth Avenue in New York City on a hot day in July. The sun is shining brightly, and the temperature is ninety degrees. Because the air is very humid, we feel even warmer than we would if it were dry. We wish that

A beach along the Atlantic coast of Delaware. Summers are hot and humid in most parts of the Northeast. Winds from the Gulf of Mexico often bring "heat waves" to this region. Some people from the cities go to the seacoast to enjoy the cooling ocean breezes.

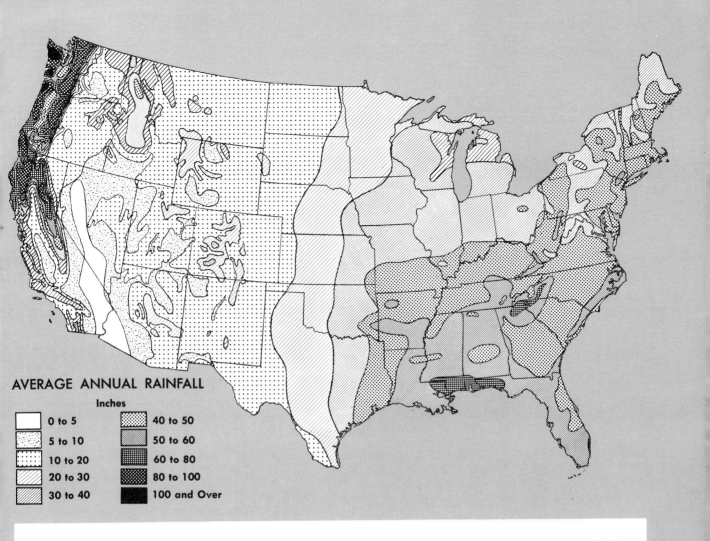

AVERAGE ANNUAL RAINFALL

Inches

☐ 0 to 5	▦ 40 to 50
▨ 5 to 10	▧ 50 to 60
⠿ 10 to 20	▩ 60 to 80
▨ 20 to 30	▦ 80 to 100
▨ 30 to 40	■ 100 and Over

The map above shows the average yearly rainfall in different parts of the conterminous* United States. As used here, the term "rainfall" includes not only the amount of water that falls as rain, but also the amount of water that falls as snow and other forms of precipitation. It may take from six to thirty inches of snow to equal one inch of rain.

In the Northeast, the average amount of rainfall per year varies from place to place, ranging from about twenty to sixty inches. In the summer, winds from the Gulf of Mexico bring hot, humid weather and frequent rains to much of the Northeast. Almost all parts of this region receive enough rainfall for growing most kinds of crops.

*See Glossary

we could drive to one of the beaches on Long Island for a refreshing swim in the Atlantic Ocean.

In the middle of the afternoon, large, dark clouds called thunderheads appear in the west. The air is very still. Suddenly we hear a loud crash of thunder, and rain begins to fall in large drops. We stand in a doorway to get out of the downpour. Within an hour, the storm is over. Now the air feels cooler.

Hot, humid days like this are common in most parts of the Northeast during the summertime. The feature on

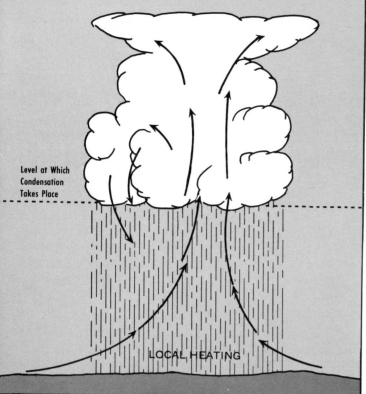

Level at Which
Condensation
Takes Place

LOCAL HEATING

Nearly all rain is formed when air, which always contains moisture, rises and cools. To understand why this happens, we must know where air gets its moisture, why rising air cools, and what happens when moist air cools.

Where air gets its moisture. Under natural conditions, all air contains moisture. This moisture, called water vapor, is water that has evaporated from the soil, vegetation, rivers, lakes, and oceans. It is mixed with the other gases that compose air, and cannot be seen.

Why rising air cools. As air rises, the weight of the air on top of it decreases. For this reason, the rising air is able to spread out, or expand. As it expands, rising air must push aside the air around it. This requires energy, which uses up much of the air's heat. Therefore, the rising air cools.

What happens when moist air cools. The amount of moisture air can hold in the form of water vapor depends on the temperature of the air. The warmer the air, the more water vapor it can hold. As air rises and expands, it cools. Therefore, the amount of water vapor the rising air can hold decreases. Its excess water vapor must condense. As it condenses, it forms tiny particles of water called cloud droplets. These droplets, as their name suggests, make up clouds.

Cloud droplets combine in several ways to form raindrops. Often droplets fall within the cloud. As they fall, they collide with other droplets, and raindrops are formed. Raindrops are also formed when some cloud droplets turn to ice particles. Other droplets tend to cling to these ice particles until they are heavy enough to fall. As the ice particles fall, they travel through warmer air, which melts them. Thus, they fall to the ground as raindrops. There may be as many as 8 million cloud droplets in a good-sized raindrop.

Types of rainfall. There are three main types of rainfall, which are associated with the reasons why air rises. Sometimes rain falls because of a combination of these reasons.

Convectional rainfall. Air expands, grows lighter, and rises as it is heated. This process, called convection, causes one type of rainfall. As you have learned, air cools as it rises. On very hot days, air rises and cools quickly. If the rising air is very moist, heavy showers may result. Convectional rainfall is especially common in humid, tropical areas. It often occurs in

Convectional rainfall (above) occurs when moist air is warmed, grows lighter, and rises. Orographic rainfall (below) occurs when moist winds are forced to rise because mountains lie in their path.

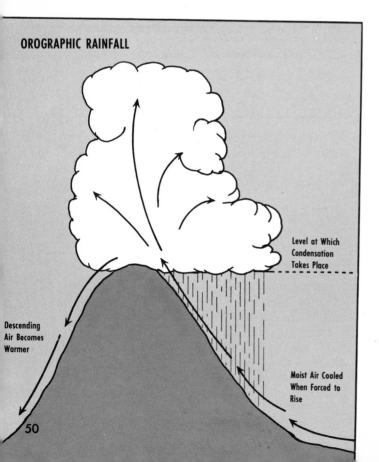

OROGRAPHIC RAINFALL

Level at Which
Condensation
Takes Place

Descending
Air Becomes
Warmer

Moist Air Cooled
When Forced to
Rise

Rainfall

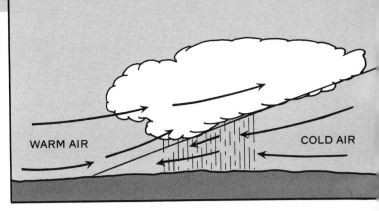

the afternoon, which is the hottest part of the day.

When convection occurs very rapidly, creating strong currents of rising air, thunderstorms may develop. As rain clouds are formed, the rising air currents sweep them upward, several miles above the earth's surface. Falling raindrops are broken up into fine particles by the rising air. These particles develop electrical charges, some negative (−) and some positive (+). Particles with the same charge collect in different parts of a cloud, or form new raindrops that fall to earth. When the difference in electrical charge becomes great enough, electricity may be discharged between different parts of one cloud, between two clouds, or between a cloud and the ground. This discharge, or flash of lightning, heats the air through which it passes. The heated air expands violently, creating the sound waves that we call thunder. Since it takes about five seconds for a sound wave to travel one mile, a person can tell how far away a storm is by counting the seconds between a lightning flash and the thunder that follows.

Orographic rainfall. A second type of rainfall is called orographic rainfall. This type results when winds are forced to rise because hills or mountains lie in their path. As the winds rise and cool, some of the moisture they contain condenses and falls as rain. (See bottom chart on opposite page.) As the winds flow down the other side of a hill or mountain, however, they become warmer and may evaporate the moisture there. The side of the mountain that receives little rain and loses its moisture is said to lie in a rain shadow.

Cyclonic rainfall. A third type of rainfall occurs when a mass of warm, moist air rises in a spiral fashion over a mass of cooler and generally drier air. The wind system that results is a type of cyclone. It should not be confused with a tornado, which is a violent, whirling windstorm that travels in a narrow path. Nor should this type of cyclone be confused with a tropical cyclone, which is also a severe storm. When the winds of a tropical cyclone reach speeds of more than 75 miles per hour, the storm is known as a hurricane or a typhoon.

A cyclone that is associated with cyclonic rainfall is much larger than a tornado, sometimes covering an area as large as one million square miles. The moist air in a cyclone rises and cools slowly enough so that cyclonic rainfall

Cyclonic rainfall occurs when a mass of warm, moist air rises in a spiral fashion over a mass of cooler and generally drier air. The area in which two air masses come in contact with each other is called a front. The two main types of fronts are warm fronts (above) and cold fronts (below).

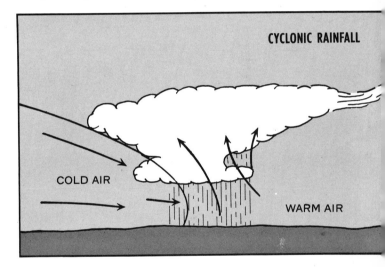

usually varies from a drizzle to a long steady rain. In some cases, however, heavy showers and even thundershowers may result.

This type of cyclone develops when two large air masses of different temperatures meet, and the warmer mass rises over the cooler. This usually occurs in the middle* latitudes, where warm air masses from tropical regions meet cold air masses from polar regions. The area in which the two masses come in contact with each other is called a front. There are two main types of fronts, called warm fronts and cold fronts. Usually, one air mass is more active than the other. In a warm front, the warm air mass is more active and rises above the cold air. In a cold front, the cold mass forces itself under the warm mass, causing the warmer air to rise. Cyclonic rainfall results in both cases as the warm, lighter air mass rises.

*See Glossary

pages 42 and 43 helps to explain why. During the summer months, the northern part of the earth is tilted toward the sun. Therefore, lands in the Northern Hemisphere receive large amounts of warm sunshine.

There is also another reason why summers are so warm in the Northeast. During the summer, many of the winds that blow across this region come from the Gulf of Mexico. (See map on page 20.) These winds are very warm and moist. They bring hot, humid weather to many parts of the Northeast.

The winds from the Gulf of Mexico also bring frequent rains to the Northeast during the summertime. As the

moist air passes over the hot land, it rises and cools quickly, losing some of its moisture in the form of rain. (See the description of convectional rainfall on pages 50 and 51.) Often this kind of rainfall is accompanied by thunder and lightning. In the summer, the Northeast gets much of its moisture during thunderstorms.

Hot, humid weather can be very unpleasant for people living in large cities, where the buildings and pavements reflect the sun's heat. Sometimes a "heat wave" may last for weeks. It is hard to work when the weather is hot and humid. Sleeping is also difficult. On hot days, city dwellers go to parks or sit on

A rainy summer day in the Northeast. Winds from the Gulf of Mexico bring rainfall to the Northeast during the summertime. As the moist air passes over the hot land, it rises and cools quickly, losing some of its moisture in the form of rain.

Camping in the Adirondack Mountains. In the summer, many people in the Northeast come to mountainous areas such as the Adirondacks to escape the heat. Summers are cooler in the mountains than they are on nearby lowlands because of the difference in elevation.

porches and balconies to get fresh air. Some people go to the seacoast or to the mountains to escape the heat.

Summers are cooler in some parts of the Northeast. From New York City we travel to the Adirondack Mountains. We find that the summer weather here is cooler and more pleasant than it is in the lowlands. Summers are also pleasantly cool in other mountainous areas in the Northeast. Many people come to these areas during the summer to enjoy the refreshing mountain air.

Mountainous parts of the Northeast are generally cooler than nearby lowlands because they are so much higher above the level of the sea. The higher you go above sea level, the cooler the

air becomes. As you may have learned in your science class, the earth gives off heat that it has received from the sun. At low elevations, much of this heat is absorbed by the moisture and particles of dust in the air. At high elevations, however, the air is much cleaner and drier. Therefore, it cannot absorb as much heat. As a result, the temperature is usually cooler at high elevations than it is at lower elevations.

Another place where summers are mild is the Atlantic coast of New England. Cool breezes from the ocean keep the temperature from becoming very hot. This is one reason why many people spend their vacations on Cape Cod or along the coast of Maine.

53

Autumn

Autumn brings cool, pleasant weather, colorful leaves, and shorter days to the Northeast.

Autumn is a pleasant season in the Northeast. Now it is October, and we are hiking through the Berkshire Hills in western Massachusetts. We are wearing lightweight coats, because the temperature here is about fifty degrees. The air here is so cool and fresh that it makes us feel very energetic. Wherever we go in the Northeast during the autumn, we are likely to find cool, pleasant weather.

The oaks, maples, and birches that cover the hillsides around us are clothed in scarlet and gold. Although the sky overhead is blue and cloudless, there is a smoky haze in the air. Farmers are busy harvesting the last of their crops. Tomorrow morning, the ground will probably have a white coating of frost.

The days are growing shorter. Each day the sun is a little lower in the sky. Winter will soon be here.

Explore the Climate of the Northeast
1. State two reasons why winters are cold in the Northeast.
2. What facts help to explain why many areas in the Northeast receive heavy snowfall?
3. How does the long growing season along the Atlantic coast help farmers here?
4. Why is the climate along Lake Ontario and Lake Erie well suited for growing fruit?

Discuss an Important Generalization

As a class, discuss the following generalization:

The climate of the Northeast affects people's lives in many ways.

To prepare for your discussion, you will need to do some research. As you carry on your research, look for ways in which the climate of the Northeast affects each of the following:
a. farming
b. the types of homes in which people live
c. the clothes people wear
d. transportation

The guidelines on page 351 will help you have a successful discussion.

Climate and You

What is the climate like where you live? How does it affect your everyday life? Think carefully about these two questions and then organize your ideas into an essay to share with your class. Follow the guidelines for good writing given on page 347.

Part 2
History

This statue of a Minuteman stands in Concord, Massachusetts, the site of one of the first battles of the Revolutionary War.

An Iroquois Indian village consisted of a group of "longhouses" made of poles and bark. Several families lived in each longhouse. The Iroquois and other Indians in the Northeast depended on the forest for many things they needed. They obtained most of their food by hunting.

4 The Coming of the White Men

A Problem To Solve

The Pilgrims, who founded Plymouth in 1620, were the first of many thousands of English settlers to make their homes in the Northeast. **Why were so many Englishmen willing to endure the dangers and hardships of life in a new land?** In forming hypotheses to solve this problem, consider how settlement in America was affected by the following:

a. religious differences in England during the 1600's
b. living conditions in England at that time
c. opportunities for a better way of life in America

See TO THE STUDENT, pages 8-10.

Indians were the first people to live in the Northeast. Five hundred years ago, dense forests covered the part of our country that we call the Northeast. In these forests lived people with straight, black hair and copper-colored skin. To-day, these people are known as Indians. Most historians believe that the Indians first came from Asia. (See opposite page.)

The Indians in the Northeast obtained most of their food by hunting. Deer and other forest animals provided

Early Peoples of the Northeast

At the time the first European settlers came to the Northeast, Indian tribes were scattered throughout most of the region. These tribes belonged to two main groups. One group spoke languages of the Algonquian family, and the other group spoke Iroquoian languages. (See map below.)

Most of the Indians along the Atlantic coast of the Northeast belonged to Algonquian tribes. These included the Wampanoag, the Pequot, and the Delaware. Massasoit, an Indian chief who helped the Pilgrims, was a Wampanoag.

The Iroquoian tribes of the Northeast lived farther inland. Five of these tribes — the Seneca, Cayuga, Onondaga, Oneida, and Mohawk — were known as the Iroquois. During the 1500's, the Iroquois had formed a league to keep peace among themselves. Hiawatha* helped to found this league, which became known as the Five Nations. About 1715, the Tuscarora tribe moved into the area from North Carolina and joined the league, which from then on was known as the Six Nations.

Over the years, many Indian tribes disappeared from the Northeast. Some were wiped out in violent wars with other tribes or with colonists. Others were forced to give up their lands and move westward. Many Iroquois who had sided with the British during the Revolutionary War moved to Canada. In the 1780's, the United States began to establish reservations for the Indians who still lived in the Northeast.

*See Glossary

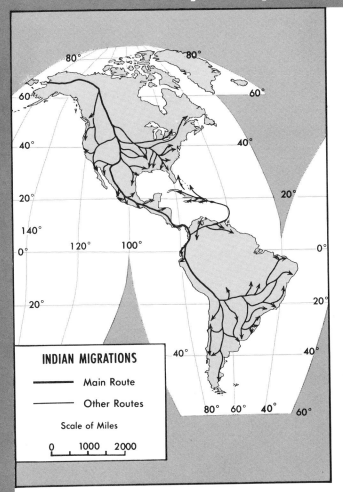

INDIAN MIGRATIONS

— Main Route
— Other Routes

Scale of Miles
0   1000   2000

Most historians believe that the people we now call Indians first came to America from Asia. The map above shows the routes that these people may have followed.

Asia and North America are very close together in the far north. Here they are separated only by a narrow stretch of water called the Bering Strait. (See left-hand inset map on page 18.) About twenty thousand years ago, the oceans of the world were shallower than they are today. At that time, a bridge of land may have connected Asia and North America. It would have been fairly easy for people to travel from one continent to the other.

The people who came from Asia were wandering hunters. They probably came to America to hunt animals for meat and for skins to make clothing. Some of these people stayed in the far north to hunt such animals as walrus and seal. However, most of them traveled southward to make their homes in warmer regions. Over the centuries, Indians settled in many parts of North and South America.

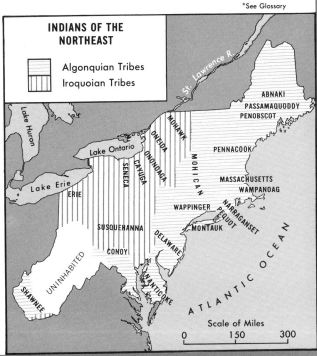

INDIANS OF THE NORTHEAST

▦ Algonquian Tribes
▥ Iroquoian Tribes

Scale of Miles
0   150   300

not only meat but also skins for making clothing. In some tribes, the Indian women tended small fields of corn, squash, and other crops. They also gathered roots, nuts, and berries for food.

The Indians used the trees of the forest for making many things they needed. Most tribes built round or oval huts called wigwams, which were usually made by stretching pieces of bark over a framework of poles. The Iroquois*

Indians lived in "longhouses." These buildings were also made of poles and bark, but they were long and narrow. The Indians traveled in canoes made from birch bark. Many of their household articles were made from bark or wood.

Most Indian tribes in the Northeast were very warlike. The Indians greatly admired anyone who showed bravery in battle. Even tribes that were closely related often fought each other.

European Explorers Come to America

While the Indians were roaming the forests of the Northeast, great events were taking place in Europe, across the Atlantic Ocean. Early in the 1400's,

Christopher Columbus left Spain in 1492 in search of an all-water route to Asia. Sailing westward, he discovered a new part of the world.

European explorers began making voyages southward along the coast of Africa. (See page 60.) These daring seamen were looking for an all-water route to the eastern part of Asia. There they could obtain spices and other precious goods.

Christopher Columbus sails westward and discovers America. An explorer named Christopher Columbus thought that he could find a better route to Asia. Like many educated Europeans at that time, Columbus believed the earth was round. He felt sure that he could reach Asia by sailing westward across the unknown waters of the Atlantic Ocean. At last he persuaded Queen Isabella of Spain to provide money and ships for his voyage.

In August, 1492, Columbus and his crew left Spain in three tiny ships. Many weeks later, they reached a small island off the coast of North America. After visiting several other islands, they returned to Spain. Columbus made three more trips to America, but he died

*See Glossary

John Cabot was hired by a group of English merchants to seek a westward route to the rich cities of Asia. He made two voyages across the Atlantic Ocean, in 1497 and 1498. Although Cabot did not find what he was seeking, his voyages gave England a claim to much of North America.

without realizing that he had reached a new part of the world instead of Asia.

Cabot and other explorers sail along the Atlantic coast. The news of Columbus' discovery soon spread from Spain to other parts of Europe. In England, a group of merchants hired an explorer named John Cabot to travel westward in search of the rich cities of Asia. Cabot made two voyages to the west, in 1497 and 1498. It is believed that he followed the routes shown on page 61.

Although Cabot did not succeed in reaching Asia, his voyages had two important results. First, they gave England a claim to much of North America. Second, Cabot discovered that the waters off the coast of North America contained large numbers of fish. Soon many fishermen were sailing westward from

Europe to visit these rich fishing grounds.

In the years that followed, other explorers came to the New World. They soon realized that Asia was much farther away than Columbus had supposed. Two great continents, North America and South America, blocked the way. To reach Asia, westbound ships had to travel all the way around the tip of South America.

Several explorers tried to find a shorter sea route between the Atlantic and Pacific oceans. One of these men was Giovanni da Verrazano, who was hired by the King of France. In 1524, Verrazano sailed along the eastern coast of North America and discovered the great bay that now forms the harbor of New York City.

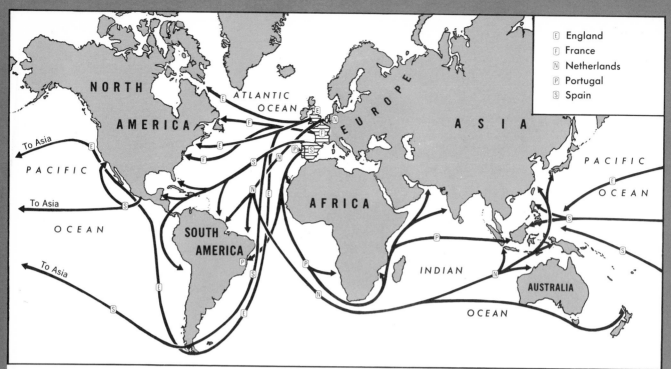

During the Age of Exploration, explorers from five small European countries sailed to many parts of the world. The map above shows the main routes of exploration.

The Age of Exploration

At the beginning of the 1400's, people in Europe knew little about the rest of the world. Educated men believed the earth was round, but no one had ever proved this. Ships were so small and unsafe that only the boldest men would sail far out to sea in them. In addition, sailors lacked instruments for determining where they were if they sailed out of sight of land.

During this same period, people in Europe heard amazing stories about travelers who had crossed rugged mountains and burning deserts in order to reach lands of southern and eastern Asia known as the Indies. Many of these people returned with spices, jewels, and other precious goods. The most famous traveler was an Italian named Marco Polo, who had spent many years in China during the late 1200's. When he returned to Europe, he wrote a book describing the rich lands he had visited. Long after Marco Polo's death, his book continued to make men want to see the Indies for themselves.

Europeans seek an all-water route to the Indies. In the early 1400's, people in Europe had to pay high prices for goods from Asia. Arab traders brought spices, silks, and other items from the Indies to ports on the eastern shore of the Mediterranean. Here, traders from the powerful Italian city of Venice loaded the goods on their ships and carried them to ports in Europe. The prices they charged for these goods were many times higher than the prices they had paid. As a result, people in western Europe wanted to

find an all-water route to the Indies, so that they could buy goods directly from merchants there. Then they would no longer have to pay high prices to Arab and Venetian traders.

The Portuguese sail to the Indies. In the 1400's, events took place that made it possible for men to sail far out to sea. European craftsmen learned to make instruments to help sailors find directions at sea. Prince Henry of Portugal did more than any other man of his time to put these instruments to good use. He organized a school where Portuguese sailors learned to use the latest charts and instruments. In addition, his shipbuilders designed faster, more seaworthy vessels. Prince Henry then encouraged Portuguese seamen to sail farther and farther south along the west coast of Africa.

In 1497, four ships commanded by a sea captain named Vasco da Gama set sail from Lisbon, Portugal. Da Gama and his men sailed southward along the west coast of Africa and rounded the continent's southern tip. Then they sailed north and east across the Indian Ocean to India. Portugal was the first European country to find an all-water route to the Indies.

Columbus discovers America. Several years before Da Gama's voyage, an Italian explorer named Christopher Columbus had tried to reach the Indies by sailing westward across the Atlantic Ocean. In August of 1492, Columbus and his men sailed from Spain in three small ships. Two months later, they sighted the island of

San Salvador, in the West Indies. (See top map at right.) Columbus was certain he had reached the Indies. Although he made three more voyages to America, he never discovered that the Indies lay thousands of miles farther west.

Magellan finds a westward route to the Indies. After Columbus' first voyage, other explorers traveled westward in search of the Indies. One of these was John Cabot, who made two voyages westward from England, in 1497 and 1498. Cabot explored part of the northeastern coast of North America. (See middle map at right.) However, Cabot, like Columbus, thought he had reached Asia. Not until the early 1500's did men realize that the lands to the west were two great continents—North and South America.

A courageous Portuguese sea captain named Ferdinand Magellan tried to find a way around North and South America. In 1519, he and his men set sail from Spain. They crossed the Atlantic and sailed southward down the east coast of South America. At last they found a water passage leading westward. This brought them to the great body of water we know today as the Pacific Ocean. They sailed on westward across the Pacific. Although Magellan was killed by natives in the Philippine Islands, his ships continued the westward voyage without him and finally arrived back in Spain. These were the first ships to sail completely around the world.

Europeans try to find a water route through North America. Other European explorers were determined to find a westward route to the Indies that was shorter than the one found by Magellan. If men could find a route through North America, they would be able to reach the Indies much faster than if they had to travel around South America. England, France, and the Netherlands sent out many explorers to find such a route. These men sailed into one inlet after another along the Atlantic coast of North America. Although the search went on for many years, no one was able to find a passage. Some of the men who tried, however, explored large areas of the Atlantic coast of North America. While exploring for France, Giovanni da Verrazano discovered the bay that is now New York City's harbor. (See lower map at right.)

Settlers come to the newly discovered lands. In time, other people in Europe besides explorers traveled to the New World. Some went in hopes of finding treasure. Others left Europe with the idea of starting a new life. Settlers from Spain and Portugal came to South America and the southern part of North America. Other parts of North America were settled by people from England, France, the Netherlands, and Sweden. Many of these settlers came to the Northeast. In this chapter, you can learn more about the settlement of this part of our country.

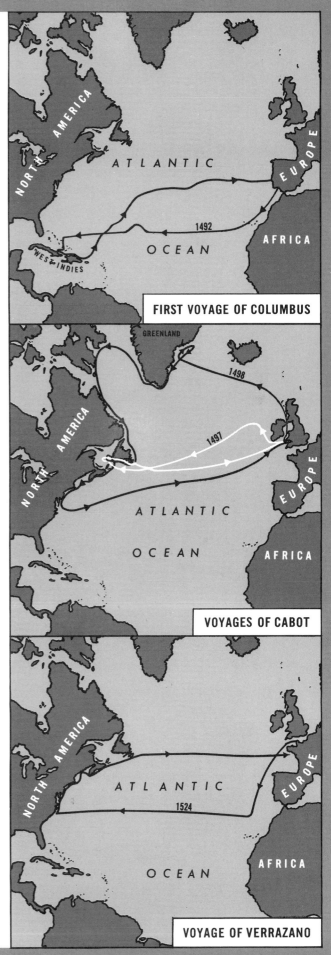

FIRST VOYAGE OF COLUMBUS

VOYAGES OF CABOT

VOYAGE OF VERRAZANO

Settlers Make Their Homes in the Northeast

The English decide to start colonies in America. Within fifty years after Columbus' first voyage, Spain had built a great empire in the New World. England, however, had not established any colonies in the lands claimed by Cabot. There were several reasons for this. In the early 1500's, England was a rather poor, weak country. It did not have a large navy to protect its merchant ships from attack by pirates or foreign enemies. Also, England had been weakened by a bitter quarrel between rival families of noblemen.

As the years passed, England became richer and more powerful. English companies sold large amounts of woolen cloth to other countries in Europe and Asia. To protect its merchant ships, England built up a strong navy. By the end of the 1500's, it had a more powerful navy than its great rival, Spain.

Gradually, English leaders became interested in starting colonies in America. Colonies could provide such articles as timber and furs, which England at that time had to buy from other European nations. English merchants would be able to sell large amounts of cloth, hardware, and other supplies to American colonists. The English government could get rid of criminals, beggars, and other troublesome persons by sending them to America. In addition, if there were English colonies along the Atlantic coast, the Spanish would be less likely to claim this territory for themselves.

English merchants thought that they could make large profits from trading with colonies in America. In 1607, English trading companies sent two groups of settlers to the New World. One group founded a settlement called Jamestown in Virginia. This became the first permanent English settlement in America. The other group started a settlement at Popham Beach on the coast of Maine. During the first winter, the settlers at Popham Beach suffered greatly from cold, hunger, and disease. In the spring, they returned to England.

The Pilgrims come to New England. On a bright September day in 1620, a tiny ship called the *Mayflower* left the harbor of Plymouth, England, and headed westward toward the New World. On board the *Mayflower* were a group of people whom we know today as the Pilgrims. To understand why the Pilgrims were willing to make the long, dangerous journey to America, you must know something about the history of England.

At the start of the 1500's, nearly all Englishmen belonged to the Roman Catholic Church. Then Henry VIII,

Build Your Vocabulary

Iroquois	colony	Puritans	Pilgrims	Roman Catholic Church
Church of England	Separatists	assembly	French and Indian War
Quakers	Appalachian Mountains	Toleration Act	proprietors

The Pilgrims celebrating the first Thanksgiving. In 1620, the Pilgrims came to America to worship God in their own way. They founded Plymouth colony. During their first winter, about half of the Pilgrims died of cold and starvation. The following autumn the harvest was good, and the Pilgrims invited their Indian friends to join them in a feast of thanksgiving.

the king of England, broke away from this church and started one of his own. This became known as the Church of England. It resembled the Roman Catholic Church in many ways, but it was headed by the king instead of the pope.*

All Englishmen were expected to belong to the Church of England. Many people, however, preferred to worship God in other ways. Some wanted to remain Roman Catholics. On the other hand, many people were opposed to the Church of England because they felt it was too much like the Roman Catholic Church. Some of these people were called Puritans because they wanted only to "purify" the Church of England. Others, who were known as Separatists,

wanted to break away from this church entirely.

James I, who was king of England during the early 1600's, often persecuted people who belonged to other churches. The Separatists were forbidden to hold their own church services. Some were put in jail for their beliefs. Finally a group of Separatists — the Pilgrims — decided to go to America. In that distant land, they could worship God as they chose.

After a long, stormy voyage, the *Mayflower* reached the coast of what is now Massachusetts. There the Pilgrims founded a settlement called Plymouth. The first winter was a hard one for the Pilgrims. They had little food, and the weather was bitterly cold. About half of the settlers died. When spring came, friendly Indians taught the Pilgrims how to plant corn and other crops. The harvest was good that year, and life became easier for the Pilgrims.

The Plymouth colony never became very large or prosperous. Still, it played an important part in our country's history. By journeying to a new land in search of freedom, the Pilgrims set an example of courage for all the settlers who came after them.

Other colonies are founded in New England. After the Pilgrims arrived, many other English settlers made the journey to America. Some, like the Pilgrims, came mainly to worship God as they pleased. Others came because they felt that the English king and his nobles had too much power over them. In America, they might be able to have a larger share in the government.

Many colonists came to the New World to seek a better life. During the early 1600's, it was hard to make a good living in England. Formerly, most Englishmen had been farmers who rented land from wealthy landowners. As time passed, the landowners found

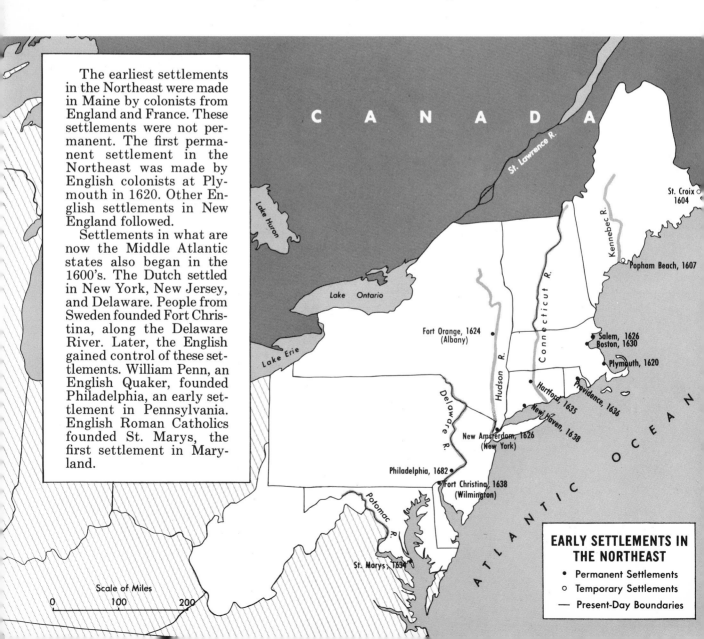

The earliest settlements in the Northeast were made in Maine by colonists from England and France. These settlements were not permanent. The first permanent settlement in the Northeast was made by English colonists at Plymouth in 1620. Other English settlements in New England followed.

Settlements in what are now the Middle Atlantic states also began in the 1600's. The Dutch settled in New York, New Jersey, and Delaware. People from Sweden founded Fort Christina, along the Delaware River. Later, the English gained control of these settlements. William Penn, an English Quaker, founded Philadelphia, an early settlement in Pennsylvania. English Roman Catholics founded St. Marys, the first settlement in Maryland.

CANADA

St. Lawrence R.

Lake Huron

Lake Ontario

Lake Erie

St. Croix 1604

Kennebec R.

Popham Beach, 1607

Fort Orange, 1624 (Albany)

Connecticut R.

Salem, 1626
Boston, 1630

Plymouth, 1620

Hudson R.

Hartford, 1635

Providence, 1636

New Haven, 1638

Delaware R.

New Amsterdam, 1626 (New York)

ATLANTIC OCEAN

Philadelphia, 1682

Fort Christina, 1638 (Wilmington)

Potomac R.

St. Marys, 1634

EARLY SETTLEMENTS IN THE NORTHEAST
• Permanent Settlements
○ Temporary Settlements
— Present-Day Boundaries

Scale of Miles
0   100   200

they could make more money by raising sheep for wool. They fenced off much of the farmland and made it into pastures for sheep. Many farmers could not find any land to rent, and it was not easy for them to get other jobs. In America, however, there was enough land for everyone.

Massachusetts Bay colony. Between 1628 and 1640, thousands of Puritans came to New England. They settled north of Plymouth and started a colony called Massachusetts Bay. Boston and other towns were established here. The Puritan settlers were serious, hard-working people, and their colony grew rapidly. In 1691, the colony of Plymouth became part of Massachusetts Bay colony.

Although the Puritans who settled Massachusetts Bay colony had left England in search of religious freedom, they were not willing to grant the same rights to others. All the people who lived in Massachusetts Bay colony had to obey the strict rules laid down by the Puritan leaders. They also had to pay taxes to support the Puritan church. Yet only church members could vote or take part in the government. People whose religious beliefs were different from those of the Puritans did not dare to state their views openly. If they did, they might be whipped or forced to leave the colony.

Rhode Island. Many people in Massachusetts Bay colony disagreed with the rules set up by the Puritans. Among these was a young minister named Roger Williams. He argued that every man should be free to worship God in his own way. Williams also said that the Puritans had no right to their land be-

Thomas Hooker and his followers journeyed to the Connecticut River valley from Massachusetts Bay colony. Hooker was one of several ministers who left the colony to start settlements of their own.

cause they had not bought it from the Indians.

Because his opinions made the Puritan leaders angry, Williams was forced to leave Massachusetts Bay colony in the winter of 1636. Helped by friendly Indians, he traveled southward to Narragansett Bay. There he founded a settlement called Providence. (See map on opposite page.) Later, other people who disagreed with the Puritans started towns nearby. All these towns eventually joined together to form the colony of Rhode Island.

Connecticut. Another minister who left Massachusetts Bay colony was Thomas Hooker. He did not like the way that the colony was governed. Also, the land was poor for farming. Hooker and his followers hoped to find better farmland farther to the west. In

1636 they journeyed to the fertile valley of the Connecticut River, where they built new homes. Later, the settlements in the Connecticut Valley were joined with several towns along Long Island Sound to form the colony of Connecticut.

New Hampshire and Maine. Meanwhile, other settlements were being started to the north of Massachusetts Bay colony. Some of these were founded by Englishmen who hoped to make money from fishing or fur trading. Others were started by people who left Massachusetts Bay for religious reasons. The land north of Massachusetts Bay colony was divided into two territories, New Hampshire and Maine. New Hampshire became a separate colony, but Maine became part of Massachusetts Bay colony.

Catholic settlers arrive in Maryland. During the 1630's, another English colony was founded in the Northeast. This was Maryland. Its founder, Lord Baltimore, was a Roman Catholic. At that time, Catholics were treated harshly in England. Lord Baltimore wanted to start a colony in America where Catholics could worship without interference. Also, he hoped to make money by renting land to colonists.

There were more Protestants than Catholics among the people who settled in Maryland. To make sure that the rights of the Catholics would be protected, Maryland's government passed the Toleration Act in 1649. This law provided that all Christians, whatever their church, could worship freely in Maryland.

The Dutch settle along the Hudson and Delaware rivers. The land between Maryland and New England was claimed by the Dutch. In 1609, a group of Dutch merchants had hired an explorer named Henry Hudson to search for a northern water route to China. Hudson explored the coast of the Northeast, looking for a sea passage through America. He sailed about 150 miles up the river that now bears his name, hoping it was the passage he was seeking.

Hudson never found a northern route to China. However, his discoveries served to establish Dutch claims in America. He also helped the Dutch to establish a profitable fur trade with the Indians.

The Dutch soon began to settle the lands they claimed. Their settlements were known as the colony of New Netherland. In 1624, Dutch colonists founded Fort Orange on the Hudson River, at the place where Albany stands today. Two years later, the Dutch

New Amsterdam was founded by the Dutch in 1626. About forty years later, this city was captured by an English fleet and renamed New York.

66

bought Manhattan Island from the Indians for about twenty-four dollars' worth of trinkets. There they established New Amsterdam. Other towns were started nearby. The Dutch also settled along the Delaware River. In 1655, they conquered the colony of New Sweden, which had been founded by Swedish settlers seventeen years earlier.

England takes New Netherland. The English King did not recognize the Dutch claims in America. He believed that John Cabot's voyages had given England a claim to all the land along the Atlantic coast. Also, the English and the Dutch were rivals in trade. In 1664, an English fleet sailed into the harbor of New Amsterdam and captured the city, which was renamed New York.

The English soon took over the remaining Dutch settlements in America. The lands that had been claimed and settled by the Dutch became the English colonies of New York, New Jersey, and Delaware.

William Penn starts a successful colony. West of the Delaware River was a large area where few people had settled. The King of England gave this land to a man named William Penn as payment for a debt owed to Penn's father. Penn belonged to a religious group called the Society of Friends. The members of this group, known as Quakers, were being mistreated in England. Penn wanted to start a colony where Quakers and other people could worship freely. In 1681, he sent the first group of settlers to his new colony, which was called Pennsylvania.

Penn was a good businessman and a wise ruler. He made friends with the Indians by buying their land instead of

William Penn founded the colony of Pennsylvania. He made friends with the Indians by paying them for their land instead of taking it away from them.

taking it away from them. People of all religions and nationalities were encouraged to settle in Pennsylvania. Colonists arrived not only from England but also from Ireland, Germany, and other countries. Pennsylvania grew rapidly and became a prosperous colony.

The English colonies in 1700. At the start of the eighteenth century, there were twelve English colonies along the Atlantic coast of America. Not all of these colonies were in the Northeast. Some, like Virginia, were in the part of our country that is now called the South. A thirteenth colony, Georgia, was founded in 1734.

About 275,000 people made their homes in the English colonies in 1700. Most of these settlers lived along the seacoast or in fertile river valleys. The rest of our country was mainly a wilderness, where the only inhabitants were scattered tribes of Indians.

How the Colonists Lived

The colonists adapted European ways of doing things to life in a new land. The people who came to America from Europe during the 1600's and 1700's brought many ideas and customs from their homelands. Since most of the early settlers came from England, it is not surprising that English was the main language spoken in the colonies. As you have learned, the colonists brought their religious beliefs with them from Europe. They also brought many ideas about law and government.

Many different skills were brought to America by the settlers. Farmers brought not only plants and livestock from Europe, but also their methods of planting and harvesting crops. The men who had been craftsmen in Europe brought their skills in making furniture and other household articles. Most of the women who came to America knew how to spin, weave, and sew. They also knew how to preserve food.

The colonists found, however, that they could not live in the American wilderness exactly as they had lived in Europe. Most of the land in Europe had been settled for many centuries. In America, dense forests covered much of the land. Trees had to be cleared away before farms could be started. In some areas, the soil was different from the soil the colonists had known in Europe. The climate, too, was different. Even many plants and animals in America were new and strange.

As a result of these differences, the colonists had to learn many new ways of doing things. For example, English houses were often made of brick. In America, however, wood was easier to obtain than brick. Therefore, most houses were built of wood. Gradually the colonists developed a way of life that was a mixture of the old and the new.

In New England, many people earned their living from the sea. During colonial days, about nine out of every ten Americans made their living by farming. In New England, however, the percentage of farmers was smaller than in other sections. The rugged hills and thin, stony soil in this area made farming difficult. In many places, summers

Reconstruction of a colonial village near Plymouth, Massachusetts. Colonists in America built homes much like the ones they had known in Europe.

New England colonists building a ship. Most of the people in colonial America were farmers. However, farming was difficult in New England, and many colonists here turned to the sea for their living. Some of them built ships. Others became fishermen, whalers, or traders.

were too short and cool for growing certain crops. Most farms in New England were small, and the people who lived on them raised just enough food for their own needs.

Although New England lacked good farmland, it did have other valuable resources. Much of the land was covered with forests, which supplied wood for building ships and houses. Along the coast of New England were many bays and inlets where ships could anchor safely. The waters of the Atlantic were rich in cod, haddock, and other fish.

With these advantages, it is not surprising that many New England colonists turned to the sea for a living. Some worked as fishermen. Others

were shipbuilders, who used wood from the forests to make sailing vessels. Still others were sailors on merchant ships that carried goods between New England and other parts of the world.

During the 1700's, Boston and other cities along the coast of New England became thriving seaports. Ships sailed from these ports with cargoes of lumber and dried or salted fish. These goods were sold in Europe and in English and French colonies in the West Indies. The ships returned to New England with sugar and molasses from the West Indies and with manufactured goods, such as silks and furniture, from Europe. Many New England merchants grew wealthy from this overseas trade.

There were prosperous farms and busy cities in the Middle Atlantic colonies. Farming was more important in the Middle Atlantic colonies than it was in New England. On the Coastal Plain and the Piedmont Plateau, there were large stretches of level land with fertile soil. Also, summers were longer and warmer here than they were in most parts of New England.

New York, Pennsylvania, New Jersey, and Delaware were often known as the "bread colonies." Here the main crop was wheat, which was ground into flour at nearby gristmills. Farmers also raised corn, oats, and other grains, as well as many kinds of fruits and vegetables. Large numbers of pigs and beef cattle were raised for meat. Although there were some huge estates along the Hudson River, most farms in the "bread colonies" were medium-sized. Farmers raised crops mainly for sale

rather than for their own use. Flour, pork, and other farm products were exported to the other colonies and to the West Indies.

Near Chesapeake Bay, in Maryland, the soil was rich and the growing season was long. Tobacco grew well there. This crop was raised on large farms called plantations, which were worked by Negro slaves. Many of the plantations were along rivers that emptied into Chesapeake Bay. Oceangoing ships could dock at the plantations to take on cargoes of tobacco. Most of the tobacco was shipped to England and other European countries, where it was sold for a high price.

The Middle Atlantic colonies were rich in resources that could be used by craftsmen. Valuable deposits of iron ore were found in eastern Pennsylvania. Large forests nearby provided wood for lumber and for charcoal,* which was used in smelting ore to make iron. In Pennsylvania and its neighboring colonies, there were many blast furnaces where iron was made. Beaver and other forest animals were trapped for their valuable furs, which were used in making hats and coats. Other types of manufacturing, such as weaving and glassmaking, also developed in the Middle Atlantic colonies.

Along the Middle Atlantic coast were many bays and river mouths that provided good harbors for ships. Seaports such as New York, Philadelphia, and Baltimore grew up along these harbors. They handled the thriving trade between the Middle Atlantic colonies and other parts of the world. By 1750, Philadelphia and New York were the largest cities in America.

A blacksmith. The Middle Atlantic colonies were rich in resources, such as iron ore and furs, that could be used by blacksmiths and other craftsmen.

70

The colonists had a large share in governing themselves. The English settlers who came to America in colonial days brought with them many ideas about freedom and self-government. At that time, people in England enjoyed more rights and freedoms than people who lived in other parts of Europe. For example, no Englishman could be punished for a crime until he had been given a fair trial by a jury. Although the king was the head of the government, he was not free to rule just as he pleased. His power to govern was limited by Parliament, which made the laws and decided what taxes everyone must pay.

Gradually, the English colonists in America began to set up governments that were similar to the one they had known at home. Each colony was ruled by a governor and a lawmaking body called a legislature. (See feature at right.) The legislature was divided into two branches called houses. The lower house, known as the assembly, was the more powerful of the two.

In each colony, members of the assembly were elected by colonists. Not all colonists could take part in the elections, however. The right to vote was usually limited to white men who owned a certain amount of land or other property. In some places, voters had to belong to a particular church or hold certain religious beliefs. In spite of these requirements, the colonists had a larger share in their government than the people of any European country at that time.

In most of the colonies, bitter quarrels often took place between the governor and the elected assembly. This

The Old State House in Boston.

COLONIAL GOVERNMENT

The English colonies in America were not all governed in exactly the same way. Each colony had a governor and a legislature, or lawmaking body. However, the way in which government officials were chosen differed from one colony to another. In the middle of the 1700's there were three types of colonies. Each type had its own form of government.

1. Charter colonies. Connecticut and Rhode Island were called charter colonies because they had charters signed by the English king, setting forth the rights of their citizens. In the charter colonies, the governor was elected by a vote of the people. Voters also chose representatives to both houses of the legislature.

2. Proprietary colonies. Maryland, Delaware, and Pennsylvania had all been founded by men known as proprietors.* These men and their descendants had the right to appoint the governor of the colony and to choose the members of the upper house of the legislature. Members of the assembly were elected by the people. In Pennsylvania, the upper house was discontinued after 1701.

3. Royal colonies. At one time, most of the other English colonies had also been charter or proprietary colonies. One by one, however, they came under the direct control of the king. In the royal colonies, the king appointed the governor and one house of the legislature. The colonists themselves elected the members of the other house.

was because the assembly represented the colonists, while the governor usually represented the king or a proprietor. (See feature on page 71.) The governor could refuse to approve legislation. He could also prevent the assembly from meeting. However, the assembly controlled the spending of public money. By threatening to withhold the governor's salary, it could force him to do as it wished. Gradually, the colonial assemblies became more and more powerful.

The colonists not only chose representatives to the assemblies but they also ran their local governments. In New England, for example, the voters of each town met at least once a year to elect officials and pass laws for the community. Through these town meetings, the colonists gained much experience in governing themselves.

A town meeting. In New England, the voters of each town met at least once a year to elect officials and pass laws. Through these meetings, colonists gained experience in governing themselves.

Ideas of freedom grew stronger. As you have already learned, many of the colonists came to America in order to worship God as they pleased. At first, however, they were not always willing to allow this freedom to others. In many colonies, only people who belonged to a certain church could vote or take part in the government. People who held different religious beliefs were sometimes jailed or forced to leave the colony. Gradually, however, many people came to believe that everyone should be able to worship in his own way. Laws were passed to allow greater freedom of worship.

The colonists also felt that they should have the right to speak and write their opinions on any subject without fear of punishment. In other words, they wanted freedom of speech and freedom of the press. In 1734, a newspaper printer named John Peter Zenger was arrested for publishing articles that criticized New York's governor. At Zenger's trial, his lawyer argued that no one should be punished for writing the truth. The jury decided that Zenger was not guilty of any crime, so he was set free. This decision helped to establish freedom of the press in America.

Not all the people in the colonies enjoyed equal rights and freedoms. The people who had the fewest rights of all were the Negroes. Many thousands of Negroes from Africa had been brought to America as slaves. Most of them lived in the South, where they worked on large plantations. However, there were many slaves in the northern colonies as well. Here, most of them were household servants or farm workers.

England controlled the colonists' trade. Although England allowed the colonists much freedom, it kept firm control over their trade. In the 1600's and 1700's, people in England felt that the main purpose of the colonies was to benefit the mother country. The colonists were expected to supply the mother country with certain raw materials and to buy English manufactured goods. English shipowners hoped to earn money by carrying goods between England and the colonies.

To achieve these goals, England had to prevent the colonists from trading freely with foreign countries such as France and the Netherlands. Otherwise, foreign merchants might be able to sell manufactured goods to the colonists more cheaply than English merchants could. This would hurt the sale of English goods. By paying high prices to the colonists, foreign countries might obtain raw materials that were urgently needed in England. In addition, foreign shipowners might take away business from English shipowners.

In the 1660's, Parliament began passing strict laws to control the trade of the colonies. One law stated that goods sent to and from the colonies must be carried in English ships. It also listed a number of articles that the colonists could not sell directly to foreign countries. These goods had to be shipped to England first. Merchants there could buy them and send them on to other countries in Europe. Another law placed high taxes, or duties, on sugar and molasses that the colonists bought from foreign colonies in the West Indies.

Parliament also passed several laws that restricted the sale of goods manufactured in the colonies. These laws provided that certain items produced in America, such as hats and woolen cloth, could not be sold anywhere except in the colony where they were made. The purpose of these laws was to prevent the colonists from taking business away from English manufacturers.

Most colonists strongly resented the trade laws. They argued that these laws hurt colonial manufacturing and forced them to pay higher prices for the goods they imported. Many colonists violated the laws by trading secretly with foreign countries. Although there were laws against smuggling, these were not strictly enforced. Some colonists made large sums of money by selling smuggled goods.

Britain and France Struggle for Power

France rules a large empire in America. During the 1600's, thousands of people came to the New World from France. Many were traders who obtained valuable furs from the Indians in exchange for knives, hatchets, beads, and other articles. Some were Catholic missionaries who came to teach the Indians about Christianity. Still others were soldiers. The people who came from France explored the lands along the St. Lawrence River, the Great Lakes, and the Mississippi River. They claimed a huge amount of territory for France.

The British defeat the French. Great Britain* disputed France's claim to some of the land west of the Appalachian Mountains. At that time, the two countries were rivals not only in America but also in Europe. Between 1689 and 1763, Britain and France fought each other in four wars. The last of these conflicts, known in America as the French and Indian War, began in 1754. French soldiers had built several forts in western Pennsylvania, on land claimed by the British. When France refused to give up these forts, the two countries went to war.

At first, the French won most of the battles. They had good military leaders, and they were helped by several Indian tribes. In 1755, a group of French soldiers and Indians attacked a British army in the forests of Pennsylvania. The leader of the British army was killed, and his troops were defeated. Later, the French captured two important British forts in northern New York.

As time passed, however, Britain began to win the war. The British had several advantages over the French. About twenty times as many people lived in the British colonies as in the French colonies. The British colonists had developed more farming and industry, so they were better able to supply their troops with food, clothing, and

George Washington (right) served as an officer in the French and Indian War. This war was fought between Great Britain and France over conflicting claims to territory in North America.

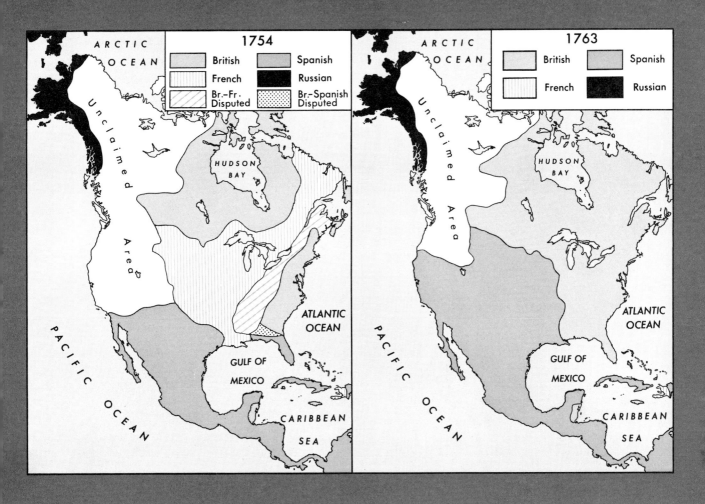

1754

British	Spanish
French	Russian
Br.-Fr. Disputed	Br.-Spanish Disputed

ARCTIC OCEAN
Unclaimed Area
HUDSON BAY
ATLANTIC OCEAN
PACIFIC OCEAN
GULF OF MEXICO
CARIBBEAN SEA

1763

British	Spanish
French	Russian

ARCTIC OCEAN
Unclaimed Area
HUDSON BAY
ATLANTIC OCEAN
PACIFIC OCEAN
GULF OF MEXICO
CARIBBEAN SEA

Before and after the French and Indian War. The maps above show the lands claimed in North America by European nations at the beginning and end of this war. Britain won the war in 1763. As a result, France lost most of her possessions in the New World, while Britain gained vast territories. Spain, an ally of France, lost Florida but received French territory west of the Mississippi River.

weapons. Britain had a stronger navy than France. Therefore the British could transport more troops and supplies to America.

After British forces captured the important cities of Quebec and Montreal in Canada, France had to admit defeat. The treaty of peace, signed in 1763, gave Britain vast territories in America. (See maps above.) Great Britain was now the most powerful country in the world.

Explore the Early History of the Northeast
1. Who were the first people to live in the Northeast?
2. Why were Cabot's voyages important?
3. When was the French and Indian War fought? What was the outcome of this war?

Make a Chart of American Colonies
Read about the history of some of the early colonies in the Northeast. Then record your findings on a chart similar to the one below.

Name of Colony	Date Founded	Founders	Reason for Settlement

You will find much of the information for your project in this chapter. Refer to pages 347-349 for help in locating additional information.

James Otis, a Boston lawyer, arguing against the writs of assistance. These documents allowed British officials to enter any home or business place in the colonies to search for smuggled goods. American colonists felt their rights were being violated by the writs of assistance and other actions of the British government. The dispute with Britain led to the Revolutionary War.

5 The Birth of Our Nation

A Problem To Solve

In 1775, American colonists revolted against British rule. After several years of fighting, Great Britain finally recognized the United States as an independent country. **Why were the Americans willing to fight for their independence?** In forming your hypotheses, consider the following:

a. British restrictions on trade
b. the Proclamation of 1763
c. British tax laws
d. changes in the attitude of the colonists toward Great Britain

Chapter 4 contains additional information that will be helpful in solving this problem.

See TO THE STUDENT, pages 8-10.

Britain and the colonists disagree on goals. After the French and Indian War, Britain began to pay more attention to its colonies in America. The war had been very costly for the British. Be-

cause British troops had helped to protect the colonists from the French and Indians, the British government felt that the colonists should pay some of the costs of the war.

Britain, you will remember, had always expected the colonies to earn a profit for the mother country. (See page 73.) British leaders now realized that if the colonies were to be profitable, they would have to be controlled more strictly than before. For example, the laws against smuggling would have to be enforced. The British felt that the colonists should be willing to obey any laws that would benefit the mother country.

Most of the colonists did not agree that the main purpose of the colonies was to benefit Britain. They had worked hard for all they had achieved, and felt that they no longer owed anything to the mother country. As long as the colonists had been threatened by the French, they had depended on British troops for protection. Now that France had been defeated, the colonists felt they could take care of themselves. What the colonists wanted was more freedom, not less.

British actions make the colonists angry. In the 1760's Britain took several steps in an attempt to strengthen its hold on the colonies. These actions greatly angered many Americans.

The Proclamation of 1763. The American colonists had expected that they would be allowed to settle west of the Appalachian Mountains after the French were defeated. Britain, however, feared that this would cause trouble with the Indians who lived in the area. In 1763,

the King issued a proclamation forbidding settlers to move west of the Appalachians. The colonists strongly resented the Proclamation of 1763. Many disobeyed the King's order and moved into the territory beyond the mountains.

Writs of assistance. The colonists were also unhappy about Britain's efforts to make them obey the trade laws. (See page 73.) British officials were sent to the colonies to hunt for smugglers. These officials were issued documents called writs of assistance, which allowed them to enter any home or business place in search of smuggled goods. The colonists insisted that the writs violated their rights as British subjects.

Food and shelter for British troops. At about the same time, the British government sent ten thousand soldiers to America. The colonists were ordered to provide the soldiers with food and shelter whenever these were needed. Although the colonists were to be repaid for their services, they did not like having soldiers in their homes.

New tax laws. The colonists became even angrier when the British Parliament* passed a number of new tax laws. One of these was the Stamp Act of 1765. It required that newspapers, legal documents, playing cards, and many other items had to be stamped with an official seal. To get these items stamped, the colonists had to pay a tax to the British government. The Stamp Act was repealed* the following year. However,

*See Glossary

Build Your Vocabulary

Proclamation of 1763   Intolerable Acts   Continental Congress   Parliament

Revolutionary War   Stamp Act   Constitution   Declaration of Independence

Articles of Confederation   federal   Bill of Rights   Industrial Revolution

A mob of New Yorkers burning a pile of stamped papers to protest against the Stamp Act. This law was very unpopular throughout the colonies.

in 1767 Parliament placed taxes on certain goods the colonists bought from Britain, such as tea, paper, and paint.

The colonists strongly objected to the new tax laws. In the past, the legislature in each colony had decided what taxes people would have to pay. Since the colonists were not represented in the British Parliament, they felt that Parliament had no right to tax them. It seemed to the colonists that Britain was trying to take away their right to govern themselves.

Americans work together to protect their rights. The colonists protested against the Stamp Act and the other new laws. In each colony, special groups were formed to see that these laws were not obeyed. The officials who sold government stamps were attacked or threatened by angry mobs. Many colonists refused to buy any more goods from Britain until the laws were changed. These boycotts caused British merchants to lose much money.

Many people in Britain felt that efforts should be made to settle the dispute with the colonies. However, Parliament at this time was controlled by friends of King George III. The King was a stubborn man, and he did not try to understand the views of the colonists. He thought they should be forced to obey the laws made by Parliament.

The Boston Tea Party. In 1773, Parliament passed a law that made it possible for the colonists to buy tea from a British trading company at a very low price. The colonists still had to pay a tax on the tea, however. Many colonists believed that the new law was a trick to make them accept the idea of being taxed by Britain. One winter night, a group of men in Boston disguised themselves as Indians. They boarded some British ships that were loaded with tea and dumped the tea into Boston Harbor.

The Boston Tea Party greatly angered the British leaders. To punish the people of Massachusetts, Parliament passed several harsh laws. One law declared that no trading ships could enter or leave Boston Harbor until the tea had been paid for. Another law took away some of the rights of self-government enjoyed by the people of Massachusetts. The colonists called these laws the "Intolerable Acts."

The First Continental Congress. The Intolerable Acts aroused strong resentment throughout the colonies. In September, 1774, twelve colonies sent delegates to a gathering in Philadelphia to discuss the growing quarrel with Britain. This gathering was called the First Continental Congress. The Congress sent a letter to the King protesting against these laws. The Congress also urged the colonists to refuse to import goods from Britain. Committees were organized in each colony to see that this trade boycott was carried out.

Many Americans were becoming convinced that they would have to fight to protect their rights. In each colony, groups of citizens began to gather weapons and to meet for military drill.

In Massachusetts, these volunteers were known as Minutemen, because they could be ready for battle only a few minutes after receiving a warning.

The Revolutionary War begins. The conflict between Britain and the colonies finally led to war. On April 18, 1775, the British governor of Massachusetts sent troops from Boston to the nearby villages of Lexington and Concord. At Lexington the troops were supposed to arrest two colonial leaders, Samuel Adams and John Hancock. Then they were to seize weapons and gunpowder that the colonists had stored at Concord.

Minutemen fighting British troops at Lexington, Massachusetts, on April 19, 1775. This battle marked the beginning of the Revolutionary War. It did not take long for the news of the fighting in Massachusetts to spread to the other colonies.

When the British reached Lexington, early the next morning, they found a group of Minutemen blocking the way. Fighting broke out between the soldiers and the Minutemen. This was the start of the Revolutionary War. (See page 81.)

Very soon the news of the fighting in Massachusetts spread to the other colonies. In May, 1775, another gathering of colonial leaders was held in Philadelphia. This was the Second Continental Congress. For almost six years, it directed the thirteen colonies in their struggle against Britain.

Many Americans come to favor independence. Even after the war began, most Americans still felt a strong loyalty toward Great Britain. They hoped that the fighting in Massachusetts would cause the British government to change its attitude. However, King George III disappointed them. He declared that the colonial leaders were traitors who should be punished severely. The King made the colonists still angrier by hiring thousands of German soldiers to help put down the rebellion in America.

Gradually, many Americans came to feel that the colonies should break away from Britain. These people asked themselves why a huge territory in North America should remain under the control of a small island thousands of miles away. They also asked why Americans should obey a king who cared little about their needs and problems. If the colonies were independent, Americans could govern themselves as they pleased. They could develop new industries and trade freely with all countries. People could settle anywhere in America without needing the King's permission.

The Declaration of Independence is adopted by colonial leaders. By the summer of 1776, most delegates to the Second Continental Congress were in favor of independence. A five-man committee was appointed to prepare a statement explaining to the world why the colonies wanted to become independent states. Thomas Jefferson did most of the actual writing of this document, which is known as the Declaration of Independence. The Second Continental Congress approved the Declaration on July 4, 1776.

Although independence had been declared, Americans were not yet free of British rule. The Revolutionary War

Preparing the Declaration of Independence. Thomas Jefferson (right) wrote most of this famous document, which was adopted on July 4, 1776.

The Revolutionary War

The Revolutionary War began in Massachusetts in April, 1775. In the years of fighting that followed, it spread northward to Canada and southward to Georgia. When it was over, the British had lost all of their important North American possessions except Canada. The map on this page shows where the main battles of the war took place.

At Lexington and Concord, the British failed to keep the rebellion from spreading. They now had to fight to keep Boston. Just outside this city, they won the Battle of Bunker Hill. At about the same time, however, a strong leader was named to head the Continental Army. He was General George Washington. In March, 1776, Washington succeeded in driving the British from Boston.

Since the British had failed to stop the rebels in New England, they decided on another plan. First, they would capture New York City. From there, they would try to gain control of the Hudson and Champlain valleys. In this way, they would cut New England off from the other colonies, and the rebellion would collapse.

Washington did his best to defend New York, but his army lacked both supplies and experience. After several battles, the British occupied the city. Washington was forced to retreat westward. In the weeks that followed, however, victories at Trenton and Princeton, in New Jersey, raised the Americans' spirits.

As part of a plan to cut off New England, General Burgoyne led a British army southward from Canada toward the Hudson Valley. He expected to get help from other British forces, but they never arrived. At Saratoga, New York, in October, 1777, Burgoyne was surrounded by the Americans and forced to surrender.

Meanwhile, another British force had occupied Philadelphia. Here, during the bitter winter of 1777-1778, British soldiers were warm and well fed. A few miles away, at Valley Forge, thousands of Washington's troops had to camp without enough food, clothing, or fuel. Many died, but those who lived were more determined than ever to win the war.

After their defeat at Saratoga, the British turned their efforts toward the South. In December, 1778, they took Savannah, Georgia. In May, 1780, they captured Charleston, South Carolina. Although the British won other victories, they were not able to end the rebellion. In the spring of 1781, General Cornwallis, the commander of British armies in the South, moved northward into Virginia. He assembled his troops at Yorktown.

Washington saw that he finally had an excellent opportunity to defeat the British. Three years earlier, the French had entered the war on the side of the Americans. Now, the French sent a powerful fleet toward Yorktown. At the same time, Washington arrived from New York with a large army of American and French troops. Cornwallis was trapped. On October 19, 1781, after several weeks of fighting, he surrendered all his forces. This defeat ended British hopes of keeping the thirteen colonies. Peace negotiations began a few months later, and in 1783 Britain signed a treaty recognizing the United States as an independent country.

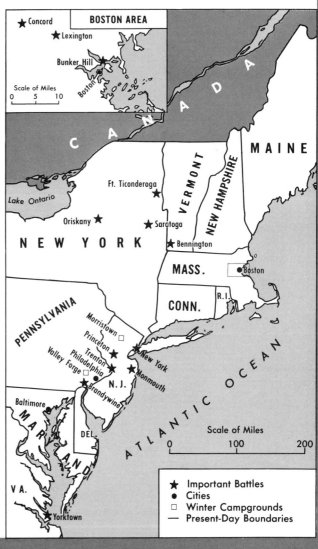

Washington and his men at Valley Forge, Pennsylvania. The Continental Army camped here during the cold winter of 1777-1778. Many of the soldiers lacked warm clothing, and there was not enough food to eat. Washington's strength and courage helped to keep the little army together.

continued for more than seven years before Britain finally recognized the United States as an independent country.

Americans face great handicaps in their fight for freedom. During the war, there were many times when victory seemed far away. The Americans were fighting a wealthy, powerful nation. Britain's army and navy were large. The British soldiers were experienced, and they were well supplied with food, clothing, and weapons.

The Americans had a small army and an even smaller navy. Most of the American soldiers did not have much training. These men had enlisted in the army for short periods only, and they felt free to leave for home whenever their terms of service were completed. The Continental Congress had little money with which to buy supplies and weapons. As a result, the American soldiers often did not have enough to eat, and many of them lacked shoes, coats, and other clothing. To make matters worse, about one third of the people in America were opposed to independence. These people, called Loyalists or Tories, sometimes gave considerable aid to the British.

Why the Americans were able to win. In spite of these handicaps, the Americans gradually began to win the war. Because the American soldiers were fighting to gain freedom and to protect their homes, they showed great bravery and determination. The commander of the Continental Army,* George Washington, was a wise and courageous leader. Most of the American soldiers were used to outdoor living, and they could bear hardships patiently. Also, they were more familiar with the countryside than the British.

The British armies were made up mostly of hired soldiers and people who had been forced into military service. These men did not generally fight with as much spirit as the Americans. The British generals were so confident of winning that they became careless and made a number of serious mistakes.

The Americans received much valuable aid from foreign countries. France joined the war against Britain in 1778, hoping to weaken its old enemy. The French loaned large amounts of money to the Continental Congress. In addition, it sent supplies and troops to America. France's ally, Spain, also entered the war against Britain. French and Spanish ships battled the British fleet in various parts of the world. Many gallant soldiers came from France, Germany, and other European countries to help the Americans in their struggle for freedom.

The Revolutionary War ends in victory for the Americans. As the years passed, the British people grew tired of the costly war in America. Finally, in 1781, they learned that an entire British army had surrendered at Yorktown, Virginia. (See page 81.) Soon afterward, a new group of leaders gained control of Britain's government. These men were eager for peace.

In 1783, Britain signed a treaty recognizing the United States of America as an independent country. By the terms of this treaty, the new nation owned all the land from the Atlantic Ocean to the Mississippi River and from Canada to Florida.

A Strong National Government Is Established

The new nation lacks a strong central government. At the end of the Revolutionary War, the American people faced a very serious problem. The thirteen states that had won their independence were not really united. Each state was almost like a separate country, with its own laws and government. Many people felt a greater loyalty to the state in which they lived than they did to the nation as a whole.

During the war, the thirteen states had adopted a plan of government called the Articles of Confederation. The Articles provided for a weak national government. The national lawmaking body, which was called the Congress, could make laws. However, it could not force

FOUR AMERICAN PATRIOTS

George Washington
(1732-1799)

George Washington is often called "The Father of His Country." The son of a Virginia plantation owner, he was trained in military skills and surveying. As a surveyor, he learned how to live in the wilderness. This training aided him when he served as a British officer during the French and Indian War. Washington's leadership during this war made people realize that they could depend on him. In June, 1775, shortly after the start of the Revolutionary War, the Second Continental Congress elected him commander in chief of the Continental Army. Washington's strength and courage during this war kept the colonial army together even when failure seemed certain. After the war, Washington continued to serve his country. He headed the group that wrote the Constitution, and in 1789 was chosen as the first president of the United States of America. The wise decisions he made as president helped the United States to meet the challenges it faced as a young nation.

Throughout his life, Benjamin Franklin used his talents to make life better for his fellowmen. Franklin was born in Boston, but he spent most of his life in Philadelphia. There, for many years, he published a newspaper and *Poor Richard's Almanac.** Franklin was also a scientist, and the inventor of such useful items as the bifocal* lens. His many achievements earned him the respect of Americans and Europeans alike. Franklin devoted most of his later life to public service. Before the Revolutionary War, he tried to settle some of the quarrels between the colonies and Britain. Later he decided that the colonies must break away from the mother country, and helped prepare the Declaration of Independence. During the war, he was minister to France, where he gained French support in the struggle against the British. After returning to America, he served as a member of the convention that drew up the Constitution. Today, Franklin is recognized as one of the outstanding men of his century.

Benjamin Franklin
(1706-1790)

John Adams
(1735-1826)

Our second president, John Adams, was born in Massachusetts. After graduating from Harvard College, he studied law. Adams opposed the Stamp Act of 1765 and other actions of the British government. People in Massachusetts admired the courageous stand he took on many different issues, and in 1771 elected him to the colonial legislature. Later, as a member of the Continental Congress, he played an important part in gaining approval of the Declaration of Independence. He also helped draw up the Treaty of Paris, which ended the Revolutionary War. After the war, Adams first served the United States as minister to Great Britain and then as vice-president under Washington. He was elected president in 1796. At that time, many American leaders wanted the United States to go to war against France. Adams helped to prevent this from happening. Although Adams was not as popular as some other patriots, he was respected as a man who did what he believed was right, regardless of the cost.

Thomas Jefferson, our third president, helped to establish our country's democratic form of government. He was born and educated in Virginia, and became a successful lawyer. Jefferson felt that the British were violating the rights of the American colonists. In 1776, he was asked to prepare a document explaining why the colonists wanted their independence. Although others helped him, Jefferson is considered the author of this document — the Declaration of Independence. During most of the Revolutionary War, he served the people of Virginia — first as a lawmaker and then as the state's governor. Jefferson served the United States after the war as minister to France, Secretary of State, and vice-president. In 1801, he became president. One of his greatest achievements while president was the Louisiana Purchase. (See page 104.) During his lifetime, Jefferson did much to strengthen our democracy and to defend the inalienable* rights of all people.

*See Glossary

Thomas Jefferson
(1743-1826)

84

people to obey them. There was no separate department of the government to carry out the laws made by Congress. Neither were there any national courts to settle disputes and to try people accused of breaking the laws.

A lack of money. Congress could ask the states for money, but it could not tax the people directly. The state governments seldom provided all the money they were asked to pay. Therefore, the national government usually lacked funds. It could not afford to maintain a large army for defense against foreign enemies and hostile Indians. Neither could it pay back the large sums of money it had borrowed from France and other European countries during the Revolutionary War.

Foreign problems. A government with so little power could not win the respect of other countries. Britain, for example, refused to give up control of several forts that were inside the United States. Spain also kept control of certain forts in American territory, and Spanish officials in Florida encouraged the Indians to attack American settlements.

Barriers to trade. Under the Articles of Confederation, trade between the states was difficult. There were two main reasons for this. Congress did not have the power to regulate trade, so each state could place taxes on goods brought in from neighboring states. In addition, each state could issue its own money. The value of money varied greatly from one state to another.

Quarrels between states. Often, neighboring states became involved in bitter disputes over boundaries or other matters. The national government was not able to settle these quarrels. It appeared that there soon might be thirteen small, weak countries instead of one strong, united nation.

A new plan of government is written. Many American leaders felt that a stronger national government was needed. In 1786, delegates from several states met at Annapolis, Maryland, to discuss some of the problems caused by the weakness of the national government. They decided that another meeting should be held the following year in Philadelphia to revise the Articles of Confederation.

In May, 1787, all of the states except Rhode Island sent delegates to the meeting, or convention, in Philadelphia. The delegates soon agreed that the Articles of Confederation were not worth revising. They decided to write an entirely new plan, or constitution, for the government.

For almost four months, the delegates argued over the provisions of the new constitution. There were many differences of opinion, and it sometimes seemed that the convention would break up without accomplishing anything. Finally, however, the work of the convention was completed. On September 17, thirty-nine of the delegates signed the Constitution of the United States.

The Constitution provides for a strong federal government. Under the new plan adopted at Philadelphia, the federal* government would be much stronger than the government under the Articles of Confederation. It would be able to tax people directly instead of having to ask the state governments for money. It would also be able to regulate trade and settle disputes between states. Only

Adopting the Constitution of the United States. The Constitution was written by a group of American leaders meeting at Philadelphia in 1787. It established a strong national government. At the same time, it allowed the states to keep control of most local affairs.

the federal government would have the power to issue money. At the same time, the states would keep control of most local affairs. They would be able to pass any law that did not conflict with federal laws.

Under the Constitution, the federal government would be divided into three branches. One branch, Congress, would make the laws. Another branch, headed by an elected president, would see that the laws were carried out. The third branch would consist of a system of federal courts.

The states accept the Constitution. Before the Constitution could go into effect, it had to be approved by at least nine of the thirteen states. There were many people who supported the new Constitution. They felt that a strong national government would be able to solve some of the country's problems. Other people, however, were opposed to the Constitution, mainly because they felt it gave too much power to the national government. They feared that a strong national government might take away some of the people's rights. To calm these fears, supporters of the Constitution promised to work for a number of amendments* guaranteeing certain rights that the government could not take away from anyone.

In each state, a convention was held to decide whether or not to accept the Constitution. One by one, the state conventions gave their approval. By the summer of 1788, the Constitution had been approved by nine of the states. In 1791, ten amendments to the Constitution were passed. These first ten amendments are known as the Bill of Rights.*

The new government begins work. Soon after the Constitution went into effect, elections were held for a president and a vice-president and for members of Congress. George Washington was elected president without any opposition. He named a group of advisors to help him run the government. This group became known as the Cabinet. The Supreme Court and other federal courts were also organized at this time. At last, the new government was ready to begin work.

When Washington became president, New York City was the capital of the United States. From 1790 to 1800, the federal government made its home in Philadelphia. Then it moved to a new capital city, Washington, which was built in an area along the Potomac River called the District of Columbia.

The United States in 1800

After it won its independence in 1783, the United States owned all the land from the Atlantic Ocean to the Mississippi River and from Canada to Florida. At first, the new nation had only thirteen states. Three more were added during the 1790's, when Vermont, Kentucky, and Tennessee joined the Union.

In 1800 there were two large areas west of the Appalachian Mountains that had not yet been divided into states. North of Kentucky was an area known as the Northwest Territory, which was still largely a forested wilderness. South of Tennessee was an area called the Mississippi Territory.

You will notice that the names of some states in the Northeast are missing from the map at the right. In 1800 Maine was still a part of Massachusetts. It did not become a separate state until 1820. West Virginia remained a part of Virginia until the time of the Civil War. (See page 107.)

Original Thirteen States

States Added to the Union by 1800

United States Territories

Disputed Between United States and Great Britain

Scale of Miles
0   200   400

Trade and Industry Develop in the Northeast

At the time our federal government was established, the Northeast was still mainly a rural region. About nine out of ten people made their living from farming. There were few cities or large towns here. The population of the country's largest city, Philadelphia, was less than 50,000, including its suburbs.

In the years that followed, however, important changes began to take place in the Northeast. The people here increased their trade with other parts of the United States and with foreign countries. Our country's first factories were started in the Northeast. As people left their farms to seek other ways of earning a living, cities such as New York and Philadelphia grew steadily in population.

Ships from the Northeast sail to distant parts of the world. When the Revolutionary War ended, merchants and shipowners in the Northeast faced serious problems. Many American ships had been captured or sunk by the British during the war. Because the people of America were no longer British subjects, they were not allowed to continue their profitable trade with British colonies in the West Indies.

To overcome these difficulties, people in the Northeast built more ships and sought new customers for their goods. Adventurous seamen soon discovered that they could make large profits by trading with China and other countries in Asia. Merchants and sea captains in the Northeast also began to build up a large trade with France and other European countries. Many of these traders became very wealthy. Coastal towns such as Salem, Massachusetts, and Providence, Rhode Island, grew into flourishing seaports.

Many New England sailors made their living by hunting whales. Ships in search of these giant sea animals set out on long, dangerous voyages to every part of the world. Oil made from whale fat, or blubber, was used as a fuel for lamps. Whalebone was used in making many different articles, such as buggy whips, fishing rods, and hoopskirts.

The Industrial Revolution comes to America. At the time the United States was founded, nearly all household articles used in our country were produced by hand. People either made their own clothing, furniture, and tools, or else bought the things they needed from local craftsmen. However, a great change was taking place in Britain. In the textile industry, machines were now being used to perform tasks that formerly had been done by hand. This was the start of the Industrial Revolution. (See pages 90 and 91.)

With the new machines, Britain could produce more textiles* than any other country in the world. The British government did not want other countries to learn how to make these machines. It passed a law forbidding people to take them out of Britain. Another law stated that textile machine operators could not move to other countries.

In 1789, a young textile worker named Samuel Slater escaped from Britain to America. He had memorized the details

Continued on page 92.

TWO REVOLUTIONS

New ways of living. People in many parts of the world still live much as their ancestors did hundreds or even thousands of years ago. We in America, however, as well as people in certain other parts of the world, are living in ways that are unlike those of our ancestors. Our lives differ from theirs in two main respects. First, we live in a democracy,* whereas our ancestors were governed by powerful kings and princes who ruled as they pleased. Second, we produce most goods by machine instead of by hand. These two basic changes have been so great that we call them revolutions—the Democratic Revolution and the Industrial Revolution.

THE DEMOCRATIC REVOLUTION

Self-government makes a start in England. At the beginning of the 1700's, most of the world's

The British surrender to the Americans at Yorktown. In the late 1700's the spread of democratic ideas led to two major political revolts — the American and the French revolutions.

people lived under rulers who inherited their positions and governed with unlimited power. In England, however, a lawmaking assembly called Parliament had more power than the king. Parliament was made up of two houses. Membership in the House of Lords was a privilege, which nobles* inherited. Members of the House of Commons, however, were chosen by landowners and wealthy merchants. Although the vast majority of the people still had no voice in governing themselves, democracy had made a start.

The idea of democracy continues to grow. During the eighteenth century, the desire for self-government became very strong in many parts of Europe, as well as in the English colonies in America. Many people came to believe that all citizens of a country should be granted equal rights. They felt it was wrong for kings and nobles to inherit special privileges. They also believed that every person has certain inalienable* rights. Freedom of speech is an example of this kind of right.

Toward the end of the century, these beliefs about equality and natural rights helped bring about two important political revolutions. One was the American Revolution, which led to the founding of a new nation based on the idea of self-government. The other was the French Revolution,* which began in 1789. During this revolution, the French people succeeded in overthrowing their king. They also took away the special privileges that had been enjoyed by the nobles.

The further spread of the Democratic Revolution. As time went on, the desire for self-government continued to spread. The growth of democracy was aided by the Industrial Revolution. (See pages 90 and 91.) As industry became more highly developed, more and more working people gained the leisure time and the education required for learning about public affairs. These people began to demand a voice in government.

Although the United States was founded on the principle of self-government, certain people were not at first granted the right to vote. For example, people who did not own property

*See Glossary

had no voice in the government. By about 1830, however, most states no longer required a person to own property in order to vote. The Fourteenth and Fifteenth amendments to the Constitution, adopted during the late 1860's, gave Negroes the right to vote. An amendment passed in 1920 gave voting rights to women.

The Democratic Revolution has now spread to many parts of the world. Most countries in western Europe and North America are democracies, as are Australia and New Zealand. In South America and Africa, a few countries are at least partially democratic. The leading democracies of Asia are Japan, India, and the Philippines.

In some parts of the world, the Democratic Revolution has had little effect. This is true in two of the world's largest countries — the Soviet Union and China. Although the people in these two countries are no longer governed by hereditary rulers, they now live under dictatorships.* The present leaders in these countries do not give the people much voice in government affairs.

THE INDUSTRIAL REVOLUTION

New ways of producing goods are developed. During the seventeenth century, most goods were produced by people in their own homes or on farms. Work was performed mainly by the muscle power of human beings or animals, although a few simple tools and machines were in general use. Wind and waterpower were used for certain work, such as the grinding of grain.

Beginning about the middle of the eighteenth century, three important developments occurred in the way goods were produced. First, many new machines were invented to help people make things more quickly and easily. Second, steam and other new sources of power came into use. Third, factories were built to house the new machines. Together, these three main developments are known as the Industrial Revolution. Like the Democratic Revolution, the Industrial Revolution began in England.

One invention leads to another. Changes in England's textile industry during the eighteenth century illustrate the way the Industrial Revolution developed. In the early 1700's, workers used spinning wheels to make thread. Other

Cotton-spinning machines in an early factory. In the 1700's, machines were invented that made it possible to produce textiles and other goods more quickly and easily. The use of such machines was part of the Industrial Revolution.

workers wove the thread into cloth on hand looms. As the result of an improvement in the loom, made in 1733, weavers began to make cloth so fast that the spinners could not provide enough thread. During the 1770's, a spinning machine was developed that could be run by waterpower. This machine speeded up the making of thread. Toward the end of the century, a power loom was invented. By using the new loom, workers were soon able to speed up the weaving process.

Steam power. Spinning was the first manufacturing process to make use of steam power. Since the early 1700's, crude steam engines had been used for pumping water out of mines. In 1769, a Scottish inventor named James Watt patented* a much-improved steam engine. Within a few years, the new engine was being used to run spinning machines. Soon, steam power was being used in making iron and pottery. In ironmaking, steam power was used to produce the steady blast of air needed to smelt* iron ore with coke,* which had largely replaced charcoal for this purpose. The iron produced by using coke and steam power was cheaper and of better quality than the iron made by older methods. Better quality iron, in turn, made it possible to build sturdier and more complicated machinery that could be run by steam engines.

The modern factory system begins. As machines became larger, heavier, and more complicated, they could no longer be placed in workers' homes. Instead, special buildings called factories were constructed, where workers could come to operate the machines. Machines run by waterpower had to be housed in factories located along streams. With the introduction of steam power, however, factories could be located anyplace fuel was available.

The Industrial Revolution spreads. The new ways of producing goods soon spread from England to other parts of the world. The United States, Belgium, France, and Germany were among the first countries to adopt the new methods. Information about the development of modern industry in America is provided in Chapters 6, 7, and 9.

The Industrial Revolution has continued to spread. Today, it is in different stages in different countries. (See map below.) In much of the world, industry is just beginning to develop. Most parts of Europe and North America, however, are already highly industrialized. This is also true of Australia and New Zealand. The United States and several countries in western Europe are now beginning to move into a new stage of the Industrial Revolution. This new stage includes automation, which is the development and use of automatic machines. Through automation, it is now possible for an entire industrial plant to be run with few human operators.

Industrialization changes people's lives in several ways. For one thing, the standard* of living is generally higher in nations that have experienced the Industrial Revolution. Also, more of the people in such nations live in cities. The people in industrialized nations are more interdependent than those who live in countries that have little industry. They depend on people in many parts of the world for raw materials. They also depend on other people to buy their products and services. We do not know just what the world of the future will be like as industrialization continues. We can be sure, however, that it will be different in many ways from the world of today.

The spread of the Industrial Revolution. The world's most highly industrialized countries are generally referred to as developed nations. Countries in which the Industrial Revolution has as yet had little or no effect are said to be underdeveloped. In the partly developed countries, industrialization is well under way.

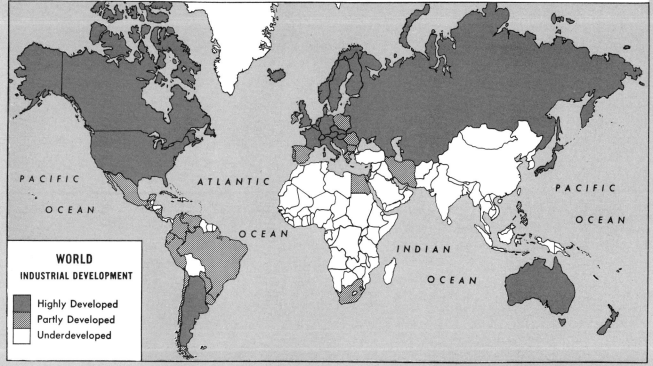

WORLD
INDUSTRIAL DEVELOPMENT

Highly Developed
Partly Developed
Underdeveloped

Old Slater Mill Museum. In 1790, a young Englishman named Samuel Slater opened a cotton spinning mill at Pawtucket, Rhode Island. Soon many other factories were started in New England. There were many waterfalls and rapids here that could be used to provide power for industry.

of some of the new machines so that he could build others just like them. In 1790, he opened a textile mill at Pawtucket, Rhode Island. This mill contained machinery for spinning cotton into yarn.* It is sometimes referred to as the first factory in the United States.

Eli Whitney develops a new method of manufacturing. In 1798, a Connecticut inventor and manufacturer named Eli Whitney received a contract to make 10,000 guns for the United States Army. At that time, guns were made slowly

and carefully by skilled gunsmiths in small shops. No two guns were exactly alike. Whitney decided to make his guns in a different way. He designed special tools and machines to make individual gun parts. For example, one machine made triggers, while a different machine bored gun barrels. All the parts made by a particular machine were exactly alike. The different parts were assembled to make a complete gun. As a result of Whitney's new method of manufacturing, guns could be produced quickly in large quantities. Mass production, as the system is called, was soon adopted by other industries.

Many factories are started in the Northeast. In the early 1800's, many factories were started in New England. There were several reasons why this was the first part of our country to develop much industry. At that time, most machines were run by waterpower. In New England, there were many waterfalls and rapids that could be used to produce power. Another reason for the development of industry in New England was that the wealthy merchants here could provide the money needed to start new factories. Because most of the land in New England was poor for farming, many people sought other ways of earning a living. As a result, there was a plentiful supply of factory workers.

Factories were established in the Middle Atlantic states also. In eastern Pennsylvania, there were many forges* where iron was made. The forges used iron ore from nearby deposits. Sawmills were built in New York and other states to cut logs from the forests into lumber. Wheat grown in Pennsylvania and New Jersey was ground into flour at nearby gristmills. Many of the factories were located along the Fall Line in order to make use of the waterpower available here. (See page 34.)

The frontier moves westward. During the early years of our nation's history, thousands of settlers moved from the Atlantic coast to new homes west of the Appalachian Mountains. The land beyond the mountains was generally more fertile than the land along the coast. In addition, many men who had fought in the Revolutionary War were given free land in the west on which to start farms. Since Britain no longer ruled the territory beyond the mountains, people were free to settle where they pleased.

New settlements grew up all along the frontier. Some pioneers made their homes on the fertile plains in western New York. Others settled in mountain valleys in western Pennsylvania and Virginia. Still others traveled down the Ohio River to the part of our country known today as the Midwest.

The pioneers found most of the western lands covered with dense forests. They cut down the trees to clear the land for farming, and used the logs to build their homes. As more people came to the frontier, some of the early settlements grew into towns or cities. By 1820, there were settlements in nearly every part of the Northeast.

Learn About the Birth of Our Nation
1. List at least four British actions or laws that angered the colonists.
2. Why did many Americans gradually come to feel that the colonies should break away from Great Britain?
3. What was the purpose of the Declaration of Independence?
4. What handicaps faced the colonists in their fight for freedom? What advantages did they have?
5. What were two important results of the treaty signed in 1783 by Britain?

Use Your Imagination
Imagine that you are one of the great Americans listed below.

George Washington   John Adams
Benjamin Franklin   Thomas Jefferson

Write a brief autobiography, or story of your life, to share with your class. The suggestions on pages 345-349 will help you locate information and write your autobiography.

New York City's waterfront in 1828. During the early 1800's, New York and other seaports along the Atlantic coast grew rapidly in population. Sailing ships from the Northeast carried goods and passengers to all parts of the world. Many new industries were started during this period.

6 The Young Nation

Problems To Solve

Solving these problems will help you to gain important understandings about the history of the United States.

1. During the 1820's and 1830's, a number of roads and canals were built in the Northeast. The first railroads were also built during this period. **How did improvements in transportation affect the people of the Northeast?** In forming your hypotheses, you will need to consider how the building of roads, canals, and railroads affected:
   a. farming
   b. the development of natural resources

   c. manufacturing
   d. trade between different areas

2. Confederate troops fought bravely during the Civil War, and they were led by outstanding generals. Yet the North finally won the war. **Why was the North able to defeat the South in the Civil War?** In forming your hypotheses, you will need to consider how the North and the South differed in:
   a. population
   b. industry
   c. farm production
   d. transportation
   e. government leaders

See TO THE STUDENT, pages 8-10.

The War of 1812

Americans fight another war against Britain. Shortly after 1800, a serious dispute arose between the United States and Great Britain. At that time, Britain was fighting a long, bitter war against France. The United States government wanted to stay out of this war. It hoped that by remaining on good terms with Britain and France it could sell large amounts of products to both countries. However, Britain and France wanted to hurt each other's trade. Therefore, the British often captured American ships carrying goods to France, and the French seized ships that were headed for Britain. Americans strongly resented this interference with their trade.

Other British actions made the American people even angrier. Britain was having trouble finding enough sailors to serve on its warships, so it often used a practice called impressment. A British warship would stop an American ship on the ocean and search it. If there were any British citizens on board, they would be taken off and forced to serve in the British navy. Sometimes the British even captured sailors who were citizens of the United States.

Many Americans felt that the United States should go to war against Britain. Among these people were a number of settlers who lived west of the Appalachian Mountains. They believed that British officials in Canada were stirring up the Indians to attack American settlements. If the United States went to war against Britain, it might be able to take possession of Canada and stop the Indian raids. Also, Americans might get control of the profitable fur trade in Canada.

In June, 1812, the United States declared war on Britain. Our country was poorly prepared for the War of 1812. Its army and navy were small and there was little money with which to buy supplies. Many people in New England were opposed to the war because they feared it would hurt their trade with Europe. Some New England states even refused to send troops to fight the British. In spite of these difficulties, the United States won a number of victories.

Several important battles of this war took place in the Northeast. In 1814, British forces headed southward from Canada to invade New York State. They were forced to turn back after American ships defeated a British fleet on Lake Champlain. During the same year, British troops captured Washington, D.C., where they burned the Capitol and the White House. However, the British failed in an attempt to capture Baltimore. The fighting at Baltimore inspired a young lawyer named Francis Scott Key to write "The Star-Spangled Banner," which is now our national anthem.

By the end of 1814, both the United States and Britain were eager for peace. American troops had failed to take Canada, and the British knew that they could probably never defeat the United States. In December, the two countries

Lake Champlain was the site of an important naval battle during the War of 1812. This war, which was fought between the United States and Great Britain, showed European countries that Americans would fight to protect their rights.

signed a peace treaty. Since that time, they have never again gone to war against each other.

The War of 1812 brings changes to the Northeast. The war against Britain caused heavy losses to merchants and shipowners in the Northeast. British warships often prevented American trading ships from leaving port. As a result, American merchants could not sell their goods to foreign countries. Rows of idle ships lined the docks at Boston, New York, and Baltimore.

Although the war hurt trade and shipping, it greatly helped manufacturing in the Northeast. Before the war, there were still few factories in the United States because people could buy manufactured goods more cheaply from Europe. During the war, however, Americans could not get European goods. Many factories were established to produce cotton cloth, iron goods, and other needed items. By the end of the war, there were hundreds of factories in the Northeast.

Build Your Vocabulary

National Road   turnpike   steamboat   clipper   tariff   Erie Canal

impressment   telegraph   secede   immigrants   the Confederacy

the Union   abolitionists   border states   states' rights   nationalism

NATIONALISM

Americans feel a growing sense of national pride. At the time the United States was founded, many Americans felt more loyal to their home states than to the country as a whole. Some even felt closer to the people of Europe than to their fellow Americans. President Washington realized that this lack of national unity might weaken the United States. In his Farewell Address,* he warned against any attempts to loosen "the sacred ties which now link together the various parts."

After the War of 1812, people in the United States began to feel a stronger sense of national pride. At that time, the country was growing rapidly. American manufacturers of goods such as textiles and iron were competing successfully with European producers. Also, the federal government was growing stronger.

What is nationalism? The feeling of national pride that developed in the United States during the early 1800's is an example of what we call nationalism. In order to understand what nationalism is, however, you must first know what is meant by the term nationality.

A nationality is a large group of people who feel they belong together and should be able to run their own affairs. Usually they live in the same geographical area, speak the same language, and have the same history, religion, and customs. All of these conditions are not necessary, however. For example, the people of Switzerland feel they are a nationality even though four different languages are spoken in their country.

Nationalism combines the two ideas of loyalty to one's nationality and love of one's country. In a country where the people are all of a single nationality, there is no conflict between the two parts of nationalism. The people develop a strong feeling of national pride in both their country and their fellow citizens. Such a country is called a nation-state.

All countries are not nation-states, however. A single country may include more than one nationality. If the different nationalities are living under the same government by choice, there is usually no serious conflict of loyalties. Sometimes, however, several different nationalities may be held together under a single government by force, or people of the same nationality may be scattered among several powerful countries. Under such circumstances, people often feel greater loyalty to their nationality than to their government. They develop a strong feeling of nationalism toward their own group and want to have an independent country of their own.

Effects of nationalism. Nationalism often leads to the creation of new nation-states. Italy, for example, was divided into a number of small territories until the nineteenth century. Then a growing feeling of nationalism helped to unite the Italian people into a true nation-state. During the present century, nationalism has led many former colonies to break away from the countries that controlled them. Most of the newly independent countries of Asia and Africa were formed in this way.

A nation-state is made stronger by the sense of nationalism among its people. For example, the widespread feeling of nationalism in the United States during the nineteenth century led many Americans to work for the good of their country. Explorers and pioneers pushed westward and opened up new lands for settlement. Sometimes, however, nationalism leads to destruction and suffering. This was the case in World War II, when the Germans and the Japanese were both strongly nationalistic. In their desire for power and glory, Germany and Japan tried to take over several weaker countries by force.

*See Glossary

Francis Scott Key wrote "The Star-Spangled Banner" during the War of 1812. This war helped to create a feeling of nationalism among Americans.

The War of 1812 had other effects as well. It showed the countries of Europe that Americans would fight to protect their rights. Also, it caused many Americans to feel a greater loyalty to their nation as a whole than to any state or region. In other words, it helped to develop a strong feeling of nationalism.

The Northeast Grows in Wealth and Population

New roads and canals are built in the Northeast. In the early 1800's, it was difficult to travel from one place to another in the United States. Most of the roads were narrow trails that were muddy in rainy weather and bumpy the rest of the time. People traveled over these roads on horseback or in wagons or stagecoaches. Land travel was slow and uncomfortable. Travel by water was sometimes more pleasant, but it, too, was slow. There was no direct water route between many cities so boats often had to go far out of their way to reach their destinations. Also, sailing ships were often delayed for days by unfavorable winds. Because it was costly to ship goods from place to place, there

The Lancaster Turnpike was America's first hard-surfaced toll road. This sixty-two-mile road from Philadelphia to Lancaster, Pennsylvania, was covered with hard-packed gravel. The owners of the Lancaster Turnpike and other toll roads collected money from people who used these highways.

was little trade between different parts of our country.

Many Americans realized that great benefits would result from better transportation. Farmers in the fertile Midwest would be able to send their crops to customers in cities along the Atlantic coast. Manufacturers in the cities could sell their products to people in rural areas. Settlers could travel more quickly and easily to new homes beyond the Appalachian Mountains.

Turnpikes. As time passed, new and better roads were built in the Northeast and in other sections of our country. Some of them were called toll roads, or turnpikes.* These roads were built by private companies, which collected a toll from anyone who used them. The first hard-surfaced toll road, the Lancaster Turnpike, was built in the 1790's. It extended from Philadelphia to Lancaster, Pennsylvania.

The National Road. In 1818, the United States government finished building a highway from Cumberland, Maryland, to Wheeling, in what is now West Virginia. This highway was eighty feet wide, and had a center strip of crushed stone covered with gravel. It was called the Cumberland Road. A Maryland highway connected this road with the port city of Baltimore.

The Cumberland Road became the main land route between the Atlantic coast and the Midwest. Thousands of pioneers traveled westward on this highway. Large herds of sheep and cattle were sent eastward over the Cumberland Road to coastal cities. By 1840, the road had been extended westward as far as Vandalia, Illinois. It was then known as the National Road.

The Erie Canal was completed in 1825. It extended from the Hudson River to Lake Erie. Large amounts of goods were carried on this waterway.

The Erie Canal. For many years, people had dreamed of a waterway that would connect the Atlantic coast of the United States with the Great Lakes. Their dream came true in 1825, when New York State finished building the Erie Canal. This man-made waterway extended from the Hudson River westward through the Mohawk Valley and the Erie-Ontario Lowland to Lake Erie. After it was completed, boats could travel from New York City, at the mouth of the Hudson River, to Buffalo and other ports on the Great Lakes.

The Erie Canal was very helpful to the Northeast. Heavy cargoes could be carried more quickly and cheaply by canalboat than they could by wagon. Soon large amounts of grain, lumber, and other products from the Midwest were being shipped over the Erie Canal to cities along the Atlantic coast. Goods manufactured in eastern cities were carried by canalboat to settlers west of

*See Glossary

the Appalachians. The canalboats also carried many passengers. Much of the cargo transported on the Erie Canal passed through New York City. Even before the canal was built, New York had become the largest city in the United States. Now it grew even more rapidly in population.

Other canals. After the Erie Canal was completed, many other canals were built in the Northeast. Some were used mainly to carry coal from mines in eastern Pennsylvania to Atlantic ports. Canals were built by Maryland and Pennsylvania to connect the Atlantic coast with the Midwest. However, they were not as successful as the Erie Canal. Because these canals passed through mountainous areas, they were difficult and expensive to build. In fact, Maryland's canal never reached the Midwest. About this time, railroads were becoming common in the Northeast. Trains could transport goods more quickly than canalboats.

The "Clermont," launched in 1807, was the world's first practical steamboat. Soon many other steamboats were traveling on the rivers of America.

Steam power is used to drive boats and trains. At the same time that canals were being built in the Northeast, a new kind of power was being used for transportation. This was steam power. The first practical steam engine had been built in the 1760's by a Scotsman named James Watt. Soon, curious people were asking themselves whether the steam engine could be used to move boats and wagons.

Steamboats. In 1786, a Connecticut clockmaker named John Fitch built the first steamboat in America. Several other inventors also built steamboats about the same time, but the first boats were not very practical. The first successful steamboat was built by Robert Fulton of Pennsylvania. It was called the *Clermont*. In 1807, the *Clermont* steamed up the Hudson River from New York City to Albany, traveling about 150 miles in thirty-two hours.

Soon many steamboats were carrying goods and passengers on the rivers of America. About fifty years passed, however, before steam-powered vessels were widely used for ocean travel. Shipping companies were more interested in building faster and better sailing ships.

During the 1840's, a new type of sailing ship called the clipper was built at ports in the Northeast. These ships had many sails. They were the fastest sailing ships ever built. For about twenty years, the clippers carried goods and passengers to every part of the world. Then steamships were developed that could travel even faster than the clippers. They could carry more cargo, and they did not have to depend on favorable winds. In the 1860's steamships rapidly took the place of the clippers.

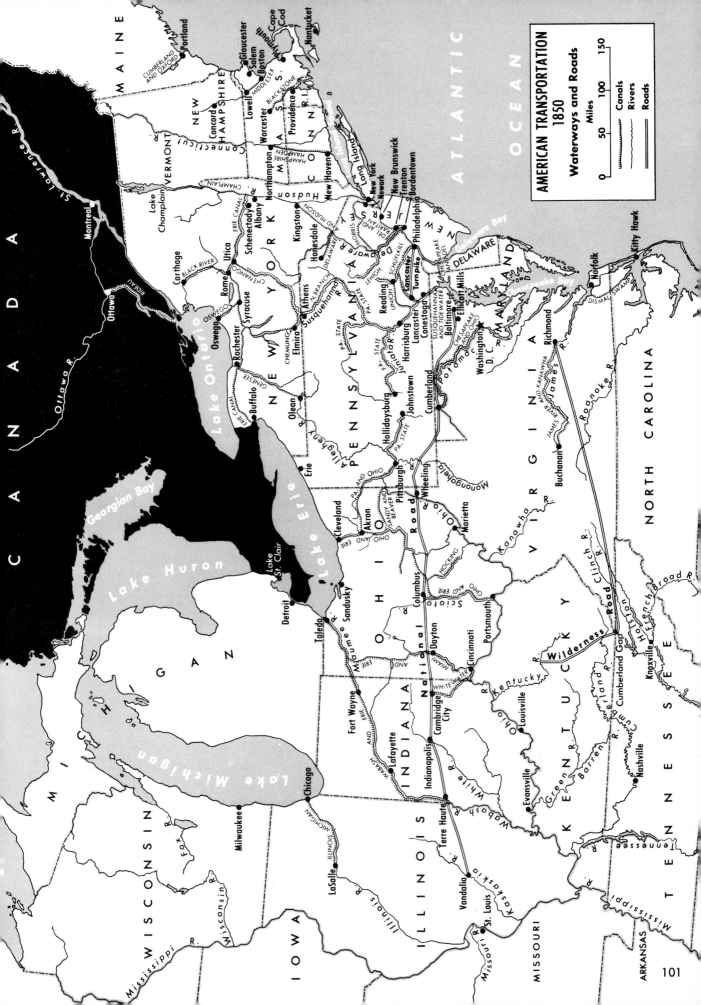

AMERICAN TRANSPORTATION
1850
Waterways and Roads

Miles
0   50   100   150

········· Canals
———— Rivers
———— Roads

101

Railroads. Meanwhile, steam power was also being used for land transportation. During the 1820's several steam locomotives were built in England. One of the first locomotives built in the United States was called the "Tom Thumb" because it was so small. In 1830, the "Tom Thumb" made a trial run on the Baltimore and Ohio Railroad in Maryland. It pulled a car with thirty-six passengers over a thirteen-mile track in less than an hour.

After steam locomotives proved successful on the Baltimore and Ohio, other railroad lines were started in the Northeast. Most of these were short, and they usually connected only two cities. One line ran between Albany and Schenectady in New York. Another crossed New Jersey, between New York and Phila-

delphia. Still others connected Boston with Providence and other cities in New England.

Early railroad travel was uncomfortable and often unsafe. However, many Americans were eager to ride on trains. They could travel faster and more comfortably by train than by wagon or stagecoach. Goods could be carried more quickly by train than by canalboat. Railroads cost less to build than canals, and they were easier to construct in mountainous areas. As the years passed, more railroads were built. They took much business away from the canals and turnpikes. By 1860, there were railroad lines in nearly every part of the Northeast.

Other inventions help the Northeast to grow. Until the 1830's the only way to

An early train on the Baltimore and Ohio Railroad. One of the first steam locomotives built in America was used to pull a car on this railroad in 1830. After steam locomotives proved successful on the Baltimore and Ohio, railroad lines were started in other parts of the Northeast.

communicate with someone a long distance away was either to visit him in person or to write a letter. Then a Massachusetts artist, Samuel Morse, invented a device for sending messages by wire. This device was called the telegraph. In 1844, Morse sent a telegraph message from Washington, D.C., to Baltimore. Soon telegraph lines connected all the main cities of the Northeast. The telegraph proved very useful to the people of this region. Newspapers could get the latest news from distant places by telegraph. Railroad companies could direct the movement of their trains. Businessmen could use the telegraph to conduct their dealings with people in other cities.

Two other useful inventions developed by people in the Northeast were the sewing machine and the elevator. Elias Howe of Massachusetts invented the first practical sewing machine in the 1840's. With this device, clothing could be made more quickly and sold more cheaply than ever before. The first successful passenger elevator was developed by Elisha G. Otis of New York in 1852. American cities were growing rapidly at that time, and it was becoming difficult and expensive to buy land on which to build apartments and offices. If people could construct buildings many stories high, they would save valuable land. The elevator made it practical to construct tall buildings.

Newcomers from Europe pour into the Northeast. Between 1820 and 1860, millions of people came to the United States from Europe. The largest numbers of immigrants* came from Ireland and Germany, but there were also many newcomers from England and other parts of Europe. The reasons why so many people came to America at this time are explained in Chapter 12.

Many of the newcomers settled in New York or other large cities of the Northeast. Because many of the immigrants had little money, they could not afford to move very far from the ports where they entered the United States. In the cities of the Northeast, they could find jobs in mills and factories. Some of them were employed in building canals or railroads. As immigrants poured into the Northeast, this region grew rapidly in population.

The Northeast leads the nation in manufacturing. During the first half of the 1800's there was much more industry in the Northeast than in any other part of our country. Many new factories were started in this region every year. Although most people in the Northeast continued to earn their living from farming, the number who worked in factories grew steadily.

Factories in the Northeast produced a wide variety of goods. Hundreds of textile mills had been started in this region, especially in New England. There were also many factories that produced hats, shoes, suits, or dresses. Large amounts of iron were manufactured in Pennsylvania and other Middle Atlantic states. Some of this iron was used by factories in the Northeast to make such items as wagon tires, stoves, and farm implements. Among the other products manufactured in this region were clocks, silverware, guns, and locomotives.

Why the Northeast became a great manufacturing region. Several facts help to explain the growth of industry

How Our Country Grew

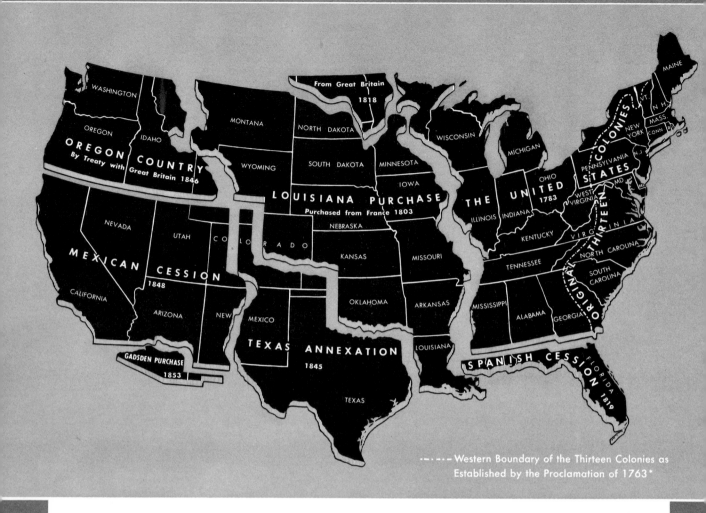

-·-··--- Western Boundary of the Thirteen Colonies as Established by the Proclamation of 1763*

The United States in 1783. At the end of the Revolutionary War, our country extended westward from the Atlantic Ocean to the Mississippi River, and southward from Canada to Florida. (See special feature on page 87.)

Louisiana Purchase. West of the Mississippi River was a huge area called Louisiana, which was owned by Spain. In 1800, France acquired Louisiana from Spain. Three years later, the United States purchased this territory from France and it became part of our country.

Treaty of 1818. In 1818, the United States signed a treaty with Great Britain, which then owned Canada. Under this treaty, the 49th parallel* became the United States-Canadian boundary from the western part of what is now Minnesota to the Rocky Mountains.

Spanish Cession. In 1763, the British gained control of Florida, which had belonged to Spain. Twenty years later, the Spanish regained Florida. In 1818, the United States sent troops here to fight Indians who had attacked American settlements. The next year, Spain signed a treaty by which the United States gained possession of Florida.

Texas Annexation. American settlers living in Texas revolted against the Mexican government and in 1836 set up an independent country. They asked the United States to annex* Texas, which it did in 1845.

Oregon Country. Both the United States and Great Britain claimed the Oregon Country, a large area west of the Rocky Mountains. In 1846, the two nations signed a treaty that gave the United States nearly all of the Oregon Country south of the 49th parallel.

Mexican Cession. Mexico was angry because the United States had annexed Texas. In 1846, the two countries went to war. The United States won the war in 1848. Mexico was forced to sell us California and other territory shown on the map above.

Gadsden Purchase. In 1853, our country bought from Mexico parts of what are now southern Arizona and New Mexico. This was known as the Gadsden Purchase.

Alaska and Hawaii. Alaska and Hawaii are shown on the map on page 18. In 1867, the United States bought Alaska from Russia. The Hawaiian Islands were annexed in 1898.

*See Glossary

in the Northeast during the first half of the 1800's. As you learned in Chapter 5, the Northeast had a "head start" in manufacturing. The South* and the Midwest had very little industry at this time. The people who lived there bought many of the manufactured goods they needed from businesses in the Northeast.

The large population of the Northeast helped industry to grow. Many of the European immigrants who settled in this region were very poor, and they were willing to work for low wages. As a result, there was a large supply of cheap labor for the factories. The cities of the Northeast provided many customers for manufactured goods.

Another reason for the growth of industry in the Northeast was the fine system of transportation in this region. As you learned earlier, many roads, canals, and railroads had been built in the Northeast. These could be used to transport raw materials to factories and to ship manufactured goods to people who wanted to buy them. In addi-tion, most of our country's leading sea-ports were located in the Northeast. Goods could be carried by ship from these seaports to other parts of the United States as well as to foreign countries.

During the first half of the 1800's, coal was becoming very important to industry. People were using steam engines not only to drive boats and loco-motives, but also to run machines in factories. Coal was burned to produce steam for these engines. It was also used in making iron and steel. In the mountains of Pennsylvania were rich coal deposits which helped the growth of industry in the Northeast.

There were still other reasons why the Northeast became a great manu-facturing region. The telegraph, the sewing machine, and other inventions developed by people in the Northeast helped industry to grow here. Also, there were many wealthy people living in the Northeast who were willing to invest money in new industries.

A War Is Fought To Preserve the Union

People in the United States disagree about slavery. At the time the Northeast was becoming an important manu-facturing region, the southern part of our country remained a region of farms. In the South, there were few large cities or towns and only a small num-ber of factories. Wherever the land was level and fertile, there were huge plan-tations on which cotton, tobacco, or other crops were grown. Many workers were needed on plantations. Most of the work was done by Negro slaves, whose ancestors had been brought from Africa in the 1600's and 1700's.

In colonial days, slavery had been permitted in the Northeast also. How-ever, slaves were not very useful in this region. Most farms in the Northeast were too small to require large numbers of workers. Also, factory owners used hired workers rather than slaves. The hired workers could be laid off if busi-ness was poor, but slaves had to be fed and clothed all the time. Many people in the Northeast felt it was wrong for one person to hold another as a slave. By about 1800, most states in this region had passed laws prohibiting slavery. Slavery was also forbidden in the states that were later formed north of the Ohio River and east of the Mississippi River.

In the early 1800's, an increasing number of people in the northern part of our country came to feel that slavery should be abolished throughout the United States. These people were called abolitionists. They often helped slaves to escape from their owners.

Most people in the South strongly resented the words and actions of the abolitionists. They realized that the South's plantation system would break down without slave labor. In addition, many southerners sincerely believed that God had intended the Negroes to be servants of white people.

People also disagree on the issues of states' rights and tariffs. Another important issue on which people disagreed was the question of states' rights. In the North,* most public leaders believed that the federal* government had final authority over the states. They felt that the states had a duty to enforce all federal laws. Many southern leaders, however, argued that the states could limit the power of the federal government whenever they considered it necessary. Some even claimed that the states had the right to leave the Union* if they wished.

A southern plantation. During the early 1800's, when the Northeast was becoming an important industrial region, the South remained a region of farms. Negro slaves did most of the work on plantations. Most people in the South resented attempts by northerners to abolish slavery.

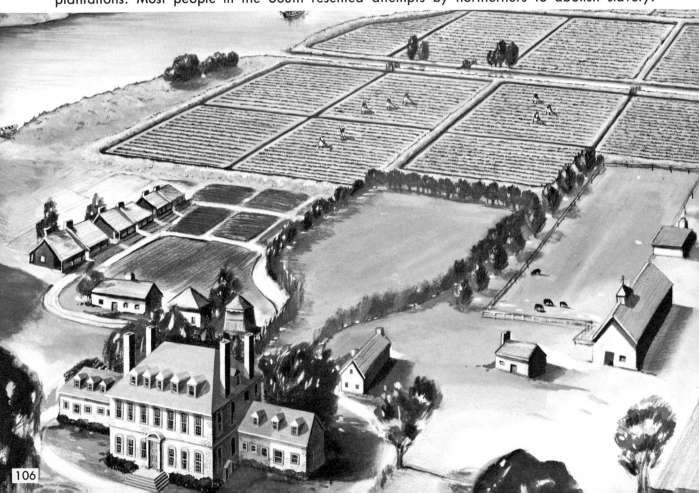

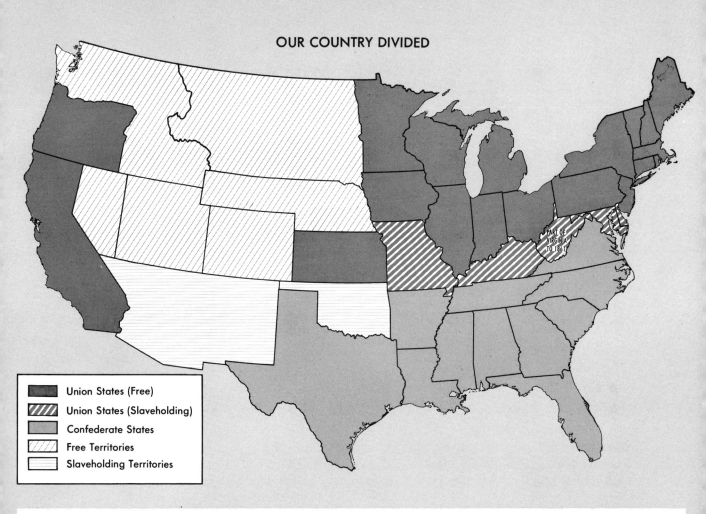

Union States (Free)
Union States (Slaveholding)
Confederate States
Free Territories
Slaveholding Territories

PART OF VIRGINIA TO 1861

From 1860 to 1865, the United States was a divided country. In 1860, Abraham Lincoln was elected president. None of the southern states had wanted Lincoln as president, however, mainly because Lincoln was against slavery in the territories and new states of our country. Shortly after the election, South Carolina seceded from the Union.

During 1861, ten more states seceded. These states, together with South Carolina, became a separate nation called the Confederacy. The western part of Virginia remained in the Union, and later became the state of West Virginia. The United States was a divided country until the Civil War ended, in 1865.

The North and the South also differed on the question of tariffs.* Many people in the North wanted the government to place a high tariff on all manufactured goods imported from Europe, so that these goods would cost more to buy. Then people in the United States would buy American goods instead. This would help factory owners and industrial workers in the North. People in the South were strongly opposed to a high tariff. They sold large amounts of cotton and other crops to Great Britain. In exchange, they bought many British manufactured products. A high tariff would force them to pay higher prices for the goods they imported from Britain. In addition, it might cause the British to buy less cotton from the South. The disagreement over tariffs

Abraham Lincoln's first inauguration, March 4, 1861. In his speech, Lincoln pleaded for peace and unity. However, seven slaveholding states had already withdrawn from the Union. The Civil War began on April 12, when Confederate troops fired on Fort Sumter.

helped cause unfriendly feelings between the North and the South.

The dispute over slavery leads to war. During the 1850's, the North and the South drew farther apart on the issue of slavery. Most northerners believed that the federal government should prohibit slavery in the new territories that were being formed west of the Mississippi River. However, most southerners felt that slavery should be permitted throughout the new territories.

Eventually, as a result of this disagreement, the United States became a divided nation. A group of northerners who wanted to prevent the spread of slavery to the territories founded the Republican Party in 1854. Six years later, the Republican candidate, Abraham Lincoln, was elected president of the United States. This led South Carolina to secede, or withdraw, from the Union. South Carolina was followed by ten other slaveholding states. These states established a separate nation called the Confederate States of America, or the Confederacy. (See map on page 107.)

President Lincoln believed that no state had the right to secede from the Union. He refused to withdraw Union troops stationed at Fort Sumter in Charleston, South Carolina. On April 12, 1861, Confederate troops fired on the fort, and the Civil War began.

The Civil War lasted four years and cost almost 600,000 lives. In this terrible conflict, the main goal of the North was to save the Union. In addition, many northerners hoped to end slavery. The South was fighting to win its independence.

During the Civil War, most of the states in the Northeast gave their full support to the Union. These states sent many thousands of soldiers to fight in the Union armies. Factories in the Northeast produced most of the equipment used by the Union forces.

Maryland and Delaware were called border states. Although they had always permitted slavery, they remained in the Union. However, many of their citizens fought for the Confederacy.

The Civil War led to the founding of a new state called West Virginia. When Virginia seceded, many people in the western part of the state remained loyal to the Union. In 1861, the western counties declared their independence from Virginia and set up a new government. Two years later, the state of West Virginia was admitted to the Union.

Although most of the Civil War was fought in the Confederate states, two important battles took place in the

President Lincoln issued the Emancipation Proclamation in 1863. This freed the slaves in areas held by Confederate forces at that time. The Civil War, which cost almost 600,000 lives, continued until the surrender of Confederate troops on April 9, 1865. A few days later, Lincoln was shot and killed. However, he had succeeded in his goal of preserving the Union.

Northeast. In 1862, Union and Confederate forces fought a bloody battle at Antietam Creek in western Maryland. The following year, a Confederate army invaded Pennsylvania. At the town of Gettysburg, it was defeated by Union forces after three days of hard fighting.

The Union is saved. In the Civil War, each side had certain advantages. The southern soldiers were more accustomed to outdoor life than many northerners, so they found it easier to get used to military service. They also had the advantage of fighting on their own territory. The Confederacy had excellent military leaders, such as Robert E. Lee and Thomas "Stonewall" Jackson. The North, however, had a much larger population than the South and much more wealth. It also had a better network of roads and railroads. Farms in the North produced a wider variety and larger amounts of crops and livestock. There were more factories to produce weapons and other supplies. The North was aided by nearly 200,000 Negro troops who fought for the Union. In addition, the North was led by a wise and strong president.

These advantages finally led to victory for the North. On April 9, 1865, Lee surrendered to General Ulysses S. Grant at Appomattox, Virginia. A few days later, President Lincoln was shot to death by an actor who sympathized with the Confederate cause. However, Lincoln had succeeded in his goal of preserving the Union.

The Civil War settled the issues of slavery and secession. Slavery was finally ended throughout the United States in 1865 by the Thirteenth Amendment to the Constitution. Since the Civil War, no state has again claimed the right to secede from the Union.

Develop Important Understandings
1. Why did the United States declare war on Great Britain in 1812?
2. List three ways in which the War of 1812 affected the United States.
3. Why was there little trade between different parts of our country in the early 1800's?
4. Why was the Erie Canal so helpful to the development of the Northeast?
5. Why did railroads take business away from canals and turnpikes?
6. What facts help to explain why industry grew rapidly in the Northeast during the first half of the 1800's?
7. In what ways did the North and South disagree over states' rights?
8. What was the main goal of the North during the Civil War? What was the main goal of the South?

Learning More About the Civil War
Although the War of 1812 gave Americans a new feeling of nationalism, the country was soon torn apart by the Civil War. Choose one of the topics below and write a report about it.

Famous Leaders of the Civil War

Famous Battles of the Civil War

Results of the Civil War

The suggestions on pages 345-349 will help you to find information and to write a good report. When you have finished your report, present it to the rest of the class. Then, when all reports have been given, write a summary of the Civil War. Use information you have learned from this book and from the reports of your classmates to write your summary.

Many new industries have grown up in the Northeast since the Civil War. One type of industry that grew rapidly was steelmaking. The picture on the left shows ironmaking in the nineteenth century; the picture on the right shows steelmaking in the twentieth century.

7 A Century of Progress

A Problem To Solve
After the Civil War, the cities of the Northeast grew rapidly in population. **Why was there such a rapid growth of cities in this region?** In forming your hypotheses to solve this problem, you will need to consider how the growth of cities was affected by:

a. new developments in farming
b. the growth of industry
c. immigration
d. improvements in transportation

See TO THE STUDENT, pages 8-10.

Imagine that you are traveling backward through time for a visit to New York City in the year 1865. When you arrive in New York, you find that it is very different from the city shown in the picture on page 29. For one thing, it is much smaller. The city covers only the southern part of Manhattan Island. In the northern part of the island, there are farms and woods. As you walk through the city, you notice that the bumpy streets are crowded with horse-drawn carriages. You do not see any tall skyscrapers made of steel and concrete. The tallest buildings are only five or six stories high, and they are built mainly of wood and stone. At night, the buildings and streets are lighted with flickering gas lamps.

Since 1865, great changes have taken place not only in New York City but throughout the Northeast. Inventions such as the electric light and the automobile have changed people's way of life. New industries have developed. Millions of people have left the farms and small towns of this region to seek jobs in the cities. Partly for this reason, the cities of the Northeast are much larger than they were one hundred years ago. Let us learn more about some of the important developments that have taken place in this region since the Civil War.

New Industries Provide Jobs for Many People

The Civil War spurs the growth of manufacturing. During the Civil War, industry grew rapidly in the Northeast. The Union forces needed large amounts of clothing, weapons, and other supplies. New factories were started to help meet these needs, and older factories increased their production.

After the war, industry continued to expand. The United States was now in the midst of the Industrial Revolution. Each year, hundreds of factories were established in the Northeast to produce a wide variety of goods. Many new factories were also started in the Midwest and the South. By 1900, the United States was producing more manufactured goods than any other nation in the world.

Steel mills are built in the Northeast. One type of industry that grew rapidly in the Northeast after the Civil War was steelmaking. Before 1860, machines and other metal goods had usually been made of iron. This metal was not satisfactory for many purposes, because it broke or bent too easily. For example, the iron rails of railroad tracks lasted only about two years. Steel was much stronger than iron, but it was difficult and costly to produce. Manufacturers had to find a way to make large amounts of steel quickly and cheaply.

During the 1850's, an English inventor named Henry Bessemer and an American ironmaker named William Kelly helped solve this problem. Each man, working by himself, discovered that steel could be produced by forcing a current of air through a vat of hot, melted iron. This method of making steel became known as the "Bessemer process." By using the Bessemer process, manufacturers could produce

Build Your Vocabulary

Bessemer process	invention	standard of living	Thomas A. Edison
financial	World War I	stocks and bonds	depression
World War II	computers	Space Age	atomic energy

A Bessemer converter, as shown in an engraving by a nineteenth century artist. The Bessemer process of changing iron into steel made possible the production of large quantities of this metal at low cost. Following the Civil War, steelmaking became a giant industry in the Northeast.

huge quantities of steel at a low cost. In the years that followed, a number of steel mills were built in the Northeast. Steel produced in these mills was used by other factories in making hundreds of products.

The steel industry was especially important in Pennsylvania. In this state were rich deposits of coal and limestone, two minerals needed for making steel. Pennsylvania was not very rich in iron ore, which was also needed for steelmaking. However, huge deposits of iron ore had been found near Lake Superior. To make steel, about two tons of coal were needed for each ton of iron ore. Therefore, it was

cheaper to bring the iron ore to the coalfields of Pennsylvania than it would have been to transport coal to the iron mines. Also, the coalfields were nearer to the large cities of the Northeast, where there were many customers for steel.

By 1880, the Great Lakes had become an important transportation route for iron ore. Large boats carried the ore from ports on Lake Superior to ports on Lake Erie. There the ore was loaded onto railroad cars that carried it to Pittsburgh and other steelmaking cities. Soon Pittsburgh was producing more steel than any other city in the United States.

Oil refining becomes a leading industry. During the early 1800's, the most important kind of oil used in the United States was whale oil. It was used to lubricate machines so that they would run smoothly. In addition, thousands of homes were lighted with whale-oil lamps. Many people knew about a dark, oily substance called petroleum, which seeped from the ground in some areas. However, no one realized that petroleum could be made into useful products. People who drilled wells in order to obtain salt were disgusted if they found petroleum instead.

In the 1850's, scientists discovered a better and cheaper fuel for lamps than whale oil. This was kerosene, which could be produced by distilling* petroleum. Suddenly, petroleum became very valuable.

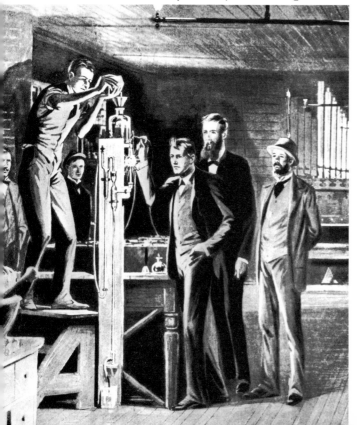

Thomas Edison experimenting in his laboratory at Menlo Park, New Jersey. One of Edison's greatest inventions was a cheap and practical light bulb.

A group of businessmen in the Northeast realized that it might be possible to obtain large amounts of petroleum by drilling wells in the same way that people drilled for salt. They hired a man named Edwin Drake to drill a well in northwestern Pennsylvania. In 1859, petroleum began to flow out of Drake's well. This was the first oil well in the United States. After Drake struck oil, hundreds of other wells were drilled in the same area. By the 1880's, oil wells in Pennsylvania and the western part of New York State were producing millions of barrels of petroleum each year.

Special plants called refineries were established in Pittsburgh and other cities. In the refineries, petroleum was changed into kerosene, wax, lubricating oil, and other products. Oil refining became a very important industry in the Northeast.

Inventors find ways to make use of electricity. At the time of the Civil War, most machines in the United States were run by waterwheels or steam engines. Buildings were lighted either with kerosene lamps or with lamps that burned coal* gas. In the late 1800's, however, a new way of producing light and power was developed.

For years, scientists had been studying the mysterious force known as electricity. Then inventors developed machines that could produce large amounts of electric power. They also found ways to use electricity in homes and factories.

The most famous of these inventors was Thomas A. Edison, who lived in the small town of Menlo Park, New Jersey. In 1879, Edison invented an

*See Glossary

electric light bulb that was inexpensive and practical. This bulb gave a much better light than lamps that burned kerosene or gas. Three years later, Edison built a power plant in New York City. In this plant, steam engines ran machines that produced electricity to light nearby houses, stores, and offices.

Soon electricity was being used in other ways. Streetcars and elevators were run by electric motors. People also began using electricity to run machines in factories. Electricity could be sent long distances through wires. Therefore, manufacturers no longer had to build their factories beside waterfalls or use clumsy steam engines to produce power. Instead, they could buy electricity from power companies. Electric-power plants were built to serve all the large cities of the Northeast. Many workers took jobs in plants that manufactured electrical machinery.

Another invention that made use of electricity was the telephone. It was developed in 1875 by Alexander Graham Bell, a young Scottish teacher living in Boston. At first, most people thought that the telephone was only a toy. Gradually, they came to realize that it could be very useful. People could talk on the telephone with friends and relatives who lived far away. They could call doctors, policemen, or firemen in times of emergency. Businessmen could telephone customers and suppliers in distant cities. By 1900, more than one million telephones were in use in the United States.

The Northeast Becomes a Great Gateway for Trade

At the same time that new industries were being established in the Northeast, great changes were taking place in other parts of our country. The Midwest was becoming an important farming and manufacturing region. The South was beginning to recover from the destruction that had been caused by the Civil War. Thousands of people were moving into the unsettled lands west of the Mississippi River. As our country grew, more and more goods were exchanged between the people of different regions.

Railroads connect the Northeast with other parts of the United States. Many short railroad lines were built in the Northeast during the 1830's and 1840's. As time passed, certain businessmen in the Northeast bought many of these small lines and combined them to form huge railroad systems. Among the railroad systems formed in this way were the New York Central Railroad and the Pennsylvania Railroad.

After the Civil War, many new railroads were built in all parts of the United States. Some of these railroads connected the Northeast with other regions. In 1869, a railroad was completed across the western part of our country from the Missouri River to the Pacific Ocean. Now it was possible to travel all the way across the United States by train.

Railroads helped make it possible for trade to develop rapidly between the Northeast and other parts of the United

New York's waterfront in the late 1800's. After the Civil War, railroads helped trade to develop rapidly in the Northeast. Trains brought goods from other regions of our country to the port cities of the Northeast. Here the goods were loaded onto ships to be sent to other parts of the world.

States. People in the Northeast could buy farm products such as beef, pork, and wheat from farmers in the Midwest. Northeastern manufacturers could obtain raw materials by train from California and other distant places. They could sell their manufactured goods to customers throughout our country.

Steamships crowd the harbors of the Northeast. In the years after 1865, the United States carried on more trade with foreign countries than ever before. Much of this trade passed through the seaports of the Northeast. Grain, meat, lumber, and other goods produced in various regions of the United States were brought to these ports by train. Here they were loaded onto ships that carried them to Europe, South America,

and other parts of the world. Foreign goods were brought to these same ports for distribution throughout the United States. The harbors of the Northeast were crowded with steamships from many lands.

New York and other cities become great financial centers. Ever since the 1700's, the Northeast had been the home of banks and insurance companies. Many business firms throughout the United States kept their money in banks in the Northeast. They felt that their money was safer there than in local banks, because the banks of the Northeast were usually larger and had more funds to take care of emergencies. If companies needed money to buy new equipment, they often borrowed it from banks in the Northeast. Thousands of people bought insurance from companies whose headquarters were in New York, Boston, Hartford, or other cities.

Between 1865 and 1915, businessmen from Great Britain and other European countries invested large sums of money in American factories and railroads. They did this by purchasing stocks* and bonds* issued by various companies. In New York and other port cities of the Northeast, there were many firms that handled the sale of stocks and bonds.

As the years passed, cities such as New York, Philadelphia, and Boston became great financial centers. Many large companies established their headquarters in these cities in order to be near the large banks and other financial agencies. Thousands of people in the Northeast were employed in banks and offices.

Great Cities Grow Up in the Northeast

Large numbers of people move from farms to cities. When the Civil War began, only about one fourth of the people in the Northeast lived in cities or large towns. During the next fifty years, however, great changes took place in people's way of life. New kinds of farm machinery and better methods of farming were developed. (See page 160.) As a result, fewer farmers were needed to supply our country with food. At the same time, more workers than ever before were needed in factories, stores, and offices. Many people from rural areas moved to the cities of the Northeast to get jobs in business and industry. These jobs usually paid them more money than they had been able to earn in farming.

In the years following the Civil War, the cities of the Northeast grew very rapidly. By 1900, New York City was four times as large as it had been in 1860. Other cities, such as Boston and Pittsburgh, also became much larger than ever before. By 1910, more than half of the people in the Northeast lived in cities or large towns.

Immigrants come from many lands. Not all of the people who came to the cities of the Northeast during this period were from rural areas in the United States. Many were immigrants from Europe. Between 1865 and 1915, more than 26 million immigrants poured into the United States. Most of them entered our country at New York City. Ellis Island in New York Harbor became world famous as a landing place for immigrants. Small numbers of immigrants entered the United States at Boston or other ports in the Northeast. In Chapter 12, you can learn more about the immigrants who came to make their homes in America.

Many of the immigrants who came to the United States after 1865 settled in the cities and towns of the Northeast. Some took jobs in factories here. Others traveled to the coalfields of Pennsylvania and West Virginia to work in the mines. All of these people helped

Immigrants entering New York Harbor in the late 1800's, as pictured in an old engraving. Between 1865 and 1915, more than 26 million immigrants came to the United States. Large numbers of these people took jobs in the factories and mines of the Northeast.

to meet our country's great need for industrial workers. Not all immigrants were employed in mines and factories, however. Some, for example, became storekeepers or office workers.

The newcomers face many problems. At first, life was not easy for most of the immigrants who came to the Northeast. These people were generally very poor, and they brought few possessions with them to America. Because most of them did not have any special skills, they could not get well-paying jobs. Usually they had to do the hardest, most unpleasant kinds of work for long hours at low pay. Because they did not have much money, they were forced to live in crowded, dirty slums.

The immigrants often found it hard to give up their old customs and adjust to a new way of life. Many of them could not speak English when they arrived from Europe. To most newcomers, America was a strange and frightening land. Therefore, people from one nation often settled together in a certain neighborhood where they would be able to feel more at home. This made it even more difficult for them to learn American customs.

Some immigrants received unfriendly treatment from native-born Americans. This was partly because the newcomers seemed strange and "foreign." Also, many Americans feared that the immigrants would take their jobs away by working for less money.

As time passed, however, life became easier for some immigrants. The children and many of the adults went to school and learned to speak English. They also learned American ways of doing things. As the newcomers gained more education and experience they were able to get better jobs. Many of them eventually moved out of the slums into better neighborhoods. Today, many leaders in government, science, the arts, and other fields are immigrants or are descended from immigrants who have come here during the last hundred years. On page 194 you can learn about some of these people.

World Events Affect the Northeast

The United States enters a war in Europe. In 1914, something happened in Europe that greatly affected the lives of people in the United States. A terrible war broke out between two groups of countries. On one side were the Central Powers, which included Germany, Austria-Hungary, Bulgaria, and Turkey. On the other side were Great Britain, France, Russia, and a number of other countries. They were called the Allies. The great struggle between the Allies and the Central Powers became known as World War I. (See feature on page 120.)

For a while, the United States government tried to stay out of the war in Europe. Before long, however, German submarines began to attack Allied ships traveling on the Atlantic Ocean. A number of American passengers on these ships were killed. Other German actions also made the American people angry. In April, 1917, the United States joined the war on the side of the Allies.

During World War I, factories in the Northeast needed large numbers of workers to produce military equipment. Hundreds of thousands of people came to the cities from rural areas to work in industry. Many of these people were Negroes from the South, who had not been able to earn a good living as farm workers or household servants. They came to the Northeast in the hope of getting better jobs in factories. The Negroes settled mainly in New York, Philadelphia, and other large cities. Even after the end of the war, Negroes

In World War I, American soldiers fought alongside other Allied troops. During this war, many people moved to the cities of the Northeast to take jobs in factories that were producing military equipment.

WORLD WAR I

World War I (1914-1918) was fought between two rival groups of countries. One group, called the Central Powers, was made up of Germany, Austria-Hungary, Bulgaria, and Turkey. The other group, called the Allies, included Great Britain, France, Russia, and many other countries. The United States entered the war on the side of the Allies in 1917.

Causes of World War I. At the beginning of the 1900's, fierce rivalries divided the countries of Europe. These rivalries were caused partly by the rise of nationalism. (See page 97.) Especially in eastern Europe, there were countries where different nationalities were being held together against their will. In addition, bitter competition for raw materials and markets was developing between the industrialized nations of western Europe. These nations hoped to meet their needs by gaining territories, mainly in Africa and Asia. Many European nations formed secret alliances. By 1914, much of Europe was divided into opposing groups of countries, which faced each other with hatred and distrust. The immediate cause of the war was the assassination of Archduke Francis Ferdinand of Austria-Hungary. This was blamed on the neighboring country of Serbia, and war broke out between these two countries. Most of Europe was soon drawn into the war.

The Allies triumph. Most of the important land battles of World War I took place in France. In the beginning, the Central Powers won victories on both land and sea. The Allies, however, had more men and materials than the Central Powers. In the end, the Allies were victorious. American troops sent to Europe near the end of the war helped bring about the victory. During the war, more than 30 million troops had been killed or wounded. Millions of people also died of disease or starvation.

The results of the war. As a result of the peace treaties that officially ended the war, much territory was taken from the defeated Central Powers. New nations, such as Yugoslavia and Czechoslovakia, were formed. Germany was forced to accept the terms of a very harsh treaty, called the Treaty of Versailles. This helped sow the seeds of an even more terrible war — World War II. (See page 124.)

from the South continued to move into the cities of the Northeast.

Automobiles and other inventions change people's lives. By the time World War I ended, life in America was changing rapidly. One reason for this was the growing use of such inventions as the automobile and the airplane.

Automobiles were developed in the 1880's and 1890's by inventors in the United States and Europe. At first, automobiles were so expensive to manufacture that only a few people could afford to buy them. In the early 1900's, however, manufacturers found ways to produce automobiles rapidly and cheaply. By 1920, there were about eight million automobiles in the United States.

The development of the automobile changed American life in several ways. Automobile manufacturing became one of our country's leading industries, employing many thousands of workers. It also helped other industries to grow. For example, large amounts of steel were used in making automobiles. Gasoline, a substance made from petroleum, was needed as a fuel in auto engines. As a result, the steel and petroleum industries greatly increased their production. Better highways, paved with concrete or asphalt, were built to handle automobile traffic. People who used cars for transportation did not have to live near the places where they worked. Many of them moved to communities called suburbs, which grew up around the cities.

The first practical airplane had been built in 1903 by Orville and Wilbur Wright, two brothers from Ohio. As the years passed, larger and better airplanes were developed. They made it

120

Assembling automobiles in the early 1900's. The development of the automobile provided Americans with a new means of transportation. Automobile manufacturing became one of our country's most important industries, employing thousands of workers.

possible for travelers to go long distances in only a few hours. During the 1920's, airports were built near the large cities of the United States. Businessmen started airlines to carry passengers, mail, and freight on regular schedules.

Other inventions changed the ways in which Americans spent their leisure time. Radio was developed in the early 1900's. In 1920, the world's first radio station began broadcasting in Pittsburgh, Pennsylvania. Within a few years, many people in the United States were listening to news broadcasts and entertainment programs on their own radio sets. Two other inventions that

provided entertainment for millions of people were the phonograph and motion pictures. These were developed largely by the great inventor Thomas A. Edison. (See pages 114 and 115.)

During the 1920's, business was good in most parts of the Northeast. Many new factories were started to manufacture household appliances and other products. People continued to move from rural areas into the cities to get jobs in business and industry. Huge skyscrapers were built in New York and other cities.

A great depression leaves many people without jobs. Not all Americans shared in the prosperity of the 1920's. Since

121

the end of World War I, farmers had been receiving low prices for their crops. Many factory employees had been working for low wages. These people could not afford to buy all the goods they needed.

About the start of the 1930's, serious business troubles developed in the United States. People were buying fewer goods than factories were producing. Many factories could no longer operate at a profit, so they were forced to close. Thousands of people lost their jobs and could not find new ones. They were not able to buy as many goods as before. As a result, stores laid off some of their clerks, and more factories went out of business. By the end of 1932, there were about thirteen million unemployed workers in the United States. Many families did not even have enough money to buy food, shelter,

Unemployed workers in New Hampshire. From about 1930 to 1940, the United States went through a period of business troubles called a depression. Many factories closed and millions of people lost their jobs.

and clothing. A period of business troubles and unemployment such as this is called a depression.

In New England, there was also another reason for unemployment and poverty. Textile manufacturing had long been a leading industry in this section. Near the end of the 1800's, however, many cotton textile mills were started in the South. These mills had several advantages over the New England factories. They were closer to the farms where cotton was grown. Workers in the South were willing to accept lower wages than New England workers. Also, taxes were usually lower in the South. For all these reasons, the southern mills could produce textiles more cheaply than those that were located in New England. During the 1920's and 1930's, many textile plants in New England were forced to close because they could not compete with the mills in the South. Thousands of textile workers in New England were left without jobs.

During the 1930's, the federal government and some of the states tried in various ways to end the depression. They provided food and small sums of money to people who did not have jobs. They employed many workers in the construction of highways, dams, and public buildings. In addition, the federal government loaned money to people who wanted to start new businesses. Gradually business improved, and more people were able to find work. By the end of the 1930's, the depression was almost over.

World War II makes heavy demands on the Northeast. As our country was recovering from the depression, another

American troops in Paris during World War II. This war began in 1939 when Germany attacked the neighboring country of Poland. It ended in 1945 with the surrender of Japanese forces. During the war, factories in the Northeast helped supply war equipment for the United States and its allies.

war was starting. In 1933, a group of people called the Nazis had taken control of Germany's government. They wanted to conquer other countries and make Germany the most powerful nation in the world. Italy and Japan were also willing to go to war in order to gain territory. These three countries became known as the Axis powers.

In 1939, Germany attacked a neighboring country, Poland. This was the start of World War II. (See page 124.) Again the leaders of the United States hoped to stay out of the war in Europe. In 1941, however, Japanese forces made a surprise attack on the American naval base at Pearl Harbor in the Hawaiian Islands. This attack brought

our country into the war against the Axis. World War II continued until the Axis powers were defeated, in 1945.

During this war, the Northeast again helped to supply many of the goods needed by the United States and its allies. Factories operated twenty-four hours a day producing ships, tanks, airplanes, and many other kinds of war equipment. Again large numbers of people came to the cities of the Northeast to get factory jobs. Some of these people were Negroes from the South. Others came from the island of Puerto Rico, which belonged to the United States. On page 193, you can learn more about these newcomers to the Northeast.

123

WORLD WAR II

World War II began in 1939 and lasted six years. The war was fought between two groups of nations called the Axis powers and the Allies. The principal Axis powers were Germany, Italy, and Japan. The Allies included the United States, the Soviet Union, Great Britain, and many other countries. Almost every part of the world became involved in World War II.

Main causes of World War II. Many different conditions helped to bring about the Second World War. The following are some of the main causes:

The Treaty of Versailles. This treaty, signed after World War I, forced Germany to greatly reduce the strength of its army and navy, to give up much of its territory, and to pay large sums of money to the victors of the war. Many people blamed this treaty for the widespread poverty and discontent in Germany during the 1920's and early 1930's.

The rise of dictatorships and militarism. A worldwide depression, strong feelings of nationalism, and various other conditions led to the rise of dictatorships in certain nations. In Germany, the Nazi* leader Adolf Hitler became an absolute dictator, with control over the German military forces. Powerful military leaders also came to power in Italy and Japan, and allied their countries with Germany.

Aggression by the Axis powers. Each of the three principal Axis powers sought to gain more territory by force. During the 1930's, Japan invaded China, Italy seized territory in Africa, and Germany sent troops into Austria and Czechoslovakia. In 1939, after Hitler's troops invaded Poland, Great Britain and France declared war on Germany. World War II had now begun. The United States was drawn into the war two years later. (See page 123.)

The Allies win the war. In the early years of the war, the Axis powers won many victories. German armies gained control over much of Europe and northern Africa. Japanese forces won victories in Asia and the Pacific. The Allies gradually grew stronger, however, and the course of the war changed. Germany was finally defeated in May, 1945. After American planes dropped atomic bombs on Japan in August, 1945, that country also surrendered.

More people were killed or wounded in World War II than in any other war in history. About fifteen million troops were killed in action. In addition, millions of civilians were killed in air raids, starved to death, or died in concentration camps. The Nazis murdered more than half the Jews in Europe, as well as vast numbers of Russians and Poles.

Results of World War II. One result of World War II was the spread of communism. Soviet armies occupied much of eastern Europe during and after the war. In several countries, these armies helped to establish Communist governments, which are still in power. The war also helped the Communists in China to gain control of the country.

World War II led to great progress in science. The development of the atomic bomb has given a new and fearful weapon to the United States, the Soviet Union, and several other countries. Peaceful uses of atomic energy, however, promise many benefits to mankind. The development of rockets during the war led to the Space Age.

Following World War II, most of the nations of the world joined together in a new organization to preserve world peace. This is the United Nations, which has its headquarters in New York City.

*See Glossary

Allied leaders meeting during World War II. This war involved most of the world. Millions of people were killed during World War II.

The Northeast Today

The Northeast is still a very important region. Since World War II, the Northeast has not grown as rapidly in population as some other regions of the United States, such as the West and the South. However, it remains the most densely populated region of our country. The cities of the Northeast are still great centers of trade, manufacturing, education, and culture. Since 1946, the Northeast has been the home of the United Nations. Most of the world's nations are members of this organization, which tries to maintain peace and solve important problems through international cooperation.

Changes in American life have brought progress and problems to the Northeast. During the last twenty-five years, great changes have been taking place in the Northeast and in other regions of the United States. Many of these changes have been brought about by the Industrial Revolution, which is still in progress today. (See page 91.) For example, machines have been invented that require few, if any, human operators. The use of such machinery is called automation. With automation, factories in the Northeast and throughout our nation can produce more goods than ever before.

In 1945, scientists working for the American government exploded the first atomic bomb on a desert in the southwestern part of the United States. Since that time, scientists have been working to find peaceful ways of using atomic* energy. In the Northeast to-day, there are several plants that use atomic energy to produce electric power for homes, offices, and factories.

In recent years, the United States has entered the Space Age. Scientists have developed rockets that can travel far beyond the earth's atmosphere. These rockets have been used to launch a number of spacecraft from the earth. Some of these spacecraft have carried astronauts to the moon. In the future, astronauts will probably be traveling even greater distances, to neighboring planets such as Mars and Venus.

Other inventions have changed the everyday lives of many Americans. Most families now have television sets to provide them with entertainment, as well as news from all over the world. Labor-saving devices such as dishwashers are making housework easier. Jet airplanes have been developed that can carry passengers at speeds of nearly ten miles a minute.

The changes brought about by science and invention have provided jobs for many people in the Northeast. As you learned earlier, New England was severely hurt by the closing of textile mills in the 1920's and 1930's. In the last few years, many new electronics plants have opened in New England. They use skilled workmen to manufacture a variety of products, ranging from television parts to large "thinking" machines called computers.* Other factories in the Northeast make equipment for our country's space program.

A modern expressway in Philadelphia. As a result of science and invention, great changes have taken place in the Northeast during the last twenty-five years. Although these changes have brought progress, they have also caused some serious problems that must be solved.

The period since World War II has been a time of great prosperity for most people in the Northeast. Today they enjoy one of the highest standards* of living in the world. In spite of this prosperity, they still face serious problems. Some of these are the result of the rapid changes that have occurred during the past century. In Chapter 14, you can learn about some of the problems facing the people of the Northeast today. You can also learn what is being done to solve these problems and to make plans for future growth.

Learning About a Century of Progress

Great changes have taken place in the United States during the past one hundred years. Listed below are certain developments that helped to bring about important changes. Do some research about these developments. Then write a brief paragraph about each, explaining how it affected the people of the Northeast.

The Bessemer process for making steel is developed.

Edison invents an inexpensive, practical electric light bulb.

Railroads are built to connect the Northeast with other parts of our country.

The automobile is developed.

The United States is involved in two world wars.

Much of the information you will need can be found in this chapter. For help in locating additional information, refer to the suggestions on pages 347-349.

Part 3
Earning a Living

A dairy farm in New England

A worker in a Pennsylvania steel plant

Coal barges on the Ohio River. Much of the coal mined in West Virginia and Pennsylvania is shipped to large steel mills in Pittsburgh. The people of the Northeast have used coal and other natural resources of this region to develop many important industries.

8 Natural Resources

A Problem To Solve

How have the natural resources of the Northeast affected the development of manufacturing in this region? To solve this problem, you will first need to learn what natural resources are found in the Northeast. Then you will need to make hypotheses that explain how these resources have affected:

a. the location of industries in the Northeast

b. the types of manufacturing that have developed here

c. the total amount of manufacturing in the Northeast

Chapters 5, 6, 7, and 9 contain additional information that will help you.

See TO THE STUDENT, pages 8-10.

It is a bright warm day, and we are watching several long barges on the Ohio River, northwest of Pittsburgh, Pennsylvania. Two of the barges are loaded with coal. Another barge is filled with crushed limestone. Both the coal and limestone will be used in Pittsburgh's huge steel mills.

Coal, limestone, and other minerals are valuable gifts from nature. These gifts are called natural resources. The people of the Northeast have used their natural resources to develop many important industries.

In addition to minerals, there are many other valuable natural resources in the Northeast. Forests cover more than half of the land. Each year, fishermen catch millions of pounds of fish in waters along the coast of this region. Rivers and lakes generally provide the Northeast with enough water for its great cities and industries. Fertile soil, sunny days, and rainfall are also valuable natural resources. (See Chapters 2 and 3.) They help farmers provide much of the food needed by the people of this region.

Water Resources

Water is one of the most valuable resources of the Northeast. The people in the Northeast, like people everywhere, use water in many ways. In their homes, they use water for drinking, cooking, and other purposes. On warm summer days they enjoy swimming and boating. Farmers in this region need water to raise crops and livestock.

Water is also important to the industries of the Northeast. It is used in the manufacture of most products. For example, as much as 65,000 gallons of water are used to make one ton of steel. In addition, many industries transport their goods on oceans, rivers, and lakes. Some factories use hydroelectricity, which is produced by the force of water. (See page 131.)

The Northeast faces the problem of obtaining enough usable water. The rivers and lakes of the Northeast are the main sources of water for the people who live here. In the past, these sources usually provided all the water that people needed for their homes, farms, and industries. Recently, however, people in many parts of the Northeast have found it more difficult to obtain a plentiful supply of usable water. During some years, water shortages have created serious problems for New York and other large cities, as well as for many smaller communities.

One reason for water shortages is that the population of the Northeast has been increasing every year. Therefore, more water is needed today than in the past. Facilities for collecting water and transporting it to the places where it is needed have not been built fast enough to keep up with the growth in population. Also, many rivers and lakes that could be used to supply water are polluted* with wastes from factories and homes. For example, factories often

*See Glossary

Build Your Vocabulary

bituminous coal   "seed trees"   reservoir   natural gas   tree farming

anthracite   drought   petroleum   ore   polluted   hydroelectricity

A polluted river in New Jersey. Many of the rivers and lakes in the Northeast are filled with wastes from homes and factories. If pollution of these water sources can be controlled, this region will have a larger supply of usable water.

dump harmful chemical wastes into nearby rivers and lakes. Wastefulness, also, has helped create water shortages. In New York City, millions of gallons of water are wasted each day through leaks in pipelines and from faucets that people have carelessly left dripping.

How a drought can affect the people of the Northeast. Another cause of water shortages is a lack of rainfall to keep lakes and rivers filled. Ordinarily, the Northeast receives plenty of rainfall. However, in 1961 a long period of dry weather, called a drought, began in the Northeast. It lasted until late 1966, when rainfall finally returned to normal.

The drought affected the people of the Northeast in many different ways.

In certain areas, people were not permitted to wash their cars or sprinkle their lawns. For other people, the drought was more serious. Farmers in some parts of Pennsylvania and West Virginia watched their crops dry up in the hot sun. Residents of some towns had to pay to have water brought in by truck.

The drought showed what might happen in the future if steps are not taken to prevent water shortages. If the supply of usable water in the great cities of the Northeast should run out, grave problems would result. Factories would have to shut down. Millions of people would be without the resource they use so freely each day.

How Electricity Is Produced

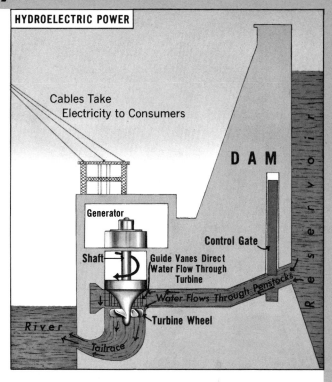

HYDROELECTRIC POWER

Cables Take Electricity to Consumers

DAM

Generator

Control Gate

Shaft

Guide Vanes Direct Water Flow Through Turbine

Water Flows Through Penstocks

Turbine Wheel

River

Tailrace

Reservoir

River

Each day, the homes and factories in the Northeast require an enormous amount of electric power. Water, coal, oil, and natural gas are used to produce most of the electricity needed by the people of this region. How are these natural resources used in the production of electric power?

Most electricity is produced in power plants by large machines called generators. These generators are usually driven by turbines. There are two main types of turbines. One type is powered by steam, while the other is powered by the force of falling water.

Steam-powered turbines are used in producing almost nine tenths of the electricity generated in the Northeast. To create steam for the turbines, water is heated in large boilers. In the Northeast, coal is the fuel most commonly used to heat the water. Oil or natural gas is used in some places, however, and a few plants use atomic energy.

About one tenth of the Northeast's electricity is produced by generators driven by water turbines. Electric power produced in this way is called hydroelectricity.

The diagram on this page shows how waterpower is changed into electrical energy. A dam has been built across a river to hold back the water and create a large reservoir.* Turbines are located at the bottom of the dam. When the control gate is opened, water rushes downward through pipes called penstocks and turns the turbines. Shafts leading from the turbines turn the generators, which produce electricity. Cables carry the electric current to customers in a large area.

Electric power is produced in different ways in different parts of the Northeast, depending on the natural resources available. For example, Pennsylvania and West Virginia are rich in coal. This fuel is used to produce almost all the electricity generated in these states. On the other hand, states such as Maine, Vermont, and New Hampshire lack coal but have abundant water resources. Much of their electric power is generated in hydroelectric plants. Some of the largest hydroelectric power projects in the country are located in New York State. The picture on page 304 shows the power plant for one of these huge projects.

*See Glossary

A turbine and generator in a nuclear power plant. Steam-powered turbines are used in producing nearly all of the Northeast's electricity. Fuels such as coal, natural gas, and oil are usually used to heat water and create steam. In nuclear power plants, however, atomic energy is used.

The people of New York City use an average of more than one billion gallons of water each day. To satisfy this enormous need, water must be collected in reservoirs* and transported long distances to the city. The map on the right shows where New York City gets its water.

Three main reservoir systems—the Delaware, the Catskill, and the Croton—store water for New York City. These three systems include a total of eighteen reservoirs. Some of the reservoirs are located more than one hundred miles from New York City.

The reservoirs receive their water from the rain and snow that fall each year. Rain and melted snow drain into creeks and rivers, which are dammed to form artificial lakes. These lakes serve as reservoirs.

Water flows through huge aqueducts* from the main reservoir systems to distribution reservoirs in and near New York City. Some of these aqueducts are about twenty feet in diameter. When the water reaches the city, it is distributed through smaller pipes to homes, office buildings, and factories.

*See Glossary

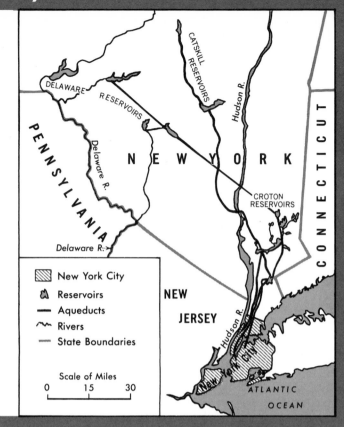

Solutions to the water problem. Experts have suggested several solutions to the water problem in the Northeast. One of these is to find new sources of water. Another is to encourage people to use water more carefully.

There are several ways in which the water supplies of the Northeast can be increased. Some of the water that falls as rain or snow seeps down through the soil until it reaches certain layers of rock far beneath the ground. Because these layers of rock are full of tiny holes and cracks, they can hold large amounts of water. Scientists believe that much water could be obtained by drilling wells that are deep enough to reach these underground deposits.

Another way to increase the water supplies of the Northeast is to reduce pollution in the rivers and lakes of this part of our country. For example, if the Hudson River were not polluted, it could supply the people of New York City with millions of gallons of fresh water every day.

Someday, people in the Northeast may be able to obtain a plentiful supply of fresh water by removing the salt from ocean water. At present, however, the process of desalting ocean water is very expensive.

Careful use of water can also help to prevent water shortages. For example, in New York City, some of the leaks in underground pipelines have been repaired. Residents of this city have been urged to use water more carefully. In addition, water meters could be installed in homes so that people would have to pay for the amount of water they use. This system, which is used in many cities in our nation, helps to make people less wasteful.

Prospects for the future. In the past, many people in the Northeast believed that there would always be an unlimited supply of water. They used water carelessly, without thinking of the future. Like people in other parts of our country, they allowed beautiful lakes and rivers to become so polluted that people can no longer swim or fish in them.

Although water shortages have caused serious problems, they may have helped to make a brighter future for the Northeast. People are beginning to realize that water is a precious resource and must be used wisely. If pollution of lakes and rivers can be controlled, the Northeast will be a healthier and more beautiful place in which to live. Also, the federal government and state governments have begun work on projects that should provide the Northeast's growing population with dependable supplies of water for years to come.

Mineral Resources

There are only a few important mineral deposits in the Northeast. Many of the minerals needed by industries in this region are brought in from other parts of the United States. Some are imported from foreign countries.

Vast amounts of coal are mined in the Northeast. Coal is the most important mineral resource of the Northeast. Deposits of high-grade soft coal, called bituminous coal, are found in the Appalachian Plateau. Deposits of anthracite, or hard coal, are located in eastern Pennsylvania. (See map on page 135.) Industries in the Northeast use much of the region's coal. Some coal is transported to Lake Erie for shipment to steel plants in the Midwest.

More bituminous coal than anthracite is mined in the Northeast. Anthracite was once used widely for heating homes. Today, most homeowners use oil or natural gas, and there is little demand for anthracite. However, bituminous coal is used for many purposes.

For example, it is needed in the manufacture of steel, chemicals, and many other products.

A coal mine in West Virginia. We are visiting a coal mine in the northern part of West Virginia. The main tunnel of the mine leads into the side of a large hill. This kind of mine is called a drift* mine.

The men working in the mine are operating machines. One of the machines is tearing pieces of coal from a wall of the tunnel. The pieces tumble onto a conveyer belt. This belt carries the coal to a "shuttle car," which resembles a long, open trailer.

When the shuttle car is loaded, it is driven to a large building near the entrance of the mine. Here, machines wash and sort the pieces of coal according to size. Then, the coal is taken by train to the Monongahela River, a few miles away. There it is loaded on barges and taken down the river to large steel mills in Pittsburgh.

Many coal miners are unemployed.
After our visit, one of the miners takes us to the small mining town nearby. Most of the houses are shabby and deserted. The miner tells us that nearly all of the people in this little town once made their living by mining coal. Gradually, machinery was invented to do the backbreaking work once done by miners using picks and shovels. As more machinery was used, fewer miners were needed. Since there were no other job opportunities in the community, many unemployed miners and their families left their homes to find jobs in other places. Several families who did not move are now living in poverty. The miner tells us that this has happened in many other coal-mining towns in West Virginia and the western part of Pennsylvania.

There is also unemployment in eastern Pennsylvania, where anthracite is mined. As you have learned, there is not much demand for this type of coal. Therefore, today very little anthracite is mined, and few workers are needed.

Some steps are being taken to solve the problem of unemployment among coal miners. Scientists are searching for new ways to use anthracite. Some of the larger coal-mining towns, such as Scranton, Pennsylvania, have brought in new industries. These industries have created new jobs. Government training programs provide unemployed workers with an opportunity to learn skills for different types of jobs. However, many

Mining coal by machine in Pennsylvania. Coal is the most important mineral resource of the Northeast. In coal mines today, machinery is used to do much of the work that was once done by hand. As a result, many coal miners have been left without jobs.

Coalfields of the United States

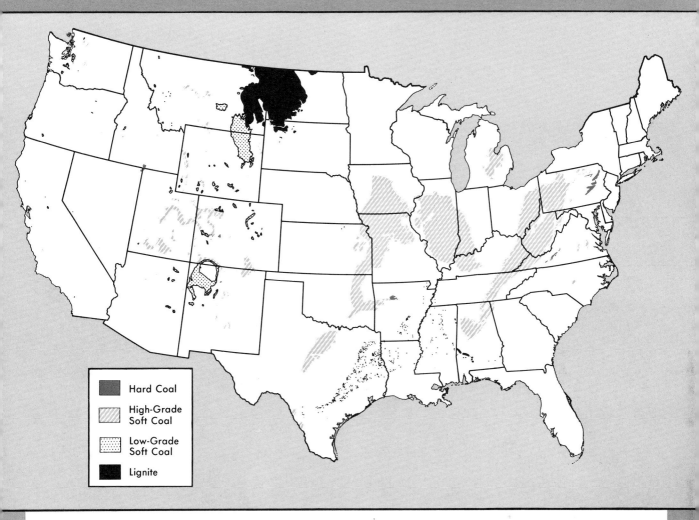

Hard Coal

High-Grade Soft Coal

Low-Grade Soft Coal

Lignite

The map above shows the main coal deposits in the conterminous* United States. Important deposits of high-grade soft coal are found in West Virginia and western Pennsylvania. They are part of a huge coalfield that stretches through much of the Appalachian Plateau. Hard coal is found in eastern Pennsylvania. West Virginia and Pennsylvania lead our country in coal mining.

Coal is one of our country's most important natural resources. It is burned as a fuel in homes, factories, and steam power plants. Coal also provides raw materials for industry. Iron and steel mills use large amounts of coke, which is made by roasting coal in large, airtight ovens. From the gases driven off during the coking process, thousands of different products are manufactured. Among these are medicines, dyes, and plastics.

Coal is a rocklike substance composed mainly of carbon* and water. It was formed millions of years ago from decayed plant matter under the pressure of overlying layers of sand, mud, and water. Different kinds of coal resulted from different kinds of plants and different amounts of pressure. The best coals are those with the most carbon, since they give off the most heat when burned.

There are four main kinds of coal. Hard coal, or anthracite, is a high-quality coal that burns without much smoke. High-grade soft coal has a high carbon content, but it gives off large amounts of smoke. It is also called bituminous coal. Low-grade soft coal, or subbituminous coal, is poor in quality. It is about three-fourths carbon and one-fourth water. Lignite, a still poorer quality coal, is about half water. *See Glossary

IRON ORE

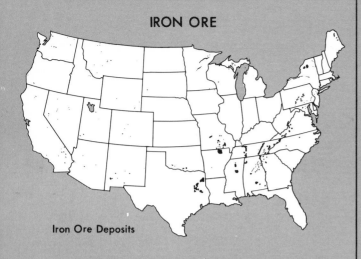

Iron Ore Deposits

LIMESTONE

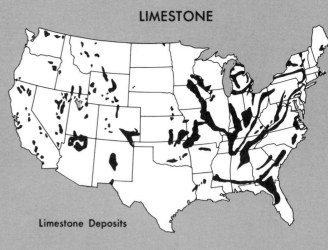

Limestone Deposits

NATURAL GAS

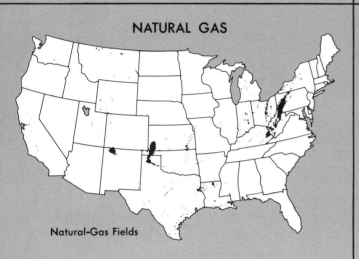

Natural-Gas Fields

OIL

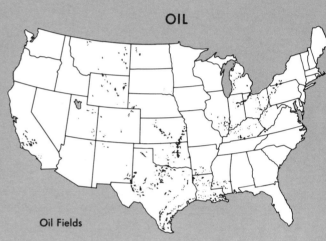

Oil Fields

The maps above show areas of the conterminous* United States where four valuable minerals are found. It is important to remember that these maps include both developed and undeveloped deposits. For example, the map at upper left shows deposits of iron ore in several states of the Northeast. Except for New York, however, none of these states produces appreciable quantities of iron ore. Pennsylvania leads the states of the Northeast in the production of oil and limestone, and West Virginia is the leading producer of natural gas.

of the men who were once coal miners are still without jobs.

Petroleum and natural gas are produced in the Northeast. There are deposits of petroleum, or oil, and natural gas in several states of the Northeast. America's first oil well was drilled in northwestern Pennsylvania in 1859. Methods of pumping and refining crude* oil were also developed here. Until 1895, west-

ern Pennsylvania and southwestern New York produced more oil than any other part of the country.

Today, other regions of our country are far ahead of the Northeast in petroleum production. However, the oil found in the Northeast is valuable because of its high quality. It is used to make lubricants,* gasoline, kerosene, and other products.

West Virginia ranks seventh in the nation in the production of natural gas. This resource has many uses. Some of it is carried by pipelines to homes, where it is used for heating and cooking. Chemicals made from natural gas are used in manufacturing many products, such as medicines and plastics.

The Northeast has few deposits of metal ores. There are only a few deposits of metal ores in the Northeast. Iron ore is found in the Adirondack Mountains of New York State. However, New York is not an important producer of this ore.

Zinc is mined in New York, New Jersey, and Pennsylvania. This metal is combined with copper to make brass. It is also used to coat iron and steel to prevent rust.

Other minerals. There are large deposits of limestone in several states of the Northeast. (See map on opposite page.) This nonmetallic* mineral has many important uses. In the Northeast, large amounts of limestone are used in the manufacture of steel. Limestone is also used in making cement. Pennsylvania, which has large deposits of this mineral, is one of our nation's leading producers of cement. Blocks of limestone are used for the foundations and walls of buildings.

Several other nonmetallic minerals are also produced in the Northeast. Sand and gravel, which are found in every state of this region, are used mainly as construction materials. Some high-quality sand is used in the manufacture of glass. Vermont produces large quantities of granite and marble. These types of stone are used in the construction of monuments and buildings. Several states of the Northeast also produce slate.*

Among the other minerals produced in the Northeast are salt and clay. New York produces large amounts of salt. Various types of clay are found throughout the region. These are used in making pottery, china, tile, bricks, and many other products.

Forests

A tree farm in Maine. It is a brisk fall day, and we are visiting a tree farm in northern Maine. Many acres of the farm are green with fir trees. There is also a large grove of brilliantly colored beech and maple trees. The farmer tells us that the beeches and maples were growing here when he bought the land. However, he planted and raised the fir trees, just as other farmers raise crops such as wheat or oats.

The farmer says that he began raising trees nearly twenty-five years ago. He thought he could make a bigger profit from raising and selling trees than from raising crops on the stony soil. The first fir trees that he planted have just been sold. They will be made into wood pulp. (See page 138.) Through the years, he has sold many of his beech and maple trees to a nearby lumber company.

We ask the farmer if tree farming takes much time and work. He tells us that after the trees are planted, they must be protected against fire and other enemies. Sometimes the trees must be sprayed to prevent damage from insects or disease. He also spends long hours pruning* and cutting them. However, he does have enough time to raise some livestock, which he sells to increase his income.

Forests cover more than half of the Northeast. Although the Northeast is our country's most densely populated region, more than half of the land is forested. Large forests are found in nearly every part of the region.

Many different types of trees grow in the Northeast. (See map on opposite page.) Softwoods, such as spruce and fir, grow mainly in the northern part of the region. Many different hardwoods, such as oak, birch, and maple, also grow in the Northeast.

The forests of the Northeast are used to make many products. The forests of the Northeast have been used in many ways since white men first came to this region. Colonists cut down forests and used the lumber to build homes, schools, and churches. They also found the lumber valuable for building ships. Much lumber was exported to other parts of the world.

Today, a variety of products are made from wood. The most important forest product of the Northeast is wood pulp. This is used to make newsprint, cardboard boxes, and other paper products. Much of the timber in the Northeast is cut into lumber, which is used to make furniture and to construct homes and other buildings.

In a Maine lumber mill. The forests of the Northeast provide raw materials that are used in making a variety of products. Much of the timber harvested in this region is made into lumber. Wood pulp, which is used in making paper, is the Northeast's most important forest product.

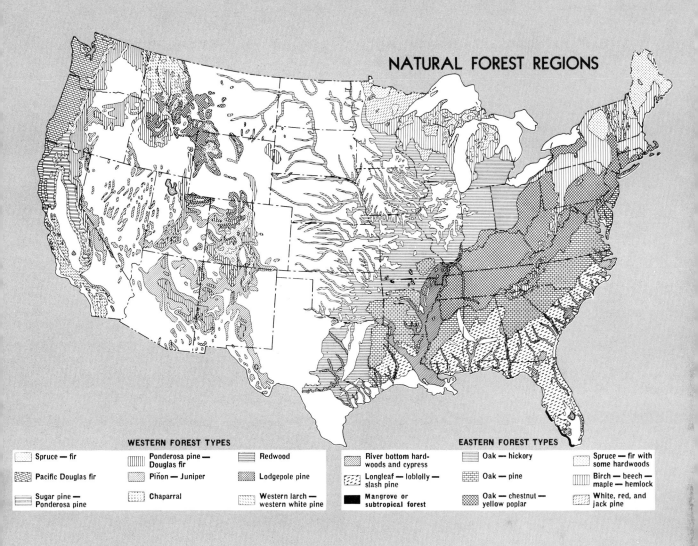

NATURAL FOREST REGIONS

WESTERN FOREST TYPES

Spruce — fir
Ponderosa pine — Douglas fir
Redwood
Pacific Douglas fir
Piñon — Juniper
Lodgepole pine
Sugar pine — Ponderosa pine
Chaparral
Western larch — western white pine

EASTERN FOREST TYPES

River bottom hardwoods and cypress
Oak — hickory
Spruce — fir with some hardwoods
Longleaf — loblolly — slash pine
Oak — pine
Birch — beech — maple — hemlock
Mangrove or subtropical forest
Oak — chestnut — yellow poplar
White, red, and jack pine

Many types of trees grow in the forests of the Northeast. At one time, forests covered nearly all of this region. Today, more than half of the land here is forested. Softwoods, such as spruce and fir, grow mainly in the northern part of the Northeast. Oak, birch, maple, and other hardwoods are found in many areas.

Maple syrup and maple sugar are also forest products of the Northeast. In late winter, when days become warmer but nights are still cold, the sap begins to flow in sugar maple trees. This sap is collected and made into maple syrup and maple sugar. Vermont and New York lead all of our states in the manufacture of these two products.

The forests of the Northeast have other uses. In addition to providing the raw materials for many products, forests are valuable in other ways. The roots of trees help hold the soil in place, preventing erosion by wind and water. Forests also provide shelter and food for wildlife.

Forests help in the conservation of water. During a heavy rainfall in open country, water often flows away quickly in ditches and streams. Where there are trees, however, rain must fall through leaves and branches. Therefore, a heavy rainfall reaches the ground more slowly in a forest than it does in open country. This gives the ground time to soak up the water. In addition, snow melts slowly in a forest and is absorbed by the soft soil. Much of the rain and melted snow that collects in the ground beneath the forest drains slowly into rivers and lakes, helping to provide them with a steady supply of water.

Forests are also important to the tourist industry of the Northeast. They provide beautiful scenery for the people of this region and for visitors from other parts of our country. People can hike, camp, or hunt in the Northeast's many state and national forests.

Conserving the forests. In the past, the forests of the Northeast, like those in many other parts of the country, were not used wisely. Trees were cut until much of the land was barren. Soil once protected by trees was carried away by wind and water. Some forests were destroyed by fire. No efforts were made to replace the trees that were cut or burned.

Today, people in the Northeast are trying to conserve their forest resources. When forests are cut, new trees are usually planted. Sometimes several large healthy trees, called "seed trees," are left standing. These trees drop their seeds, and new trees begin to grow where others were cut. Better ways of controlling insects and disease are continually being discovered. In addition, much land that is unsuitable for growing food crops is now used for raising trees. For these reasons, forests will be an important natural resource in the states of the Northeast for many years to come.

Fisheries

The Northeast is an important fishing region. Fishing has been an important occupation in the Northeast for more than three hundred years. The eastern part of the region borders on the Atlantic Ocean. One of the world's best fishing grounds lies in the coastal waters that extend from Massachusetts northward to the Canadian island of Newfoundland. In addition, the Northeast has fine natural harbors where fishing boats can anchor.

Fishing in New England. Each year, fishermen bring more than 300,000 tons of fish to ports in New England. Massachusetts leads the states of the Northeast in the value of fish caught. (See graph on page 142.) Boston, Gloucester, and New Bedford, Massachusetts, are the leading New England fishing ports. Portland, Maine, is also an important port. Some of the fish that are brought to ports in New England are sold fresh in the large eastern cities. Others are frozen or canned and sent to other parts of our country.

New England fishermen catch many different kinds of fish. Whiting, ocean perch, haddock, and cod are brought to the Boston and Gloucester ports. Flounder and scallops are the most important types of fish brought into the port at New Bedford. New England fishermen also catch thousands of tons of lobsters and clams.

A visit to Gloucester Harbor. We are visiting the busy harbor of Gloucester, Massachusetts. Several fishing boats are entering or leaving the harbor. Others are docked here. Many of the boats that we see are trawlers. Some of these boats are as long as one hundred feet and are powered by diesel engines.

A fisherman working on the deck of his trawler invites us to come aboard. He shows us a huge net called an otter trawl. This net is towed along the bottom of the ocean with long cables. Two boards, called otter boards, keep the mouth of the net open so that fish can swim in. When the net is full, the fishermen hoist it into the boat with a machine called a winch.

The fisherman tells us that he and his crew travel northward toward Newfoundland to fish for haddock, cod, and ocean perch. As soon as the fish are caught, they are refrigerated so that they will be fresh when the ship arrives back in port.

Problems face the fishing industry in New England. We learn from the fisherman that fishing is no longer as important in New England as it was in the past. Some areas have been fished so heavily that the supply of fish is low. Fleets from other nations, such as Japan and the Soviet Union, fish in many of the same areas as New England fishermen. These ships have far better equipment than most New England fishing boats. For example, some have electronic equipment that locates schools of fish. Others have complete canning factories aboard.

Gloucester fishermen. Each year, fishermen bring more than 300,000 tons of fish to Gloucester and other ports in New England. Fishing is an important industry in several Middle Atlantic states, also.

There are other problems facing the fishing industry. Wages are so low that young men do not want to become fishermen. Also, boats have to travel longer distances to find good fishing grounds. This raises the cost of fishing trips.

We ask the fisherman why he continues to fish. He smiles and explains that both his father and grandfather were fishermen. For his family, fishing has always been a way of life. After working on the sea for so many years, he would not be happy with any other job. The fisherman tells us that the federal government is now trying to help solve some of the problems that face the fishing industry. For example, it is helping New England fishermen to buy modern equipment. Therefore, he feels hopeful about the future of the fishing industry.

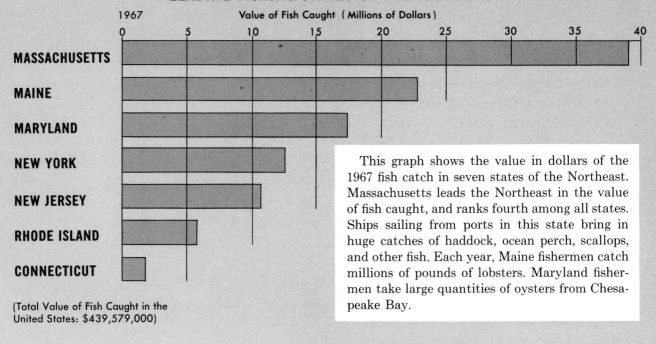

LEADING FISHING STATES OF THE NORTHEAST

1967   Value of Fish Caught (Millions of Dollars)

State	Value
MASSACHUSETTS	(to ~38)
MAINE	(to ~22)
MARYLAND	(to ~17)
NEW YORK	(to ~13)
NEW JERSEY	(to ~11)
RHODE ISLAND	(to ~7)
CONNECTICUT	(to ~2)

(Total Value of Fish Caught in the United States: $439,579,000)

This graph shows the value in dollars of the 1967 fish catch in seven states of the Northeast. Massachusetts leads the Northeast in the value of fish caught, and ranks fourth among all states. Ships sailing from ports in this state bring in huge catches of haddock, ocean perch, scallops, and other fish. Each year, Maine fishermen catch millions of pounds of lobsters. Maryland fishermen take large quantities of oysters from Chesapeake Bay.

Fishing in the Middle Atlantic states. Fishing is also important in several Middle Atlantic states. In 1967, Maryland fishermen brought in more than seventeen million dollars' worth of fish. Many of these fish were caught in Chesapeake Bay.

Fishermen from the Middle Atlantic states catch several kinds of fish. Each year, thousands of tons of oysters and other kinds of shellfish are harvested from Chesapeake Bay. Large amounts of menhaden are also caught in the coastal waters of the Middle Atlantic states. The oil from menhaden is used in making such products as soap and paint. Menhaden are also ground and used as fertilizer.

Investigate the Northeast's Water Problem
Read about the water resources of the Northeast. Then use each of the statements below as the topic sentence of a brief paragraph. In each paragraph, explain and support the facts given in the topic sentence.

1. Water is one of the most valuable resources of the Northeast.
2. The Northeast faces the problem of obtaining enough usable water.
3. The people of the Northeast are trying to increase their water supplies.

On page 347, you will find guidelines that will help you in writing your paragraphs.

Explore Relationships
Read to find out about the important resources that come from the mines, forests, and fisheries of the Northeast. Then find out how these resources are used. Make a chart of your findings to share with your class. You may wish to make your chart similar to the one below.

Resources	Uses
limestone	used in making cement and steel

You will find much useful information for this project in the chapters about the individual states of the Northeast, as well as in this chapter.

A United States Steel Corporation plant near Morrisville, Pennsylvania. Oceangoing ships travel up the Delaware River to bring iron ore to this plant. Good transportation routes, huge markets, and the availability of capital, workers, and power have all helped to make the Northeast one of the world's great manufacturing regions.

9 Industry

A Problem To Solve

The Northeast is one of the most important manufacturing regions in the United States and the world. Why is this true? In forming hypotheses to solve this problem, you will need to consider how the growth of industry in the Northeast has been affected by:

a. the location of this region
b. the history of the Northeast
c. the raw materials available here
d. the markets for manufactured goods in this region
e. transportation routes here
f. the sources of power available
g. the skills of people here

Chapters 7, 8, and 11 contain additional information that will be helpful in solving this problem.

See TO THE STUDENT, pages 8-10.

A tour through a Pennsylvania steel plant. We are driving along a modern highway in Pennsylvania, about thirty miles northeast of Philadelphia. In the distance, we can see a row of tall smokestacks and the towers of three giant blast furnaces. These are part of one of the largest steel plants in the

Northeast. We will take a tour of this plant to learn how steel is made. (See opposite page.)

This plant is owned by a large steel company. Before we begin the tour, our guide gives us some information about the plant we are visiting. He tells us that the plant belongs to the United States Steel Corporation. This is a huge company with factories and offices in many parts of our country. Only a company with large amounts of capital* could afford to build a plant like this one, which cost about 400 million dollars.

Our guide tells us that this company was started more than sixty years ago by a group of businessmen in the Northeast and the Midwest. Several small steel companies were combined to form one large corporation. Shares of stock* were issued to the founders of the new company. Additional shares were sold to other people who wanted to invest their money. These investments helped the company to grow and brought profits to the stockholders. Today, more than 300,000 people own stock in the United States Steel Corporation. Much of the money needed to start new plants comes from profits. The company may also borrow money from banks or offer additional shares of stock for sale.

The plant employs thousands of workers. Many workers are needed to produce steel. We learn that about 9,000 people are employed in this plant.

Some of these workers run the machines. Others are managers or office workers. Most of them live in towns or cities that are located within twenty miles of the plant.

Raw materials come from far and near. We ask the guide where this steel plant gets the iron ore and other raw materials that it needs. He says that the plant is in a good location for obtaining iron ore. In the past, most of the iron ore used for steelmaking in the United States came from mines near Lake Superior. Today, however, these mines do not produce enough iron ore to meet the needs of industry. Large amounts must be imported from Venezuela, Canada, and other countries. The cheapest way to transport iron ore over long distances is by water. Our guide explains that this steel plant is on the Delaware River, which empties into Delaware Bay, an arm of the Atlantic Ocean. Ships bringing iron ore from foreign countries can travel up the river and unload their cargo at the plant.

This plant is also well located for obtaining the other raw materials it needs. Coal is brought by train from rich deposits in western Pennsylvania and West Virginia. Trucks bring limestone from quarries in central Pennsylvania.

Electricity is used to run machinery. As we tour the plant, we see that many kinds of machinery are needed for making steel. These machines are run by

*See Glossary

Build Your Vocabulary

raw materials	electronic	capital	refinery
blast furnace	ingot	market	corporation
open-hearth furnace		stock	basic chemicals

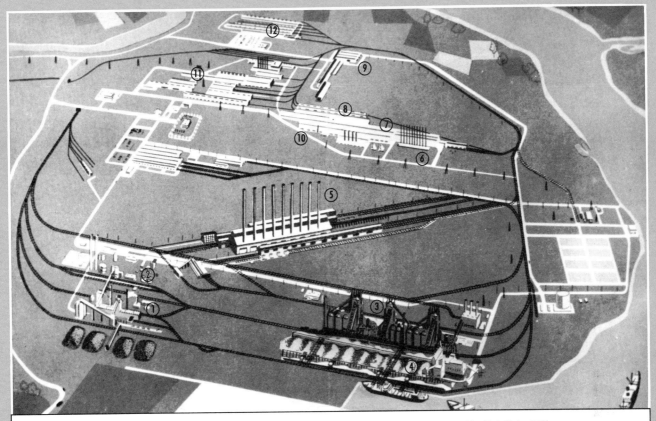

1. Coke Ovens
2. Coal-Chemicals Plant
3. Blast Furnaces
4. Docks and Ore Storage Yard
5. Open-Hearth Building
6. Soaking Pits
7. Slab—Bloom Mill
8. Billet Mill
9. Bar Mill
10. Hot-Strip Mill
11. Sheet and Tin Finishing Mill
12. Pipe Mill

A STEEL PLANT

Our tour of the steel plant illustrated above will show us how iron ore, coal, and limestone are used in making steel. This plant also appears in the picture on page 143.

We begin our tour at the coke ovens (1). Here, coal is unloaded from trains and heated in airtight ovens. The heat drives gases from the coal, leaving a hard, gray substance called coke. This is a fuel that burns with a hot flame, necessary in the making of iron and steel. The gases given off when the coal is heated are piped to the coal-chemicals plant (2), where they are made into valuable chemicals. A conveyor belt more than a mile long carries the coke from the ovens to the blast furnaces (3).

Now we visit the docks along the Delaware River (4), where we watch a ship unloading a cargo of reddish-brown iron ore. Large amounts of iron ore, coke, and limestone are fed into the three giant blast furnaces nearby. Powerful machines then blow a blast of extremely hot air into each furnace. This air makes the coke burn with an intense heat that melts the iron ore. The limestone combines with waste materials in the ore to form slag, which rises to the top. Molten iron containing carbon and other substances col-lects at the bottom of the furnace. The iron is now ready to be made into steel.

Our next stop is the open-hearth building (5), where steel is made. Here we watch iron ore, limestone, and steel scrap* being loaded into a huge open-hearth furnace. These materials are heated until they melt. Then molten iron, transported from the blast furnace in huge containers, is added to the mixture. Small quantities of special metals may also be added. The mixture is cooked for several hours to burn out excess carbon and other unwanted materials from the iron. Finally, molten steel is drained from the furnace and poured into molds. As the steel cools, it hardens into huge blocks called ingots. The molds are removed and the ingots are taken to the soaking pits (6). Here they are reheated until they are an even temperature throughout.

The steel now goes to the mills (7-12) where it will be formed into various shapes that can be used in manufacturing steel products. Some of the steel is rolled into thin sheets or strips. Some is formed into more bulky shapes. In one mill, sheets and strips of steel are used in making tinplate.* Steel pipes and tubes are made in another mill.

*See Glossary

electric power. Our guide says that the plant has its own powerhouse. There, gas from the blast furnaces and coke ovens is burned to heat water, which turns to steam. The steam is used to run generators* that produce electricity for the steel plant. About two thirds of the electricity needed by this plant is produced in the powerhouse. The rest is bought from a company that supplies power to many homes, stores, and factories in eastern Pennsylvania.

The Delaware River supplies water. Large amounts of water are needed in steelmaking. Our guide says that this plant uses about 250 million gallons of Delaware River water every day. After the water has been used, it is treated to purify it and then is returned to the river.

Many factories in the Northeast buy steel from this plant. A factory cannot operate without customers to buy its products. In other words, every factory must have a market. This steel plant is in a very good location because it lies between the two largest cities in the Northeast, New York and Philadelphia. There are many factories in this area. Some of them use large quantities of steel in making their products. For example, automobile plants use sheets of steel in making cars. Other factories make cans from steel that has been coated with a thin layer of tin. Steel is also used in making

Manufacturing tin-coated steel. The manufacture of iron and steel is one of the most important industries in the Northeast. Much of the steel produced in this region is used by factories here to make products such as automobiles, tools, and electrical appliances.

such things as tools and electrical appliances.

Trucks and trains carry the steel to customers. After the steel has been produced, it must be delivered to the people who buy it. This steel plant is near several excellent highways and railroad lines. Most of the steel manufactured here is shipped to customers by train or truck.

The Northeast is a great manufacturing region. The steel mill we have just visited is only one of many factories in the Northeast. Altogether there are more than 100,000 factories in this region. They make a great variety of products, ranging from nails and buttons to jet airplanes and ocean liners. The total value of goods manufactured each year in the Northeast is more than eighty billion dollars. No other part of our country except the Midwest has so much industry.

Why there is so much industry in the Northeast. Our tour of the steel plant showed us that a factory needs many things. First, capital is needed to start the factory and to keep it operating. Skilled people are needed to run the machines and to work in the factory offices. In addition, managers are needed to direct the other workers. The factory must have raw materials. It must also have power to run its machinery. Trucks, trains, and other means of transportation are needed to bring raw materials to the factory and to ship manufactured goods to customers. Finally, every factory must have a market for its products.

The Northeast is an important manufacturing region because it has most of the things that factories need. The

Assembling airplanes. Factories in the Northeast make a great variety of products, ranging from nails and buttons to jet airplanes and ocean liners.

things it does not have can be obtained from other regions of the United States or from foreign countries. Let us learn more about the reasons why the Northeast is so industrialized.

The Northeast had a "head start" in manufacturing. The history of the Northeast helps explain why this region has so much industry today. As you learned in Chapter 5, the first factories in our country were started in the Northeast. Therefore, the people of this region have long been experienced in producing manufactured goods. Also, people in other regions have grown accustomed to buying many articles from factories in the Northeast. Many companies that were started in the Northeast during the early 1800's are still in business there today.

Throughout its history, the Northeast has been the home of skillful,

Workers leaving a factory. The industries of the Northeast need many skilled workers. There is a large labor supply in this densely populated region. In addition to skilled craftsmen, the Northeast is well supplied with experienced managers and office workers.

inventive people. Some of these people developed new methods of production or new devices that have greatly influenced our lives. (See Chapters 6 and 7.) Inventions such as the telephone and the electric light were first tried out in the Northeast. They led to the development of several new industries in this region.

In the Northeast, industries can get the capital they need. Ever since colonial times, the Northeast has been the home of wealthy businessmen who were willing to invest money in new industries. Today it is still well supplied with capital. In this region are many banks and other agencies that lend money to businessmen who want to

build new factories. Here, too, are large stock* exchanges, where people can buy and sell shares in various companies.

The Northeast has a large labor supply. The Northeast is well supplied with industrial workers, for there are more than 55 million people living in this region. Many of these people have the skills needed to operate complicated machinery or to produce delicate articles by hand. New England is especially noted for its skillful, hardworking craftsmen. The Northeast also has a plentiful supply of experienced managers and office workers.

To produce goods of high quality, workers and managers must be well trained. There are many fine schools and colleges in the Northeast that train people for jobs in industry.

Some of the raw materials needed by industry are found in the Northeast, but some must be obtained from other places. As you learned in Chapter 8, the Northeast is supplied with a number of raw materials that factories need. The most important of these is coal. Other minerals found in the Northeast include limestone, natural gas, and salt. In some areas, there are large forests that supply wood for certain industries. Important raw materials also come from the farms and fisheries of the Northeast.

At the same time, the Northeast lacks many of the raw materials needed by industry. For example, it does not produce nearly enough oil to supply the needs of its refineries. It is also poorly supplied with iron ore, bauxite, and other metal ores. Many kinds of farm products cannot be raised in the Northeast because the land and climate are not suitable.

This lack of raw materials has not been a great handicap to the Northeast, however. Most raw materials that are not produced in this region can be obtained from other regions or from foreign countries. Also, people in the Northeast have made good use of their region's advantages for manufacturing. New England, for instance, is very poor in mineral resources, but it has a large supply of skilled workers. Therefore, many New England factories specialize in making products that require much skilled labor but only small amounts of raw materials. Among these items are clocks, machine tools, and electronic* instruments.

The Northeast is well supplied with power. Nearly all machines in northeastern factories are run by electric power. Most of this power is supplied by steam plants, but some is produced in hydroelectric plants. (See page 131.) The coal deposits in Pennsylvania and West Virginia provide vast quantities of coal for steam power plants. Hydroelectric plants are located along many rivers in the Northeast.

Industry got an early start in New England partly because there were many small streams here to provide waterpower. As time passed, however, New England's factories needed more power than these streams could provide. Today, most factories in New England use electricity produced in steam power plants. Coal for these plants is brought by train and ship from Pennsylvania and West Virginia.

In a steam power plant. The Northeast is well supplied with power for industry. In most factories, machines are run by electricity produced in steam power plants. Some power is produced in hydroelectric plants.

Loading cargo at Newark. Industries in the Northeast are served by excellent transportation routes. Ships can load and unload goods at ports along the Atlantic coast. In addition, the Northeast has a widespread network of inland waterways, roads, railroads, and airways.

Good transportation is available. The Northeast is served by a large network of roads, railroads, airways, and waterways. (See Chapter 11.) Because this region borders on the Atlantic Ocean, raw materials can be shipped here from all parts of the world. Factories in the Northeast can send finished products by ship to foreign buyers.

There is a huge market for manufactured products in the Northeast. If you were a businessman choosing a location for a new factory, you might decide to build it in the Northeast to take advantage of the enormous market there. The millions of people who live in the Northeast are constantly buying large amounts of manufactured products. Also, many factories in the Northeast use the goods that other factories produce. This large market is one of the main reasons why there is so much industry in the Northeast today.

Where most of the Northeast's factories are located. Factories are not distributed evenly throughout the Northeast. There is little industry in some areas, such as the Adirondack Mountains and the northern part of New England. Other areas are heavily industrialized.

The map on the opposite page shows the main industrial areas of the Northeast. You will notice that many industrial areas are located along the Atlantic coast, between New Hampshire and Virginia. This is a densely populated area, with several large cities. (See map on page 197.) The millions of people who live here buy huge amounts of

Main Industrial Areas

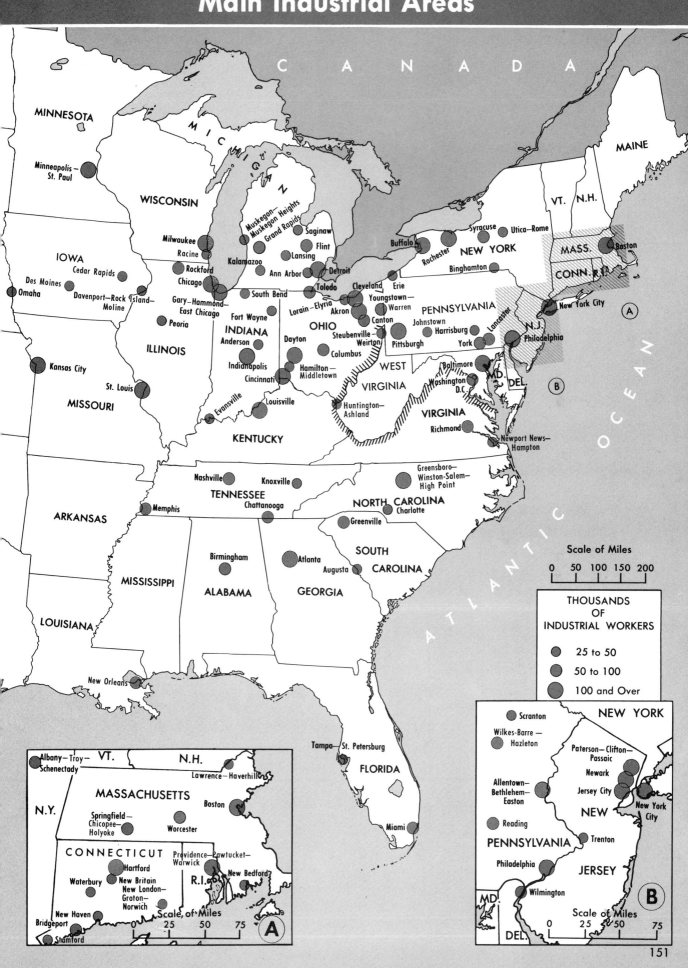

CANADA

MINNESOTA

Minneapolis – St. Paul

WISCONSIN

MICHIGAN

MAINE

VT. N.H.

Syracuse Utica – Rome

MASS.

Boston

CONN. R.I.

Muskegon – Muskegon Heights – Grand Rapids

Saginaw

Milwaukee

Flint

Buffalo

NEW YORK

Racine

Lansing

Rochester

IOWA

Kalamazoo

Ann Arbor

Binghamton

Cedar Rapids

Rockford

Detroit

Des Moines

Chicago

Toledo

Cleveland Erie

PENNSYLVANIA

New York City

Omaha

South Bend

Lorain – Elyria

Youngstown – Warren

N.J.

A

Davenport – Rock Island – Moline

Gary – Hammond – East Chicago

Akron

Johnstown

Lancaster

Philadelphia

Peoria

Fort Wayne

OHIO

Canton

Harrisburg

INDIANA

Steubenville – Weirton

York

ILLINOIS

Anderson

Dayton

Columbus

Pittsburgh

Kansas City

Indianapolis

Hamilton – Middletown

Baltimore

MD. DEL.

B

St. Louis

Cincinnati

WEST

Washington D.C.

MISSOURI

Evansville

Louisville

VIRGINIA

KENTUCKY

Huntington – Ashland

VIRGINIA

Richmond

Newport News – Hampton

Nashville

Knoxville

Greensboro – Winston-Salem – High Point

TENNESSEE

Chattanooga

NORTH CAROLINA

ARKANSAS

Memphis

Charlotte

Greenville

SOUTH

Birmingham

Atlanta

CAROLINA

MISSISSIPPI

ALABAMA

Augusta

GEORGIA

LOUISIANA

Scale of Miles

0   50   100 150 200

THOUSANDS OF INDUSTRIAL WORKERS

- 25 to 50
- 50 to 100
- 100 and Over

New Orleans

Tampa St. Petersburg

FLORIDA

Miami

ATLANTIC OCEAN

Inset A

Albany – Troy – Schenectady

VT.

N.H.

N.Y.

MASSACHUSETTS

Lawrence – Haverhill

Boston

Springfield – Chicopee – Holyoke

Worcester

CONNECTICUT

Providence – Pawtucket – Warwick

Hartford

R.I.

New Bedford

Waterbury

New Britain

New London – Groton – Norwich

New Haven

Bridgeport

Scale of Miles

25   50   75

Stamford

A

Inset B

Scranton

NEW YORK

Wilkes-Barre – Hazleton

Paterson – Clifton – Passaic

Newark

Allentown – Bethlehem – Easton

Jersey City

New York City

Reading

NEW

PENNSYLVANIA

Trenton

Philadelphia

JERSEY

MD.

Wilmington

Scale of Miles

0   25   50   75

DEL.

B

151

manufactured goods. Many of these people have the skills needed by industry. There are a number of good harbors along the Atlantic coast, where ships can dock.

Another great manufacturing belt extends across the central part of New York State from Albany to Buffalo. This area lies along one of the main transportation routes through the Appalachian Highlands. Cities that have grown up in this area are served by roads, railroads, and the New York State Barge Canal.

There are also many factories in western Pennsylvania and West Virginia. This area is rich in coal, natural gas, and other minerals used in industry.

Products of Northeastern Factories

Metals. The manufacture of iron and steel is one of the most important industries in the Northeast. There are more than 300 steel plants in this region, employing many thousands of workers. These plants produce more than one third of all the steel made in the United States.

The greatest steelmaking area in the Northeast is located around the city of Pittsburgh, in western Pennsylvania. Steel plants in this area can get coal and limestone from large deposits nearby. Iron ore can be brought here cheaply from mines near Lake Superior. There are many customers for Pittsburgh's steel in the great manufacturing cities of the Northeast and Midwest. The Pittsburgh area is well served by railroads, waterways, and other means of transportation.

Not all of the steel plants in the Northeast are in the Pittsburgh area. There are also several plants in eastern Pennsylvania, including the one we visited earlier in this chapter. Other large plants are located near Buffalo and Baltimore. There are no large steel plants in New England, however. This area lacks both coal and iron ore for steelmaking. Factories here must buy most of their steel from plants in other parts of the Northeast.

Other metals besides iron and steel are also produced by factories in the Northeast. There are two large aluminum plants in northern New York State and another in West Virginia. Factories along the Atlantic coast produce more than half of all the copper refined in the United States. They use ore that is brought by ship from the West and from foreign countries. Zinc smelters* are located in Pennsylvania and other states.

Products made from metal. Factories in the Northeast use steel and other kinds of metal to produce thousands of useful articles. Let us learn more about some of these metal products.

Machinery. In the Northeast, more workers are employed in the manufacture of machinery than in any other industry. Electrical machinery such as motors and generators are important products of this region. Air conditioners, washing machines, toasters, and other household appliances are also produced here.

Workers in a machine-tool factory in Vermont. The manufacture of machine tools is one of the most important industries in New England. Other kinds of machinery produced in the Northeast include household appliances, parts for electronic products, and office equipment.

Many factories specialize in making parts for electronic products such as radios, television sets, tape recorders, and computers.* There are also factories that make equipment needed by the telephone industry.

Many other kinds of machinery are also manufactured in the Northeast. Among these are various kinds of office equipment, such as typewriters and adding machines. One of the most important industries in New England is the manufacture of machine tools. These are power-driven machines that cut, grind, and shape metal to produce parts needed in making other machines. Other types of factory machinery are also produced in the Northeast. For ex-

ample, textile and shoemaking machinery is manufactured in New England. New York City is a leading producer of presses and other printing machinery.

Transportation equipment. Some of the metal produced in the Northeast is used in making transportation equipment. Shipbuilding has been an important industry in this region since colonial days. (See page 69.) Today there are large shipyards near Boston, New York, Philadelphia, and Baltimore. They build all types of vessels, from tugboats to huge naval ships and passenger liners. Nuclear* submarines and helicopters are manufactured in Connecticut. Many factories in Connecticut, Maryland, and other states make airplanes or airplane parts. There are plants that produce automobile parts near Buffalo and other cities. Factories in New York State, New Jersey, and Pennsylvania manufacture locomotives and railroad cars.

Other metal products. Factories in the Northeast make a great many other products from metal. Steel sections used in building bridges are manufactured in Pennsylvania. Many northeastern factories produce nails, saws, locks, and other hardware. Connecticut is noted for products made from copper and brass. Here, too, are factories that produce ball and roller bearings* for industry. Rifles and other firearms are manufactured in New England.

Petroleum products. In the Northeast, there are many refineries* that make gasoline, fuel oil, and other products from petroleum. Although these plants do not employ many workers, the goods they produce are very important to people in the Northeast. Several huge refineries are located along the Atlantic coast, near Philadelphia and other cities. They use petroleum that is brought by ship from other states and from foreign countries. There are a number of small refineries near the oil fields of northwestern Pennsylvania and New York State.

Chemicals and chemical products. The chemical industry is another important manufacturing industry in the

Chemists working in a research laboratory in West Virginia. In the Northeast are many plants that manufacture basic chemicals and chemical products. Among the chemical products manufactured in this region are plastics, paint, nylon, and explosives.

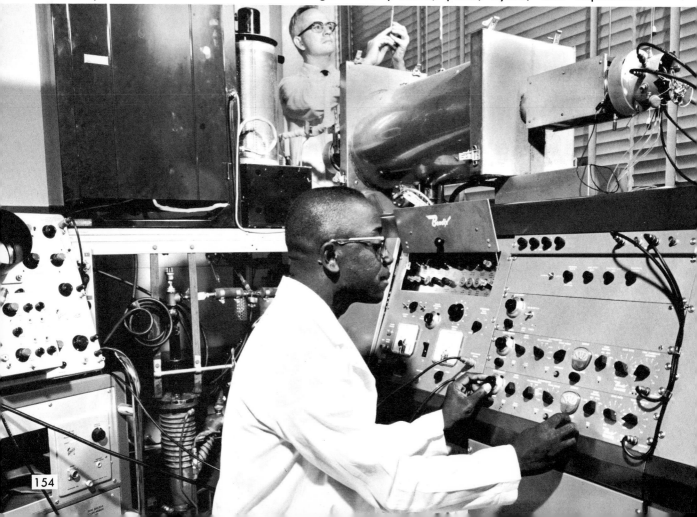

Northeast. Many plants in this region produce basic chemicals, such as ammonia, sulfuric acid, and chlorine. Basic chemicals are used in making a great variety of products, including plastics, synthetic fibers, soap, medicines, paint, fertilizer, and explosives.

Many of the Northeast's chemical plants are located in the New York City area or along the Delaware River. Some of these plants use products from nearby oil refineries to make chemical products. Other raw materials used by the chemical plants come by ship from distant places. The great cities along the Atlantic coast provide an enormous market for chemical products.

Chemical plants in other parts of the Northeast are usually located near sources of raw materials or power. In West Virginia, for example, there are a number of plants that use local supplies of coal, natural gas, and other minerals. Certain chemical plants that need large amounts of electricity are located in the Buffalo area, where they get cheap hydroelectric power from Niagara Falls.

Textiles, clothing, and shoes. As recently as 1920, textile manufacturing was the most important industry in New England. Then, during the 1920's and 1930's, many New England textile plants were forced to close because they could not compete with mills in the South. Even today, however, textile manufacturing is important in New England, as well as in other parts of the Northeast. Some textile mills spin natural or synthetic fibers into yarn. Others use yarn to make cloth. There are also factories that use textiles to make such items as sheets, blankets, tablecloths, and clothing.

Garment workers. The Northeast produces most of the clothing worn by people in our country. Dresses, coats, and many other kinds of garments are made here.

Most of the clothing worn by people in the United States is produced in the Northeast. New York City is the center of our country's clothing industry. There are several reasons for this. Because fashions in clothing are always changing, manufacturers need to be aware of the latest styles. They find it helpful to be located near one another. In the New York area, there are many workers with the skills needed by the clothing industry. There are also millions of customers for clothing. Factories in New York make dresses, suits, coats, and many other kinds of garments. Clothing is also manufactured in Philadelphia, and other cities.

More shoes are produced in the Northeast than in any other region of the United States. Among the nation's leading shoe-manufacturing cities are Boston

155

and New York. There are also many shoe factories in the smaller cities and towns of New England. Many animal skins used in making shoe leather are brought by ship from Argentina and other foreign countries.

Food. The millions of people who live in the Northeast eat great quantities of food every day. It is not surprising, then, that food processing is a leading industry in this region.

The farms and fisheries of the Northeast provide many raw materials for the food industry. Canneries and freezing plants are located in New Jersey, Maryland, and other states. They process fruits and vegetables that are grown on farms nearby. Cattle raised on West Virginia and Pennsylvania farms are butchered in meat-packing plants. Other factories process chickens grown on nearby poultry farms or seafood caught by northeastern fishermen. Dairy farms in the Northeast supply milk to creameries, cheese factories, and ice cream plants.

Some factories in the Northeast use farm products that are raised outside this region. There are large sugar refineries in New York, Baltimore, and other seaports. They process raw* sugar that is brought by ship from the West Indies. Buffalo is noted for its flour mills and breakfast-food plants. These plants use grain that is shipped over the Great Lakes from farming areas in the Midwest and Great Plains. Bakeries in many northeastern cities use flour from Buffalo in making bread, pies, cakes, and other products.

Develop Important Understandings
The Northeast is one of the great manufacturing regions of our country. Do research to find out why this is so. As you read, look for information about the six things listed below, which are needed by any factory in order to operate successfully:
a. capital
b. skilled workers
c. raw materials
d. power to run machines
e. good transportation
f. markets

Explore Industry in the Northeast
1. State two ways in which companies in the Northeast obtain the money they need for building factories and keeping them in operation.
2. Why is the area around the city of Pittsburgh, Pennsylvania, a good location for steelmaking?
3. What three areas of the Northeast are the most heavily industrialized?

Take Your Class on an Imaginary Tour
Imagine that you work in one of the following places:
    a shipyard near Baltimore
    a steel plant near Pittsburgh
    an electronics plant in Connecticut
    an oil refinery in New Jersey

Take your class on a "guided tour" through your place of work. First, you will need to do some research about the industry in which you work. Notes and charts will help you remember the information you find. On your tour, try to tell your class something about each of the following:
1. the product, or products, made there
2. the main raw materials used
3. the main steps in manufacturing
4. some of the special skills needed by workers

You may also wish to include information about who buys your products and how shipment is made.

Tomatoes are produced on many truck farms in the Northeast. Farmers in this region produce great quantities of vegetables, milk, poultry, and eggs. Most of these products are sold in the large cities of the Northeast. Some are processed and shipped to other parts of our country.

10 Farming

Problems To Solve

Solving these problems will help you to gain a better understanding of farming in the Northeast.

1. **Why is dairying the most important type of farming in the Northeast?** In forming hypotheses to solve this problem, you will need to consider:
   a. the climate of the Northeast
   b. the land features of this region
   c. the markets for dairy products

2. There are many truck farms on the Coastal Plain of the Northeast. **Why is truck farming so important there?** In forming hypotheses to solve this problem, you will need to consider each of the following:
   a. the soil and climate of the Coastal Plain
   b. the nearness to markets
   c. workers available there

See TO THE STUDENT, pages 8-10.

A New Jersey truck farm. It is a hot summer afternoon, and we are driving across the level countryside of southern New Jersey. On both sides of the highway are green fields of crops. A sign tells us that we can buy fresh tomatoes at a roadside stand just ahead.

We stop at the stand and pick out a bushel of ripe, red tomatoes. As we are making our purchase, the man who owns this farm comes over to talk with us. We ask him whether he grows any crops besides tomatoes. The farmer says that he also raises green beans, peppers, and cauliflower. He explains that raising vegetables for sale is known as truck farming.

We learn that this farm is very small in area compared with many farms in the United States. It covers only thirty acres. Even a small farm, however, can provide a good living if the farmer uses his land carefully. He must grow crops that sell for high prices. In addition, he must make each acre of land produce a large yield.

The farmer tells us that vegetables are a profitable crop. He explains that his farm is only forty miles from Philadelphia and one hundred miles from New York City. In both of these cities, there are many people who are willing to pay high prices for fresh vegetables. This farmer never sees most of the people who eat his products. Instead, he sells his crops mainly to large chains of grocery stores. He must harvest his vegetables and ship them as quickly as possible so they will still be fresh when they reach his customers in the cities. Trucks can deliver the farmer's vegetables to markets in New York or Philadelphia on the same day they are picked.

To produce large yields, the farmer must give his crops a great deal of care. In the spring, he and his two sons plow and fertilize the land. Then they set out the young vegetable plants. As the plants grow, they are weeded and sprayed with chemicals that kill weeds and harmful insects. If the weather is dry, the plants must be irrigated. At harvesttime, the farmer has to hire additional workers to pick the vegetables before they spoil.

As we tell the farmer good-bye, he smiles and says he wishes all his sales were this easy. He tells us that it takes as much skill to sell his vegetables as it does to grow them. The farmer must listen to the radio and read the newspaper to keep up with the latest prices for fresh vegetables. In this way, he knows when to sell his crops in order to get the best price. If he sells his crops at the wrong time, he will not make a good profit. From time to time, the farmer must buy fertilizer or insect spray, or some new farm machinery. To meet these expenses, he must manage his money carefully. We can see that a grower of truck crops must be a good businessman as well as a good farmer.

Not all farms in the Northeast are like the one we have just visited. Some of them are much larger, covering hundreds or even thousands of acres. There are farms that raise fruit, tobacco, or other crops. Many farms here specialize in raising livestock, such as cattle or poultry. In spite of these differences, however, many northeastern farms have

Build Your Vocabulary

broilers	truck farm	irrigate	mixed farming
intensive farming	fertilizer	vineyard	silage

MAJOR TYPES OF FARMING IN THE UNITED STATES

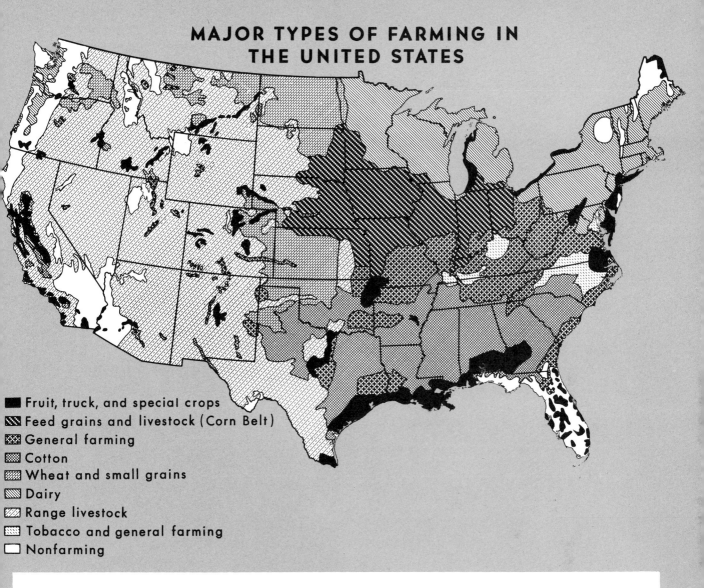

■ Fruit, truck, and special crops
▨ Feed grains and livestock (Corn Belt)
▩ General farming
▨ Cotton
▨ Wheat and small grains
▨ Dairy
▨ Range livestock
▨ Tobacco and general farming
□ Nonfarming

The map above shows the major types of farming in the conterminous United States. To locate the Northeast, compare this map with the one on page 21. As this map shows, dairying is the main type of farming in most parts of the Northeast.

In some parts of the Northeast, other types of farming are more important than dairying. For example, fruit growing is most important on the Erie-Ontario Lowland. A few areas, such as the Adirondack Mountains, are not suitable for farming of any kind.

certain things in common. You will learn what some of these likenesses are as you read more about agriculture in the Northeast.

The amount of farmland in the Northeast is shrinking. There are fewer farms in the Northeast today than there were one hundred or even fifty years ago.

Also, less land is being used for farming. New England, for example, has only about half as many farms and half as much farmland as it had in 1880.

Several facts help explain why there is less farmland in the Northeast today than there used to be. Much of the land in this region is poor for growing crops.

159

A REVOLUTION IN FARMING

Farming has changed greatly since the early days of our country. At that time, most farmers produced barely enough food for themselves and their families. Today, the average farmer in our country produces enough food for about thirty people.

There are many reasons why farm production has increased. Scientists have developed new varieties of plants that produce larger yields than older varieties. Better breeds of livestock have also been developed. It is now possible for farmers to enrich their soil with more effective chemical fertilizers. They can also kill harmful insects with newly developed chemicals. As a result of such advances, larger yields are now produced on each acre of farmland. The invention of new farm machines has also helped increase production. For example, a harvesting machine called a combine not only cuts grain but also threshes* and cleans it. With modern equipment, one man can farm much more land than in the past.

Increased farm production in the United States has resulted in two important trends. First, the number of farmers needed to feed our people is decreasing. In the early years of our country, about nine out of every ten persons worked on farms. Today, only about six out of every one hundred workers are farmers. Second, the size of farms is increasing. This is partly because a farmer must produce a large amount of farm products in order to earn an adequate living. Also, most farm machines are too large and expensive to be used effectively on small farms. Today, the size of the average farm in the United States is about three hundred acres.

Machinery helps farmers to produce more.

Some of it is too rugged and stony to be cultivated easily with farm machines. The soil in many areas is lacking in fertility. In some parts of the Northeast, summers are too short and cool for growing corn and certain other crops successfully.

In the early years of our country, these disadvantages were not as important as they are today. At that time, about nine out of every ten people in the United States earned their living by farming. Most families raised barely enough food for their own needs. If they had any food left over, they sold it in nearby towns and cities.

In the middle of the 1800's, this way of life began to change. New machines and farming methods made it possible for a farmer to produce more crops than before. (See feature on this page.) As a result, fewer farmers were needed. Meanwhile, people were moving to new farmlands in the Midwest. There the soil was generally fertile. The climate was well suited to growing corn, wheat, and other grains. In the Midwest were large stretches of level land that could be cultivated easily with the farm equipment of that time. It is not surprising that midwestern farmers could produce more grain at a lower cost than northeastern farmers could. The Midwest grain was shipped to all parts of the country by railroad. People in the Northeast could buy grain from the Midwest more cheaply than they could buy grain produced on farms nearby.

As time passed, many northeastern farmers moved to the Midwest to obtain better land. Others gave up farming and went to work in factories or offices,

Truck farms in New Jersey. Although less land in the Northeast is being used for farms today than in the past, farmers here produce larger amounts of farm products than ever before. In order to do this, they must plan carefully how to make the best possible use of each acre of land.

where they could earn more money. Many abandoned farms in New England and other parts of the Northeast became overgrown with trees and bushes.

Especially in recent years, the amount of farmland in the Northeast has been shrinking for another reason. Cities and their suburbs are spreading over larger and larger areas. (See Chapter 13.) Much land that was once used for farming is now occupied by houses, factories, highways, or shopping centers.

Farmers in the Northeast use efficient methods. Although the Northeast has less farmland today than in the past, it produces larger quantities of farm products than ever before. Northeastern farmers are able to get large yields because they use their land very effi-

ciently. They try to select the finest varieties of plants and livestock. To make their land produce as much as possible, they use large amounts of fertilizer. Chemicals are used to destroy weeds and insect pests. When the weather is dry, the farmers irrigate their fields.

Planting, fertilizing, spraying, and harvesting crops all require a great deal of labor. Much work is also needed to care for livestock. Nowadays, farmers in the Northeast have machines to help them do much of their work. For example, milking machines are now used on most dairy farms. Many kinds of vegetables can be planted and harvested by machine. However, men are still needed to run the machines and

Irrigating cabbages. Irrigation is one of the methods used by farmers in the Northeast to get large yields. They also use modern machinery and much fertilizer.

Delaware may plant green beans in a certain field as soon as the soil warms up in the spring. By the end of June, the beans will be ready to pick. After they have been harvested, the farmer will plow the land again and fertilize it. Then he will plant some other vegetable that will ripen before the first frost of autumn.

The use of labor, machinery, and efficient methods to produce a large yield in a small area is called intensive farming. Much of the farming done in the Northeast is intensive.

Farm products are sold in nearby cities. Farmers in the Northeast have benefited greatly from their location in the most densely populated part of our country. Millions of people live in the great cities of the Northeast. Each day these people buy vast quantities of perishable foods, such as milk, eggs, vegetables, and fruit. All of these products must be sold and used quickly before they spoil. Therefore, farms that are close to market have an advantage over farms that are located farther away. It is not surprising that there are many dairy and poultry farms, orchards, and truck farms in the Northeast. Farmers here make use of trucks and trains to rush their products to customers in the cities.

to do work that machines cannot do, such as harvesting peaches and other delicate fruits.

Another reason why farmers in the Northeast are able to get large yields per acre is that they use their land throughout the growing season. In some places along the Atlantic coast, the frost-free period is long enough for growing two crops on the same land in a single year. For example, a truck farmer in

Livestock

Dairy cattle. The raising of cows for milk is the most important type of farming in the Northeast. Farmers here earn more money from milk than from any other product. Dairy farms can be found in nearly all parts of this region. (See map on page 159.) However, the main dairy-farming areas are the Appalachian Plateau in New York and northern Pennsylvania, the Piedmont Plateau in Pennsylvania and Maryland, and the Champlain Valley in Vermont.

There are several reasons why dairying is so important in the Northeast. People in the large cities of this region use huge quantities of fresh milk every day. Milk is a bulky product and spoils quickly. Even with fast, refrigerated trucks and trains, fresh milk is usually not shipped farther than two hundred miles. Therefore, most dairy farms are located near urban areas.

The land and climate of the Northeast also help to explain why there is such a large number of dairy farms in this region. Land that is too rugged for growing crops can often be used as pasture for dairy cows. Grasses used for hay and grazing grow well in places where summers are too short and cool for raising most other kinds of crops. Cows give more milk if the weather is not too hot in the summertime. In the Northeast, there is usually enough rainfall to provide drinking water for cattle.

Most dairy farms in the Northeast are rather small in area. A typical farm covers about one hundred acres. Dairy farmers use most of their land for pasture, or for growing hay and other feed crops. In addition, some farmers feed their cattle grain from the Midwest. In

Milking cows by machine. Raising cows for milk is the main type of farming in the Northeast. The land and climate in many parts of the region are well suited to dairying, and dairy farmers find a ready market for their products in the many large cities of the Northeast.

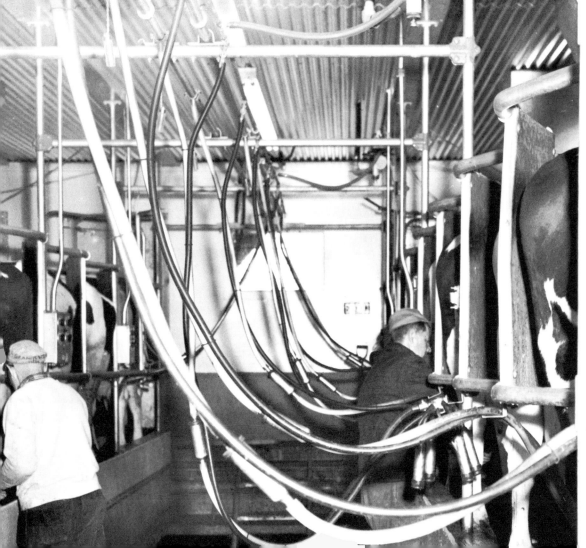

this way, they do not need to own as much land as they would if they grew their own feed crops.

Dairy farming requires skill and care. On a typical farm, there may be as many as forty cows. These cows must be milked twice a day throughout the year. Milking machines and other equipment must be kept spotlessly clean. The cows have to be given just the right quantities of certain feeds if they are to produce large amounts of high-quality milk.

Farmers who live near cities usually sell their milk to dairies, which pasteurize it and put it into bottles or cartons. Some of this milk is sold to grocery stores, and some is delivered to people's homes. If a farmer is far from a large city, he may sell his milk to a nearby processing plant. There the milk is made into butter, cheese, or other products that do not spoil as easily as fresh milk.

Poultry. Poultry and eggs rank second in value among the farm products of the Northeast. Like dairy cows, poultry can be raised in areas where the land and climate are poor for growing most crops. Also, farmers can raise a lot of poultry on only a few acres of land. There is an enormous market for eggs and fresh poultry in the large cities of the Northeast.

Broiler chickens are among the main types of poultry raised in the Northeast. These are chickens that are butchered when they are six to twelve weeks old. At that age, their meat is tender and very good to eat. The Delmarva Peninsula* was the first area in our country to produce broiler chickens on a large scale. Today the South produces more broilers than any other region. However, Maryland and Delaware are still important broiler-producing states. In some years, nearly 100 million broilers are raised in Maryland alone.

Many farmers in the Northeast raise chickens for their eggs. Pennsylvania and New York are the main egg-producing states in this region. There are also many chicken farms in the southern part of New England. Each day, these farms supply many thousands of eggs to customers in nearby cities.

Other kinds of poultry are also raised in the Northeast. Farms on Long Island produce about half of the ducks raised in the United States. Large numbers of turkeys are raised in Pennsylvania and West Virginia.

Although people who specialize in other types of farming sometimes raise a few chickens as a sideline, most

A duck farm. Poultry and eggs are important farm products in the Northeast. Each year, the region produces millions of broiler chickens, as well as large numbers of ducks and turkeys.

*See Glossary

164

poultry farming in the Northeast today is a full-time business. Some farmers care for many thousands of birds. To do this successfully, a farmer must have a great deal of knowledge and skill. He must select breeds of poultry that will provide the most meat or eggs at the lowest cost. He must spend much money to build poultry houses and to furnish them with automatic feeders and other modern equipment. The farmer must make sure that his birds receive the right amounts of food and water. He must protect them from disease by giving them "shots" and keeping their houses clean. It is also important for the farmer to know how to market his poultry and eggs so that they will bring good prices. Otherwise, he will not be able to make a profit.

Beef cattle. The raising of cattle for beef is less important in the Northeast than the raising of dairy cattle. How-ever, many herds of beef cattle graze on hillside pastures in West Virginia. Much of the land in this state is too rugged for growing crops, but it can be used for pasture.

The cattle raised in West Virginia are usually lean, because they feed mainly on grass. They must be fed corn and other grains to fatten them before they can be sold for meat. Although it is difficult to grow corn and other grains on the rugged land of West Virginia, these crops grow well on the fertile, rolling Piedmont Plateau. Each fall, large numbers of lean beef cattle are shipped by train or truck from West Virginia to farms on the Piedmont in Maryland and southeastern Pennsylvania. There they are kept in feedlots* and fed a rich diet of hay and grain. When they are fat enough, they are shipped to meat-packing plants in New York and other cities of the Northeast.

Vegetables and Fruits

Vegetables. In the Northeast, there are thousands of truck farms like the one we visited at the start of this chapter. Many truck farms are located in southern New Jersey, on Long Island, and on the Delmarva Peninsula. All three of these areas are in the Coastal Plain region of our country.

The land and climate of the Coastal Plain help explain why truck farming is so important here. Most of the land is level enough for growing crops. The loose, sandy soil is easy to cultivate, even though it must be fertilized heavily to produce good yields. This kind of soil is especially well suited to growing root crops, such as carrots and beets. The Coastal Plain has a long growing season. Also, the sandy soil warms up quickly in the spring. As a result, farmers here can plant their crops earlier than farmers in other parts of the Northeast. They can harvest their vegetables and send them to market earlier in the season. In this way, they are likely to get a better price.

Many different kinds of vegetables are raised on the Coastal Plain. Among the most important are tomatoes, potatoes, beans, peas, and cucumbers.

A large part of the vegetable crop is sold fresh in nearby cities. The rest is sent to canning or freezing plants.

Not all truck farms are as small as the one we visited. Some of them cover thousands of acres. These large farms may specialize in growing a single vegetable, or they may raise a variety of crops. Some of them are owned by food-processing companies. The large farms use many special kinds of machinery for planting, cultivating, and harvesting their crops.

The Coastal Plain is not the only truck-farming area in the Northeast. Large crops of cabbages, beans, and other vegetables are grown on the Lake Ontario plain in New York State. Northern Maine is one of the chief potato-farming areas in the United States. (See page 260.)

Fruit. In some parts of the Northeast, fruit growing is an important type of farming. There are many orchards on the Erie-Ontario Lowland in western New York and Pennsylvania. The climate here is very favorable for growing fruit. (See page 47.) Among the leading kinds of fruit grown here are apples, peaches, pears, and cherries. In western New York, there are also many vineyards. Grapes grown here are used mainly for grape juice and wine.

Apples are grown in every state of the Northeast. They can be raised in places where the climate is too cold for other kinds of fruit. In fact, they grow best where summers are not extremely hot. Some of our country's best apple-growing areas are on the sloping lands of the Appalachian Ridges and Valleys section in Pennsylvania, Maryland, and West Virginia. In the

Picking apples. Fruit growing is important in several parts of the Northeast.

Exploring Agriculture With Maps

The maps below provide information about some of our country's important farm products. Test your skill at map reading by trying to answer the following questions about farm products in the Northeast. To locate the states of the Northeast, compare these maps with the map on page 233.

1. Which of these products bring more money to farmers in the Northeast — dairy products or fruits and nuts?
2. Which state raises more cattle — New York or Maine?
3. Which state earns more money from the sale of vegetables — New Jersey or Vermont?

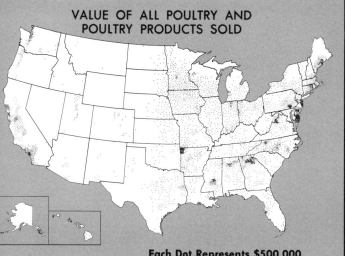

VALUE OF ALL POULTRY AND POULTRY PRODUCTS SOLD

Each Dot Represents $500,000

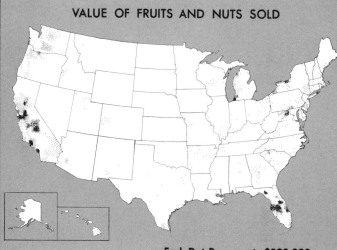

VALUE OF FRUITS AND NUTS SOLD

Each Dot Represents $500,000

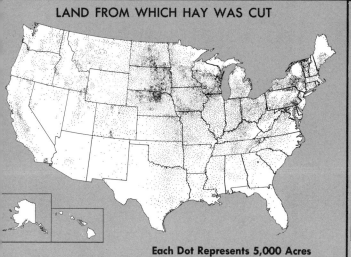

LAND FROM WHICH HAY WAS CUT

Each Dot Represents 5,000 Acres

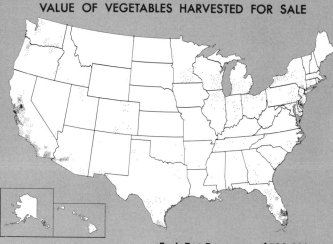

VALUE OF VEGETABLES HARVESTED FOR SALE

Each Dot Represents $500,000

CATTLE

Each Dot Represents 5,000 Head

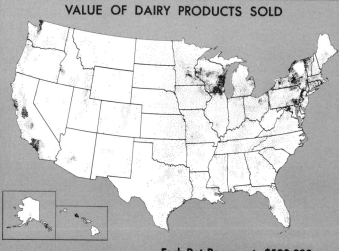

VALUE OF DAIRY PRODUCTS SOLD

Each Dot Represents $500,000

167

springtime, many hillsides and mountain slopes here are covered with white rows of blossoming apple trees.

Among the other fruit crops grown in the Northeast are blueberries and cranberries. Large amounts of blueberries are grown in New Jersey and along the eastern coast of Maine. In these places, the soil is especially well suited to this crop. More than half of the nation's cranberry crop is grown in southeastern Massachusetts. You can learn more about the growing of cranberries on pages 277 and 278.

Other Crops

In addition to vegetables and fruits, many other crops are produced in the Northeast. Among these are tobacco, wheat, corn, and hay. In some parts of the Northeast, several different crops are grown on one farm. This is called mixed, or diversified, farming.

Mixed farming in Lancaster County. To learn more about mixed farming, we will visit Lancaster County in south-

Farms in Lancaster County, Pennsylvania. This county lies in one of the most fertile farming areas in the United States. Farmers here grow several different kinds of crops. Members of certain religious groups in Lancaster County, such as the Amish, still travel by horse and buggy.

Cutting corn for silage. In some parts of the Northeast, summers are too short and too cool for corn to ripen fully. Farmers in these areas harvest corn while it is still green and store it in silos. During cold winter months, silage* is fed to cattle and other livestock.

eastern Pennsylvania. This part of Pennsylvania is one of the most fertile farming areas in the United States. The soil here is very rich, and the land is gently rolling. Rainfall is plentiful, and the growing season is long enough for many kinds of crops.

It is a bright morning in June as we drive through the rolling countryside of Lancaster County. All around us are golden fields of wheat and bright-green rows of corn and tobacco plants. Here and there we see neat farmhouses and large, sturdy barns. The people who own these farms are mainly of German descent. Many of them are members of a religious group known as the Amish.

They are noted for their hard work and their love of farming.

The main crops grown in Lancaster County are tobacco, wheat, potatoes, corn, and hay. To help keep the soil fertile, farmers rotate their crops. One year a farmer may plant tobacco on a certain piece of land. The next year he may use the same land for wheat. He may plant clover or alfalfa the third year, and corn the fourth. Then the land will be ready for growing tobacco again. Many farmers in Lancaster County raise beef cattle. In the fall, after their crops are harvested, they buy lean cattle from West Virginia and other states. They feed the cattle corn and other grains that they have grown on their own farms. When the cattle are fat enough, the farmers sell them for meat.

Tobacco. Lancaster County is one of three main tobacco-raising areas in the Northeast. The others are in the Connecticut Valley and in southern Maryland. Tobacco is a crop that needs much care, so it is usually grown on small patches of land with the help of many workers. Although farmers must spend much money for labor and equipment, they usually make a good profit.

Grain crops. As you have learned, much of the Northeast is not well suited to growing corn, wheat, and other grains. However, these crops are important in some areas. Wheat is raised on the Erie-Ontario Lowland and the Piedmont Plateau. Some of it is used in making flour, and some is fed to livestock. In many parts of the Northeast, dairy farmers raise corn for silage.* Other grain crops grown in the Northeast include barley, oats, and rye.

Nursery and greenhouse products. Near the large cities of the Northeast, there are many nurseries and greenhouses. Nurseries are places where trees, shrubs, and flowering plants are grown for sale. People buy these plants for their lawns and gardens. Flowers, vegetables, and other delicate plants are raised in greenhouses the year around. Many of the orchids, carnations, and gardenias sold in the United States come from greenhouses in southeastern Pennsylvania. This is also the chief mushroom-growing area in the United States.

Explore Farming in the Northeast
1. Why is the amount of farmland in the Northeast shrinking?
2. Explain what the term "intensive farming" means.
3. Why is dairy farming the most important type of farming in the Northeast?
4. Why are many of the truck farms in the Northeast located on the Coastal Plain?
5. Why are poultry and eggs important farm products of the Northeast?

Investigate Truck Farming in the Northeast
Imagine that you are a truck farmer in the Northeast and have been asked to write an article about your farm for a leading farm magazine. Before writing your article, you will need to do some general reading. Take careful notes and then make an outline before beginning to write. Some of the things your readers will be interested in are:
1. where your truck farm is located
2. why your location is good for truck farming
3. what crops you grow

4. how your farm products are shipped to market and who buys them
5. what kinds of work you do on the farm

Feel free to use your imagination, but be sure the statements you make are based on facts. This chapter contains much useful information for this project. If you wish to do outside research, refer to the suggestions on pages 347-349.

Learn About Special Crops of the Northeast
Choose one or more of the topics below, and do research to find the answers to the questions about it.

Cranberries: Where are cranberries grown in the Northeast? What special kind of soil do they need? How are they grown and harvested?

Mushrooms: Where are mushrooms grown in the Northeast? What special conditions do they require?

Blueberries: How are blueberries raised? How are they harvested and processed for market?

Ships in New York Harbor. Since colonial days, trade and transportation have been important to the growth of the Northeast. Today, more trade is carried on here than in any other region of our country. The Northeast's excellent network of water, land, and air transportation has helped it become an important trading region.

11 Trade and Transportation

Problems To Solve

Solving these problems will help you to develop your understanding of the concept "trade."

1. **A good transportation network is important to the progress of any region. Why is this true?** In forming your hypotheses you will need to consider:

   a. how factories get raw materials

   b. how farm products and manufactured goods are distributed to the people who use them

   c. how people get from their homes to the places where they work

2. Each year, thousands of ships from foreign countries visit ports in the Northeast. **Why is foreign trade important to the people of this region?** The following questions suggest hypotheses:

   a. Where do factories in the Northeast get their raw materials?

   b. Where do the people of the Northeast sell the goods that they produce?

   c. How does foreign trade affect ways of earning a living in the Northeast?

   See TO THE STUDENT, pages 8-10.

Trade

A visit to a great department store. It is a snowy day in December, and we are doing our Christmas shopping in New York City. Our shopping trip takes us to one of the largest department stores in the United States. At Christmastime, more than twelve thousand people work in this huge store, which covers an entire city block. Each year, about 45 million shoppers visit the store. They buy millions of dollars' worth of goods.

As we walk through the crowded aisles, we see many different kinds of merchandise. A clerk tells us that some items, such as women's hats and dresses, were made right here in New York City. There are also many articles that were manufactured in other parts of our country. For example, we notice furniture from North Carolina and sportswear from California. We also see many items that were produced in foreign countries, such as Italy, Great Britain, and Japan. Among these items are typewriters, chinaware, and transistor radios. In this one store, we can buy goods from nearly every part of the world. To understand why this is possible, you must know something about trade.

What is trade? Trade is exchanging one item of value for another. When you give a friend a stack of your comic books in exchange for some of his, you are carrying on trade. A shopper in a department store is carrying on trade when she gives the clerk some money in exchange for the goods that she wishes to buy. Trade takes place not only between individuals and business firms, but also between states, regions, and countries.

Trade helps everyone to live better. People can have a better life through trade than they could without it. By trading with each other, they can obtain goods that they would not be able to produce themselves. For example, oranges and coffee cannot be grown in New York because of the cold winters there. However, oranges can be raised in southern California, where the weather is mild the year around. Trade between New York and California makes it possible for New York children to have fresh orange juice for breakfast. Their parents can have coffee to drink because our country trades with Brazil and other coffee-producing countries.

When the first settlers came to America, they carried on very little trade. Each family grew or made nearly everything that it needed. If you were to do this today, you would have to give up most of the things that people consider necessary for modern living. With a

Build Your Vocabulary

trade	advertising	export	retail	wholesale
standard of living		merchant		St. Lawrence Seaway
Great Lakes – St. Lawrence Waterway		import	turnpike	lock

Christmas shoppers throng Macy's department store in New York City. This is one of the largest department stores in the United States. People who buy goods in a store are carrying on one form of trade. Trade helps everyone to live better.

great deal of effort, you might be able to grow your own food and make your own clothing. You might even be able to build a house for yourself. However, you would have neither the skill nor the equipment to make such things as automobiles, refrigerators, and television sets.

Today, hardly anyone in our country tries to make everything that he needs. Instead, each person usually does only one kind of work. With the money he earns from his job, he can buy goods that other people produce. In this way, he can obtain a larger quantity and a greater variety of goods than he could

if he had to produce everything that he needed. Also, he can specialize in doing a kind of work that he enjoys and that suits his abilities.

Just as people differ in their abilities, so do states, regions, and countries differ in their natural resources and the skills of their people. Trade makes it possible for each state, region, or country to specialize in producing the goods that it is best suited to produce. Without trade, all of us would have a much lower standard* of living than we enjoy today.

The Northeast is an important trading region. More trade is carried on in the

Northeast than in any other region of our country. Each year, merchants and business firms in the Northeast sell about 200 billion dollars' worth of goods. More people in this region are employed in trade than in any other kind of work except manufacturing. Let us learn more about the different kinds of trade carried on in the Northeast.

Foreign trade. Much of the trade between the United States and foreign countries is carried on by firms in the Northeast. In New York, Boston, and other port cities, there are many companies that make a business of importing and exporting goods.

Each year, large quantities of goods produced in Europe, South America, and other parts of the world are brought by ship to the ports of the Northeast. The merchandise is stored in large warehouses until it is ready to be delivered to the people who will use it. Then it

is sent by train or truck to all parts of our country. Among the chief imports are food products, such as coffee and sugar, and raw materials, such as oil and copper. Our country also imports manufactured goods, including machinery, clothing, watches, toys, and sports equipment.

Goods produced in various sections of the United States are brought to ports in the Northeast for shipment to many parts of the globe. The leading exports of the United States are manufactured products, such as machines, automobiles, and textiles. Our country also exports large amounts of farm products, such as wheat and corn.

Trade with other parts of the United States. The Northeast also carries on much trade with other parts of our country. For example, wheat grown in the Midwest and Great Plains is brought to Buffalo and other northeastern cities to be made into flour. During the winter, fresh fruits and vegetables produced in California and Florida are shipped to customers in the Northeast. This region, in turn, sells large quantities of goods to other regions. Among these products are many manufactured items, such as electrical appliances, machine tools, and clothing.

Retail and wholesale trade. Any store that sells goods directly to the people who use them is carrying on retail trade. There are hundreds of thousands of retail stores in the Northeast. They range in size from the department store that we visited earlier in this chapter to tiny shops that employ a single person. Most of the Northeast's retail trade is carried on in large cities, such as New York and Philadelphia. In

Ore mined in Africa is loaded onto a train at Baltimore. Large amounts of the goods traded between the United States and foreign countries pass through the great port cities of the Northeast.

addition to large department stores, these cities have many luxury shops that sell expensive items such as furs and fine jewelry. People may come from hundreds of miles away to shop in the great cities of the Northeast. Here they can find many goods that they cannot buy in their home towns.

A company that sells large quantities of goods to retail stores and other business firms is said to be carrying on wholesale trade. Many wholesale firms have their offices in the large cities of the Northeast. Wholesale trade has been important in this region since the 1700's, when all of our country's main seaports and manufacturing cities were located in the Northeast.

Advertising. To carry on trade successfully today, products must be advertised. People will not usually buy a product unless they know something about it. Therefore, business firms often employ advertising agencies to make their products known to the public. Advertising appears in newspapers and magazines as well as on radio and television.

Many of our country's largest advertising agencies are located on or

Televising a commercial. Many business firms employ advertising agencies in New York City to advertise their products in newspapers and magazines as well as on radio and television.

near Madison Avenue in New York City. Here they are close to the main offices of many large manufacturing firms. They are also near the headquarters of the large radio and television broadcasting companies. In addition, several large newspapers and a number of magazines are published in New York City.

Transportation

Good transportation is important to everyone. Trade between different states, regions, and countries would not be possible without good transportation. Goods must be shipped from the places where they are produced to the people who use them.

Our visit to a Pennsylvania steel plant in Chapter 9 showed us some of

the ways in which transportation is important to industry. We learned that much of the iron ore used in this plant must be brought long distances from other countries. Trains and trucks are needed to bring the other raw materials — coal and limestone — from the places where they are produced. The products manufactured in this steel plant must be delivered to customers. In addition, the thousands of workers employed here must have a dependable way of traveling to and from work every day.

Industrial workers are not the only people who need good transportation. Farmers must have a way to send their products to the people who buy them. Salesmen and other people engaged in trade must be able to travel from one place to another to conduct their business. Policemen and firemen need transportation to carry out their work of protecting the community.

Transportation is important to our lives in many other ways. People must have some means of transportation if they want to visit friends or relatives in distant places, or if they want to spend their vacations away from home. Students who do not live close to the

schools they attend must have some way of traveling to and from their classes. Often people need transportation to movie theaters, athletic stadiums, and other places of recreation. It is hard for us to imagine what our lives would be like without cars, airplanes, and other modern means of transportation.

Natural transportation routes have helped make the Northeast a great trading region. The Northeast has benefited greatly from its location along main transportation routes. This region borders the great Atlantic Ocean. Along the Atlantic coast are many bays and river mouths that provide excellent harbors. The seaports that have grown up around harbors in the Northeast are closer to Europe than those in any other region of the United States. This fact is important because our country carries on a huge amount of trade with Europe. Also, most of the people who settled America came here from Europe. Ever since our country was founded, the Northeast has been the main "gateway" to the United States.

From the Atlantic coast, several river valleys lead through the Appalachian Mountains. The most important of these is the Hudson-Mohawk Lowland in New York State, but there are others in Pennsylvania and Maryland. In the early days of our country, roads and canals were built through these lowland passageways. (See pages 99 and 100.) Later, railroads followed the same routes. Today, these natural passageways are still important transportation routes between the Atlantic coast and the interior of our country.

West of the Appalachians are two waterways that connect the Northeast

A modern subway train in Hoboken, New Jersey. Good transportation is important to everyone. In some of the Northeast's large cities, many people travel on underground trains, called subways.

with the interior of the United States. One is the Ohio River, which begins in western Pennsylvania. The other is the Great Lakes–St. Lawrence Waterway. This long water route is formed by the St. Lawrence River, the five Great Lakes, and the straits, rivers, and canals that connect them. As you will discover, both the Ohio River and the Great Lakes–St. Lawrence Waterway are important to the Northeast.

The Northeast has a well-developed network of transportation. The people of the Northeast have made good use of the region's natural advantages for transportation. Today the Northeast has one of the best systems of transportation in the world. It is served by roads, railroads, airways, and waterways. Ships from every part of the globe anchor in the fine harbors of the Northeast.

Roads. There are more than 400,000 miles of roads in the Northeast. They range from narrow strips of gravel to broad, modern expressways paved with concrete or asphalt. Hardly any place in the Northeast is more than a few miles from a paved highway. The only large area that is not served by a network of roads is the forested wilderness of northern Maine.

Each year, millions of vehicles use the highways of the Northeast. Most of these vehicles are automobiles. In addition, there are many buses that carry people between cities and towns in the Northeast. Trucks haul large quantities of goods from farms, forests, and mines to the cities, and from one city to another.

To handle all this traffic, the states of the Northeast have been building many highways in recent years. Some

A modern superhighway near Washington, D.C. The states of the Northeast have been building many highways in recent years. Today, hardly any place in this region is more than a few miles from a paved highway.

of the new highways are at least four lanes in width, and they do not have any traffic lights or crossroads. On these broad superhighways, people can travel quickly and safely.

Certain highways in the Northeast are called toll roads, or turnpikes. To use these highways, motorists must pay a fee called a toll. Among the most heavily traveled toll roads in the Northeast are the Pennsylvania Turnpike, the New Jersey Turnpike, and the New York State Thruway.

The federal government is now spending billions of dollars to help our states construct a nationwide system of superhighways. These new roads are called interstate highways. By 1974, interstate highways are scheduled to be completed between the main cities of the Northeast.

A railroad yard in New Jersey, across the Hudson River from New York City. Goods from all parts of our country are brought here by train and sent by ferry to New York or loaded onto oceangoing ships for export to other countries. Railroads carry much of the freight that is moved from place to place in the Northeast, since it is often cheaper to haul bulky goods by train than by truck.

Railroads. Some of the first railroads in our country were built in the Northeast more than one hundred years ago. (See page 102.) At the beginning of the twentieth century, the best way to travel from one place to another was by train. Today, more people travel by car and bus than by train. This is partly because highways serve more towns than railroads do. However, railroads are still used by many travelers. More than 100 million passengers enter and leave New York City by train every year.

Railroads carry much of the freight that is moved from place to place in the Northeast. It is often cheaper to haul bulky goods by train than by truck. Large amounts of beef, fruit, vegetables, and other foods produced in various parts of the United States are brought to cities in the Northeast by railroad. Trains also carry raw materials, such as coal and iron ore, to northeastern factories. Goods produced in some of these factories are carried by train to customers throughout the nation.

Airways. We are standing on the observation deck of a large passenger terminal at John F. Kennedy International Airport in New York City. This is one of the largest and busiest airports in the world. From the observation deck, we see airplanes landing or taking off every few seconds. The noise of the jet engines is almost deafening. We also notice several helicopters, which transport passengers to and from downtown New York City, nearly fifteen miles away.

More than fifty different airlines serve the cities of the Northeast. The planes of some of these airlines fly only to cities within the region. The planes of other airlines fly to many parts of the United States. Many planes fly between the Northeast and foreign countries, such as Great Britain, France, and Germany.

Airplane travel is faster than land or water transportation. Businessmen and other people travel by plane when they want to get from one place to another very quickly. It is relatively expensive to ship freight by airplane. However, planes are often used to carry lightweight or perishable goods that must be delivered quickly. Much mail from the Northeast is sent to other regions or to foreign countries by air. Airplanes are also used to transport products such as live lobsters and cut flowers over long distances.

Ocean shipping. Some of our nation's largest ports are located along the Atlantic coast of the Northeast. The largest port of all is the one that serves the New York metropolitan* area. About 21,000 ships enter and leave this port every year. Other leading ports are at Philadelphia, Baltimore, and Boston.

John F. Kennedy International Airport, in New York City. This is one of the largest and busiest airports in the world. More than fifty different airlines serve the cities of the Northeast. Planes fly not only between cities in the region but also to other parts of the United States and to foreign countries.

Most of the ships that dock at ports in the Northeast carry freight. Some of these ships travel between the United States and other parts of the world, such as Europe, Africa, and South America. There are also many ships that carry cargoes between the Northeast and other parts of the United States. For example, tankers bring large amounts of petroleum from oil-producing areas in Texas and Louisiana. Ships also carry much freight between the Northeast and the Pacific coast of our country by way of the Panama Canal.*

Many large passenger liners dock at New York City and other ports in the Northeast. Some of these luxurious ships, such as the *Queen Elizabeth 2* and the *Michelangelo*, carry travelers between the United States and Europe.

Others travel to South America and other parts of the globe.

Inland waterways. People in the Northeast also use lakes, rivers, and canals for transportation. Although water travel is usually slow, it is one of the cheapest means of transportation. Therefore, boats are often used for transporting heavy goods that do not need to be moved in a hurry. In the early 1800's, when there were few roads or railroads, many people traveled by boat on lakes, rivers, and canals. Today, few passenger boats use these inland waterways.

New York and Pennsylvania border on one of the greatest inland waterways in the world. This is the Great Lakes–St. Lawrence Waterway. Many long, low ships travel between ports on the

A ship traveling through a lock in the St. Lawrence Seaway. Each year, thousands of ocean-going ships travel between the Northeast and other parts of the world. The region's leading ports are located along the Atlantic coast. There are also several important ports on Lake Erie and Lake Ontario. Ships reach these ports by traveling on the Great Lakes – St. Lawrence Waterway.*

Waterways of the Northeast

Legend:
- Main Rivers
- Navigable Part of Main Rivers
- Main Ports
- New York State Barge Canal
- Other Canals

CANADA

Lake Huron

Lake Ontario

Lake Erie

St. Lawrence R.

Lake Champlain

Canal

Great Sodus Bay

Niagara R.

Welland Ship Canal

Buffalo

New York State Barge Canal

Mohawk R.

Albany

Genesee R.

Hudson R.

Connecticut R.

Housatonic R.

Merrimack R.

Kennebec R.

Penobscot R.

Androscoggin R.

Searsport

Portland

Portsmouth

Salem

Boston

ATLANTIC OCEAN

Fall River

Providence

Cape Cod Canal

Erie

Allegheny R.

Susquehanna R.

Delaware R.

Schuylkill R.

Bridgeport

Norwalk

New Haven

New York

Port Jefferson

Hempstead

Aliquippa-Rochester

Pittsburgh

Clairton-Elizabeth

Ohio R.

Monongahela R.

Kanawha R.

Huntington

Penn Manor

Trenton

Wilmington

Philadelphia

Chesapeake and Delaware Canal

Baltimore

Washington, D.C.

Potomac R.

Chesapeake Bay

James R.

ATLANTIC OCEAN

Scale of Miles
0 50 100 150

WILMINGTON — PHILADELPHIA AREA

Schuylkill R.

Delaware R.

Philadelphia

Camden-Gloucester

Marcus Hook

Paulsboro

Wilmington

New Castle

Scale of Miles
0 10 20

This map shows the main seaports, river ports, and waterways of the Northeast. These ports and waterways have helped the Northeast become our country's leading trading region.

A number of cities along the Atlantic coast have fine deepwater harbors. Ships from all over the world come to these harbors, bringing goods of many kinds to the Northeast. Ships also carry cargoes from these harbors to many distant ports. New York City is our country's busiest seaport.

Inland waterways are also important in the Northeast. Part of the Great Lakes–St. Lawrence Waterway borders this region. Ships use this waterway to travel between lake ports in the Northeast, such as Buffalo, and ports in the Midwest and Canada. This waterway also connects the Northeast's lake ports with the Atlantic Ocean. Another important inland waterway is the Ohio River, which connects the Northeast with parts of the South and the Midwest. Many port cities within the Northeast are linked by smaller rivers and canals. For example, the Monongahela River and the New York State Barge Canal carry large amounts of freight between ports in the Northeast.

Great Lakes. Some of them carry iron ore from Minnesota or limestone from Michigan to Buffalo and other ports on Lake Erie. These minerals are used by steel plants in the Northeast. (See page 145.) Other ships bring wheat to Buffalo to be made into flour. On their trip westward, some of the lake ships carry coal that was mined in the mountains of Pennsylvania.

Until a few years ago, large ocean-going ships could not travel between the Atlantic Ocean and the Great Lakes. Their way was blocked by rapids and shallow places in the St. Lawrence River, between Lake Ontario and the city of Montreal, Canada. In 1959, the governments of the United States and Canada finished building a series of canals and locks that allow ships to bypass the rapids and shallow water in the river. This system of canals and locks is known as the St. Lawrence Seaway. By using the Seaway, ocean-going ships from every part of the world can reach ports located on the Great Lakes.

Several rivers in the Northeast are important transportation routes. Coal, oil, and other raw materials are carried by barge on the Ohio River and its main tributaries, the Allegheny and the Monongahela. Powerful towboats can push as many as ten or twelve barges at one time. Boats and barges also carry large amounts of goods on the Hudson River between New York City and Albany, and on the Delaware River as far north as Trenton.

People in the Northeast have built several canals to connect different bodies of water. The New York State Barge Canal links all the main rivers and lakes in the state. (See map on page 181.) It is used for transporting oil, wheat, and other raw materials. Two other canals serve as shortcuts between seaports along the Atlantic coast. One of these, the Cape Cod Canal, shortens the sailing distance between Boston and New York City. Another canal, which extends across the Delmarva Peninsula, connects Chesapeake Bay with the Delaware River.

Explore Trade and Transportation
1. What is trade? Give some examples.
2. What is the difference between retail and wholesale trade?
3. Why are many large advertising agencies located in New York City?
4. What is the St. Lawrence Seaway? Why was it built? What is the Great Lakes–St. Lawrence Waterway? Why is this waterway important to the Northeast?
5. What kinds of goods are transported by train in the Northeast? Why?

Hold a Trade Fair
As a class, learn more about trade by holding a trade fair. First, do research to find out where different products in your homes came from. Bring samples of some of these to class, and make drawings to represent others. Try to include products from other countries as well as from other states. Label each product and tell where it came from. Then arrange your samples and drawings in an attractive exhibit. You may also wish to make an exhibit of products that are exported from your community or state to other parts of the world. After you have studied all of the exhibits, hold a class discussion based on the following question:

How does trade help people have a better life?

The guidelines on page 351 will help you have a successful discussion.

Part 4
The People and Their Way of Life

Wooded countryside in Vermont

Skyscrapers in New York City

A crowded street in New York City. About one fourth of the people in the United States live in the Northeast. Most of them live in or near large cities. The people of the Northeast represent a variety of races, religions, and nationalities.

12 People

A Problem To Solve

Ever since the United States became a nation, people from many different lands have come to the Northeast to live. **Why have so many immigrants made their homes in the Northeast?** In forming hypotheses to solve this problem, you may wish to consider each of the following questions:

a. What facts about religious and political freedom in the United States help to solve this problem?

b. What facts about job opportunities in the Northeast help to solve it?

c. How has the location of the Northeast affected the number of immigrants who have come to this region?

See TO THE STUDENT, pages 8-10.

The Northeast is the most densely populated part of our country. More than 55 million people live in the Northeast. This is about 25 percent of the entire population of the United States. However, the Northeast covers only about 6 percent of the area of our country. This region is smaller than the state of Texas. If all the people in the Northeast were evenly distributed throughout the region, there would be about 268 persons for each square mile. No other region of the United States is so densely populated. (See top map on page 190.)

Where the people of the Northeast live. About three fourths of the people in the Northeast live in or near large cities. Many others live in the hundreds of towns and villages that are scattered through this region. The remainder of the people in the Northeast live in rural areas.

Most of the Northeast's towns and cities have grown up in the lowland areas along the Atlantic Ocean and the Great Lakes, or in river valleys. Many early colonists settled near the fine natural harbors along the coast. Others settled along rivers, which provided convenient water transportation routes. As people moved westward, they settled mainly on plains or in river valleys. In these areas, they generally found the land and climate well suited to farming. Also, it was easier to build roads and railroads through plains and valleys than through the highlands. Few people settled in the mountainous sections of the Northeast, such as the Adirondacks in New York or the highlands of Maine. Today, these areas are still thinly populated. (Compare map on page 27 with top map on page 190.)

The Northeast has three main areas of dense population. The most densely populated part of the Northeast begins in southern New Hampshire and extends southward along the Atlantic coast. This area of dense population is known as Megalopolis, or the "super city." (See Chapter 13.) Megalopolis includes the great Atlantic port cities of Boston, New York, Philadelphia, and Baltimore, as well as Washington, D.C. It also includes the many smaller cities, towns, and suburban communities between these larger cities.

Another heavily populated part of the Northeast is in western Pennsylvania, along the Ohio River and its tributaries. Abundant supplies of coal have helped this to become one of our country's leading industrial sections. More steel is made here than in any other part of the Northeast. Pittsburgh is the largest city in western Pennsylvania, and one of the oldest.

The Northeast's third heavily populated area extends from east to west across central New York. It lies along the route of the Erie Canal. (See page 99.) This area includes the cities of Albany, Utica, Syracuse, Rochester, and Buffalo.

People from many lands have made their homes in the Northeast. Most people in the Northeast are native-born citizens, just as most people are in other regions of the United States. In our country, however, almost all native-born citizens are descended from immigrants who have come to America during the last four hundred years. Indians, Eskimos, and Hawaiians* are the only exceptions. In the Northeast, by far

*See Glossary

Build Your Vocabulary

suburban   quota   foreign stock   native-born   religious freedom

population density   nationality   descent   migrate   immigration

the largest number of native-born citizens are of European descent. Their ancestors came to America from many different countries in Europe. The Negroes in the Northeast are descended from people who lived in various parts of Africa.

Immigration during the early years of our country's history. As you learned in Chapter 4, people from several different European countries came to America during the colonial period. Most of the colonists in the Northeast came from England. Others came from Scotland and Ireland. There were Dutch settlers in New York and New Jersey, Germans in Pennsylvania, and Swedes in Delaware. French Huguenots* also settled in the Northeast, mainly in New York. In addition to the settlers who came to the Northeast from Europe, there were also many Negroes who were brought from Africa to work as slaves.

During the period that followed the Revolutionary War, few settlers came to the United States. People in Britain were not greatly attracted to the country that had so recently been their enemy. In fact, none of the countries of Europe had much faith in the future of America. Few people wanted to leave their homelands to settle in a new and untried country. Britain, France, and several other countries in Europe were busy fighting a long series of wars. These wars did not end until 1815. Also, with the rise of manufacturing in England, the British government had passed a law that prevented many skilled workers from leaving the country. (See page 88.) This law was not repealed until the 1820's.

The Statue of Liberty, in New York Harbor, represents the promise of freedom.

Immigration from 1820 to 1900. About the year 1820, immigration to America began to increase very rapidly. By this time, the United States had established itself as a successful, prosperous democracy. It was not only a land of freedom, but also a land of opportunity. Many Americans were moving from the east into the vast new lands that had been opened up for settlement in the west. This westward movement left a shortage of workers in the many new factories that were springing up in the Northeast.

At this same time, many people in Europe were becoming discontented and restless. There were two main reasons for this. One reason was that thousands of workers were unable to find jobs. Everywhere in Europe the population was increasing rapidly. No new land was available for farming, and the cities could not provide factory jobs for all the people who needed work. Second, many Europeans were dissatisfied with the governments under which they lived. Democracy and religious freedom were unknown in most of the countries in Europe.

Soon, people from northern and western Europe began to pour into the United States. Between 1840 and 1860,

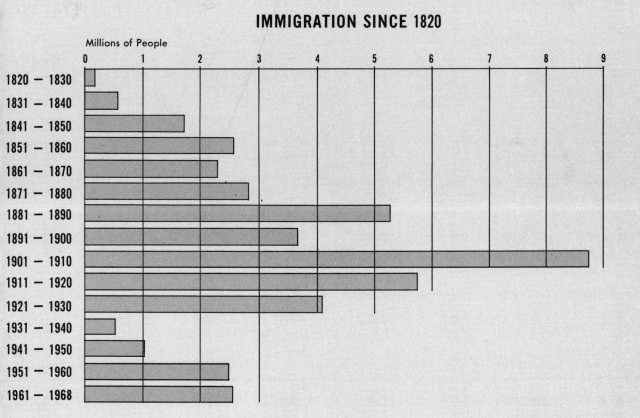

IMMIGRATION SINCE 1820

Millions of People

Since 1820, about forty-five million immigrants have settled in the United States. During the 1800's, most immigrants came from Germany, Ireland, and other parts of northern and western Europe. About 1890, however, large numbers of Italians, Russians, and other people from southern and eastern Europe began coming here. Immigration decreased sharply after 1917, mainly as the result of various laws passed by the United States Congress. Quotas were established limiting the number of immigrants who could come from certain countries. In 1965, however, Congress voted to revise this quota system. (See pages 192 and 193.)

more than one and one-half million people left their homes in Ireland and moved to America. Many came to avoid a widespread famine that occurred in Ireland during this period. This famine resulted mainly from a blight* that struck potato crops in the 1840's. Since the potato was the main food of the Irish people, the blight caused terrible hardship and suffering.

A steady stream of German immigrants came to America during the second half of the nineteenth century. Political discontent caused much of this German migration, especially in the 1850's and 1880's. Crop failures also caused many Germans to migrate to the United States. Some of the German immigrants had saved enough money to buy farmland. These people generally moved farther west, where more land was available. Many Germans settled in the towns and cities of the Northeast, however.

In addition to the large number of immigrants from Ireland and Germany, people came to America from many other parts of the world. They came from England as they always had. They also came from Sweden, Norway, Finland, and the Netherlands. After the Civil War, many French Canadians also came to the United States. Most of them settled in New England.

Altogether, more than twenty million immigrants came to America between

Immigrants arriving in the Northeast. Between 1820 and 1900, more than twenty million immigrants came to the United States. Most of these people entered our country through ports in the Northeast. Many immigrants were poor, and were seeking a better way of life.

A foreign quarter of New York City, about 1900. In many large cities, immigrants of the same nationality lived close together, speaking their native language and following their own customs.

1820 and 1900. Most of these people entered our country through the great port cities of the Northeast. Large numbers of these immigrants found jobs in the cities where they landed. Some moved on to other parts of the Northeast or to other regions of our country.

Immigration in the twentieth century. During the first ten years of the twentieth century, almost nine million immigrants came to the United States. (See chart on page 187.) By that time immigration from the countries of northern and western Europe was decreasing. More people were coming from southern and eastern Europe. Each year, thousands of Italians, Poles, Greeks, Russians, Jews, and Czechs turned their backs on Europe and came to America. Most of these immigrants became industrial workers in the great cities of the Northeast and the Midwest. Some found jobs in the coal mines of West Virginia and western Pennsylvania.

Many people feared that our country would become less "American" if we continued to allow so many immigrants to come here. Most immigrants, these people said, would never adopt American ways. In many cities, immigrants of different nationalities lived in separate sections. The people in each little community spoke their native language instead of English, and followed the customs they had brought with

189

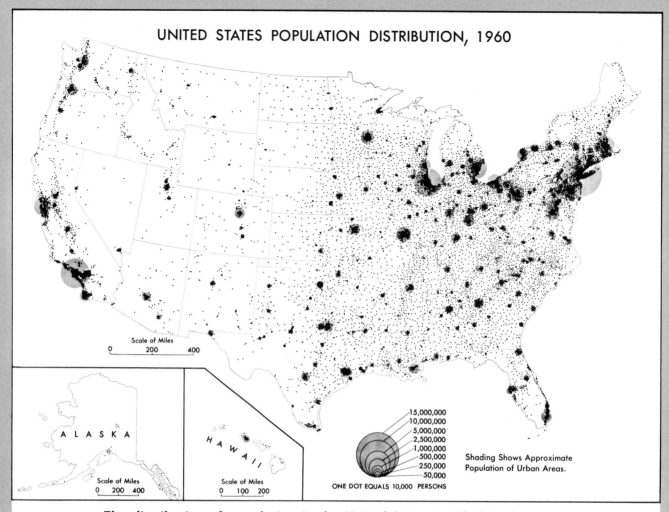

UNITED STATES POPULATION DISTRIBUTION, 1960

Scale of Miles
0 200 400

ALASKA

Scale of Miles
0 200 400

HAWAII

Scale of Miles
0 100 200

15,000,000
10,000,000
5,000,000
2,500,000
1,000,000
500,000
250,000
50,000

ONE DOT EQUALS 10,000 PERSONS

Shading Shows Approximate
Population of Urban Areas.

The distribution of population in the United States in 1960 is shown on this map. The Northeast is the most densely populated part of our country. Twenty-nine cities in this region have populations of 100,000 or over.

Exploring Population

The people of the United States. The map on this page shows where the people of the United States live. Each tiny black dot stands for ten thousand persons. On some parts of the map, the dots are far apart. These are thinly populated areas such as farmlands, deserts, or mountains. On other parts of the map, the dots are closer together. These areas are more densely populated.

In many places on the map, the dots are so close together that they form irregular black spots. These spots show the location of densely populated communities such as cities and towns. The gray circles indicate the approximate number of people who live in each urban area that has a population of more than fifty thousand.

In 1960, about 180 million people lived in the United States. By 1970, this number had grown to more than 205 million. The general pattern of distribution has not greatly changed, however. The Northeast is still the most densely populated part of our country. (Compare map above with map on page 21.) About one fourth of the population of the United States lives in this region. In recent years, however, many people have been moving to the West. California now has the largest population of any state in our country.

The world's population is increasing rapidly. Today there are more than three and one-half billion people in the world. This is more than four times the population of the world in the year 1800. One reason for this increase in population is that more and more babies are being born. Also, people generally are living longer. This is mainly because of improvements in medical care and sanitation. In addition, more and better food is available.

The number of people in the world is still growing rapidly. At the present rate, the world's population will double every thirty-five years. In general, population is increasing most rapidly in those parts of the world where there is little industry and the standard* of living is low. Many countries such as China and India are barely able to feed their own people. These nations are faced with the problem of providing a better life for their present populations. They must also plan ahead for the even larger populations they will undoubtedly have in the future.

The distribution of the world's population. If all the world's three and one-half billion people were evenly distributed over the earth, there would be more than sixty people to each square mile of land. The map below shows that this is not the case, however. Much of the world's population is crowded into four main areas. The three most heavily populated areas are eastern Asia, southern Asia, and Europe. The fourth area of dense population is the eastern half of the conterminous* United States. Although the population density of the United States as a whole is only about fifty-five, some urban areas along the Atlantic coast have an average of more than one thousand persons per square mile.

All four of the world's most heavily populated areas have land and climate that are well suited to farming. Europe and the eastern part of the United States, however, have much more industry than the other two. In general, the people in these areas also enjoy a much higher standard of living.

*See Glossary

The distribution of the world's population is shown on the map below. The four most heavily populated parts of the world are eastern Asia, southern Asia, Europe, and the eastern half of the conterminous United States. These areas all have land and climate well suited to farming.

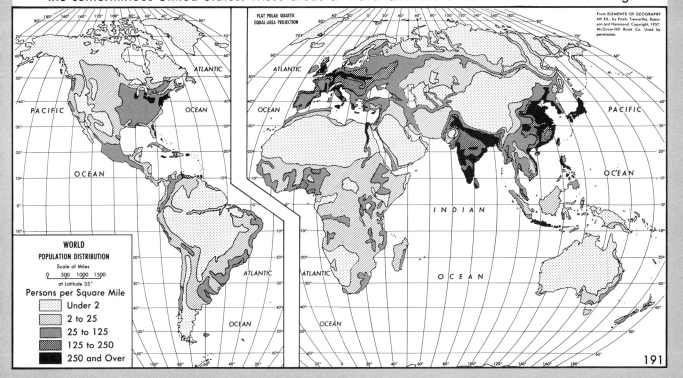

WORLD
POPULATION DISTRIBUTION
Scale of Miles
0   500   1000   1500
at Latitude 35°
Persons per Square Mile
Under 2
2 to 25
25 to 125
125 to 250
250 and Over

From ELEMENTS OF GEOGRAPHY 4th Ed., by Finch, Trewartha, Robinson and Hammond. Copyright, 1957. McGraw-Hill Book Co. Used by permission.

191

them from Europe. Many Americans had forgotten that their own forefathers had come to America from other lands. They failed to realize that without the labor, skills, and ideas of immigrants, the United States could never have become such a large and prosperous nation.

Mainly as a result of such attitudes, Congress passed several laws to restrict immigration. One of these laws, passed in 1917, kept adults who could not read or write from coming to the United States. Laws passed in the 1920's established immigration quotas,* limiting the number of people who could come to the United States from each country in a single year. These quotas favored immigration from the countries of northern and western Europe. No limit was placed on the number of people who could come from the countries of the Western Hemisphere.

These laws caused a sharp decrease in immigration, especially from Europe. (See chart on page 187.) Since 1920, more immigrants have come to the United States from Canada than from any other country. After World War II, many displaced* persons and refugees from Europe and Asia were permitted to settle in the United States, even though the quotas had been filled.

Congress has recently revised the old quota system. Today, immigrants from

Immigrants becoming United States citizens. During this century, immigrants have come to the United States from many parts of the world. Today, three out of every ten people in the Northeast are either foreign born or have at least one foreign-born parent.

Children playing in Harlem. This part of New York City is made up largely of Negroes and Latin Americans. Since World War II, many Negroes from the South and Spanish-speaking people from Puerto Rico have moved to the Northeast. More than two million have come to New York City.

the countries in northern and western Europe and the Western Hemisphere are no longer given preference over people from other countries.

Americans move into the Northeast from other areas. Although immigration from Europe declined after 1920, the great industrial cities of the Northeast continued to grow. Many farm workers left rural areas to take the factory jobs that were available in the cities. Thousands of Negroes moved from the South to New York and other cities of the Northeast, hoping to find work in industry. In the late 1930's, Spanish-speaking Americans from the island of Puerto Rico* also began to move into

the cities of the Northeast. Since World War II, more than two million Negroes and Puerto Ricans have moved into New York City.

Who lives in the Northeast today? As we have seen, people have been coming to the Northeast from other places for hundreds of years. Today, three out of every ten persons in the Northeast are either foreign born or have at least one foreign-born parent. These people are said to be of foreign stock. The largest group of people of foreign stock in the Northeast is made up of Italians. The next largest groups are the Poles, Canadians, Germans, and Russians.

More than nine tenths of the people of the Northeast are white. Almost all the rest are Negroes. Fewer than one out of every one thousand people in the Northeast belong to other races. A total of about 100,000 people of Asian descent live here. These people are mainly Chinese, Japanese, or Filipino. There are also about 30,000 American Indians living in the Northeast.

Every major religion may be found among the people of the Northeast. Although there are more Protestants than Catholics, Roman Catholics make up the largest single religious group. The Eastern Orthodox churches, which are similar to the Roman Catholic Church, also have many members. Among the leading Protestant denominations are the Methodist, the Presbyterian, and the Baptist.

Another large religious group in the Northeast is made up of Jews. There are hundreds of Jewish congregations in this region, especially in New York and other large cities. In addition, a few people of other faiths such as Islam and Buddhism live in the Northeast, mainly in the cities.

The people of the Northeast are Americans all. Life in the Northeast, as in all of America, is more interesting because of the variety of races, religions, and nationalities that are represented among the people. Each group, in its own way, has had an influence on the culture of our country.

People of almost every different group in the Northeast have made important contributions to American life. For example, Andrew Carnegie, an immigrant from Scotland, helped to develop America's steel industry. Gian-Carlo Menotti, who came to the Northeast from Italy, is a world-famous composer. One of America's finest singers, Marian Anderson, is a Negro who was born in Philadelphia. Irving Berlin, a Jew who has written many of America's most popular songs, was born in Russia. The German-born scientist Albert Einstein was also a Jew. John F. Kennedy, whose grandparents came from Ireland, was our first Roman Catholic president. John L. Sullivan, one of America's early world boxing champions, was also of Irish descent.

The people of the Northeast, through their labor, their skills, and their talents, have all helped to make the United States the strong and prosperous country it is today. Whatever their race, religion, or national origin, the people of the Northeast have one very important thing in common. They are all Americans.

A Jewish religious observance. People of every major world religion live in the Northeast.

194

Marian Anderson, an outstanding singer, is one of many Negroes from the Northeast who have made important contributions to American life. Life in our country is more interesting because of the variety of races, religions, and nationalities that are represented among the people.

Practice Your Research Skills

Do research to find as many facts as you can that support or explain each of the following statements:

1. Few immigrants came to the United States right after the Revolutionary War.
2. More than twenty million immigrants came to our country between 1820 and 1900.
3. In the last fifty years, there has been a decrease in immigration from countries outside the Western Hemisphere.
4. People of many different races, religions, and national origins make their homes in the Northeast.
5. People of the Northeast have made important contributions to American life.

Explore Immigration in a Discussion

Some countries allow people of any nationality and religion to settle there. Other countries have very severe restrictions. Recently, the immigration laws of the United States have undergone changes that will make it easier for people to enter our country. As a class, discuss the following question:

Should a country restrict immigration?

To prepare for your discussion, do some careful reading and thinking about this question. Make notes of information you find that will help you support your opinion. Pages 347-351 contain suggestions that will be helpful in locating and evaluating information.

195

Boston, Massachusetts, is part of a long chain of cities, towns, and suburbs that extends along the Atlantic coast of our country from southern New Hampshire into northern Virginia. This densely populated part of the Northeast is known as Megalopolis, or the "super city."

13 Great Cities

A Problem To Solve

In the Northeast, as in other regions of our country, urban areas have been growing rapidly in recent years. **Why have so many people been moving from rural to urban areas?** You will need to make several hypotheses to solve this problem. In forming your hypotheses, you will need to consider each of the following:

a. the basic human needs that all people have

b. how cities help people to meet these needs

See TO THE STUDENT, pages 8-10.

The Northeast is a region of great cities. If you were to go by train from Washington, D.C., to Boston, Massachusetts, you would travel through an almost unbroken series of cities, towns, and suburbs. Although you would see patches of open countryside and farmland from time to time, you would sometimes find it difficult to tell where one city ends and another begins.

Main Cities of the Northeast

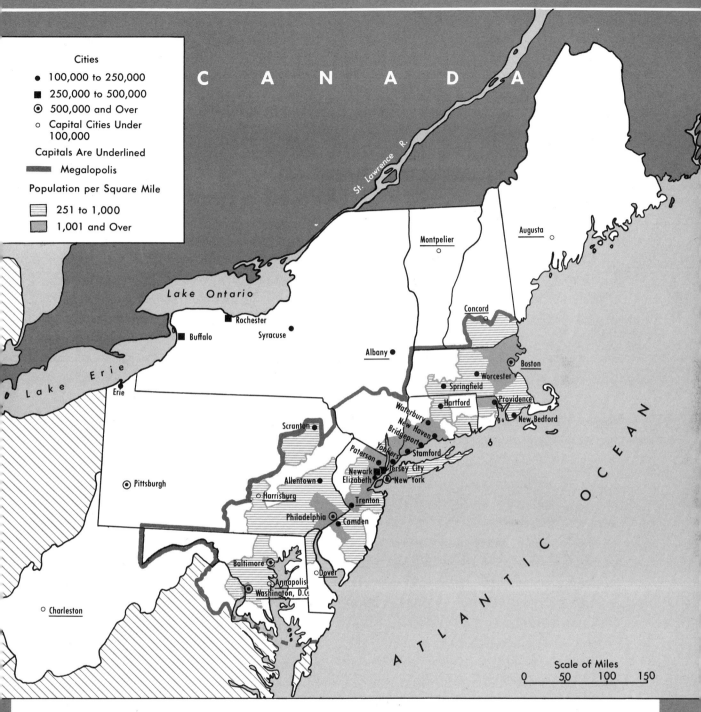

The map above shows the main cities of the Northeast. It includes all cities that have a population of 100,000 or more. All capitals are also shown, including those with a population of less than 100,000.

The heavy dark line on the map indicates the border of Megalopolis — the "super city." (See page 198.) Almost forty million people live in this area. The map shows that many parts of Megalopolis have a population density of at least 250 persons per square mile

and others more than 1,000. In the section of New York City called Manhattan, the density is nearly 74,000 persons per square mile. By comparison, the population density of the United States as a whole is only about 55 persons per square mile.

Six cities in the Northeast have populations of 500,000 or more. By comparing this map with the chart on page 201, you will see that each of these cities is the center of a great metropolitan area.

197

The entire area along the Atlantic coast from southern New Hampshire into northern Virginia appears to be a single immense city. For this reason, this area has been called Megalopolis, or the "super city." (See feature on page 197.) Several of the largest metropolitan* areas in the Northeast form part of the super city. In addition to these great metropolitan areas, there are many smaller urban areas in Megalopolis.

There are also large cities in other parts of the Northeast. The Pittsburgh and Buffalo metropolitan areas each have populations of more than one million. There are also several large cities on the Hudson-Mohawk Lowland in New York State. (See map on page 301.)

The Northeast has not always been a region of great cities. Three hundred years ago, most of the region was a forested wilderness. Only along the coast and in some of the river valleys were there small towns and settlements. Today four out of every five people in this region live in cities or small towns. Let us learn how the Northeast became a region of great cities.

How Cities Grew Up in the Northeast

Cities do not grow up in a certain place by accident. There are always reasons for their development. To understand why the Northeast has developed into a region of great cities, we need to know about the history of some of these cities.

Many early settlements were made along the coast or in river valleys. Many of the Europeans who came to the Northeast in early colonial days settled along bays and inlets on the Atlantic coast. Some of these settlers turned to the sea for their living. (See pages 68 and 69.) They became shipbuilders, sailors, and fishermen. Many of the early settlements along the coast became seaports. Some ships sailed from these ports to the nearby fishing grounds in the Atlantic. Others made long voyages to trade with Europe and the West Indies. This trade helped the seacoast towns to grow. Even before the Revolutionary War, seaports such as Boston, New York, and Philadelphia had become important cities.

Some early settlements were made in the river valleys of the Northeast. Since there were no roads through the dense forests, the early settlers usually traveled by river. They found some sites along the rivers favorable for starting settlements. For example, Albany, New York, started as a fur-trading post on the west bank of the Hudson River. Pittsburgh, in western Pennsylvania,

*See Glossary

Build Your Vocabulary

commute   finance   New York Metropolitan Region   borough

Megalopolis   human needs   central city   metropolitan area   suburbs

also began as a trading post. It grew up at the point where the Allegheny and Monongahela rivers flow together to form the Ohio River.

Industrial cities develop in the Northeast. As a result of the Industrial Revolution (see pages 90 and 91), many of the first settlements in the Northeast became important manufacturing cities. In the early 1800's, textile mills and other factories were established in this region. Many of these were started in port cities. Here, there were merchants and shipowners who had money to invest in factories. Also, most of the people lived near the coast. The large population here provided workers for factories and customers for manufactured goods.

Some industrial cities grew up around factories located near waterfalls. The force of falling water was used to run machines in certain types of factories, such as gristmills* and textile mills. Lowell, in Massachusetts, Pawtucket, in Rhode Island, and many other industrial cities in New England grew up near waterfalls.

Good transportation routes helped cities to grow. Some cities in the Northeast benefited from good transportation routes. From three of the region's largest cities — New York, Philadelphia, and Baltimore — natural passageways led through the Appalachian Highlands. In the 1800's, roads, canals, and railroads were built through these passageways.

Many people from the Northeast moved westward along these transportation routes. They established farms and settlements in the lands beyond the mountains. A brisk trade began between

HOW PEOPLE MEET THEIR NEEDS IN CITIES

The world's urban areas are growing larger. Today, throughout the world, huge numbers of people are moving from rural areas into urban areas. As a result, the proportion of the population living in urban areas is steadily increasing. In the United States, for example, more than two thirds of the people now live in or near large cities. All of the world's urban areas are growing rapidly. They will continue to grow as long as people feel they can meet their needs more easily and more satisfactorily in urban areas than in rural areas.

What are the basic human needs? All human beings have certain basic needs that are almost exactly the same, whatever their race, national origin, or religion may be. There are three kinds of basic human needs. (1) Physical needs are so important that a person may become seriously ill or die if these needs are not met. For example, you must have air to breathe, food to eat, and protection from extremes of heat and cold. (2) Every person also has social needs. You need to feel that you belong to a group of people, such as your family, who respect you and whom you respect. You also need important goals to work for and an opportunity to develop and use your abilities. (3) Every human being also needs faith. You may be sustained by different kinds of faith, such as faith that your life will be happy and useful, faith in the orderliness of the universe, or faith in God.

Cities provide many opportunities for people to meet their needs. Most people who live in cities have many opportunities to satisfy their needs. The variety of jobs available makes it fairly easy for people to earn enough money to meet their physical needs. Workers are able to use the money they earn to buy food, clothing, and shelter for themselves and their families.

People in cities may satisfy their social needs in various ways. Most large cities provide many opportunities for young people and adults to continue their education as long as they wish. Clubs and other organizations give people a chance to work together toward important goals, such as neighborhood improvement. People who live in cities also have many opportunities to express their faith in God by worshiping with others who share their beliefs.

The Erie Canal. In the 1800's, people in the Northeast built canals, roads, and railroads westward. Trade helped some of the settlements along these routes, such as Buffalo and Rochester, to grow into important cities. Trade also helped New York and other coastal cities to grow.

the manufacturing cities near the coast and farming communities in the interior. This trade helped the coastal cities to grow. It also helped settlements along the transportation routes to develop rapidly. For example, the small settlements of Buffalo, Rochester, and Syracuse became important cities after the Erie Canal was finished. (See pages 99 and 100.)

Immigrants and people from rural areas came to the cities. About the middle of the 1800's, the cities of the Northeast began to grow very rapidly. Between 1840 and 1870, Philadelphia and Boston

more than tripled in population. New York grew even more rapidly. By 1900, it had become the second largest city in the world. Only London, England, was larger.

There were several reasons for the rapid growth of cities during this period. One reason was the great increase in the number of immigrants coming to the United States. Between 1850 and 1900, more than sixteen and one-half million people left their homes in other lands to come to this country. Most of the immigrants entered the United States through ports on the Atlantic coast.

Large numbers of these immigrants settled in the cities of the Northeast, where many jobs were available.

During this same period, thousands of people came to the cities of the Northeast from rural areas. Fewer people were needed on the farms as a result of great changes that were taking place in agriculture during this period. (See page 160.) At the same time, industry was growing rapidly in the cities of the Northeast. Many of the people who left the farms came to the cities to find work in factories.

The Great Cities Today

Cities have continued to attract many people during the twentieth century. During the present century, the cities of the Northeast have continued to grow. Between 1900 and 1920, more than fourteen million immigrants came to this country. In the 1920's, however, laws were passed that greatly limited the number of people who could enter the United States from certain foreign countries. Partly as a result of these laws, fewer immigrants came to this country. (See Chapter 12.)

People from other parts of the United States have also been coming to the cities of the Northeast. The excitement of big-city life is an attraction to many young people living in smaller cities or in rural areas. Large cities also offer wider job opportunities. Many people move to the cities in search of a career in business or the arts. Some families move to urban areas because they feel their children have a better chance to receive a good education there.

In recent years, many Negroes from the South and Spanish-speaking Americans from the island of Puerto Rico have moved to New York and other cities in the Northeast. Most of these people are poor and have come to the cities in search of a better life. Many Negroes and Puerto Ricans are unskilled and uneducated, and it is difficult for them to find jobs. Often these people are forced to live in crowded slums.

Many people are moving from the central cities to the suburbs. Although people are still coming to the great cities of the Northeast, fewer people live in the

NINE METROPOLITAN AREAS		
Metropolitan Area	Population of Entire Area	Population of Central City (or Cities)
New York	11,410,000	8,110,000
Philadelphia	4,690,000	2,050,000
Boston	2,740,000	638,000
Pittsburgh	2,380,000	546,000
Washington	2,620,000	850,000
Baltimore	1,980,000	897,000
Newark	1,860,000	402,000
Buffalo	1,320,000	482,000
Paterson-Clifton-Passaic	1,320,000	280,000

The metropolitan* areas shown above are the largest in the Northeast. Each has a population of more than one million. The central cities are generally much smaller. Today the metropolitan areas are growing in population, but most of the central cities are declining.
*See Glossary

EDUCATION IN THE NORTHEAST

Every child in the United States has an opportunity to obtain an education in our public schools. All of the states provide free elementary and secondary schools, which are supported by state and local taxes and governed by local school boards. State laws require all children to attend school, generally until they are sixteen. However, parents may send their children to private schools instead of public schools, if they prefer to do so.

State and local taxes may also be used to support colleges and special schools. For example, many state and community colleges are largely tax supported. Students who wish to continue their education beyond high school may attend such colleges free or at a reasonable cost. Most states also provide various special institutions, such as schools for the handicapped.

The Northeast has played an important part in the history of American education. Many significant events in the history of American education have occurred in the Northeast. During colonial days, most of the schools and colleges in America were run by churches or other private organizations. As early as 1647, however, Massachusetts passed a law that required every town of more than fifty families to establish an elementary school and every town of more than one hundred families to establish a secondary school. Soon, other New England colonies passed similar laws. The schools established under these laws were not much like our present-day public schools, for their main purpose was to teach religion. However, they mark the beginning of the idea that schools should be the concern of the local community.

Public education did not really get started in America until the end of the colonial period. Pennsylvania, Vermont, and Massachusetts were among the first states to include provisions for education in their constitutions. For some time, however, none of the states made any attempt to carry out such provisions. Finally, in 1837, Massachusetts established the first state board of education, with Horace Mann* as secretary. By the end of the nineteenth century, the people of America had accepted the idea of paying taxes to support public education through high school.

Many opportunities for education are available in the Northeast. Today, the Northeast has many fine schools and colleges. About thirteen and one-half million young people in this region attend elementary and secondary schools. Opportunities for higher education are available in more than seven hundred colleges and universities. In addition, there are many business colleges, vocational institutes, and other special schools.

Excellent opportunities for education have helped some of the cities in the Northeast become important cultural centers. Boston, for example, is famous for its many fine schools, museums, and libraries. More than thirty colleges and universities are located within fifty miles of downtown Boston. One of the best known is Harvard,* which is America's oldest institution of higher learning. Another is the Massachusetts Institute of Technology.

*See Glossary

A view of Harvard University, in Cambridge, Massachusetts. Harvard was founded in 1636.

central cities today than fifteen years ago. In recent years, many people have left the crowded cities and moved to homes in the suburbs. As a result, the population of the central cities is declining. However, the metropolitan areas continue to grow in population.

There are several reasons for the movement from the cities to the suburbs. Many factories have been built in the suburbs. Industries that require large, sprawling buildings, such as aircraft factories, steel mills, and oil refineries, cannot afford the high cost of land in the central cities. Therefore, they build their plants in less-crowded areas, outside the cities. Many people have moved to the suburbs to be near the factories where they work.

Many people who work in the crowded central cities prefer to make their homes in the suburbs. Before automobiles, buses, and subways became available, this was difficult to do. People who worked in the cities had to live close to the offices, stores, and factories where they worked. Today, however, people can commute* between their homes in the suburbs and their places of work in the central cities.

In this chapter you have learned how settlements started in the Northeast. You have also learned how some of these settlements grew to be the great cities of today. To learn more about the great cities of the Northeast, we shall make a case* study of the largest city of all — New York.

New York City

A visit to New York. We are flying northward along the coast of New Jersey. Soon we see the tall buildings of a great city. This is New York. Below us, we see a wide harbor. Miles of docks line the waterfront, and in the harbor we see many ships of all kinds. Most of the city is located on islands. On one small island in the harbor stands the Statue of Liberty. As far as we can see, the land is covered with tall buildings, factories, and homes.

New York is located in the southeastern part of New York State, at the mouth of the Hudson River. Across the Hudson from New York City is New Jersey. Here are several densely populated cities. They are part of the New York Metropolitan Region. (See page 205.)

New York is our country's largest city. New York, with a population of more than eight million, is the largest city in the United States. In addition to the people who live in the central city, millions of others live in cities and suburbs close to New York, such as Yonkers. More people live in the New York Metropolitan Region than in any other urban area in the world.

A city of trade, finance, and manufacturing. New York is the world's wealthiest city. No other city compares with it as a center of trade, finance, and manufacturing.

Trade. New York is our country's greatest seaport. Each year, about 21,000 ships carrying goods and passengers enter and leave New York Harbor.

New York is our country's largest city. Most of New York is located on islands. (Compare this photograph with the lower map on the opposite page.) New York is the largest seaport and most important manufacturing city in the United States. It is also the financial capital of the world.

Much of the cargo entering New York is shipped to other parts of the country. Goods produced in the Northeast and other regions of the nation are shipped to all parts of the world through New York's port. In addition, most of the freight that is shipped by air between the United States and other countries passes through New York's John F. Kennedy International Airport.

More wholesale* and retail* trade is carried on in New York than in any city in our country. Wholesale firms in New York employ more than 300,000 people. These companies sell goods to custom-ers throughout the United States and in many foreign countries. The value of products sold by wholesale firms in New York every year is more than fifty billion dollars. This makes up more than one seventh of the wholesale trade of our entire country.

There are more than 75,000 retail stores in New York City. They sell food, clothing, furniture, and hundreds of other products needed by people in the city. Some of the country's largest department stores, such as Macy's and Gimbels, are located in New York. Along Fifth Avenue in Manhattan* are

New York Metropolitan Region

New York is the largest city in the United States. More than eight million people live here. As the map below shows, the city is made up of five separate sections called boroughs. These are Manhattan, Brooklyn, Queens, the Bronx, and Richmond.

New York is the central city of a huge urban area called the New York Metropolitan Region. (See map at right.) This region includes the New York metropolitan* area as well as other urban areas nearby. Some of these are located in New York State, while others are in New Jersey and Connecticut. Many of the people who live in the New York Metropolitan Region work in the central city. Others come to the city frequently for shopping or entertainment. About sixteen million people make their homes in the New York Metropolitan Region. More people live here than in any other urban area in the world.

*See Glossary

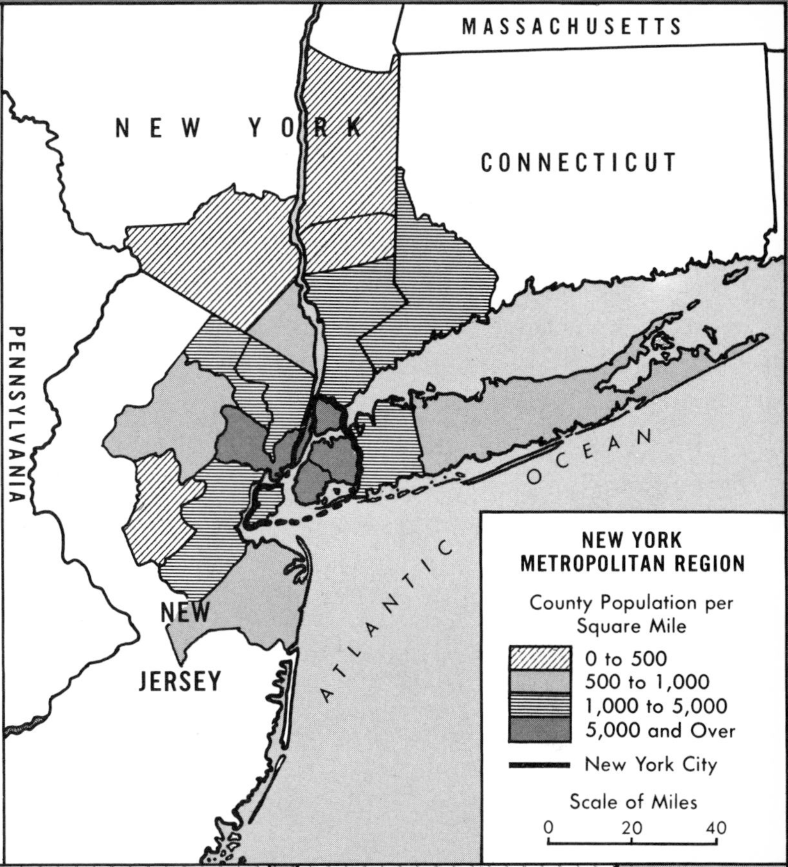

NEW YORK METROPOLITAN REGION

County Population per Square Mile

- 0 to 500
- 500 to 1,000
- 1,000 to 5,000
- 5,000 and Over
- ——— New York City

Scale of Miles
0   20   40

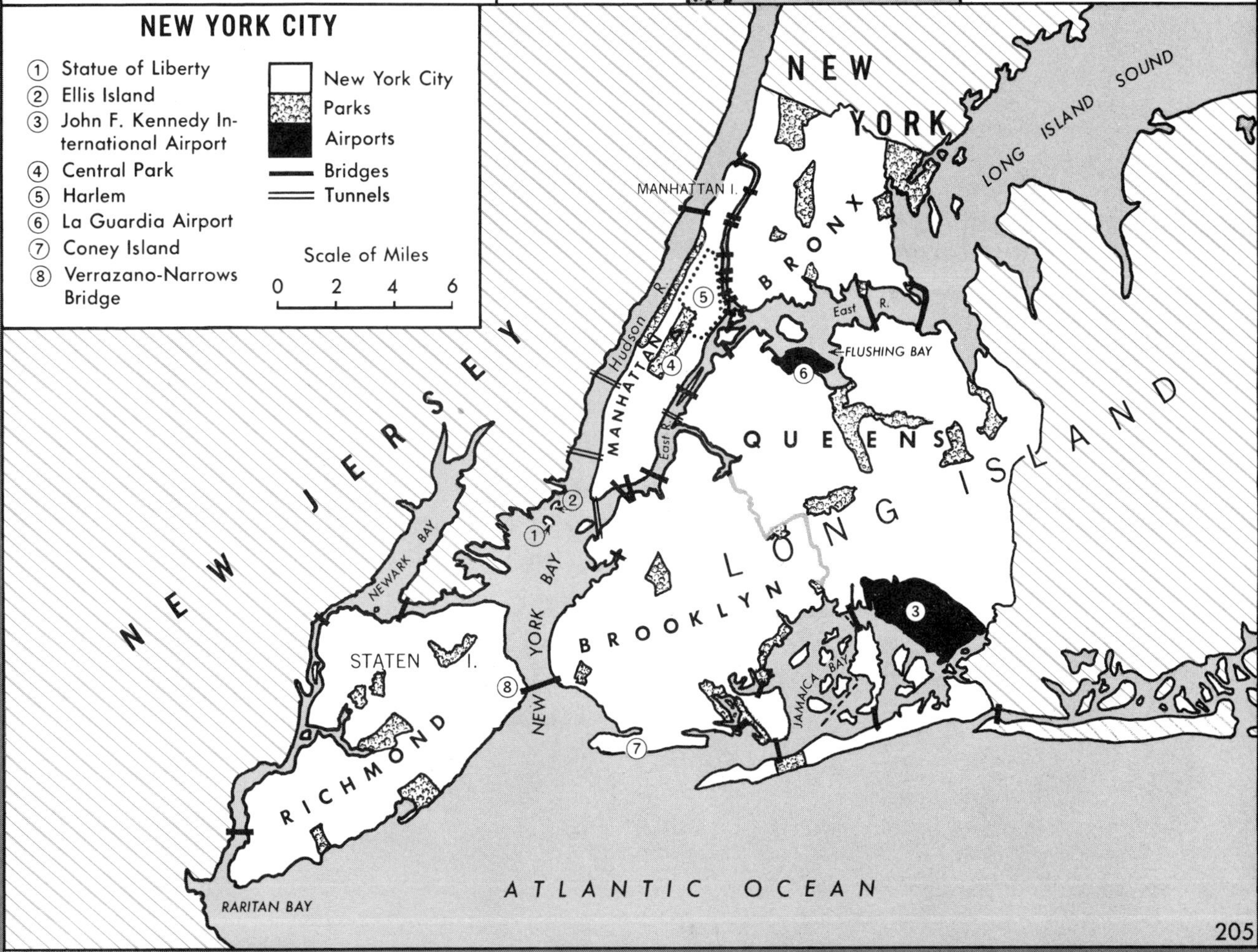

MASSACHUSETTS

NEW YORK

CONNECTICUT

PENNSYLVANIA

NEW JERSEY

ATLANTIC OCEAN

NEW YORK CITY

1. Statue of Liberty
2. Ellis Island
3. John F. Kennedy International Airport
4. Central Park
5. Harlem
6. La Guardia Airport
7. Coney Island
8. Verrazano-Narrows Bridge

- New York City
- Parks
- Airports
- ——— Bridges
- ═══ Tunnels

Scale of Miles
0   2   4   6

NEW YORK

LONG ISLAND SOUND

MANHATTAN I.

BRONX

East R.

FLUSHING BAY

QUEENS

LONG ISLAND

Hudson R.

NEW JERSEY

NEWARK BAY

NEW YORK BAY

STATEN I.

RICHMOND

BROOKLYN

JAMAICA BAY

ATLANTIC OCEAN

RARITAN BAY

many fine clothing stores and other shops. People from hundreds of miles away come to shop in stores in New York City.

Finance. New York is the financial capital of the world. Some of the nation's largest banks, trust* companies, and insurance companies are located here. They provide money for businesses throughout our country and in many foreign countries as well. Many of the banks and insurance companies are located in Manhattan, on or near Wall Street. This part of the city is known as the financial district. The country's two leading stock exchanges are also located here. At these exchanges, stocks* and bonds* of our country's largest corporations are traded each day.

Manufacturing. Most people who visit New York do not realize that it is a great manufacturing city. They see few tall smokestacks or sprawling factories such as they would see if they visited Detroit, Pittsburgh, or other industrial cities. Yet New York earns more money from manufacturing than any other city in the world. Because of the high cost of land in the city, New York specializes in industries that do not require a large amount of factory space. Printing and publishing and the manufacture of clothing are the city's leading industries.

How New York became a great city. As you have learned, there are several reasons why great cities have grown up in the Northeast. New York has enjoyed a combination of advantages that help a city to grow. It has an excellent harbor on the Atlantic coast. Most European immigrants coming to the United States entered the country through New York. Many of them settled here and took jobs in industry. Some of them started businesses that helped the city to grow. Others helped build New York's buildings, streets, subways, and bridges.

New York has enjoyed another natural advantage. The Hudson-Mohawk Lowland extends from New York City to central New York. This passageway provides an excellent route through the Appalachian Highlands. New York's location has made it a natural center for trade not only with Europe but also with cities and farming districts in the interior of our country.

New York is a city of five boroughs. The central city of New York is made up of five separate sections called boroughs. These are Manhattan, Brooklyn, Queens, the Bronx, and Richmond. (See bottom map on page 205.)

Manhattan is the smallest borough in area, but in many ways it is the most

New York's garment district produces dresses, coats, and other clothing. The city specializes in industries that do not require a large amount of factory space.

important. Nearly all of this borough is located on a small island, which is also called Manhattan. This island is only about two and one-half miles wide and thirteen miles long. Yet, more than one and one-half million people live here. Most of New York City's trade and manufacturing are carried on in this borough.

Because Manhattan is so crowded, land here is very expensive. As a result, many buildings have been built high into the sky. The world's tallest buildings are located in Manhattan. People from other boroughs and from nearby areas of New York State, New Jersey, and Connecticut work in Manhattan's giant skyscrapers.

Manhattan is a great industrial center. Most of the city's publishing and clothing firms are located in this borough. In addition, many large national corporations have their main offices in the skyscrapers of Manhattan. Businessmen here direct the operations of oil companies, railroads, steel mills, and thousands of other great industries. In Manhattan, they are close to banks, advertising agencies, law firms, and other organizations that are helpful to them in running their businesses.

Manhattan is the cultural center of our nation. It is the home of the country's leading publishers of books and magazines. Radio and television networks broadcast from studios in Manhattan to all parts of the United States. If you were to visit New York, you might enjoy seeing some of the world's great works of art. In Manhattan, you could visit the Metropolitan Museum, the Museum of Modern Art, and several other famous art galleries. To enjoy

Manhattan skyline. In the foreground is the headquarters of the United Nations. Many skyscrapers have been built in Manhattan because land here is so scarce and expensive.

good music, you could go to the opera or ballet, or listen to a concert by one of the world's great symphony orchestras. You could also see many plays and musicals. Because of the many cultural activities in Manhattan, young people seeking a career in writing, painting, music, or the theater come here from all parts of the country.

The headquarters of the United Nations is located in Manhattan. (See picture on this page.) Here, representatives from most of the world's nations meet to discuss world problems.

Some of the people who live in Manhattan are very wealthy, but others live in poverty. On the east side of midtown Manhattan are some of the most expensive apartments and homes in the country. However, in other parts of the borough, people live in crowded slums.

One of the worst slums is in a section of Manhattan called Harlem. (See map on page 205.) Here, hundreds of thousands of people, mostly Negroes and Latin Americans, are crowded into a slum area of only three and one-half square miles. In Chapter 14, you can learn about the problems of slums in the great cities.

Brooklyn is located on the western end of Long Island. (See map on page 205.) It is connected to Manhattan by several bridges and tunnels. More people live in Brooklyn than in any other borough. This borough was a separate city until 1898, when it became part of New York. If Brooklyn were a separate city today, it would be the fourth largest in the country. Many of the people who live here work in Manhattan.

The people of Brooklyn live in more than twenty different neighborhoods. These neighborhoods were once separate villages. Today, each neighborhood is like a small city with its own shopping and business district. Some neighborhoods, such as Brooklyn Heights and Bay Ridge, have attractive homes and quiet, treelined streets. The most heavily populated neighborhood in Brooklyn is Bedford-Stuyvesant. Here, thousands of people live in crowded slums. However, efforts are now being made to improve housing in this area.

Brooklyn is one of our country's largest shipping and manufacturing centers. Hundreds of docks, factories, and warehouses line the waterfront. Ships bring large quantities of grain, coffee, cocoa beans, and raw* sugar to processing plants along the waterfront. Food processing is one of Brooklyn's leading industries. Other important industries here include the manufacture of textiles, toys, paint, and machinery. Two of the country's largest shipyards are also located in Brooklyn.

Queens is the largest borough in area. It is more than five times as large as Manhattan, but its population is only slightly larger. Like Brooklyn, Queens is located on Long Island. (See map on page 205.)

Queens grew rapidly in the first part of the twentieth century. In 1900, this borough was made up mainly of scattered towns and villages separated by stretches of farmland and open countryside. In the 1920's, subways were built connecting Queens with other boroughs. After this cheap means of transportation became available, many people moved from crowded sections in other boroughs into new homes and apartments in Queens.

Today, almost two million people live in Queens. Many of them work in Manhattan. Some are employed in stores, factories, and offices in commercial and industrial districts of Queens, such as Jamaica and Long Island City.

New York City's two largest airports are located in Queens. La Guardia Airport, on Flushing Bay, handles passengers and freight being carried between New York and other cities of our country. Most people who travel by air between the United States and Europe pass through John F. Kennedy International Airport at Idlewild. This is one of the largest, most modern airports in the world.

The Bronx is the only borough that is located on the mainland. (See map on page 205.) It is separated from

Manhattan Island by the narrow Harlem River. The Bronx is mainly a residential area. Many people who live here travel by subway to work in Manhattan. Some of the people in the Bronx live in expensive apartment houses overlooking the Hudson River. However, in the southern part of the borough there are crowded slum areas.

Richmond occupies Staten Island and several smaller islands in New York Bay. This borough is located very close to New Jersey. (See map on page 205.) Only about a quarter of a million people live in Richmond. Parts of the borough are still rural. Farmers here plant crops within sight of the skyscrapers of Manhattan, across the bay. Lack of transportation has been the main reason for the fact that Richmond is thinly populated. Until recently, there were no bridges or tunnels connecting this borough with the rest of New York City. People traveled across the bay by ferry. However, in 1964, the Verrazano-Narrows Bridge was completed. (See picture at right.) This is one of

The Verrazano-Narrows Bridge extends across New York Bay. This bridge, which is one of the longest suspension bridges in the world, connects the boroughs of Brooklyn and Richmond.

the longest suspension bridges in the world. It extends across New York Bay, connecting Richmond with Brooklyn. Since the opening of this bridge, many people have begun to move to Richmond from other parts of the city.

Learn About the Northeast's Great Cities

1. What does the term Megalopolis mean?
2. What is included in the section of the Northeast that is called Megalopolis?
3. Why does New York City specialize in industries that require a small amount of factory space?
4. Name three ways in which New York City is the most important city of our country.
5. What areas are included in the New York Metropolitan Region?

Solve an Interesting Problem

The Northeast is a region of great cities. **Why have so many great cities grown up in this region?** To solve this problem, you will need to make hypotheses. (See To the Student, pages 8-10.) In forming your hypotheses, consider the following:

a. the location of early settlements in this region
b. effects of the Industrial Revolution
c. natural transportation routes in the Northeast
d. immigration to our country

Chapters 4, 5, 6, and 7, as well as this chapter, contain much useful information for solving this problem. If you wish to do outside research, refer to the suggestions on pages 347-349.

Polluted air blankets much of New York City. The cities of the Northeast face many problems, ranging from slums and unemployment to crowded streets and air pollution.

14 Problems of the Cities

A Problem To Solve

In the great cities of the Northeast, large numbers of families are living in poverty. **Why do so many people live in poverty at a time when our nation as a whole is generally prosperous?** In forming hypotheses to solve this problem, you will need to consider how the following affect people's ability to earn an adequate income:

a. automation

b. lack of education

c. physical and mental illness

d. belonging to a minority group

See TO THE STUDENT, pages 8-10.

Many city dwellers are unable to meet their basic needs. The great cities of the Northeast grew up because they helped satisfy basic human needs. (See page 199.) People moved from rural areas to the cities in order to earn a better living or to have a more interesting and enjoyable way of life. Today people are still coming to the cities of the Northeast for the same reasons.

However, there are many people living in the cities of this region who do not have a chance to satisfy some of their important needs. For example, some people lack the opportunity to develop their abilities or to accomplish worthwhile goals. Others, through no fault of their own, cannot provide adequate food, clothing, or shelter for themselves and their families.

Conditions that prevent large numbers of people from meeting their basic needs are called social problems. On the following pages, you will learn about some of the major social problems affecting city dwellers in the Northeast.

Major Social Problems

A city slum. We are taking a bus ride through one of the large cities in the Northeast. Our bus turns down a narrow street lined with tall apartment buildings that shut out most of the sunlight. The buildings on this street are run-down and shabby. Paint is peeling from the walls, and several of the buildings have broken windows. Some boys are playing in the street, which is littered with bottles and other rubbish. In a nearby alley, huge rats are scurrying between overflowing garbage cans.

Our bus driver tells us that the neighborhood we have just visited was not always in such poor condition. Many years ago, when the buildings on this street were new, this was one of the finest residential areas in the city. As the buildings grew older, however, it became harder to keep them in good repair. Several large warehouses and factories were built nearby. As a result, the neighborhood became a less pleasant place in which to live.

Gradually, most families who had enough money moved to newer, more attractive neighborhoods. People who lacked jobs or who worked for low wages usually remained here, because they could not afford better housing. They were joined by others who did not have much money. To make more money from renters, the owners of some buildings divided large apartments into smaller ones. Sometimes a family with several children moved into a single room of a run-down tenement. These buildings became more and more dilapidated,

Slums exist in all the large cities of the Northeast. Many people who live in these run-down areas suffer from poverty, disease, and discrimination.

because the owners could not or would not spend money to improve them. By this time, the neighborhood had become a slum.

There are slums in all the great cities of the Northeast. In the Northeast, as in other regions of our country, there are many neighborhoods like the one we have just visited. In New York City, for example, about one fifth of the people live in slum areas.

Most slum dwellers do not lead very pleasant or satisfying lives. Slum tenements are usually run-down, dirty, and overcrowded. They are likely to be hot and stuffy in the summertime and cold and drafty during the winter. Many of them lack running water for drinking and bathing. Fires start easily and spread quickly in these ramshackle buildings. Broken stairs and railings are also threats to the safety of slum dwellers. In addition, there are many rats and insects that carry disease germs. Altogether, it is not surprising that illness and crime flourish in such neighborhoods.

What do you think can be done to eliminate slums and prevent new slum areas from developing? Before you can offer solutions to these problems, you must know more about the people who live in the slums.

Many people live in poverty because they cannot find good jobs. As you have seen, most of the people who live in slum tenements usually do not have enough money to pay for better housing. Some of these people are unable to find steady jobs. Others have jobs that pay them very little money.

In the Northeast today, about one million persons are unemployed. Some live in places where few jobs are available, such as the coal-mining areas of Pennsylvania and West Virginia. (See pages 134 and 136.) However, large numbers of unemployed people live in cities where there are many jobs. In New York City, for example, there are thousands of jobs that are open at the present time. Yet New York City has many thousands of unemployed workers.

There are several reasons why people in the cities cannot find employment. Some are too elderly for certain jobs, or their health is too poor. Others cannot find jobs because of discrimination. (See page 215.) Probably the main reason why city people are unemployed, however, is that they lack the education or the special skills needed to hold the jobs that are available.

In the past, many jobs were open to people who did not have much education or who lacked special skills. Today, however, many jobs that used to be done by unskilled or partly skilled workers are performed by automatic machinery. Automation has greatly affected the kinds of jobs that can be obtained in our country. On the one hand, it has created many new and different

Build Your Vocabulary

discrimination   civil rights   minority groups   segregation   tenement

prejudice   pollution   Job Corps   slums   poverty   social problems

Looking for work in a large city is a disappointing experience for many people. Residents of slums are often unable to find steady employment because they lack the education or the special skills needed to hold the jobs that are available.

jobs for highly trained workers. For example, many engineers and other technical workers are needed to build the new machines and to keep them running. On the other hand, the number of jobs open to unskilled workers is steadily growing smaller. This helps to explain why so many people are unemployed in a time of prosperity.

Thousands of city dwellers are not receiving the education they need. In today's world, people need more education than ever before if they are to earn a good living. Education is also important for other reasons. Without education, people cannot fully develop their talents and abilities. They find it hard to win the respect of others or to accomplish worthwhile goals.

At the present time, many people in the Northeast are not receiving the education that would enable them to satisfy their physical and social needs. This is especially true in slum areas. Some cities spend less money on schools in poor neighborhoods. These schools are likely to be overcrowded and in poor condition. Many do not have adequate libraries or other facilities. Often there are not enough teachers.

Even if they attend good schools, most slum children have trouble gaining an education. This is because their home life has not prepared them to do schoolwork. In many cases, their parents have had little education themselves. Also, the parents may not realize the importance of education, or

213

Responsible positions are available to most people who have developed their talents and abilities. Although many people in the Northeast have not had a chance to accomplish these goals, efforts are now being made to improve their opportunities for education.

have the time to teach their children the things they must know in order to succeed in school. Many homes lack toys, books, and writing materials. Children from such homes usually know fewer words than other children do. It is not surprising that they make less progress in school, even though they may be just as intelligent as any other children.

As slum children grow older, they often become discouraged at their lack of progress in school. Some of them grow to dislike schoolwork so much that

they constantly make trouble for their teachers and the other students. As a result, an entire class may make less progress than it should.

Many young people leave school before they have gained the knowledge and the skills they need to earn a good living. In New York City, for example, about four out of every ten high school students fail to graduate. Some students drop out of school because they feel it is a waste of time. Others leave school to go to work. These young people do not realize that they must have a good education if they are to succeed in later life. On the other hand, many students who would like to continue their education beyond high school cannot afford to do so.

Physical and mental illnesses bring suffering to many people. Sickness is another problem that affects many city dwellers in the Northeast. According to government figures, about five million people in this region suffer from long-lasting illnesses or handicaps that prevent them from leading normal lives. Many are adults who can work only part of the time or not at all. Others are children who cannot attend regular schools.

The rate of sickness is particularly high in slum areas. To have good health, people need plenty of sunlight, fresh air, pure water, and wholesome food. They also need protection from contagious* diseases, such as tuberculosis and diphtheria. People who live in the slums lack most of these things. Some babies born in slum areas die because they have not received the proper care.

Thousands of people in the Northeast suffer from some form of mental illness. Experts believe that mental problems are often made worse by slum conditions, such as overcrowding, noise, and filth. Mental illness may also result from worry or from feelings of discouragement.

Many people are trapped in the "vicious circle of poverty." Large numbers of people in the great cities of the Northeast remain poor all their lives. They grow up without ever gaining the education or the special skills needed to

*See Glossary

215

PREJUDICE AND DISCRIMINATION

A serious social problem. Throughout the world, there are people who suffer because their religion, their national origin, or their race is different from that of the majority of the people in their society. An unfavorable attitude toward a person just because of the group to which he happens to belong is generally called prejudice. Often, people who are prejudiced act in ways that prevent members of minority groups from enjoying all their rights or freedoms. This is called discrimination.

Prejudice and discrimination in the United States. In our country, prejudice and discrimination prevent many people from meeting all their basic needs. Among the groups of people who are most seriously affected by prejudice and discrimination are Negroes, Jews, American Indians, Latin Americans, and people of Asian descent.

In recent years, much progress has been made toward ending certain forms of discrimination. For example, our courts have ruled that segregation* in public schools is unconstitutional.* The federal government and some of the states have passed laws to prevent discrimination in employment and housing and to end segregation in public places.

In spite of these measures, discrimination remains a serious problem throughout our country. Negroes and other minority-group members often have difficulty purchasing homes in certain sections of our cities. Because children usually attend the school nearest their home, segregation in housing has resulted in segregated schools as well.

Many people in our country are trying to solve the problem of prejudice and discrimination. Better education and laws against discrimination have helped, but much remains to be done. Progress will come faster as more people accept responsibility for solving this problem.

hold a good job. As a result, they earn little money or are unemployed. Most of them live in slums. These people may never have quite enough food, or the proper food for good health. When they become ill, they cannot afford medical care. Some develop serious illnesses that prevent them from ever holding full-time jobs. Others lose their ambition or their self-confidence. They find it easier to accept help from the government than to try to solve their own problems. These people are sometimes said to be caught in the "vicious circle of poverty."

Some minority groups suffer from prejudice and discrimination. Many of the people who live in the slums of the Northeast are Negroes or Puerto Ricans. There are several reasons for this. First, many Negroes or their parents came to the Northeast from rural areas in the South. Most of them have never had a chance to gain the knowledge or skills that are needed to obtain well-paying jobs. The rate of unemployment is twice as high among Negroes as it is among white people. Like the Negroes, many of the Puerto Ricans also came from rural areas. They, too, often lack the skills needed by modern industry.

There is another reason why so many Negroes and Puerto Ricans live in poor neighborhoods. They are the victims of prejudice and discrimination. (See feature on page 215.) Negro families often cannot buy or rent homes outside the slums even though they have enough money to pay for better housing. This is because some white people do not want to have Negroes living near them. If a Negro family moves into their neighborhood, they may try to make trouble for the newcomers. When a white homeowner moves out of the neighborhood, he may try to avoid selling his house to Negroes because he feels his neighbors would not like it.

Puerto Ricans also suffer from discrimination in housing. In some cases, this is because their skin is dark, or because they speak Spanish instead of English. Also, Puerto Ricans have customs that seem strange and "foreign" to some other Americans.

In recent years, a great change has been taking place in the cities of the Northeast. Large numbers of white people have been moving from the central cities to the suburbs. At the same time, as you have learned, thousands of Negroes and Puerto Ricans have been moving into the central cities. Today, Negroes make up about two thirds of the population of Washington, D. C. In Newark, almost one half of the people are Negroes. Philadelphia, New York, and Baltimore also have large Negro populations. At the same time, many of the suburbs that have grown up around these cities are made up almost entirely of white people.

Segregation* in housing has often resulted in segregated schools. In large cities, many Negro children attend all-Negro schools because they live in areas where there are no white children. Many other schools are attended only by white children because no Negroes live in the area.

Segregation makes it difficult for different groups of people to understand each other. If children do not have a chance to work and play with children of different races and nationalities, they may grow up with strong feelings of prejudice toward other groups. When they become adults, there is less chance that they will be able to cooperate effectively in solving common problems and achieving important goals.

Crime and violence often result from unsolved social problems. When problems such as poverty and discrimination remain unsolved, a breakdown in law and order may result. For example, the crime rate in city slums is much higher than it is in other sections. Every day, serious crimes such as murder and armed robbery take place in the slums of large cities.

There are several reasons why so many crimes are committed in slum areas. Poor people sometimes steal in order to get food, clothing, and other things they need. Many young people become involved in crime because they do not have any constructive way to spend their time. They cannot find steady jobs, and there are few opportunities for wholesome recreation in the slums. People may also turn to crime because they are unhappy with life in the slums, or because they are envious of people who are more fortunate.

The frustration felt by many people in slums because of problems such as unemployment, poor living conditions, and

Handing out leaflets at a civil-rights meeting. Many Americans have been working to end discrimination in the United States. The federal government and some of the states have passed laws to prevent segregation and to provide equal job opportunities for minority-group members.

discrimination has sometimes led to rioting. In recent years, riots have broken out in the slum areas of many cities in our country. People have set fires to stores and homes, sometimes destroying entire city blocks. Rioters have entered stores and carried away valuable merchandise. Many people have been killed or seriously injured during these riots.

Unsolved social problems are everyone's concern. All the people in our country are harmed by unsolved social problems. The crime and violence that often accompany these problems are a threat to lives and property. Also, the cost of government is higher than it would be if major social problems were solved. For example, more policemen are needed in slums than in other sections of our cities. Since many more fires break out when people live under crowded conditions, the cost of fire protection is very high in slums. Higher taxes are needed to pay for these services. Therefore, our citizens have less money to spend on themselves.

Unsolved social problems represent a great waste of human resources. People who have never had a chance to develop their abilities cannot do their full share of the nation's work. They are not able to produce the goods and services needed by themselves, their families, and other people in our country. The result is a lower standard* of living for everyone.

Solving Social Problems

The cities of the Northeast, like those in other regions of our country, are making a great effort to solve urgent social problems. They are working to eliminate slums and to find jobs for unemployed workers. They are also trying to provide greater opportunities for education and to improve the health of their citizens. Efforts are being made to end prejudice and discrimination against minority groups. If all these goals can be achieved, the cities of the Northeast will become safer and happier places in which to live.

The battle against slums. With the help of money provided by the federal government, many cities have been carrying out huge urban-renewal projects. They have been tearing down entire neighborhoods of run-down tenements, stores, and warehouses. These old structures are being replaced by modern housing, stores, and office buildings. In some cities, there are rows of up-to-date apartment houses where people can live comfortably without paying high rent.

Urban-renewal projects are transforming the appearance of many cities in the Northeast. In New York, for example, huge slum areas have been cleared away to provide low-cost housing for more than 500,000 people. Philadelphia has rebuilt much of its downtown area. Other cities, such as Pittsburgh, Baltimore, and Washington, have also replaced slum sections with new skyscrapers and apartment houses.

Although projects like these have provided better housing for hundreds of

Urban-renewal projects are transforming many northeastern cities. In some places, slums are being cleared away and replaced with new buildings. In others, old buildings are being remodeled. People are also attacking the basic causes of slums, such as unemployment and discrimination.

thousands of city dwellers, they have not fully solved the problem of slums. In some cities, old tenements have been torn down and replaced with expensive apartments that only people with higher incomes can afford. Poor families who lived in these neighborhoods have been forced to look for homes in other run-down sections, so they are no better off than before.

Even where low-cost housing is available, it does not always meet the needs of city dwellers. Public housing developments are often drab and unpleasant, and buildings may be poorly constructed. Also, the people who move into these developments are not always accustomed to taking good care of their apartments. As a result, apartment buildings may become so run-down

and unsightly that they are little better than slums.

Some people believe that it is better to remodel older homes and apartment buildings than to tear them down and replace them with new housing developments. This has been done in some parts of Boston, New Haven, and other cities in the Northeast. Some of the people living in run-down sections have decided to improve their homes and clean up their neighborhoods by themselves. Banks or government agencies have loaned them the money to make necessary improvements. By working together, these people have succeeded in turning slum areas into pleasant, attractive neighborhoods.

Cities are trying not only to get rid of present slums but to prevent the growth of new ones. Most cities have passed laws that forbid the construction of factories, warehouses, and similar buildings in residential areas. There are also laws that require landlords to keep their buildings in good repair and to provide certain services to tenants. Such laws may help to prevent older neighborhoods from becoming slums. Some cities have inspectors who check houses and apartment buildings to make sure they are safe and reasonably clean.

These measures alone cannot fully solve the problem of slums. Steps must also be taken to attack the basic causes of slums, such as unemployment and discrimination.

Helping unemployed workers to get jobs. Earlier in this chapter, you learned that many people are poor because they do not have the skills or the education needed to hold good jobs. Today, Americans are trying in various ways to solve the urgent problem of unemployment.

"Head start" programs in many communities prepare slum children for school. Efforts are also being made to help older children remain in school.

In 1964, the United States Congress passed the Economic Opportunity Act. This act established several programs to help unemployed workers. For example, it set up an agency called the Job Corps. Young men and women who are unemployed can attend special Job Corps centers located in various parts of our country. In these centers, they are given a chance to do useful work and to learn valuable job skills. Under another program of this act, young people are given jobs and vocational training in their own hometowns. The government has also set up programs to teach job skills to adults who are unemployed.

These are not the only steps being taken to lower the rate of unemployment. Many cities in the Northeast and other regions have started their own job-training and hiring programs to help young people and adults. Also, a number of private business firms have started programs to retrain workers who have lost their jobs because of automation.

Providing greater opportunities for education. As you have learned, many children who live in slums make slow progress in school because they are not prepared to do schoolwork. Experiments have shown, however, that these children can be helped by sending them to nursery school when they are three or four years old. There they can be taught the things that most other children learn at home. With the help of government funds, many communities have started nursery schools or special classes for slum children. These programs are designed to give children a "head start" that will prepare them for kindergarten or first grade.

Efforts are also being made to provide older children with the education they need. Many communities, for example, offer special programs to help students who have difficulty keeping up with their schoolwork. These programs are usually run by churches, clubs, or other community organizations. In some communities, there are special classes for high school dropouts. Many schools, both public and private, offer programs for handicapped children or for young people who are talented in certain fields.

Today, more and more students from poor families are receiving a chance to continue their education beyond high school. Each year, millions of dollars' worth of loans and scholarships are awarded to young people who want to go to college. Money for these loans and scholarships comes from churches, business firms, labor unions, private individuals, the federal government, and various other sources. Recently the government also started a program to help needy students work their way through college.

Improving the health of city dwellers. Communities throughout the United States have been taking steps to improve the health of their citizens, often with the help of the federal government. Most children receive inoculations to protect them from certain diseases. These inoculations are often given free or at a very low cost. Many communities provide clinics and other medical services for people who do not have much money. Some clinics treat physical diseases and handicaps, while others help people who have mental problems. Today, millions of American families

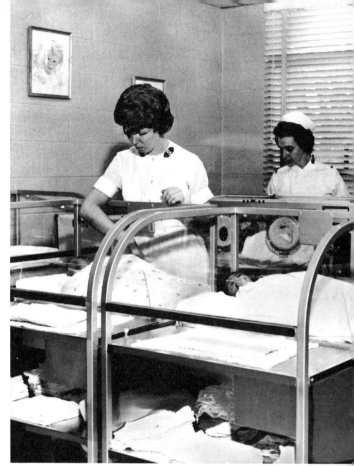

Hospital care is available in many communities for people who do not have much money. There is still a need for more adequate medical care, however.

are able to meet the costs of serious illness through insurance benefits from private companies or government agencies. Much remains to be done, however, to provide adequate medical care for all the people who need it.

Fighting prejudice and discrimination. The people of the Northeast have made much progress toward ending discrimination against minority groups. Throughout this region, Negroes and other minority-group members can exercise their right to vote, to serve on juries, and to run for public office. Federal and state laws have helped to end segregation in public places such as parks, swimming pools, hotels, and restaurants.

Job discrimination is also lessening. The Civil Rights Act passed by Congress in 1964 states that companies engaged in interstate commerce must hire workers without regard to race or religion. This law also forbids labor unions to discriminate against members of minority groups. Several states in the Northeast have passed "fair employment" laws and have set up special commissions to see that the laws are enforced. Many business firms and community organizations have worked hard to ensure equal employment opportunities for minority-group members.

Some progress has also been made toward ending discrimination in housing. In 1968 the United States Congress passed a "fair housing" law. This law forbids discrimination against minority groups in the sale or rental of most houses and apartments. "Fair housing" laws have also been passed by some states and cities.

Many people are opposed to "fair housing" laws. They believe that such laws take away a person's right to use his property as he pleases. However, others argue that no one should be denied the right to live where he pleases just because of his skin color.

In addition to the "fair housing" laws, various other steps are being taken to end segregation in housing. Some organizations have started programs to teach people the harmful effects of prejudice and discrimination. In many communities in the Northeast, there are agencies that try to find suitable housing for Negro families. Sometimes churches and other community organizations have provided money to help build integrated housing developments. Public housing projects are open to people of all races.

People in the Northeast have also been seeking answers to the problem of segregated schools. In New York City, for example, some Negro children are taken by bus to schools in white neighborhoods and some white children are transported to schools in Negro areas. This plan has aroused strong opposition, however. Many parents prefer to have their children attend schools closer to their homes. It seems likely that the problem of school segregation will remain unsolved as long as there is segregation in housing.

Other Urban Problems

In this chapter, you have learned about some of the major social problems that affect the lives of people in the Northeast. People who live in the large urban areas of this region also face other serious problems. Among these are poor transportation and the pollution of air and water.

Many cities lack adequate systems of transportation. In every urban area, there is a need for good transportation. Many of the people who work in central cities live in suburbs miles away. These people need a fast, dependable way of getting to and from work. Good transportation is also needed by people who come to the central cities for shopping or for entertainment.

In all the large cities of the Northeast, there are buses, trains, or other

Heavy traffic in New York City. All the large cities of the Northeast have problems with automobile traffic and parking. In order to reduce the number of cars entering cities from the suburbs, city officials try to encourage more people to use public transportation.

forms of public transportation. However, these are often crowded, dirty, and inconvenient. Many city dwellers prefer to travel by car. During the hours when most people are going to work or coming home, there are often so many cars on the streets that traffic comes to a standstill. Drivers often have difficulty finding a parking place, and all-day parking is likely to be expensive. In New York City, for example, some parking lots charge five dollars a day.

In recent years, cities in the Northeast have been trying to improve their transportation facilities. Many cities have built broad highways called expressways, which have few traffic lights or crossroads. Cars can usually travel

more rapidly on these expressways than on ordinary streets. Some cities have built large garages, where drivers can park their cars at a reasonable cost. These projects have not been entirely successful, however. Sometimes the new expressways and parking garages have merely attracted more cars to the business areas, creating worse traffic jams than before.

Some cities are trying to encourage more people to use public transportation. In Washington, D.C., for example, work has started on a new system of subways and surface railway lines. Other cities in the Northeast are planning to expand or improve their present transportation networks. As more people begin to use public transportation

223

instead of private cars, there may be fewer traffic jams on city streets.

Air pollution threatens the health of city dwellers. Another serious problem facing people in the large urban areas of the Northeast is air pollution. This often results from the burning of fuel or waste materials. For example, people burn oil, gas, or coal to heat houses and other buildings. These fuels are also burned to produce electric power. Trash is often destroyed by burning it. Smoke from all these fires enters the atmosphere, together with exhaust fumes from motor vehicles and locomotives. In addition, factories may give off harmful fumes in the manufacture of certain products.

Sometimes the atmosphere in a particular area contains so many impurities that it is dark and smoky. Polluted air often has an unpleasant smell. It may cause a person's eyes to water and his nose and throat to feel scratchy. Sometimes it can produce serious illness. A smoky fog that settled over the mining town of Donora, Pennsylvania, in 1948, is believed to have caused the deaths of twenty persons.

Today in the Northeast, as well as in other parts of the United States, a number of steps are being taken to reduce air pollution. Many industrial firms are using new methods to keep harmful smoke and fumes from entering the air. Federal, state, and local governments are also working to solve the problem of air pollution. For example, the federal government has passed a law that requires all new cars to have devices for controlling exhaust fumes. In some cities, there are laws that restrict the burning of trash.

Rivers and lakes contain large amounts of harmful waste materials. Water pollution occurs when cities or factories dump waste materials into rivers and lakes. The polluted water may contain disease germs or harmful chemicals, and it may have a very unpleasant odor. It must be specially processed before people can use it in their homes. Pollution often kills the fish in rivers and lakes. It also makes water unsafe for swimming.

Water pollution is an urgent problem throughout the Northeast. As Chapter 8 explains, New York and other cities have suffered from shortages of usable water in recent years. The Hudson River could easily supply all the water needed by the people of New York. However, it is so heavily polluted with wastes from homes and factories that it is unfit for human use. Other rivers, such as the Delaware and the Potomac, also contain large quantities of harmful wastes. Pollution has almost ruined Lake Erie. Tons of waste materials are dumped into the lake every day. Most of the fish in Lake Erie have disappeared, and a number of public beaches have been closed because of pollution.

Government agencies as well as private companies are now trying in various ways to reduce water pollution. A law passed by Congress in 1965 allows the federal government to take court action against cities and factories that pollute interstate rivers and lakes. The federal government also provides money to help cities pay for the safe disposal of waste materials. New York State has started a program to reduce pollution of the Hudson River. Industrial firms have been trying out new methods for disposing of chemicals and other factory wastes. If these efforts are successful, the polluted rivers and lakes of the Northeast may again be clean enough to be used to supply water for the people of this region.

Cooperation is needed to solve the problems of the cities. This chapter has described some of the problems facing the great cities of the Northeast. The people who live in these cities need to think about their problems and to work together to solve them. This can be done partly through clubs, churches, and other community organizations. Citizens can also work to solve problems through government.

In a democracy like the United States, each unit of government is only as good as its citizens make it. The people of the Northeast, like those in other regions, have the responsibility of electing local, state, and federal government officials who are honest, capable, and hardworking. In order to use their votes wisely, citizens must learn as much as possible about the problems that

Political campaigning. In a democracy, citizens have the responsibility of learning as much as they can about political issues and candidates.

face their communities. Only through hard work, careful planning, and cooperation will the problems of the Northeast's great cities be solved.

Investigate Social Problems
1. What are some of the reasons why a neighborhood may become a slum?
2. Why do children in slum areas often have difficulty gaining an education?
3. What are some of the reasons why many people in the cities of the Northeast cannot find employment?
4. Explain what happens to a person who is trapped in the "vicious circle of poverty."
5. What are some of the effects of discrimination?
6. In what ways do unsolved social problems harm our country as a whole?

Share Ideas in a Discussion
As a class, discuss the following question:
How can social problems be solved?
To prepare for your discussion, do some background reading about social problems. Take notes so you will be able to participate in the discussion. To start you thinking, consider what could be done to help solve each of the following social problems:
a. lack of education
b. unemployment
c. prejudice and discrimination
To have a successful discussion, follow the guidelines given on page 351.

In New York City's Guggenheim Museum, visitors can view paintings by contemporary* artists. The Northeast offers many opportunities for people to enjoy cultural activities. Cities throughout the region have fine museums, art galleries, theaters, and concert halls.

15 The Arts

A Problem To Solve

How do the arts of the Northeast help us to better understand our country's history? In forming hypotheses to solve this problem, you will need to consider the works of art created since colonial times by each of the following:

a. writers of the Northeast
b. painters of the Northeast
c. composers of the Northeast

As you try to solve this problem, you may wish to do research in Chapters 4-7 as well as in other books.

See TO THE STUDENT, pages 8-10.

The arts help tell America's story. The arts are much more than collections of paintings, books, and music for people to enjoy. Arts also reflect a country's way of life and express people's thoughts, emotions, and goals. Study-ing America's arts can bring us to a richer understanding of our country and its history.

The Northeast has made important contributions to the arts of America. Many of America's greatest writers, painters,

*See Glossary

and musicians have lived and worked in the Northeast. In the early years of our country's history, almost all of our large cities were located in this region. Some of these early cities, such as New York, Boston, and Philadelphia, developed into cultural centers where artists, writers, and musicians came to study and to work.

The arts in colonial America. During the early years of our country's history, most people had little time for the arts. The early colonists spent a great deal of their spare time in church. Most writing was done for sermons and religious pamphlets, and hymns were almost the only kind of music heard in the colonies. A number of colonial artists were able to earn their living as portrait painters, however. John Singleton Copley is considered the best American painter of this period.

Many useful articles made by the colonists for their homes were very beautiful, even though they were not thought of as works of art. The men made fine pieces of furniture. Colonial women made colorful quilts and rugs for their homes, in addition to making clothing for their families.

The arts of a new nation. The period of the American Revolution was full of unrest. American writers became less concerned with religious subjects and more interested in political issues. For example, Thomas Paine, an Englishman who lived in the Northeast, wrote articles to encourage the American people in their struggle for independence. One of these was called *Common Sense.*

A few years after the war, three of our country's political leaders wrote an important series of articles called *The Federalist.* The authors were John Jay and Alexander Hamilton of New York State and James Madison of Virginia. *The Federalist* was written to explain the newly written Constitution.

The interest that Americans felt in their history and their leaders was expressed in paintings of this period. Gilbert Stuart and Charles Willson Peale were two of the many artists who painted portraits of George Washington and other outstanding Americans. John Trumbull recorded some of America's great historical events on canvas. Among his paintings are "The Battle of Bunker Hill" and "Signing of the Declaration of Independence."

America's Arts in the Nineteenth Century

During much of the nineteenth century, the arts of America were romantic in style. Writers, painters, and musicians glorified the beauty of nature and the natural goodness of man. Many works of art were concerned with such subjects as heroism, patriotism, and folklore. Toward the end of the century, the romantic period came to an end and art became much more realistic.

American literature gains the respect of Europe. In the first years of the nineteenth century, Europeans generally felt that the United States was an uncivilized, uncultured country. They pointed out that no important literature had been produced in the New World. Americans were anxious for their writers to create literary works that would impress Europeans.

Three American writers who lived in New York State were the first to produce literature that was well received in Europe. Washington Irving wrote several popular books based on American themes. One of these was a collection of tales called *The Sketch Book.* This book includes "The Legend of Sleepy Hollow" and "Rip Van Winkle." James Fenimore Cooper was also a successful writer of the early 1800's. Cooper wrote several novels* about life on the frontier, such as *The Deerslayer* and *The Last of the Mohicans.* William Cullen Bryant was important both as a poet and a newspaper editor. Perhaps you have read his poem "To a Waterfowl."

Literature in the middle of the century. By the mid-1800's, American writers were respected in Europe as well as at home. Their works were widely read. The Northeast produced many of the finest American writers of this period.

Hawthorne, Melville, and Poe. Nathaniel Hawthorne was one of New England's best-known writers. He wrote several novels, including *The House of the Seven Gables,* and also many short stories. Herman Melville wrote a number of books. Melville's *Moby Dick* is one of the greatest American novels. It is the story of a sea captain who spends much of his life in pursuit of a great white whale called Moby Dick.

The return of Rip Van Winkle. Washington Irving, the author of "Rip Van Winkle," was born in New York State in the late 1700's. He was one of the first American writers to win respect in Europe. Since the days of Washington Irving, the Northeast has produced a number of world-famous writers.

Edgar Allan Poe wrote both short stories and poetry. He was especially interested in the way a writer could use words to create different moods. Some of his tales, such as "The Fall of the House of Usher," give the reader a feeling of mystery and terror. Many of Poe's poems are hauntingly musical.

From "The Bells"

Hear the sledges with the bells —
Silver bells!
What a world of merriment their melody
foretells!
How they tinkle, tinkle, tinkle,
In the icy air of night!
While the stars, that oversprinkle
All the heavens, seem to twinkle
With a crystalline delight . . .

— Edgar Allan Poe
(1809-1849)

New England poets. Several of America's most popular poets of the 1800's lived in New England. One was John Greenleaf Whittier, who wrote "Snow-Bound" and many other famous poems. Another was Henry Wadsworth Longfellow. You probably know some of Longfellow's poems, such as "The Village Blacksmith" and "Paul Revere's Ride." Other popular New England poets were James Russell Lowell and Oliver Wendell Holmes.

Emily Dickinson wrote poetry unlike that of the other New England poets. This was partly because she lived alone during much of her life and had little to do with the outside world. Miss Dickinson wrote hundreds of poems that explored her own feelings about life and death. In many of her poems she used unusual rhymes. Sometimes she used words in unusual ways.

I Never Saw a Moor

I never saw a moor,
I never saw the sea;
Yet know I how the heather looks,
And what a wave must be.

I never spoke with God,
Nor visited in heaven;
Yet certain am I of the spot
As if the chart were given.

— Emily Dickinson
(1830-1886)

Whitman. Another important poet of the Northeast was Walt Whitman. His poetry, too, was very different from that of other American poets of the 1800's. Whitman wrote in a freer style than poets before him. His poems did not follow regular patterns. Whitman's poetry shows his love of America and democracy.

From "Song of Myself"

Alone far in the wilds and mountains I
hunt,
Wandering amazed at my own lightness
and glee,
In the late afternoon choosing a safe spot
to pass the night,
Kindling a fire and broiling the fresh-
kill'd game,
Falling asleep on the gather'd leaves
with my dog and gun by my side.

— Walt Whitman
(1819-1892)

Writers of nonfiction in the 1800's. The Northeast also produced several of America's leading writers of nonfiction during this period. George Bancroft and Francis Parkman wrote important books about our country's history. Ralph Waldo Emerson and Henry David Thoreau were thinkers who believed that all men are basically good and should follow their own best instincts. Emerson's essay* "Self-Reliance" and Thoreau's book *Walden* are among the best-known literary works of our country.

Painting and music during the romantic period. George Inness and James McNeill Whistler were two of America's great nineteenth-century painters. Inness, who was born in New York, painted such famous pictures as "Peace and Plenty." His early work was influenced by an important group of painters called the "Hudson River school." These artists painted peaceful, dreamy landscapes. Whistler was a native of New England, although he spent much of his life in Europe. In many of his paintings, Whistler used color in new and different ways.

Perhaps the best-known songwriter of the nineteenth century was Stephen Foster. Although Foster lived in the Northeast, his songs were about the South. He wrote "Old Folks at Home," "Oh! Susanna," and other songs for traveling minstrel shows.

Edward MacDowell, one of America's greatest nineteenth-century composers, was born in New York City. He wrote piano and orchestra music. Some of his compositions, such as *Indian Suite* and *New England Idyls,* were based on American themes.

The century draws to a close. Near the end of the 1800's, some American novelists began to write in a new style. These men were not interested in picturing the glories of the past or the beauties of nature. Instead, they wanted to describe the common, everyday events of life. Because they tried to portray life as it "really" is, these writers are called realists.

Stephen Crane, William Dean Howells, and Henry James were three important realists who lived in the Northeast. In *The Red Badge of Courage,* Crane vividly described the fear and the courage of soldiers in the Civil War. James wrote many novels about Americans in Europe, describing in detail the lives of persons of wealthy and cultured backgrounds. Although Howells was not born in the Northeast, he spent much of his life there. His novels describe the everyday life of people in the Northeast.

During this period, painters also began to use a realistic style. Thomas Eakins painted such subjects as hospital scenes and sporting events in exact detail. Winslow Homer, one of our country's most famous artists, was also a realist. He was especially interested in the power and drama of the sea. His paintings include "The Herring Net" and "The Gulf Stream."

The Arts of Modern America

During the twentieth century, there have been many different styles in America's literature, painting, and music. These styles reflect vast changes that have taken place in our country. (See Chapter 7.)

Literature. Much of the literature of the twentieth century has explored the values and the problems of people living in the modern world. The work of Eugene O'Neill reflects this trend. O'Neill, who lived in New York City, is considered one of America's greatest playwrights. Many of his plays, such as *The Emperor Jones* and *The Hairy Ape,* show people in hopeless situations.

Perhaps the most famous American poet of the twentieth century was Robert Frost. Although Frost was born in San Francisco, he spent much of his life in New England. Frost's simple and meaningful poetry shows both the beautiful and tragic sides of life.

The Pasture

I'm going out to clean the pasture spring;
I'll only stop to rake the leaves away
(And wait to watch the water clear, I may):
I sha'n't be gone long. — You come too.

I'm going out to fetch the little calf
That's standing by the mother. It's so young
It totters when she licks it with her tongue.
I sha'n't be gone long. — You come too.

— Robert Frost
(1874-1963)

Several other modern American poets have lived in the Northeast. One of these was Edwin Arlington Robinson. Many of his poems describe people who

A scene from the opera "Porgy and Bess." Although this opera is about Negroes living in the South, its composer, George Gershwin, was born in the Northeast. Like many other American composers, Gershwin based much of his music on American themes.

are lonely and confused. Poets such as Wallace Stevens, William Carlos Williams, and E. E. Cummings have expressed their personal ideas about life and art in their works.

The Northeast has also produced several other important writers during the present century. Some of these, such as John Marquand, have written novels that explore America's changing values. Walter Edmonds and others have written novels about the history of the Northeast. Writers of nonfiction include Samuel Eliot Morison. One of his books is *Admiral of the Ocean Sea,* a biography of Columbus.

Painting and music. Never before has there been such a variety of styles of painting as in the twentieth century. Some artists have painted in a realistic style. Others have painted in an abstract* style. Artists have also used many different methods or techniques, such as pasting scraps of paper or other materials on their canvases.

Important twentieth-century painters from the Northeast include John Marin and Andrew Wyeth. Marin painted many pictures of the Maine seacoast and New York City that were somewhat abstract. Wyeth paints in a very realistic style. One of his famous paintings is "Christina's World."

Two of America's greatest composers of the twentieth century have come from the Northeast. Aaron Copland's works include the music for two important ballets—*Billy the Kid* and *Rodeo.* You are probably familiar with some of the music written by George Gershwin. Gershwin combined jazz and classical music in works such as "Rhapsody in Blue." He also composed the famous American opera *Porgy and Bess.* Among the popular songs from this opera is "Summertime."

The people of the Northeast enjoy many cultural activities. Today, people in the Northeast have opportunities to enjoy many cultural activities. There are many famous museums and art galleries in New York and other large cities of the Northeast. In these cities, people can also attend operas, ballets, and concerts of all types. In addition, there are theaters where fine plays are presented. Most cities in the Northeast have large public libraries.

In New York City there is an important group of new buildings planned especially for cultural activities. This is Lincoln Center. It includes theaters, museums, and concert halls. A similar center is being built in Washington, D.C., as a memorial to President John F. Kennedy.

Express Your Opinion
Choose one of the following poems to read in class:
  "Annabel Lee," by Edgar Allan Poe
  "The Runaway," by Robert Frost
  "Chansons Innocentes," by E. E. Cummings
As a class, discuss the poem. Consider the following questions in your discussion:
1. How did the poem make you feel?

2. Did you like the poem? Why, or why not?

Learn by Doing Research
Do research about the life and work of a painter who lived in the Northeast, such as Winslow Homer or Gilbert Stuart. Then write a report about him to share with your class. You will find suggestions for locating and organizing information on pages 345-349.

Part 5

States of the Northeast

States of the Northeast. Part 5 of this book provides information about the twelve states in the Northeast. Here you will find the facts you need for solving many problems about this region of our country. The text, the maps, and the vivid pictures will give you the most important information about the land, climate, people, and resources in each state of the Northeast. Chapter 18 gives information about the District of Columbia, which is also part of the Northeast.

Reading the fact tables. The following explanation will help you understand the information in the fact table at the beginning of each state chapter. The figures in these tables are the latest that were available from the United States government at the time this book was published. Some of these figures are amounts of money. These tell how many dollars the people of the state received in a year from such activities as farming, mining, and fishing. The figures for manufactures show the actual value added to goods or raw materials by factories in the state. The value added in manufacturing was figured out in an interesting way. From the amount of money received from the sale of goods, the cost of the materials needed to make them was subtracted. The amount of money left is the value added by the factories.

The fact tables also show the rank of each state in comparison with all the other states of our country. In cases where figures were not available, the rank is not given.

16 Connecticut

Facts About Connecticut		
	Number or Value	Rank
Area (square miles)	5,009	48
Population	2,963,000	24
Capital—Hartford		
Admission Date:		
January 9, 1788		5
Colleges and Universities	47	21
Farm Products	$ 161,880,000	42
Dairy products	45,217,000	34
Poultry and eggs	42,006,000	27
Tobacco	26,885,000	8
Fish	$ 1,768,000	23
Timber Harvested (cubic feet)	11,038,000	44
Minerals	$ 23,876,000	45
Stone	12,729,000	31
Sand and gravel	9,321,000	35
Clays	325,000	32
Manufactures	$6,184,996,000	12
Transportation equipment	1,272,800,000	7
Nonelectrical machinery	951,803,000	11
Electrical machinery	628,114,000	10

Land. Connecticut is our country's third smallest state. Only Rhode Island and Delaware are smaller. Most of Connecticut lies in the highlands of New England. There are only two small lowland areas in the state. One stretches along Long Island Sound, which borders Connecticut's southern coast. The other is the valley of the Connecticut River. This river, which begins in New Hampshire, flows southward through Connecticut and empties into Long Island Sound. (See map on page 236.)

The highlands. More than three fourths of Connecticut is made up of rolling hills and low mountains. The land is highest in the northwestern corner of the state. Here several low mountains rise about two thousand feet above sea

Forested hills in western Connecticut. Rolling hills and low mountains make up more than three fourths of Connecticut. The state has only two small lowland areas. One extends along the southern coast. The other is the valley of the Connecticut River.

Sailboats and other pleasure craft on Lake Candlewood, the largest lake in Connecticut. Scattered among the Connecticut highlands are more than one thousand lakes and ponds. In the summertime, many tourists come to these lakes to enjoy boating, swimming, and fishing.

level. Forests of oak, birch, pine, and other kinds of trees cover most parts of the highlands. The soil here is generally stony and not well suited to raising crops.

More than one thousand lakes and ponds dot the Connecticut highlands. Most of these were formed by glaciers thousands of years ago. (See page 38.) In the summertime, tourists come to the lakes for swimming, fishing, and boating. Some lakes are used as reservoirs to store water for nearby urban areas. The largest lake in Connecticut is Lake Candlewood. This is a reservoir that was formed by damming a tributary of the Housatonic River.

The lowlands. The lowland along the Connecticut coast is one of the most beautiful parts of the Northeast. In summer, the many wide bays here are dotted with sailing craft and small yachts. Fine summer homes line the sandy beaches.

The irregular coastline of Connecticut provides several excellent natural harbors. Port cities such as New Haven, Bridgeport, and New London have

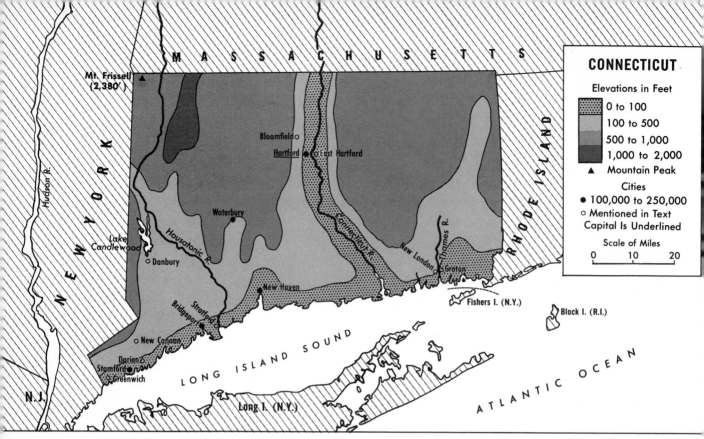

Connecticut is the third smallest state in our country. The Connecticut River flows southward through the state and empties into Long Island Sound, a narrow arm of the Atlantic Ocean. Connecticut's irregular coastline provides several excellent natural harbors.

grown up here. The harbor at New London is one of the deepest on the Atlantic coast. It is located at the mouth of the Thames River. Many of our country's atomic-powered submarines are based at Groton, a town just across the river from New London.

The Connecticut Valley is one of the most important sections of Connecticut. Here, some of the most fertile farmland in the Northeast is found. The Connecticut Valley is also an important manufacturing area. Hartford, Connecticut's leading manufacturing city, is located here.

Climate. Winters are generally milder in Connecticut than in the New England states that lie farther north. The lowland that is bordered by Long Island Sound receives less snowfall and has milder winter temperatures than other parts of the state. This area usually receives less than thirty-five inches of snowfall each year. Breezes from the Sound help keep the coastal temperatures mild. Also, Long Island shelters this part of Connecticut from winter storms that may blow in off the Atlantic Ocean.

Snowfall is heaviest in the highlands in the northwestern part of the state. This area sometimes receives as much as eighty inches of snowfall in a year. Many people come to this part of the state in winter for skiing and other winter sports.

Summer weather is generally pleasant along the coast and in the highlands of Connecticut. There are many resorts on the seashore and along inland lakes. Each year, thousands of visitors come to these resorts from New York and other cities in the Northeast to escape the heat. In the Connecticut Valley, summers are generally much warmer than elsewhere in the state. The hot summer weather here makes it possible for farmers to grow fine crops of tobacco.

Spring and autumn in Connecticut are the most beautiful seasons of the year. In May and early June, pink and white dogwood blossoms brighten the woodlands. In autumn, leaves turn to beautiful shades of yellow and scarlet. During both of these seasons, the days are mild and the nights are comfortably cool.

Natural resources. Connecticut has few mineral resources. Metal ores, coal, oil, and natural gas must be imported. The only minerals produced in fairly large quantities in Connecticut are stone, sand, and gravel. These are used as building materials. They have been very useful in constructing Connecticut's excellent highways.

Connecticut also lacks other natural resources. Waterpower is used to produce less than one tenth of the electricity needed in the state. There are some oysters, lobsters, and other fish in the waters off the coast. However, Connecticut is not an important fishing state. More than half of the state is forested, but most of the trees are not suitable for making lumber. The forests are used mainly as recreation areas.

Industry. Despite its small size, Connecticut is an important manufacturing state. Nearly two fifths of all its workers are employed in industry. This proportion is one of the highest of any of the states.

The history of manufacturing in Connecticut helps to explain why industry is so important here today. Manufacturing began in Connecticut in the early 1700's. There was little good farmland outside the Connecticut Valley. Because the early settlers found it difficult to earn their living by farming, some of them began to make articles for sale. They used iron and copper, obtained from small mines within the colony, to make nails, pins and needles, kettles, and many other useful articles. Much of the early manufacturing in Connecticut was carried on in the settlers' own homes, or in small shops and mills.

During the first half of the nineteenth century, the products of Connecticut factories became well known throughout the United States. As our country expanded westward, manufacturers in Connecticut sent peddlers on foot or horseback to find new markets for their products. These men traveled the western frontier, peddling such articles as brass buttons, kettles, hats, combs, and clocks to the settlers there.

The craftsmen in Connecticut's factories were usually able to make anything needed by the settlers. Connecticut established a reputation throughout the country for the skill and inventiveness of its people. In the 1800's, a large number of America's inventors lived and worked in Connecticut.

Today, factories in Connecticut continue to produce goods requiring highly skilled labor. This state has almost none of the natural resources needed by modern industry. Steel, copper, and other raw materials must be imported from other states and from foreign countries. Skilled workers in Connecticut use these materials to make many valuable products.

Assembling helicopters at Stratford, Connecticut. The manufacture of transportation equipment is Connecticut's leading industry. In addition to helicopters, factories in the state make submarines, aircraft propellers, and jet-aircraft engines.

Transportation equipment. Connecticut's leading industry is the manufacture of transportation equipment. Factories here make helicopters, submarines, aircraft propellers, and jet-aircraft engines.

In 1915, a United States Navy submarine base was established at Groton. The world's first submarine powered by atomic energy was launched here in 1954. Today, Groton is one of our country's leading producers of submarines.

Connecticut is also a leading aircraft manufacturer. One of the largest aircraft-engine plants in the nation is located at East Hartford. Helicopters are built at Bridgeport, Stratford,

and Bloomfield. Reentry vehicles for spacecraft are also produced at Stratford. In many parts of the state, there are factories that make aircraft parts and accessories.

Machinery. More than one and one-half billion dollars' worth of machinery is manufactured in Connecticut each year. In many cities there are factories that make machine tools. These are power-driven machines that cut, grind, and shape metal to produce parts needed in making other machines. Connecticut leads the nation in the production of ball and roller bearings.* Typewriters and other office machines are also made in Connecticut.

*See Glossary

Connecticut is also a leading producer of electrical and electronic* equipment. Factories here make light fixtures, household appliances, electric switches, and many other electrical products. Electronic devices, such as transistors and vacuum tubes, are also manufactured in Connecticut. These devices are used in equipment such as radar, electronic computers, and television sets. The design and manufacture of electronic equipment requires highly skilled engineers and workers.

Other manufactured products. Connecticut's factories make a great variety of other products. Large firms such as Winchester, Colt, and Remington make firearms and ammunition for use by our country's armed forces and by sportsmen. Connecticut is our country's leading producer of silverware, and a leader in the production of brass and copper products. Clocks, cutlery, tools, and hardware made in Connecticut are used throughout the nation.

Farming. In most of Connecticut, the land is too hilly and the soil is too stony for raising crops. However, the broad Connecticut Valley is one of the best farming areas in the Northeast.

A silversmith at work. Connecticut has long been noted for the skill and inventiveness of its workers. Factories in the state manufacture silverware, clocks, electronic equipment, and many other products that require highly skilled workmanship.

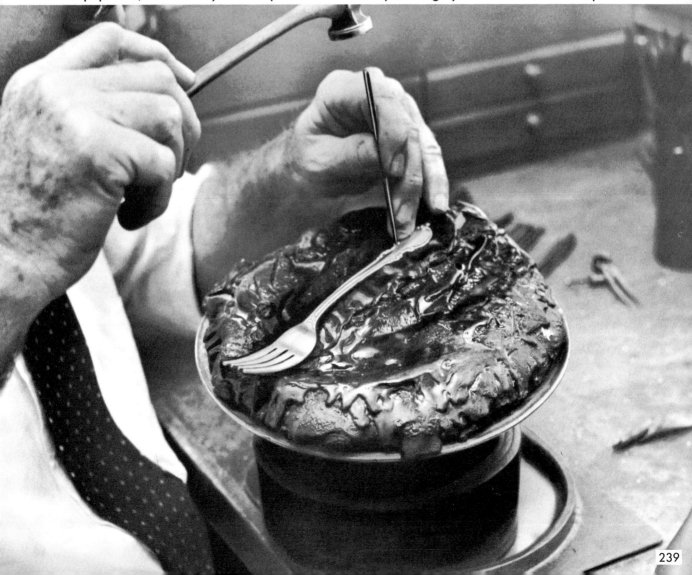

Hanging leaves of tobacco to dry. Tobacco is the most valuable crop grown in the Connecticut Valley. This valley is one of the most productive farming areas in the Northeast.

The sale of dairy products and poultry and eggs accounts for more than half of Connecticut's farm income. Livestock can be raised in areas that are not suitable for other types of farming. Also, there are many customers for fresh milk and eggs in heavily populated urban areas of the state. Millions of dollars' worth of tender, young chickens called broilers are raised on Connecticut's poultry farms each year.

The fertile soil of the Connecticut Valley attracted the first English settlers to Connecticut in the 1630's. This lowland has been an important farming area ever since. Tobacco is the leading crop grown in the Connecticut Valley. The most valuable tobacco grown here is the type that is used for making the outer wrappers of cigars. It must be grown under cheesecloth, and is very expensive to produce. For this reason,

large corporations own many of the farms where this tobacco is raised. The picture on page 28 shows tobacco farms in the Connecticut Valley.

Several other crops are also important in Connecticut. There are many small truck farms and fruit orchards in the Connecticut Valley. Apples, potatoes, sweet corn, and tomatoes are grown here. In many parts of Connecticut, flowers, plants, and trees are grown in greenhouses and nurseries. This type of agriculture is especially important in residential areas in the southwestern part of the state. Here, many people have fine homes with large, rolling lawns. In this area, millions of dollars are spent each year for plants and shrubbery.

People and cities. About four out of every ten people in Connecticut were born in foreign countries or have at least one parent who came to this country as an immigrant. Before the Civil War, most people in this state were of English or Irish descent. In the last hundred years, immigrants from Canada and from southern and eastern Europe have been attracted to Connecticut by the many manufacturing plants in the state. Today, many people of Italian, Canadian, and Polish descent live in Connecticut.

The per capita* income of Connecticut is one of the highest in the United States. This is partly because so many of the people here are well-paid workers in industry. Also, many successful business and professional people who work in New York City make their homes in Fairfield County, in the southwestern part of the state. Several of the suburban towns here are only about an

240

hour's train ride from the city. Some of these towns, such as Greenwich, Darien, and New Canaan, are among the wealthiest communities in the entire country.

About eight out of every ten people in Connecticut live in cities or their suburbs. Most of these cities are located along the coastal lowland or in the Connecticut Valley. The largest cities in Connecticut are Hartford, Bridgeport, and New Haven.

Hartford (population about 164,000) is the capital and largest city of Connecticut. It is located on the west bank of the Connecticut River, about forty miles north of Long Island Sound.

The first permanent settlement on the site of present-day Hartford was established by people from Massachusetts Bay colony in 1635. This settlement became a trading center for the farm products of the fertile Connecticut Valley. Oceangoing ships were able to sail up the Connecticut River as far as Hartford. In the 1700's, the town became an important port. Insurance companies were started in Hartford to sell fire insurance and to insure ships' cargoes. Although shipping declined in the 1800's, the insurance business in Hartford continued to grow. Today, about thirty insurance companies have their home offices here. For this reason,

Hartford, the capital and largest city of Connecticut, is located along the Connecticut River. There are many modern, attractive office buildings and factories here. Because a large number of insurance companies have their home offices in Hartford, it is known as the "insurance city." Factories in the Hartford metropolitan area make such products as firearms and typewriters.

Hartford has often been called the "insurance city."

Manufacturing is important in and near Hartford. A leading industry here is the manufacture of aircraft engines. These are made in huge plants across the Connecticut River, in the town of East Hartford. The manufacture of firearms is another important industry. A Hartford inventor, Samuel Colt, designed the first successful revolver in the 1830's and later established a plant here. Other important products made in factories in Hartford are typewriters and machine tools.

Hartford does not have the appearance of most manufacturing cities. Its businesses and factories are not all clustered in one area. Many of them are modern, attractive buildings in the suburbs of the city. The downtown section of Hartford is also clean and modern. In recent years, parts of this area have been torn down and new buildings have been erected. (See picture on page 241.)

Bridgeport (population about 154,000) is the second largest city in Connecticut. It is located along an excellent harbor on Long Island Sound. (See map on page 236.) Bridgeport was once an important seaport, but today it is mainly a manufacturing city. Bridgeport, like many other cities in Connecticut,

Bridgeport, the second largest city in Connecticut, is located along an excellent harbor. Although Bridgeport was once an important seaport, today it is mainly a manufacturing city. Important industries here are the manufacture of helicopters, machine tools, and ammunition.

produces a wide variety of manufactured goods. Important products of Bridgeport's factories are helicopters, copper wire and cable, machine tools, hardware, and ammunition. One of the few steel mills in New England is located at Bridgeport.

New Haven (population about 140,000) is Connecticut's third largest city. It is located on Long Island Sound about seventeen miles northeast of Bridgeport. New Haven is the home of Yale University, one of the oldest schools in our country.

New Haven is one of Connecticut's leading manufacturing cities. In 1798, the inventor Eli Whitney started a plant near New Haven to manufacture guns. (See page 92.) Today, many of New Haven's workers are employed in factories that make firearms and ammunition. These plants manufacture weapons for our country's armed forces. They also produce a large share of the guns used by hunters throughout the United States. In New Haven, there are also factories that make clocks, toys, locks, and aircraft-engine parts.

Buildings of Yale University, in New Haven. Yale is especially noted for its fine school of law. New Haven is Connecticut's main seaport and also one of its important manufacturing cities.

New Haven is Connecticut's main port city. Its harbor has been deepened to permit oceangoing vessels to dock here. More imports than exports pass through the port of New Haven. The chief imports are petroleum, coal, and other raw materials needed by Connecticut's many factories.

Learning From Maps

Study the map of Connecticut on page 236, and then answer the following questions:

1. What is the capital of Connecticut?
2. What body of water borders Connecticut on the south?
3. What main rivers flow through the state?
4. What three states border Connecticut?

Questions To Help You Learn

1. Where are Connecticut's two important lowland areas located?
2. How is the hot summer weather in the

Connecticut Valley helpful to farmers there?

3. Why is only a small part of Connecticut suitable for farming?
4. How does history help to explain why manufacturing is important in Connecticut?
5. What are some of the most important products made in Connecticut factories?
6. Why are there many wealthy communities in southwestern Connecticut?
7. How did the insurance business develop in Hartford?

243

17 Delaware

Facts About Delaware		
	Number or Value	Rank
Area (square miles)	2,057	49
Population	534,000	46
Capital—Dover		
Admission Date:		
December 7, 1787		1
Colleges and Universities	6	47
Farm Products	$125,518,000	45
Poultry and eggs	73,562,000	19
Vegetables	13,891,000	29
Corn	10,066,000	24
Fish	$ 259,000	34
Timber Harvested (cubic feet)	11,316,000	43
Minerals	$ 1,996,000	50
Sand and gravel	1,483,000	50
Stone	500,000	47
Clays	12,000	44
Manufactures	$955,501,000	37
Chemicals	Not available	
Food and kindred products	137,569,000	35
Fabricated metal products	32,521,000	37

Land. Delaware is smaller than any other state in our country except Rhode Island. It is located mainly in the northeastern part of the Delmarva Peninsula* (See map on page 245.) On the east, it is bordered by the Delaware River, Delaware Bay, and the Atlantic Ocean.

Nearly all of Delaware lies in the Coastal Plain region of our country. The northernmost tip of the state is in the Piedmont Plateau.

The Coastal Plain. In Delaware, the Coastal Plain is generally low and flat. Hardly any point rises more than sixty feet above sea level. Low marshes and sandy beaches extend along much of Delaware's coast. Along the southern border of the state is a large freshwater marsh called Great Pocomoke Swamp.

*See Glossary

A small town on Delaware's Coastal Plain. All but the northernmost tip of Delaware lies in the Coastal Plain region of our country. Here, the land is generally low and flat. The soil of the Coastal Plain in Delaware is good for growing a variety of crops.

The sandy loam of the Coastal Plain in Delaware is good for growing a variety of crops. It warms up more quickly than other kinds of soil. Partly for this reason, farmers in Delaware can plant their crops early in the spring. If you were to visit the Coastal Plain of Delaware during the summer months, you would see many fields of vegetables, soybeans, and other crops.

The Piedmont Plateau. Rolling hills and fertile valleys make up the Piedmont Plateau section of Delaware. The highest point in the state is located here. It is only 440 feet above sea level. Fine herds of dairy cattle graze on hillside pastures in the Piedmont. In some places, there are large estates owned by wealthy businessmen. Wilmington, Delaware's largest city, is located along the Fall Line, which separates the Piedmont from the Coastal Plain. (See feature on page 35.) About two thirds of the people in Delaware live in the Wilmington metropolitan* area.

Climate. Because Delaware is a small state without any mountains, the climate does not differ very much from one part of the state to another. Winters here are generally short and mild. Breezes from the Atlantic Ocean help to prevent severely cold weather. (See page 45.) Also, the mountains of Pennsylvania help to shelter the state from icy northwest winds. Snowfall is light, and daytime temperatures during the winter months are often above freezing. Summers in Delaware are warm and quite humid. The temperature is usually several degrees cooler along the seacoast than it is farther inland. During the summer, many people in Delaware

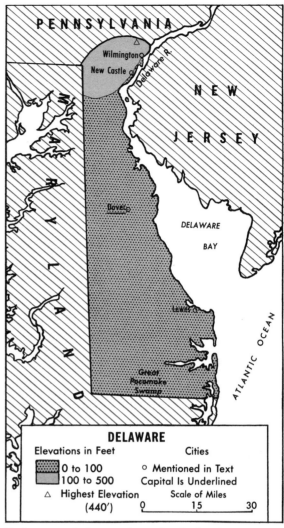

Delaware is located on the Delmarva Peninsula. This state, the second smallest in our country, is made up mostly of lowlands.

go to the seashore to enjoy the refreshing ocean breezes.

In most parts of Delaware, the growing season is about six months long. The long growing season is very helpful to farmers here. They can plant their crops earlier than farmers in most other parts of the Northeast. As a result, they can ship fresh fruits and vegetables to market before the crops grown in colder areas are ready to harvest. With this head start, Delaware farmers are likely to get a better price for their products. Also, farmers in this state

245

can often grow more than one crop on the same land in a single year.

Natural resources. The state of Delaware is poor in natural resources. Although forests cover about one third of the state, lumbering is not a major industry. Sand, gravel, and clay are taken from pits in northern Delaware. Small amounts of granite are also quarried in this part of the state.

Each winter, hunters trap thousands of muskrats in the marshes along the coast of Delaware. The muskrat pelts are sold at fur markets in New York and other cities.

Fisheries were once an important natural resource for this state. Recently, however, the menhaden and oysters that were formerly plentiful in Delaware's waters have become very scarce. The oyster beds in Delaware Bay are now being reseeded so that oysters may again become a valuable resource for the state.

Industry. About one third of all workers in Delaware are employed in manufacturing. Although Delaware does not rank high among the states in the value of manufactured products, a large number of companies have their headquarters here. Delaware's laws have made it easy to organize corporations* in this state. Also, taxes on corporations are lower here than in most other states. For these reasons, many people have set up corporations in Delaware even though their manufacturing plants may be located in other states.

Delaware earns more money from the manufacture of chemicals and chemi-

A Du Pont experimental plant, near Wilmington. The Du Pont company, the world's largest chemical company, was started in Delaware in 1802. Making chemicals and chemical products is Delaware's chief industry. Many other goods are also made here, ranging from cars to clothing.

cal products than from any other industry. The chemical industry has been important in Delaware since the early days of our nation. In 1802, a French immigrant named E. I. du Pont de Nemours built a mill near Wilmington to make gunpowder for the United States Army. This was the start of the Du Pont company, which has become the largest manufacturer of chemicals in the world. The company still has its home offices in Delaware. Here, too, are laboratories where scientists carry on experiments with chemicals. Although most of the Du Pont company's plants are in other states, there are some in Delaware that make nylon, paints, dyes, and other chemical products. Two other large chemical companies also have offices, laboratories, and manufacturing plants in this state.

Food processing is the second most important industry in Delaware. Many fruits and vegetables grown on Delaware farms are packaged, canned, or frozen at factories in the state. Canning factories in Dover process chickens raised on nearby farms. Gelatin and other food products are also produced in Dover. Much of the food processed in Delaware is shipped to buyers throughout the United States.

Another important industry in this state is the manufacture of metal products. Most of the factories that make these products are located in northern Delaware. A large plant in this area manufactures plumbing fixtures and fittings. Other factories here produce large quantities of sheet metal and wire. Coat hangers produced in factories in northern Delaware are sold throughout the United States.

Delaware has a variety of other industries. There are clothing factories and textile mills in various parts of the state. In Wilmington are several factories that process the skins of kids, or young goats, to make leather for gloves and shoes. A large oil refinery on the Delaware River uses crude oil brought by ship from Texas. Two automobile-assembly plants are also located in northern Delaware. Other factories in this part of the state manufacture products such as rubber hose, rubber gloves, and space suits for astronauts. Factories here also produce foam plastic for various uses, such as egg cartons. In southern Delaware, factories make luggage, boxes, and other goods.

Farming. There are many prosperous farms in Delaware. As you have already learned, the land and climate in this state are well suited to growing a variety of crops. Philadelphia, Baltimore, and other cities in the Northeast provide a large market for Delaware's farm products.

Farmers in Delaware earn more money from poultry than from any other product. Although some chickens in Delaware are raised for their eggs, a much larger number are grown for sale as broilers. These chickens are butchered when they are between six and twelve weeks old. At that age, their meat is still tender and very tasty. After the broilers have been cleaned and packaged, they are shipped to the cities on fast trains or trucks. Within a day after leaving the poultry farms, they can be bought in grocery stores and meat markets. Farmers in Delaware raise more than 100 million broiler chickens every year.

Several facts help to explain why Delaware produces so many broilers. In the large cities of the Northeast, there are many people who enjoy eating fresh chicken. Winters are mild in Delaware, so farmers in this state spend less money for building poultry sheds than do farmers in colder areas. Delaware farmers were among the first in our country to raise broilers on a large scale. The broiler industry was started here in the early 1920's. In recent years, however, Delaware farmers have had to face much competition from poultry farmers in the South. Several southern states, including Georgia and Alabama, now produce more broilers than Delaware.

Other kinds of livestock are also raised in Delaware. There are many dairy farms in the northern part of the state. They supply fresh milk to Wilmington and other cities nearby. Many farmers in Delaware raise hogs or beef cattle for meat.

Broiler chickens. Farmers in Delaware raise more than 100 million broiler chickens every year. Most of these chickens are sold in northeastern cities.

The sandy loam of southern Delaware is especially good for growing vegetables. Potatoes are the state's leading vegetable crop. Other vegetables raised in Delaware include lima beans, tomatoes, peas, and asparagus. Some of the vegetables grown in Delaware are sold fresh in nearby towns and cities, but a large part of the crop is sent to canning or freezing plants.

Corn and soybeans are the main field crops in Delaware. Farmers in all parts of the state grow corn to feed poultry and other livestock. Delaware is one of the leading producers of soybeans in the Northeast.

People and cities. Delaware's population has been growing faster than that of any other state in the Northeast. In 1950, fewer than 320,000 people lived in Delaware. By 1968, the population had grown to about 534,000. This rapid increase is due mainly to the development of new industries in the state.

Wilmington is the only large city in Delaware. No other town has more than 20,000 people. Dover (population about 15,000) is the state capital.

Wilmington (population about 86,000) lies in the northern part of Delaware. It is located at the place where the Christina River flows into the Delaware River. The first settlement here was Fort Christina, which was founded by Swedish colonists in 1638. This settlement eventually was taken over by the English.

During the late 1700's, several kinds of industry grew up in Wilmington. This town was located in a fertile farming area that stretched into Pennsylvania and Maryland. Waterfalls on streams in this area provided power for flour mills. Many farmers brought their wheat to Wilmington to be ground into flour. Some of this flour was sent by ship to other colonies as well as to Europe and the West Indies. Because the Christina River was deep near its mouth, ships could load their cargo near the mills. As time passed, these advantages attracted other mills and factories to Wilmington. Among these were paper mills, textile mills, and the Du Pont gunpowder works.

Today Wilmington is still an important seaport and manufacturing city. Large oceangoing ships dock here and at New Castle, about five miles down the Delaware River. These ships bring petroleum, wood, and other raw materials for the city's factories. They carry away textiles, chemicals, and other manufactured goods. Many of the industries described earlier in this chapter are located in the Wilmington area.

Wilmington is the largest city in Delaware. It is a busy seaport and manufacturing city, located on the Delaware River in the northern part of the state.

Questions To Guide Your Study

1. What is the highest elevation in Delaware?
2. What is Great Pocomoke Swamp? Where is it located?
3. Why is the climate of Delaware much the same throughout the state?
4. How is the long growing season in Delaware helpful to farmers?
5. Why are so many broiler chickens raised in Delaware?
6. Give one reason why many people have set up corporations in Delaware even though their manufacturing plants are in other states.
7. Name some of the chemical products made in Delaware.
8. Give two reasons why many industries have been attracted to the Wilmington area.

Explore an Interesting Topic

Choose one of the following topics and write a report to share with your class.

The Story of E. I. du Pont de Nemours and Company
Chicken Farming
The Development and Uses of Nylon
Muskrat Trapping
The Early History of Wilmington

You will find the suggestions on pages 347-349 helpful in locating information about the topic you have chosen. In writing your report, remember to begin each paragraph with a topic sentence. Also, use words that will create clear images in the mind of the reader. Other guidelines for good writing are given on page 347. To make your report more interesting, illustrate it with pictures or drawings.

What is the District of Columbia? The District of Columbia is a small section 'of our country that is not part of any state. It is the seat of the federal government and is therefore called a federal district. The District of Columbia covers about sixty-nine square miles. It lies along the Potomac River, between Maryland and Virginia. (See map on page 252.)

Washington, our national capital city, has the same boundaries as the District of Columbia. It is the central city of a densely populated metropolitan* area that spreads into Maryland and Virginia. Nearly two and one-half million people live in Washington and its suburbs, but only about 850,000 live within the central city.

The early history of our national capital. In 1790, the first Congress of the United States voted to establish a permanent national capital along the Potomac River. A capital on the Potomac would be centrally located, about halfway between the northern and southern borders of the country. Also, convenient transportation routes would connect the capital with the Atlantic Ocean and the western frontier.

At the request of Congress, President Washington selected the exact location for the capital city. Along both sides of the river, surveyors laid out

*See Glossary

Washington, our national capital city, has the same boundaries as the District of Columbia. It lies along the Potomac River, between Maryland and Virginia. By comparing this photograph with the map on page 252, you may be able to identify some of the city's famous landmarks.

a district covering one hundred square miles. Maryland and Virginia gave up to the federal government their rights in this area.

The capital city was built in the heart of the newly established federal district. It was named Washington in honor of the President. Major Pierre Charles L'Enfant, a French engineer, was hired to draw up plans for the new city. Major L'Enfant chose the sites for the Capitol* and the president's house. His plans included several broad avenues that radiated from these sites like the spokes of a wheel.

Slowly the new city began to take shape. After meeting in Philadelphia for ten years, the government moved to Washington in 1800. Although the Capitol was still under construction, Congress was able to meet in a completed section of the building. The president's house was also unfinished. Only a few years later, during the War of 1812, both of these structures were partly destroyed by fire. (See page 95.) After the war, they were rebuilt. The smoke-stained walls of the president's house were painted white, and the building later became known as the White House.

Our national capital becomes a great city. By the time of the Civil War, about 75,000 people lived in the District of Columbia. However, the district was now much smaller in area than it had been at first. In 1846 the government had returned to Virginia the portion of the federal district that had originally been part of that state.

After the Civil War, Washington's population grew very rapidly. Many former slaves moved to the city in search of jobs and a better way of life.

With the growth of the nation, many more people were needed to run the federal government. Thousands of workers moved to the capital with their families.

As its population increased, Washington also changed in other ways. New buildings were erected to provide the office space needed for running the government. Many libraries, museums, and colleges were established in the city. New parks were developed by reclaiming land from swamps and tidal* flats along the Potomac.

The city of Washington today. The central section of Washington still follows the original plan of the city fairly closely. Northwest of the Capitol, on Pennsylvania Avenue, is the White House. A broad, green park, called the Mall, stretches straight westward from the Capitol. There are many government buildings along Constitution and Independence avenues, north and south of the Mall. Between Pennsylvania and Massachusetts avenues lies Washington's downtown shopping district.

Each year, more than ten million people visit our national capital. Many come in April to see Washington's famous Japanese cherry trees in bloom. (See picture on page 45.) These trees border the blue waters of the Tidal Basin and extend for two miles along the Potomac. On the southeast shore of the Tidal Basin stands a circular building erected as a memorial to President Thomas Jefferson. Most of the people who visit Washington go to see the Lincoln Memorial, which contains a fine statue of President Lincoln.

Other interesting places to visit lie across the Potomac from Washington,

Our Nation's Capital

The Washington Monument

PLACES OF INTEREST

1 Union Station
2 Senate Office Buildings
3 Supreme Court
4 **Library of Congress** — contains more than 40 million books, pictures, maps, and other items.
5 Capitol
6 House of Representatives Office Buildings
7 White House
8 Department of State
9 Site of John F. Kennedy Center for the Performing Arts
10 Department of the Interior
11 Treasury Department
12 Department of Commerce
13 Department of Labor
14 Post Office Department
15 Internal Revenue Service
16 Department of Justice
17 **National Archives** — contains important government records. The Declaration of Independence and the Constitution are on display.
18 Department of Agriculture
19 Department of Health, Education, and Welfare
20 National Gallery of Art
21 Museum of Natural History
22 Museum of History and Technology
23 **Smithsonian Institution** — established to encourage the spread of knowledge. Includes a group of museums.
24 Washington Monument
25 Jefferson Memorial
26 Lincoln Memorial
27 Grave of President Kennedy
28 Tomb of the Unknowns
29 **The Pentagon** — Department of Defense

Parks and Cemeteries   Railroads

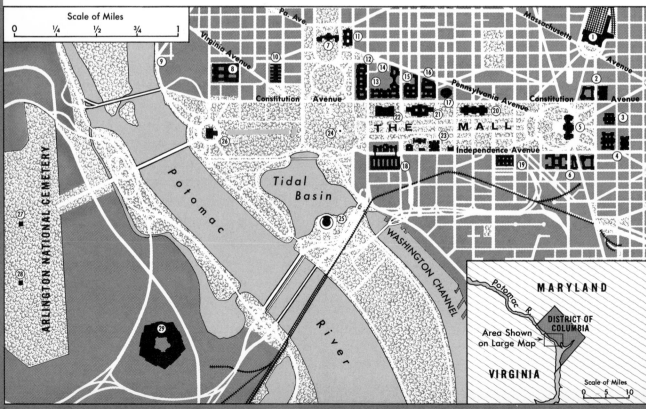

in Virginia. One of these is Arlington National Cemetery. Among the many famous Americans buried here is the late President John F. Kennedy. Not far from the cemetery is the Pentagon. This is the enormous five-sided office building of the Department of Defense. About 27,000 people work here.

The people of Washington. Many of the people who live in Washington are not permanent residents of the city. This is partly because some government workers hold their jobs only while their own political party is in power. Also, many people come here to have the experience of living and working in our national capital for awhile. After a short time, these people leave Washington to take jobs elsewhere.

Except for the representatives of foreign governments, most of the people who live in Washington were born in the United States. About two thirds of them are Negroes. No other major city in our country has such a large proportion of Negroes.

The federal government employs about one third of all the workers in Washington. Most of the others have jobs in trade, in services, or in construction. For example, many people earn their living by providing food and lodging for the millions of tourists who visit the city each year. Compared with other cities the same size, Washington has very little industry. Only about 26,000 workers are employed in manufacturing, mainly in food processing and printing.

The people who live in our national capital have little voice in local affairs. Washington residents are not represented in Congress, which makes most

Visiting the Capitol. The government buildings, monuments, and other interesting places in Washington, D.C., attract many tourists. Each year, more than ten million people visit this impressive city.

of the laws for the District of Columbia. The district is governed by a mayor and a nine-member city council appointed by the president of the United States with the approval of the Senate. Many Washington residents believe they should have more voice in their city's affairs. Some people are trying to change the system entirely. Others are working to gain representation in Congress.

Until 1961, permanent residents of the District of Columbia were also unable to help choose our country's president and vice-president. In that year, the Twenty-third Amendment to the United States Constitution was ratified.* This amendment makes it possible for the people who live in Washington to vote in presidential elections.

Clearing slums in Washington. Work is underway to improve the appearance of our nation's capital. As part of this redevelopment, slums are being replaced with modern apartment buildings.

Washington's problems and opportunities. Washington has had to face most of the same problems as other American cities. (See Chapter 14.) These include the problems of providing pure water, convenient transportation, and other services. They also include social problems such as poverty, crime, prejudice, and discrimination.

Our national capital is considered one of the world's most beautiful cities. In the past, however, much of Washington grew in a careless fashion. Over the years, large slum areas developed. Also, many ugly buildings were erected in the downtown business and shopping districts. Efforts are now being made to improve the appearance of Washington. Through various urban-renewal projects,

the old buildings in slum areas are being torn down and replaced with modern apartment houses. Plans have been drawn up for redeveloping Pennsylvania Avenue between the Capitol and the White House. If these plans are carried out, many old buildings will be torn down or rebuilt to give the avenue a more unified appearance. A splendid, treelined public square will also be built near the White House. By planning carefully for the future, the people of America will be able to preserve their national capital's magnificent historical heritage.

Questions To Help You Learn

1. What is the District of Columbia? Where is it located?
2. Why was this location chosen for our national capital?
3. Who drew up the plans for the city of Washington?
4. How did the president's residence come to be called the White House?
5. What is the Mall?
6. Why do many people visit Washington during the month of April each year?
7. Who makes most of the laws for the District of Columbia?
8. Why are plans being made to rebuild parts of Washington?

Use Your Imagination

Take your class on an imaginary tour of our nation's capital. First, do some general reading about the city. Then decide which places of interest you will visit on your tour. Make a large diagram of Washington on poster board or other heavy paper, naming these places. As you take your tour, refer to this diagram. Describe the places you visit and tell the class some interesting facts about each. To locate the information you need, refer to the suggestions on pages 347-349.

19 Maine

Facts About Maine		
	Number or Value	**Rank**
Area (square miles)	33,215	39
Population	976,000	38
Capital—Augusta		
Admission Date:		
March 15, 1820		23
Colleges and Universities	15	38
Farm Products	$209,807,000	39
Poultry and eggs	94,335,000	12
Vegetables	50,757,000	14
Dairy products	37,529,000	37
Fish	$ 22,973,000	8
Timber Harvested (cubic feet)	369,149,000	14
Minerals	$ 17,810,000	47
Sand and gravel	5,978,000	44
Stone	3,205,000	43
Clays	65,000	39
Manufactures	$980,292,000	36
Paper and allied products	286,495,000	13
Leather and leather products	181,096,000	5
Food and kindred products	128,395,000	37

Land. Maine is located on the Atlantic coast of New England, in the northeastern corner of the United States. It is the first state to see the sunrise each morning. Although Maine is smaller in area than most other states of our country, it is almost as large as the rest of the New England states combined.

Most of Maine lies in the New England highlands. There is only one lowland area in the state. This is a narrow plain that extends from northeast to southwest along the Atlantic coast.

The highlands. Plateaus, hills, and mountains make up more than three fourths of the land in Maine. Most highland areas are covered with forests of birch, fir, spruce, and other trees. This

Forest-covered hills in Acadia National Park. This scenic park is located on Maine's coastal lowland and on two islands off the coast. Although most of the state's coastal lowland is level or gently rolling, steep hills rise in some places.

sportsmen who come to fish, or to hunt deer, bear, and other wildlife.

Several mountain peaks in Maine rise more than four thousand feet above sea level. Most of them are in the White Mountains, in the northwestern part of the state. The highest point in Maine is not in the White Mountains, however. It is Mount Katahdin, which rises sharply above the surrounding land in the central part of the state. This mountain, a monadnock,* is almost a mile high.

Most of the land in the highlands of Maine is not suited to farming. Glaciers have left many rocks, which must be removed from the soil before the land can be cultivated. However, there is one large, fertile farming area in Maine. This is in the northeastern part of the state, in Aroostook County.

The coastal lowland. A narrow lowland extends along the coast of Maine for about 230 miles. Most of this lowland is a level or gently rolling plain. However, in some places steep hills rise from the seacoast. In the waters off the coast are more than one thousand islands. Many of the islands are wooded and mountainous. On the largest of these, Mount Desert Island, one peak rises more than a thousand feet above sea level.

Maine's coastal lowland is noted for its beauty. In the southern part of the state, white sand beaches extend for miles along the coast. Northeastward from the mouth of the Kennebec River, the shoreline is more rugged. Here, white surf crashes against rocks and cliffs. There are many quiet coves and inlets along the coast from which fishermen put out to sea in their small boats.

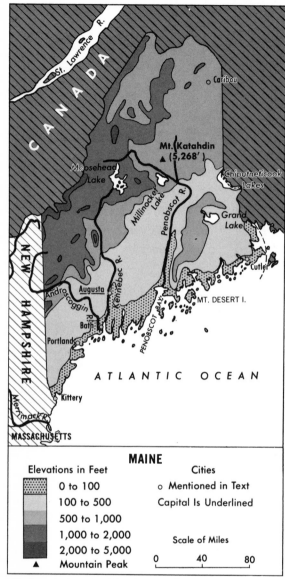

MAINE

Elevations in Feet

| 0 to 100 |
| 100 to 500 |
| 500 to 1,000 |
| 1,000 to 2,000 |
| 2,000 to 5,000 |
| ▲ Mountain Peak |

Cities

o Mentioned in Text

Capital Is Underlined

Scale of Miles

0   40   80

Maine is located in the northeastern corner of our country. Most of the state is hilly or mountainous. A narrow lowland borders the coast.

is one of the most heavily wooded states in our country.

More than one thousand clear, sparkling lakes dot the wooded highlands. These lakes were formed many centuries ago by glaciers. (See page 38.) The largest lake in Maine is Moosehead Lake, in the west central part of the state. (See map above.) The lakes and forests of Maine attract thousands of

256

*See Glossary

Most of Maine's people live on the coastal lowland. The southwestern part of this lowland is the most densely populated section of the state. Portland, Maine's largest city, is located here. Fewer people live in the northeastern part of the coastal lowland. Many of the people here earn their living as farmers or fishermen. Others work in fish canneries or in pulp and paper mills.

Climate. Maine has a cooler climate than most other states of the Northeast. This is mainly because the state lies so far north. In addition, winds from the ocean are chilled by cold currents that flow along the coast of Maine.

Winters in Maine are long and cold. In the northern part of the state, temperatures sometimes drop as low as fifty degrees below zero. One hundred inches of snow may fall in a single winter, and the land is white for several months. Because of the long winters, the growing season in northern Maine lasts only about three months. (See map on page 46.) Few areas in the United States have a shorter growing season than this.

In southern Maine, winters are not so severe. For example, the city of Portland receives only about seventy inches of snow each year. Here, the growing season is about five months long.

Summers in Maine are mild and invigorating. The average July temperature is only about sixty-five degrees. Summer nights are usually cool. The

A plywood factory near Moosehead Lake in central Maine. The vast forests that cover Maine are one of the state's most important natural resources. Factories in Maine make a wide variety of wood products, including plywood, pulp and paper, skis, canoes, and furniture.

pleasant summer weather helps attract thousands of tourists to Maine each year.

Maine receives thirty or more inches of rainfall each year. The rainfall is very evenly distributed throughout the four seasons.

Natural resources and industry. Maine has several valuable natural resources. There are deposits of a variety of minerals in the state. However, mineral production is not important at the present time. Forests, fisheries, and rushing rivers are Maine's most important natural resources. Forests cover more than four fifths of the state. Fish abound in waters off the Atlantic coast. Maine's many rivers are used to produce hydroelectricity. These resources provide raw materials and power for some of Maine's leading industries.

Maine lobster fishermen bring in the nation's largest catches of these shellfish. The state's fishermen also catch many herring, cod, and other fish.

Forest products. Both softwood and hardwood trees make up Maine's vast forests. Softwoods, such as spruce, fir, and pine, are used in building houses. Wood pulp and paper are also made from softwoods. Each year, millions of evergreen trees are harvested and shipped to other states for use as Christmas trees. Hardwoods, such as oak, birch, and maple, are used in making furniture, flooring, baseball bats, and many other products.

The manufacture of paper and paper products is Maine's leading industry. There are several large pulp and paper mills in the state. In these mills, wood from the state's forests is made into pulp, which in turn is used in making paper. Most of the mills are located beside rivers. Hydroelectric plants supply power to run machinery in some of the mills. Much of the paper manufactured in Maine is newsprint.* Many newspapers in New York, Philadelphia, and other large cities of the Northeast are printed on newsprint made in Maine.

Industries in Maine manufacture many other products from wood. Logs are sawed into lumber in more than two hundred mills. Other factories make plywood, canoes, skis, and many other wood products. Maine is our country's leading producer of wooden toothpicks.

Fishing and food processing. Maine is one of the leading fishing states in the Northeast. Thousands of tons of lobsters are taken from the cold waters of the Atlantic Ocean each year. Maine is noted for its fine lobsters. Millions of these tasty shellfish are shipped live to restaurants and fish markets in other parts of our country. Others are canned in processing plants in cities

258

Packaging fish at Portland. Processing food is an important industry in Maine. Along the coast are plants that freeze or can fish caught by Maine fishermen. Other plants prepare and package fruits and vegetables, including large quantities of potatoes from Aroostook County.

along the Maine coast. Herring, cod, scallops, and other fish are also brought to port by Maine fishermen. Tiny herring caught off the coast of Maine are canned and sold as sardines.* Plants in Maine pack millions of cans of these fish each year.

Processing plants in Maine also freeze and can fruits and vegetables. At the small town of Caribou in northeastern Aroostook County, workers prepare and package millions of dollars' worth of frozen french fries and instant mashed potatoes each year. Other plants freeze or can apple juice, blueberries, corn, and other fruits and vegetables. Food processed in Maine is sold in stores throughout our country.

Other industries. Maine has several other important industries. It is one of the leading states in our nation in the production of shoes. Textile mills in Maine produce large quantities of cotton and wool fabrics. Shipbuilding has been an important industry in Maine since colonial times. Shipyards at Bath and Kittery employ thousands of workers who build and repair vessels for the United States Navy. Pleasure yachts and fishing boats are also built in Maine.

Farming. Maine's land and climate are generally not well suited to farming. The land in most parts of the state is hilly or mountainous, and the soil is too thin and stony for growing crops.

259

In addition, the short growing season and cool summer weather make it impossible to grow many types of crops. The only large area of fertile farmland in Maine is in Aroostook County.

Aroostook County is one of the leading potato-producing areas of the United States. Farmers here harvest millions of bushels of potatoes each year. The cool, moist climate of Aroostook County, and the loose, loamy* soil found here are just right for growing this crop. Maine potatoes are shipped to many other states. Some Maine potatoes are grown to be sold as seed* potatoes. They are shipped to potato growers in more than twenty other states and in some foreign countries as well.

Several other crops are grown in Maine. Apples, sweet corn, and lettuce come from farms in the southwestern part of the state. Millions of pounds of blueberries are picked along the coast northeast of the Kennebec River. Many Maine farmers grow hay and oats to feed their livestock during the long winter months. None of these crops requires a long growing season.

Poultry, eggs, and dairy products are among Maine's leading farm products. Poultry farming has become very important in recent years, especially the raising of broiler chickens. Dairy farms in Maine supply milk needed by the people of the state. Farmers also ship milk to nearby Massachusetts.

Harvesting potatoes in Aroostook County. This county is one of the leading potato-producing areas of the United States. Farmers in Maine must raise crops, such as potatoes and hay, that grow well even in a cool climate. Chickens and milk are also important farm products in Maine.

People and cities. More than nine tenths of the people in Maine were born in the United States. Immigrants from Canada make up a large part of the state's foreign-born population. Many French-speaking farmers from the nearby Canadian province of Quebec have settled in Aroostook County.

Maine is less densely populated than any other state east of the Mississippi River. Large areas in the northwestern part of the state are uninhabited. There are few large towns or cities in Maine. Almost half the population lives in rural areas or in villages and towns with fewer than 2,500 people.

Portland (population about 78,000) is the largest city in Maine, and the only city in the state with a population of more than 50,000. It is located on beautiful Casco Bay, in the southwestern part of the state.

Portland is Maine's leading seaport and manufacturing city. It is also the main trading center for northern New England. Coal and petroleum are Portland's leading imports. These fuels are distributed to many communities in Maine and New Hampshire. Petroleum is also pumped to Canada through a pipeline that extends from Portland to Montreal. Portland's exports include canned fish, wood pulp, leather goods, and other products made here.

Augusta (population about 23,000) is the capital of Maine. It is located on the Kennebec River in the south central part of the state, about forty miles from the Atlantic coast. The Kennebec is used to produce electric power for shoe factories, textile plants, paper mills, and other manufacturing plants in Augusta.

Portland, Maine's largest city, lies along Casco Bay. It is the state's leading seaport and industrial city as well as an important trading center.

Learn About Maine With Maps

Study the map of Maine on page 256, and then answer the following questions:

1. What is the capital of Maine?
2. What country borders this state on the north?
3. What is the only state that borders Maine?
4. Name the highest point in the state and give its elevation.

Questions To Help You Learn

1. Why does Maine have a cooler climate than most other states of the Northeast?
2. What facts help to explain why food processing is an important industry in Maine?
3. Why are so many potatoes grown in Aroostook County?
4. Where have many of the foreign-born people in Maine come from?
5. What is Maine's largest city? About how many people live here?

20 Maryland

Facts About Maryland		
	Number or Value	Rank
Area (square miles)	10,577	42
Population	3,754,000	18
Capital—Annapolis		
Admission Date:		
April 28, 1788		7
Colleges and Universities	48	20
Farm Products	$ 346,514,000	35
Poultry and eggs	105,638,000	10
Dairy products	91,566,000	19
Cattle and calves	28,067,000	39
Fish	$ 17,356,000	10
Timber Harvested (cubic feet)	85,137,000	29
Minerals	$ 71,844,000	38
Stone	26,606,000	19
Sand and gravel	17,157,000	18
Coal	5,318,000	18
Manufactures	$3,587,852,000	20
Primary metal industries	555,563,000	12
Food and kindred products	503,364,000	16
Chemicals and allied products	402,883,000	17

Land. Maryland is a small state in the southern part of the Northeast. About half of Maryland lies in the lowland region of our country called the Coastal Plain. The rest of the state is in the Appalachian Highlands.

The Coastal Plain. Southern and eastern Maryland lie in the Coastal Plain. This region is divided into two parts by a long arm of the Atlantic Ocean called Chesapeake Bay. The part of the Coastal Plain that lies east of the bay is called the Eastern Shore. A small section of the Eastern Shore is bordered by the Atlantic Ocean. West of Chesapeake Bay, the Coastal Plain is called the Western Shore. Along both sides of the bay, the coast is cut by hundreds of smaller bays and inlets.

Chesapeake Bay divides Maryland's Coastal Plain into two parts — the Eastern Shore and the Western Shore. The Eastern Shore is low and flat. The Western Shore is slightly higher. Along both sides of Chesapeake Bay, hundreds of smaller bays and inlets cut into the coast.

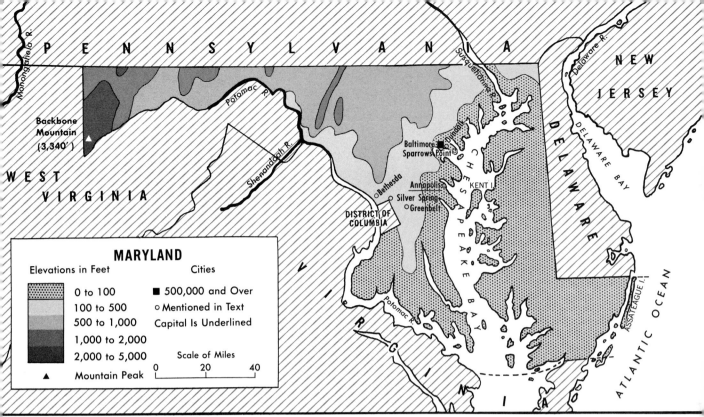

Maryland is located in the southern part of the Northeast. About half of the state lies in the Coastal Plain. The rest of Maryland lies in the Appalachian Highlands. The land rises from sea level along the coast to more than three thousand feet in the western mountains.

The Eastern Shore is low and flat. The land slopes gently from sea level in the south to only about one hundred feet above sea level in the north. Along the bay, fishing boats lie anchored in sheltered harbors. Neat dairy barns and poultry sheds dot the landscape. In the southern part of the Eastern Shore, the soil is sandy and well suited for growing tomatoes and other truck crops. In the northern part, the soil is better suited for raising crops such as corn and wheat.

The Western Shore is slightly higher than the Eastern Shore. In the southern part of this area, fields of green tobacco plants cover the countryside. Farther north, there are many busy cities and towns. This is the most heavily populated part of the state. Maryland's largest city, Baltimore, is located in this part of the Western Shore.

The Appalachian Highlands. The northern and western parts of Maryland lie in the Appalachian Highlands. Four sections of this great highland region extend through Maryland. These are the Piedmont Plateau, the Blue Ridge, the Appalachian Ridges and Valleys, and the Appalachian Plateau.

About one fourth of Maryland lies in the gently rolling Piedmont Plateau. The land here slopes gradually upward toward the west, to about one thousand feet above sea level. This is a fertile farming area. Field crops such as corn and wheat are raised here.

West of the Piedmont, the land becomes higher and more rugged. A range of forest-covered mountains extends from north to south through this part of Maryland. This range is part of the Blue Ridge. (See page 34.) West of the Blue Ridge is the Appalachian Ridges

263

and Valleys section of the state. Pastures and orchards cover the lower slopes of the ridges. In the fertile valleys are fields of hay and other crops.

Near the western border of the Appalachian Ridges and Valleys, a deep gorge called the Narrows forms a gateway through the highlands. In the 1800's, westward-bound pioneers traveled through this pass on the National Road. (See page 99.) Today, railroads and a modern highway follow the same route.

The extreme western part of Maryland lies in the Appalachian Plateau. Few people live here. Most of this section is too mountainous for farming. Coal mining and lumbering are the main occupations. Here, Backbone Mountain rises more than three thousand feet above sea level. This is the highest point in the state.

Climate. In most of Maryland, winters are mild and summers are warm. Changes in the weather from season to season are not as great here as in most other parts of the Northeast. Temperatures are usually higher in eastern Maryland than in western Maryland.

In winter, winds are warmed as they blow over the Atlantic Ocean and Chesapeake Bay. These winds bring mild weather to eastern Maryland. Temperatures rarely drop below freezing. When snow falls here, it usually melts quickly.

Winters are colder and much snowier in the highlands of western Maryland. As much as eight feet of snow may fall here in winter.

Spring comes early to eastern Maryland. Peach trees burst into bloom in early April. During this month, farmers on the Eastern Shore begin planting

A deep gorge called the Narrows forms a gateway through the highlands of western Maryland. In the 1800's, many pioneers traveled through this pass on their way westward. Today, railroads and a modern highway follow the same route.

snap beans, cucumbers, and other vegetables. They can grow more than one crop on the same land each year because the growing season here is more than six months long. Spring comes later to western Maryland, where the growing season is about five months long.

Summers are warm and humid in eastern Maryland. Many people flock to the shores of Chesapeake Bay to enjoy the cooling sea breezes. Small fishing vessels, sailboats, and cabin cruisers dot the bay in summer.

In western Maryland, summers are cooler. Farmers in this part of the state raise buckwheat and other crops that do not need hot weather to grow well.

Natural resources. Maryland produces small quantities of several important minerals. Limestone, granite, and other kinds of stone are quarried in the northern and western parts of the state. Coal is mined in the Appalachian Plateau. Some of the limestone and coal are used by steel mills in Maryland. Sand and gravel from pits on the Western Shore are used in building roads and in making concrete.

Forests cover nearly one half of Maryland. In the western and southeastern parts of the state, loggers harvest oaks, pines, and other trees. Most of the logs are made into lumber. The rest are used in the manufacture of pulp and other products.

From the waters of Chesapeake Bay, Maryland's fishermen take large catches of shellfish, such as oysters, crabs, and clams. Maryland leads all the states of the Northeast in the production of oysters and soft-shelled clams. Much of this seafood is canned or frozen in pro-

Hauling in oysters from Chesapeake Bay. Maryland fishermen bring in large catches of oysters, crabs, clams, and other shellfish.

cessing plants on the Eastern Shore. Fishermen also bring in large catches of shad, alewives, menhaden, and striped bass. Shad, alewives, and striped bass are used for food. Menhaden are used to make fertilizer and livestock feed.

Industry. Good transportation routes and nearby markets have helped industry to grow in Maryland. Baltimore is one of the Northeast's leading port cities. (See map on page 181.) Here oceangoing ships unload raw materials for Maryland's factories and load manufactured goods to carry to other states and countries. A fine system of roads and railroads links Maryland with other regions of our country. In addition, Maryland is located near many of the great cities of the Northeast. These cities provide excellent markets for goods produced in Maryland.

A steel plant at Sparrows Point. This is one of the largest steel plants in the world. Much of the steel produced here is used in Maryland factories to make products such as airplanes, ships, and tin cans. Processing ores to obtain metals is Maryland's leading industry.

Plants and mills in several parts of Maryland process ores to obtain metals. This is the leading industry in the state. Steel is the most important metal produced in Maryland. One of the world's largest steel mills is located near Baltimore, at Sparrows Point. Ships bring iron ore to this mill from Venezuela. Much of the steel made here is used in Maryland factories to make products such as airplanes, ships, tin cans, and bottle caps. Some of the steel is sent to other states and countries. Plants in Maryland also refine large quantities of copper.

Maryland's second most important industry is the processing of foods.

Many people work in plants where seafood, poultry, or vegetables are canned or frozen. Others work in dairy plants, where products such as butter and cheese are made from milk.

Another important industry in Maryland is the manufacture of chemicals and chemical products. Factories in the Baltimore area make a variety of agricultural chemicals such as fertilizers and insecticides. Other factories in the state make paints.

Transportation equipment is also made in Maryland. One of our country's largest shipyards is located on Chesapeake Bay. The manufacture of railroad equipment has been important in this state ever since the nation's first public railroad, the Baltimore and Ohio, was begun here in 1828. Plants in Maryland also make airplanes and aircraft parts.

Farming. Fertile soil, plentiful rainfall, and a long growing season make most of Maryland well suited to farming. Nearby large cities provide many customers for fresh foods, such as vegetables, eggs, and milk.

Farmers in Maryland earn more money from the sale of broiler chickens than they do from the sale of any other farm product. Most of these tender, young chickens are raised on poultry farms on the Eastern Shore. Maryland leads all the states of the Northeast in the production of broilers.

Milk is Maryland's second most important farm product. Dairy farms on the Piedmont and on the Eastern Shore help supply fresh milk for the millions of people who live in the Baltimore and Washington, D.C., metropolitan* areas.

In western Maryland, many farmers raise beef cattle. They graze their herds on the steep slopes of ridges and mountains where crops cannot be grown. Most of the cattle raised here are sent to feedlots* on the Piedmont to be fattened for market.

Many farmers on the Eastern Shore grow vegetables. Truck farms here supply tomatoes, snap beans, and other vegetables for people in nearby cities. The sandy soil and the long growing

*See Glossary

Feeding dairy cows. Most of Maryland is well suited to farming. The state's leading farm products are broiler chickens and milk. Vegetables, corn, tobacco, and other crops are also raised here. The millions of people in the Baltimore and Washington, D.C., metropolitan areas provide a good market for Maryland's farm products.

season make this area well suited to truck farming. Large amounts of the vegetables grown here are frozen or canned in nearby processing plants.

Corn and tobacco are the most important field crops grown in Maryland. Corn is raised mainly on the Piedmont and on the Eastern Shore. It is used as feed for beef and dairy cattle. Tobacco has been grown in southern Maryland since colonial days. Most of this tobacco is used in making cigarettes.

Farmers in Maryland also grow fruit. The two leading fruit crops are apples and peaches. Most of the orchards are located in the Blue Ridge and Appalachian Ridges and Valleys sections of the state.

Government work. Many people who live in Maryland work for the federal government. Some of these people work in Washington, D.C. Others are employed in government bureaus or research centers in Maryland. The National Institutes of Health is located at Bethesda. Here, scientists carry on research to find ways of curing and preventing diseases such as cancer and arthritis. At Greenbelt is the Goddard Space Flight Center, run by the National Aeronautics and Space Administration. Here, engineers and scientists plan, build, and test satellites that are designed to carry out scientific experiments in space.

People and cities. Nearly three fourths of Maryland's people live in cities or large towns. Most of them make their homes in the Baltimore and Washington, D. C., metropolitan areas. These two urban areas include many of Maryland's larger towns and cities. For example, the city of Dundalk (population about 82,000) is part of the metropolitan area of Baltimore. Silver Spring (population about 66,000) is part of Washington's metropolitan area.

Baltimore (population about 897,000) is located along a deep, wide harbor, where the Patapsco River empties into Chesapeake Bay. This city was planned in 1729 by Maryland's colonial government as a port from which to export tobacco. The mouth of the Patapsco River provided an excellent harbor for oceangoing ships.

Baltimore's settlers soon discovered another advantage of this location. Here, the Fall Line* lies close to the coast. Falls in the river could provide waterpower to run mills. Gristmills were built here to grind wheat that was grown on farms in Maryland. Baltimore soon became an important flour-milling town.

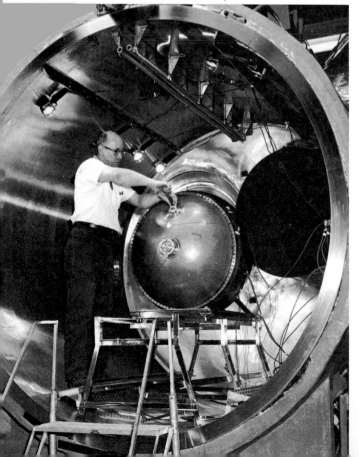

Working on a satellite. Many people who live in Maryland work for government agencies, such as the National Aeronautics and Space Administration.

268

Baltimore is Maryland's largest city. It lies along a deep, wide harbor at the mouth of the Patapsco River. Baltimore is one of our country's leading seaports and is an important manufacturing city. Many fine schools and colleges are located here.

In the 1800's, Baltimore grew as a seaport and trading center. Ships from many different countries stopped here to load and unload goods. Trade with settlements in the Midwest began to grow after the National Road was completed. (See page 99.) In 1858, the Baltimore and Ohio Railroad was completed from Baltimore to the Ohio River. Now Baltimore could exchange goods more quickly and easily with settlements in the Ohio Valley. The growth of trade encouraged the development of industry in the Baltimore area.

Today, Baltimore is part of the chain of cities in the Northeast called Megalopolis. (See map on page 197.) It is also one of the leading port cities of this region. Many of Maryland's important

manufacturing plants are located in the Baltimore metropolitan area. These include steel mills, copper refineries, and aircraft plants. In addition, Baltimore produces a variety of other goods, such as bottle caps, umbrellas, spices, and clothing.

Baltimore is noted for its many fine schools and colleges. Young people from all over the United States and from foreign countries come here to study medicine at Johns Hopkins University. Others study music at the Peabody Conservatory of Music.

Baltimore is a mixture of the old and the new. Some parts of the city have not changed much since the 1800's. Many people live in narrow red or yellow brick buildings with white marble

The United States Naval Academy is in Annapolis, the capital of Maryland. Annapolis is a very old city on the western shore of Chesapeake Bay.

steps, called row houses. These line street after street in some areas. In other parts of the city, there are modern houses and apartment buildings. Tall skyscrapers rise above the main business district.

Annapolis (population about 32,000) is the capital of Maryland. It is located on the western shore of Chesapeake Bay, near the mouth of the Severn River. Annapolis became the capital of the colony of Maryland in 1694. The state capitol building here is the oldest still in daily use in the United States. Maryland's legislature has met here to make laws for more than 180 years. Much of Annapolis looks the same as it did in colonial days. Large, red-brick mansions line narrow, tree-shaded streets.

Annapolis is the home of the United States Naval Academy. Here, young men are trained to serve as officers in the Navy or Marine Corps.

Discover Important Facts About Maryland

Read to find the answers to the following questions about Maryland:

1. In what main land regions of our country does Maryland lie?
2. What large body of water divides Maryland into two parts?
3. Why can farmers on the Eastern Shore grow more than one crop on the same land each year?
4. In what two large urban areas do most of Maryland's people live?
5. For what purpose was Baltimore founded?

Explore Maryland's History

Some important events in Maryland's history are listed in the next column. These events were also important to the rest of our country. Choose one of these, and then imagine you are a newspaper reporter sent to write an article about the event for your paper.

Francis Scott Key writes "The Star-Spangled Banner."

The first colonists arrive in Maryland from England.

The Baltimore and Ohio Railroad is completed.

An important battle of the Civil War is fought at Antietam Creek.

Do research about the event you have chosen. The suggestions on pages 347-349 will help you locate the information you need. Remember that a good newspaper story always tells:

a. who	d. what
b. when	e. how
c. where	f. why

When you feel you have all the information you need, write your article. Follow the guidelines for good writing given on page 347. Read your article to your class.

21 Massachusetts

Facts About Massachusetts		
	Number or Value	**Rank**
Area (square miles)	8,257	45
Population	5,469,000	10
Capital—Boston		
Admission Date:		
February 6, 1788		6
Colleges and Universities	108	6
Farm Products	$ 161,026,000	43
Dairy products	47,413,000	33
Greenhouse and		
nursery products	26,904,000	9
Poultry and eggs	26,521,000	30
Fish	$ 39,068,000	4
Timber Harvested (cubic feet)	27,210,000	38
Minerals	$ 43,340,000	43
Sand and gravel	20,106,000	17
Stone	19,501,000	26
Lime	3,380,000	13
Manufactures	$8,378,212,000	10
Electrical machinery	1,265,062,000	8
Nonelectrical machinery	1,152,850,000	8
Fabricated metal products	629,430,000	8

Land. Massachusetts extends across New England from New York State on the west to the Atlantic Ocean on the east. (See map on page 272.) A coastal lowland makes up the eastern third of the state. In the southeast, a long strip of sandy land curves like a giant fishhook far out into the Atlantic. This is Cape Cod. South of the cape are two fairly large islands that are part of the coastal lowland. These are Martha's Vineyard and Nantucket. The state's only other lowland area is the valley of the Connecticut River. This valley cuts from north to south through the highlands that cover most of western Massachusetts.

Highlands. The section of highlands west of the Connecticut Valley is the highest part of Massachusetts. In this

The island of Nantucket is part of the coastal lowland of Massachusetts. This lowland area also includes Cape Cod, a long, sandy strip of land that curves far out into the Atlantic Ocean. In summer, thousands of people come to cottages and resorts along the Massachusetts coast.

271

section are the Berkshire Hills. The state's highest peak, Mount Greylock, is in the Berkshires. This beautiful, wooded mountain rises about 3,500 feet above sea level. Each summer, thousands of tourists come to the Berkshires to fish, to swim, or to enjoy the magnificent scenery. Tourists also come in winter to ski.

The main farming and manufacturing area of the western highlands is a valley that runs north and south through the Berkshires. Dairy cattle graze on many grassy slopes in the valley. Pittsfield is the area's largest and most important city.

The highlands east of the Connecticut Valley are lower than the western highlands. The eastern highlands slope gradually downward to the coastal lowland. Many lakes and ponds dot the hilly land of these highlands. Quabbin Reservoir, the largest lake in Massachusetts, is located here. The city of Worcester is about twenty-five miles east of the reservoir.

Lowlands. The Connecticut Valley, which separates the western and eastern highlands, is broad and flat. The most fertile farmland in Massachusetts is found here. Several important manufacturing cities, such as Springfield and Holyoke, are situated along the Connecticut River.

The coastal lowland slopes downward from the eastern edge of the highlands to the ocean. Along the coast are many bays and inlets. In the north,

Massachusetts extends across New England from New York State on the west to the Atlantic Ocean on the east. The eastern third of Massachusetts and the valley of the Connecticut River are lowland areas. The rest of the state is made up of highlands.

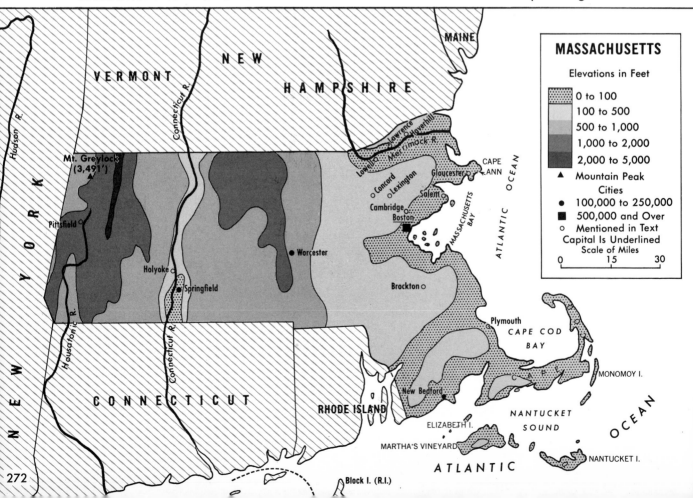

rocky cliffs rise above the ocean. Farther south, the land along the coast is low and sandy. About three fourths of all the people in Massachusetts live on the coastal lowland. Boston and several other manufacturing cities are located here. Much of the coast is lined with cottages, summer resorts, and parks. Cape Cod, with its beautiful sandy beaches, attracts many people in the summertime. Tourists come here to enjoy sports such as swimming, fishing, and sailing.

Climate. In Massachusetts, winters are longer and colder in the highlands than in the lowlands. This is mainly because temperatures are usually cooler at higher elevations. (See page 53.) The highest parts of the Berkshires may receive as much as seventy-five inches of snow during the winter. Much of the snow remains on the ground until spring. Along the coast, winters are generally milder. Here, winds that blow in from the Atlantic Ocean keep the weather from becoming very cold. (See pages 44 and 45.) The Boston area receives about forty inches of snow in winter, and an even smaller amount falls on Cape Cod.

Throughout the state, summers are short but fairly warm. Ocean breezes bring cool and pleasant summer weather to Cape Cod and other coastal areas, even during July and August. In the Berkshires, summer weather is also mild and comfortable.

The growing season is longer in some parts of Massachusetts than in others. (See map on page 46.) It is longest on the coastal lowland. Here, warm winds from the Atlantic help to delay the coming of frost. Along the state's south-

Canoe racing is one of the sports enjoyed by visitors to the highlands of Massachusetts. Each year, thousands of tourists visit the Berkshire Hills.

ern coast, for example, the growing season usually lasts more than six months. Farmers here can plant their crops earlier and harvest them later than farmers in any other part of the state. Therefore, two crops may be grown on the same land each year. In the fertile Connecticut Valley, crops can be grown outdoors for about five and one-half months. Most of the highland areas have a growing season of less than five months.

Natural resources. Massachusetts ranks fourth in the nation, after Alaska, California, and Texas, in the value of fish caught. Fishing boats of all kinds and sizes put out to sea from Gloucester, Boston, New Bedford, and other ports. (See pages 140 and 141.) Large amounts of fish such as whiting and flounder are caught in the Massachusetts coastal waters. Scallops, clams, lobsters, and other shellfish are also

Drying fishnets. Massachusetts is our nation's fourth most important fishing state. Fishermen return to ports in Massachusetts with huge quantities of cod, whiting, flounder, and other fish.

caught near the coast. Some Massachusetts fishermen sail north along the coast of Canada. They remain away from home for many days. If fishing is good, they return with large catches of haddock, ocean perch, cod, or flounder. Some of the fish caught by these fishermen are sold fresh. Most of the fish are frozen or canned and shipped to stores throughout the country.

About six out of every ten acres of land in Massachusetts are wooded. Forests of maple, birch, beech, oak, and other hardwoods grow in many parts of the state. In the western highlands, softwood trees, such as pine and hemlock, grow among the hardwood trees. Each year, some of the trees are harvested for making lumber and other wood products. Massachusetts forests cannot supply all of the wood needed by industries in the state, however.

Massachusetts has only a few mineral resources. Several kinds of stone are cut from quarries in the state. One of these is granite, which today is used mainly for monuments and tombstones. Large quantities of sand and gravel are dug from open pits. These minerals are used for various purposes, such as road building and other construction work.

Rivers and lakes have long been important resources in Massachusetts. Today, one of their most important uses is irrigation. For example, farmers in the Connecticut Valley use water from the Connecticut River to irrigate their land. Many ponds, lakes, and reservoirs in the state supply water to nearby cities and towns. At one time, swift-flowing streams provided waterpower for manufacturing. Today, some businesses in the state use these rivers to produce hydroelectricity for their factories.

Industry. Massachusetts has long been an important manufacturing state. Early in the nineteenth century, many factories were built along the Connecticut and Merrimack rivers. These streams provided waterpower for running machinery. Industry has continued to grow in Massachusetts ever since, even though machines are now run by electricity instead of by waterpower.

The most important kind of product manufactured in Massachusetts today is machinery. Although the state does not produce much of the steel or other metals needed for the manufacture of machines, these raw materials can be imported from other states of the Northeast. Also, many kinds of machinery do not require large amounts of raw materials. Instead, skilled workmanship is the main requirement. Massachusetts has a good supply of skilled workers to meet this need.

Both electrical and nonelectrical machinery are produced by factories in Massachusetts. Electrical machinery includes such products as lighting equipment, temperature-control devices, and switchboards. In addition, many small factories make radar equipment, television picture tubes, and other electronic products. Nonelectrical machinery produced in Massachusetts includes machine tools and machinery for textile mills and shoe factories.

The fabrication of metal products is also important in Massachusetts. The state ranks eighth in the nation in this industry. Metal products made in the Boston area include such items as knives and hand tools.

Many people in Massachusetts work in factories that make food products. Freezing and canning plants in the state process large quantities of fish each year. Other plants freeze or can fruits and vegetables, such as cranberries and sweet corn. These food products are sold throughout the nation.

Textile mills and clothing factories bring large amounts of money to Massachusetts. Although North and South Carolina lead the nation in the production of cotton textiles, Massachusetts manufactures more woolen textiles than any other state. The raw wool is imported from states in the West,

Skilled workers assemble an electrical laboratory in Springfield. Machinery is the most important kind of product manufactured in Massachusetts. Much of this is electrical machinery, such as lighting equipment, switchboards, and electronic products.

Machines making hosiery. Massachusetts produces large amounts of textiles and clothing. More woolen textiles are made here than in any other state.

or from Australia, Argentina, and other wool-producing countries. Woolen fabrics made in Massachusetts are sold in stores throughout the world. Large amounts of these materials are also used by factories in the state to make clothing. Some factories also make clothing from cotton or synthetic fabrics.

Massachusetts also leads the nation in the production of leather and leather products. In the eastern part of the state are many tanneries, where animal hides are treated to make leather. Much of this leather is made into shoes by factories in the Boston and Brockton metropolitan areas.

Many other products are made in Massachusetts. A number of plants here produce tires, raincoats, and other goods

made of rubber. Holyoke produces high-quality writing paper. Springfield is famous for its firearms. Printing and publishing is also an important industry in the state.

Farming. Only about one percent of the workers in Massachusetts earn their living by farming. Dairy farming is the most important kind of agriculture carried on in the state. The mild summers and regular rainfall in Massachusetts are well suited for growing grass and hay for cattle. The animals are also fed small amounts of grain, such as corn and oats, which farmers buy from the Midwest.

Dairy farms are located in all parts of Massachusetts. Dairying is especially important in the highlands, however, because the land and climate here are not well suited for growing most crops. Much of the milk produced in the state is sold to dairies in Boston and other large cities. The rest is made into products such as butter and cheese.

Farmers in Massachusetts also earn large amounts of money from the sale of poultry and eggs. Chicken farms are located in both the highlands and the lowlands. Turkeys are raised in the southeastern part of the state. The many people who live in cities and towns provide a large market for products from poultry farms. In Massachusetts, farmers earn more money from eggs than from poultry.

Massachusetts farmers raise many other farm products. Tobacco is the main crop grown in the fertile Connecticut Valley. Most of the tobacco grown here is used in making cigars. Beets, carrots, and other vegetables are raised on the coastal lowland as well as in the Connecticut Valley. Nurseries and greenhouses produce a variety of trees, plants, flowers, and shrubs. Each year, homeowners spend large sums of money for greenhouse products, such as trees and flowering shrubs, to landscape their yards. Tomatoes, green peppers, and certain other vegetables are often started from seed in greenhouses. The young plants are later transplanted outdoors.

Massachusetts leads the nation in the production of cranberries. In the southeastern part of the state there are many low, marshy places called bogs. Cranberries grow well in the wet, acid soil of these bogs.

Raising cranberries is hard work. Farmers keep their bogs covered with several inches of sand to prevent the growth of weeds. Sections of cranberry vines are pushed through this layer of sand into the soil beneath, where they take root.

Whenever frost threatens the cranberry crop, farmers must flood their bogs. This is done by allowing water from a pond or marsh to flow into a system of ditches, which cut across the bog. Besides keeping the berries from freezing, flooding provides moisture needed by the cranberry vines and also helps check the growth of weeds. When it is no longer needed, the water is allowed to drain away.

Harvesting cranberries. The nation's largest crops of cranberries come from bogs in southeastern Massachusetts. Dairying and poultry raising are important types of farming in the state. In lowland areas, farmers raise such crops as tobacco and vegetables.

In late September, the cranberry farmers hire pickers to harvest the ripe, red berries. Some of the cranberries are packaged and sold fresh. However, large quantities are sent to nearby plants where they are canned as sauce, juice, or jelly. These canned goods are shipped to stores in all parts of the United States.

People and cities. More than five million people live in Massachusetts. About five out of every six of these people live in cities and towns. The entire state lies within the densely populated part of the Northeast called Megalopolis. (See map on page 197.) However, the coastal lowland is much more thickly populated than the rest of Massachusetts. Here, many cities and towns are so close together you cannot tell where one of them ends and another one begins.

Massachusetts was settled by English colonists early in the seventeenth century. Since then, thousands of immigrants from many different countries have come here to live. Today, there are many people of foreign stock living in Massachusetts, especially in Boston and other large cities. Among these are people of Irish, Italian, French-Canadian, and Russian descent.

The Boston metropolitan area. More than one half of the entire population of Massachusetts lives in the Boston metropolitan area. This enormous urban area covers nearly one thousand square miles. In addition to the central city of Boston, there are about seventy-five smaller cities and towns included in the area. The largest of these is Cambridge, which has a population of about 93,000.

Boston (population about 638,000) is the capital of Massachusetts and the state's largest city. It is located on the Atlantic coast, at the place where the Charles River empties into Massachusetts Bay. (See map on page 272.) Boston is one of the leading seaports in the Northeast. It has an excellent deep-water harbor and more than forty miles of docks. Ships from other ports in the United States and from foreign countries steam into Boston Harbor carrying many different kinds of goods. The most important are petroleum and other raw materials. In addition, many fishing boats use Boston as their home port.

Boston is also a busy trading and manufacturing city. Many of the raw materials brought here by ship or train are reshipped to industrial plants in other cities and towns. Wholesale dealers in Boston sell products manufactured in the state to retail stores throughout the country. Boston's many industries include the manufacture of electronic equipment and other electrical machinery, food processing, and printing and publishing.

Since colonial times, Boston has been a leading center of education and the arts. Our country's first secondary school was established here by the colonists. Our country's oldest college — Harvard — is located in Cambridge, across the Charles River from Boston. Harvard, which was founded by the colonists in 1636, has become one of our leading universities. Today, the Boston metropolitan area has many fine colleges and universities besides Harvard, such as the Massachusetts Institute of Technology and Boston

Boston, the capital and largest city of Massachusetts, has long been an important Atlantic seaport. It is also a busy trading and manufacturing city. More than half of the state's population lives in the Boston metropolitan area. Here, also, are many fine colleges and universities.

College. Boston also has a number of museums and other cultural attractions. Many people enjoy viewing exhibits in the Museum of Fine Arts or listening to a concert by the Boston Symphony Orchestra.

Each year, large numbers of tourists are attracted to Boston because of its historic landmarks. One of these is Paul Revere's house, which was built about three hundred years ago. There are also several historic churches and meetinghouses in Boston. One of the best known is the Old State House. The Declaration of Independence was read from the balcony of this building in 1776. At the Boston Naval Base is the famous ship *Constitution,* nicknamed "Old Ironsides."

Today, the entire Boston metropolitan area is growing and changing rapidly. Many new buildings have been completed or are under construction. For example, in the city of Boston is an enormous new government center, where much of the work of running the state is carried on. Slums are being replaced with modern housing projects, parks, and playgrounds. Suburban residential communities are springing up almost overnight.

Worcester (population about 180,000) is the second largest city in Massachusetts. It is located in the eastern highlands. Highways and railroads connect Worcester with many other parts of the Northeast. These transportation routes have helped the city's industries to

Worcester is a thriving industrial city in central Massachusetts. It is served by several main highways and railroads. Worcester's industries have attracted workers from many foreign countries.

grow. Trucks and trains bring raw materials to plants in Worcester and deliver goods manufactured here to customers in Boston and other cities and towns.

Worcester is known for its wide variety of manufactured products. The city is one of the nation's leading producers of machine tools. Factories here also make nails and other wire products, looms, envelopes, shoes, and revolvers. The city's thriving industries have attracted workers from many foreign countries, such as Ireland and Canada.

Springfield (population about 174,000) is the third largest city in Massachusetts. It is located on the Connecticut River, not far from the Connecticut border. Settlers first came here in 1636. In the early 1700's, several sawmills and gristmills were established in Springfield. The Connecticut River provided waterpower for running these mills. During the Revolutionary War, Springfield produced firearms for the Continental Army. Today, factories in the city make a great many different kinds of goods, from matches to books. Firearms, machinery, and other metal products are especially important.

Learn About Massachusetts With Maps

Study the map on page 272 and then answer the following questions:
1. What is the capital of Massachusetts?
2. Name the largest peninsula in Massachusetts.
3. Name two islands that lie off the southeastern coast of Massachusetts.

Questions To Help You Learn

1. What scenic highlands lie west of the Connecticut Valley in Massachusetts?
2. In what part of Massachusetts is the growing season the longest? Why?
3. State one reason why many factories were established in Massachusetts in the early 1800's.
4. Why is raising cranberries hard work?

Learn More About Boston

Do research about the great city of Boston and then prepare an oral report about it for your class. Include information such as the following in your report:
1. interesting facts about Boston's founding and early history
2. places of interest in the city today
3. why Boston is considered a center of education and the arts
4. the development of the electronics industry in the Boston area
5. why Boston is one of the leading seaports of the Northeast

Pages 345-349 contain suggestions that will be helpful to you in finding information and in preparing your report.

22 New Hampshire

Facts About New Hampshire		
	Number or Value	Rank
Area (square miles)	9,304	44
Population	702,000	42
Capital—Concord		
Admission Date:		
June 21, 1788		9
Colleges and Universities	21	34
Farm Products	$ 56,403,000	48
Dairy products	22,208,000	41
Poultry and eggs	16,044,000	39
Greenhouse and		
nursery products	3,959,000	33
Fish	$ 683,000	29
Timber Harvested (cubic feet)	56,150,000	31
Minerals	$ 9,166,000	48
Sand and gravel	5,698,000	45
Stone	3,377,000	42
Clays	41,000	40
Manufactures	$ 866,114,000	39
Electrical machinery	139,518,000	23
Nonelectrical machinery	127,932,000	26
Leather and leather products	123,785,000	8

Land. New Hampshire is a small state in the northern part of New England. Nearly all of this state is made up of hills and mountains. A narrow coastal plain extends along the Atlantic Ocean.

The White Mountains. In the northern part of New Hampshire are several ranges of rugged mountains. These are the White Mountains. (See map on page 282.) Several peaks here rise more than one mile above sea level. The highest, Mount Washington, has an altitude of 6,288 feet. Mount Washington is less than half as high as many peaks in the western part of the United States, but it is the highest mountain in the entire Northeast.

Mount Washington, in the White Mountains of New Hampshire. This mountain, which rises more than 6,000 feet above sea level, is the highest peak in the Northeast. Few people make their homes in the White Mountains. However, many tourists come here each year to enjoy the beautiful scenery.

The White Mountains are noted for their beauty. Although the tops of the highest peaks are bare, the lower slopes are covered with dense, green forests of pine and other softwood trees. The mountains are separated by deep valleys. In these valleys are rushing rivers and clear, sparkling lakes.

Few people make their homes in the White Mountains. There is less industry here than in the southern part of the state, and most of the mountain

New Hampshire is a small state in northern New England. Nearly all of this state is made up of hills and mountains. A coastal plain borders the Atlantic Ocean.

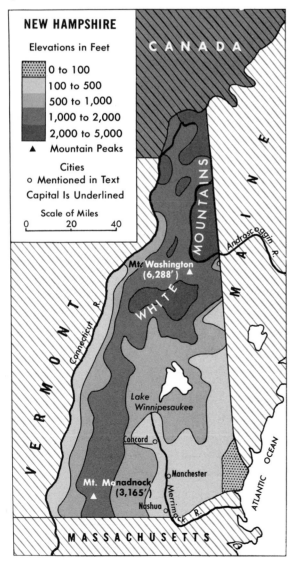

NEW HAMPSHIRE

Elevations in Feet

0 to 100
100 to 500
500 to 1,000
1,000 to 2,000
2,000 to 5,000
▲ Mountain Peaks

Cities
o Mentioned in Text
Capital Is Underlined

Scale of Miles
0   20   40

CANADA

VERMONT

Connecticut R.

WHITE MOUNTAINS

MAINE

Androscoggin R.

Mt. Washington (6,288')

Lake Winnipesaukee

Concord

Manchester

Mt. Monadnock (3,165')

Nashua

Merrimack R.

ATLANTIC OCEAN

MASSACHUSETTS

slopes are too steep for farming. However, many visitors come to the White Mountains each year to enjoy the beautiful scenery.

The plateau section. Most of southern New Hampshire is a hilly plateau. Millions of years ago, this area was quite mountainous. Through the centuries, most of the mountains have been worn away by wind and rainfall. A few peaks remain, however, because they are formed of very hard rock that does not wear away easily. Because one of these peaks is named Mount Monadnock, all mountains formed in this way are called monadnocks.

The plateau section of New Hampshire is dotted with hundreds of lakes and ponds, which were formed long ago by glaciers. (See page 38.) The largest body of water is Lake Winnipesaukee, which contains nearly three hundred islands.

The Merrimack River flows southward through the plateau section of New Hampshire, and the Connecticut River borders the state on the west. In both of these rivers are falls and rapids that provide waterpower for industry. New Hampshire's three largest cities — Manchester, Nashua, and Concord — all lie along the Merrimack River.

In the plateau section of New Hampshire, most of the soil is stony and poor for growing crops. The only fertile soil is in the narrow valleys of the Connecticut and Merrimack rivers.

The coastal lowland. New Hampshire's Atlantic coast is only about fifteen miles long. Sandy beaches stretch along the ocean. A gently rolling lowland extends westward from the coast for about fifteen miles. On this lowland are many towns and farms.

Climate. Winters in New Hampshire are long and cold. On winter nights, the temperature often drops below zero. In the White Mountains, the average yearly snowfall is more than one hundred inches. The heavy snowfall and the cold, clear winter days are excellent for skiing and other outdoor sports. Winter temperatures are highest and snowfall is lightest along the Atlantic coast, because of mild breezes from the ocean. (See pages 44 and 45.)

Spring comes late in most parts of New Hampshire. The growing season in the White Mountains is only about four months long. Along the Atlantic coast, the frost-free period lasts for about six months. When spring comes, millions of colorful wildflowers bloom in New Hampshire's woods.

Summers are mild and pleasant in most parts of New Hampshire, especially in the White Mountains and along the seacoast. Many vacationers from the large cities of the Northeast come to New Hampshire in the summertime to escape hot weather at home.

Fall is a lovely time of year to visit New Hampshire. The leaves of sugar maples and other hardwood trees turn to brilliant shades of orange, red, and gold. Autumn skies are usually bright blue. Nights are chilly, but days are pleasantly mild.

The climate on Mount Washington is one of the harshest to be found anywhere in the United States. This peak lies in the path of storms coming from many parts of North America. Winds blowing more than two hundred miles an hour have struck Mount Washington.

Skiing in the White Mountains. Winters in New Hampshire are long and cold. The growing season in most of the state is less than five months long.

These are the strongest winds ever recorded on the earth's surface. On top of the mountain is a government station where scientists study the weather.

Natural resources. Forests cover about four fifths of New Hampshire. They are among the state's most valuable resources. The trees in southern New Hampshire are mainly hardwoods, such as oaks, maples, beeches, and birches. In the northern part of the state, the forests are made up largely of pines, spruces, firs, and other softwoods. Much of the wood from the state's forests is cut into lumber. The rest is used mainly for making pulp and paper. White Mountains National Forest, in northern New Hampshire, is one of the largest national forests in the Northeast.

A paper mill in the forests of northern New Hampshire. Forests cover about four fifths of New Hampshire. They are one of the state's most valuable natural resources. Much of the wood from the forests is cut into lumber. Most of the rest is used in manufacturing pulp and paper.

Waterpower is another important resource of New Hampshire. In the early 1800's, many mills and factories were built along the Merrimack River to make use of the waterpower there. Today there are more than fifty hydroelectric plants on New Hampshire's swiftly flowing rivers. They supply almost half of the state's electric power. The rest is provided by steam power plants. The two largest hydroelectric plants in New England are on the Connecticut River in northern New Hampshire.

New Hampshire does not produce large amounts of minerals. Long ago, it was nicknamed the "Granite State" because of its rich deposits of granite. Today, however, little granite is being quarried. One reason is that most large buildings are now made out of steel and concrete instead of stone. Sand and gravel are now the chief minerals produced in New Hampshire. They are used mainly in building roads.

Manufacturing. Since the early 1800's, manufacturing has been important in New Hampshire. The earliest mills and factories were located along rivers such as the Merrimack to make use of the waterpower. Today, New Hampshire offers other advantages for industry. The state has a large supply of skilled workers. Also, it is close to Boston and other large cities of the Northeast, where there are many customers for manufactured products. About two fifths of all the workers in New Hampshire are employed in factories.

One of New Hampshire's leading industries is the manufacture of leather goods. Shoes have been made here for more than 140 years. There are leather tanneries* and many small shoe factories in the southern part of the state.

During the 1800's and early 1900's, textile manufacturing was New Hampshire's leading industry. In Manchester and other cities along the Merrimack River, there were many plants that manufactured cotton and woolen cloth.

The world's largest cotton mill was in Manchester. However, this mill was closed in the 1930's because of business troubles. During the next twenty years, a number of other textile companies shut down their plants in New Hampshire. Some of these companies moved their businesses to the South. (See page 122.) For a time, there were large numbers of unemployed workers in the state.

During recent years, business and government leaders have succeeded in attracting new industry to New Hampshire. In some cases, they did this by buying the empty textile mills and renting the buildings to other companies. Today, many companies that produce electrical and electronic equipment are

*See Glossary

Assembling small electric motors. Electrical machinery is one of New Hampshire's most important products. Factories in this state also make leather goods, precision tools, plastics, and chemicals. Like other New England states, New Hampshire has a good supply of skilled workers.

located in New Hampshire. Electrical machinery brings more money to the state than any other product. Other items now made in New Hampshire include precision tools, plastics, and chemical products.

The forests of New Hampshire provide raw materials for several industries. There are sawmills throughout the state. Lumber from these mills is used in making furniture, boats, sports equipment, and other products. In the northern part of the state are several large mills that manufacture pulp and paper.

The tourist industry. The beautiful scenery and healthful climate of New Hampshire attract more than three million tourists every year. Many people visit the White Mountains during the summertime to enjoy camping, hiking, and sight-seeing. During the winter,

Poultry raising and dairying are the two most important types of farming in New Hampshire. The land and climate of this state are generally not well suited to growing crops.

people come to the mountains for skiing and other winter sports. The shores of many lakes in New Hampshire are lined with summer cottages. Vacationers also come to the beaches along the Atlantic coast. Many people in New Hampshire operate hotels, restaurants, and other businesses that serve the needs of tourists.

Farming. There are fewer farms in New Hampshire today than there were fifty years ago. In much of the state, the soil and climate are not suitable for producing good crops. Many people have left their farms to seek jobs in industry. Today fewer than five out of every one hundred workers in New Hampshire earn their living from farming.

About half of all the farms in New Hampshire are too small to provide a good living for a family. The people who live on these farms usually work in nearby towns or cities, although they may earn extra money by raising a few chickens or growing some fruits and vegetables for sale. Some farmers earn money by selling trees on their land for lumber or pulpwood, or by growing Christmas trees.

Dairying and poultry raising are the most important kinds of farming in New Hampshire. They can be carried on even where the growing season is short or the land is poor for growing crops. Together they provide about two thirds of all the money earned by farmers in this state. Most of the dairy and poultry farms are in the southern part of the state, near the largest cities and towns.

Apples, potatoes, and hay are the main farm crops in New Hampshire. There are many apple orchards in the southern part of the state. Hay and potatoes are grown even in northern New Hampshire, where the growing season is too short for most crops. Most of the hay is fed to dairy cattle.

People and cities. Before the Civil War, most of the people in New Hampshire were of English, Scottish, or Irish descent. As industry grew during the late 1800's, large numbers of immigrants came to New Hampshire to work in factories. Many of the newcomers were French-speaking people from Canada. Today about one fourth of the people in New Hampshire are of French-Canadian descent. During the past hundred years, many immigrants have also come to New Hampshire from Poland, Greece, and other European countries. About three fifths of the people in New Hampshire live in cities or large towns.

Manchester (population about 94,000) is New Hampshire's largest city. It lies along the Merrimack River in the southern part of the state. The first settlers came here in the 1720's. Manchester began to grow rapidly in the early 1800's, after canals were built connecting it with Boston, Massachusetts. Waterfalls on the Merrimack River attracted a number of spinning and weaving mills.

Today Manchester is still an important industrial city. Among the products made in factories here are cotton and woolen textiles and leather goods such as shoes and boots. Other items manufactured in Manchester include electrical equipment, automobile accessories, and food products.

Concord (population about 27,000) is the capital of New Hampshire, and a trading center for people who live in rural areas of the state. During the 1800's, this city was noted for the manufacture of fine stagecoaches. Many travelers throughout our country rode in Concord coaches before the coming of railroads and automobiles. Today, a leading industry in Concord is printing. A number of magazines that are sold throughout the United States are printed here. In Concord there are also factories that make electrical goods, textiles, and leather and wood products. Many people in this city work for the state government.

Gain Important Understandings

1. What is a monadnock?
2. Why do few people make their homes in the White Mountains?
3. Why is the climate on Mount Washington so harsh?
4. How is the timber that is harvested from New Hampshire's forests used?
5. Why might New Hampshire's nickname be considered out of date today?
6. Why are dairying and poultry raising the most important kinds of farming in New Hampshire?
7. What is New Hampshire's largest city? About how many people live here?

Share an Imaginary Adventure
Imagine that you are taking a vacation trip to the White Mountains in New Hampshire. Do some research and then write a story about your trip to share with your class. Include the following in your story:
1. the route you will follow from your home
2. a description of the countryside as you travel through New Hampshire
3. a description of the weather here
4. your activities during your stay in the White Mountains
The guidelines on pages 345-349 will be helpful to you in locating information and in writing your story.

23 New Jersey

Facts About New Jersey		
	Number or Value	**Rank**
Area (square miles)	7,836	46
Population	7,093,000	8
Capital—Trenton		
Admission Date:		
December 18, 1787		3
Colleges and Universities	55	16
Farm Products	$ 248,016,000	37
Vegetables	75,341,000	10
Dairy products	49,006,000	30
Poultry and eggs	34,308,000	29
Fish	$ 10,716,000	13
Timber Harvested (cubic feet)	16,328,000	41
Minerals	$ 77,466,000	36
Sand and gravel	33,570,000	8
Stone	30,343,000	18
Clays	1,008,000	27
Manufactures	$12,246,302,000	7
Chemicals and allied products	2,799,914,000	1
Electrical machinery	1,671,922,000	6
Food and kindred products	1,106,223,000	7

Land. The small state of New Jersey is located on the Atlantic coast. As the map on the opposite page shows, most of this state's boundaries are formed by waterways. On the west and south, New Jersey is bordered by the Delaware River and Delaware Bay. To the east, it is bordered by the Hudson River and the Atlantic Ocean.

Slightly more than half of New Jersey lies in the Coastal Plain region of our country. The rest of the state is in the Appalachian Highlands.

The Coastal Plain. The low, sandy Coastal Plain extends across the southern part of New Jersey. The land here seldom rises more than one hundred feet above sea level. Off the Atlantic coast lies a long chain of narrow, sandy

The Piedmont Plateau of northern New Jersey is an area of gently rolling land. In the western Piedmont are many farms and small towns. Most of New Jersey's largest cities are located in the eastern Piedmont. This is the most densely populated part of the state.

islands. Shallow bays and lagoons separate these from the mainland. New Jersey's Atlantic coast has many miles of white, sandy beaches bordered by seashore resorts.

Much of the Coastal Plain is not suitable for farming. Marshes and forests cover large areas. In the southeastern part of the state is a huge wasteland called the Pine Barrens. Here, scrubby pine trees and swamps cover thousands of acres.

Other parts of the Coastal Plain are better suited for farming. The soil in the western part of this lowland is good for growing vegetables. In spring and summer, rows of green tomato plants, asparagus, and other growing vegetables cover thousands of acres here.

The Appalachian Highlands. North of the Coastal Plain, the Piedmont Plateau section of the Appalachian Highlands extends across New Jersey. This gently rolling plateau makes up about one fifth of the state. Some of the hills here rise to nine hundred feet above sea level.

The eastern part of the Piedmont is very densely populated. Newark, New Jersey's largest city, is located here. Newark is surrounded by a huge urban area that includes most of New Jersey's other large cities. The Hudson River, New York Bay, and several smaller waterways separate this area from New York City.

The western part of the Piedmont is less densely populated, although there are numerous small towns in this area. In the fertile red soil here, farmers grow corn, hay, and other field crops. Herds of dairy cattle graze on green hillside pastures.

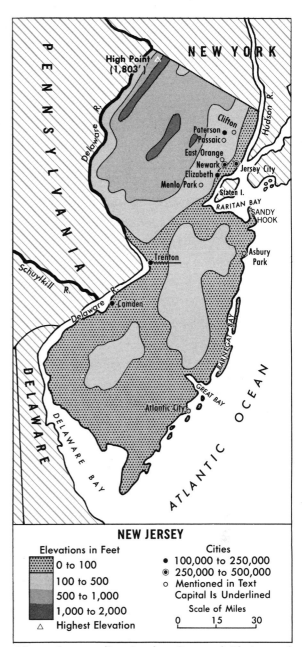

New Jersey lies in the Coastal Plain and Appalachian Highlands regions. Waterways form most of the state's boundaries.

Northwestern New Jersey is made up of long ridges and valleys. Forests of oak, birch, and other trees cover the ridges. In the valleys are fertile farmlands. Hundreds of lakes and ponds dot the countryside. These attract many vacationers each year. Many of the ridges here rise to about one thousand feet above sea level. At one point, the Delaware River has cut a deep gorge through the highlands. This is called the Delaware Water Gap.

Climate. In most of New Jersey, the climate is mild. Winds blowing in from the Atlantic Ocean help to keep temperatures from going very high in summer or very low in winter.

Summers are warm throughout New Jersey. Refreshing sea breezes make summer days pleasant along the coast. The mild summer weather here has helped to make the New Jersey shore a popular resort area. From late spring until early fall, millions of vacationers visit the seashore resorts that line the coast. Inland from the coast, summers are warmer. The weather is sometimes uncomfortably hot and humid, especially in the cities. Many city dwellers have summer cottages on the lakes in northern New Jersey, or at the sea-

shore. They spend weekends and vacations here.

The waters along New Jersey's coast stay warm until late in the fall. Ocean breezes help to delay the first killing frost in coastal areas until about the first of November. The growing season here is more than six months long. Farther inland, the frost-free season is shorter. (See map on page 46.)

Winters are mildest along the southeastern coast of New Jersey. Here, daytime temperatures are usually above freezing, and snowfall is light. In the rest of the state, winters are colder and snowfall is heavier. The northwestern highlands receive an average of more than forty inches of snow. Iceboating and ice-skating are popular sports on frozen lakes and rivers here.

Natural resources. Deposits of several important minerals are found in New Jersey. In the northern part of the state, workers quarry basalt,* granite, and other kinds of stone. The basalt is used mainly in the construction of roads. Large quantities of sand and gravel are taken from pits throughout the state. These materials are used in making concrete and in building roads. Some of the sand is used in making glass. Bottles and other glassware have been made in southern New Jersey since colonial days. There are also valuable deposits of zinc in New Jersey.

Many different kinds of fish are found in the waters off New Jersey's coast. Some of New Jersey's fishermen take large catches of shellfish, such as clams, crabs, and oysters, from the shallow waters along the coast. Other fishermen go far out into the Atlantic Ocean and bring back boatloads

The Delaware Water Gap is a gorge cut through the highlands by the Delaware River. It forms part of the border between Pennsylvania and New Jersey.

290   *See Glossary

A large chemical plant at Elizabeth. New Jersey is a leading industrial state. Chemicals and chemical products are the state's most important manufactured goods. Manufacturing electrical machinery and processing foods are also important industries here.

of menhaden, flounder, and other fish. Much of the seafood is frozen or canned in processing plants in the state.

Forests cover about half of New Jersey. However, few trees are cut today. Many of the original forests were cut down. The trees that grow here now are not suitable for being made into lumber. In addition, large areas of forest land are owned by the state. Many of these serve as recreation areas. The forests are also important for the conservation of soil, water, and wildlife.

Industry. New Jersey is one of our country's leading manufacturing states. Although this small state ranks only forty-sixth in area among all the states, it ranks seventh in the value of its manufactures.

New Jersey offers many advantages for industry. The entire state lies within the huge urban area of the Northeast called Megalopolis. Nearby great cities such as New York and Philadelphia provide huge markets for New Jersey's manufactured goods. Densely populated urban areas in New Jersey supply many skilled workers for industry.

New Jersey has several other advantages for industry. For example, there is more land available here than in nearby New York City, and it is less expensive. Factory owners who want to expand their businesses often build plants in New Jersey instead of in New York City. In addition, good transportation routes link New Jersey with other parts of the United States and with foreign countries. Excellent networks of highways and railroads cross the state. Oceangoing ships can travel up the Delaware River or into New York Bay to ports in New Jersey.

The most important branch of manufacturing in New Jersey is the chemical industry. The state is our country's leading producer of chemicals and chemical products. This industry is very important to other industries because chemicals are used in the manufacture of so many different products.

The chemical industry began to develop rapidly in New Jersey during World War I. Before that time, certain kinds of chemicals needed by the United States were produced mainly in Europe. During the war, when our country could not import these chemicals, several plants were established in New Jersey to manufacture them.

Today, New Jersey produces a wide variety of chemicals and chemical products. Some plants here make basic* chemicals. These are made from such raw materials as coal, petroleum, and natural gas. Other plants use basic chemicals in making insecticides, paints, drugs, soaps, and other products.

Another important industry in New Jersey is the manufacture of electrical machinery. Many of New Jersey's workers have jobs in plants that produce

Sorting tomatoes at a plant in Camden. Many workers in New Jersey have jobs in food-processing plants. Some of these plants make soups or juices from vegetables. Others process seafood. Foods processed in New Jersey are sold in many parts of our country.

The boardwalk and beach at Atlantic City. Thousands of tourists visit New Jersey's seaside resorts each summer. Atlantic City and Asbury Park are the state's best-known resorts. Large numbers of workers in New Jersey are employed in providing goods and services for tourists.

parts used in making television sets or radios. Others work in factories that make household appliances, such as air conditioners and sewing machines.

The food-processing industry employs many of New Jersey's workers. Some of these people work in plants that can or freeze seafood. Others have jobs in plants where fresh vegetables are packaged and frozen or made into soups and juices. Still others work in bakeries, dairies, or meat-packing plants.

New Jersey is one of the leading oil-refining states in the Northeast. Crude oil produced in Texas and Oklahoma flows to refineries in New Jersey through giant pipelines. Some crude oil is also brought here by ship. In New Jersey, the oil is refined to make many valuable products, such as gasoline and fuel oil.

New Jersey also produces many other kinds of manufactured goods. Some plants here make metal products such as tin cans and hand tools. Others make parts for giant earth-moving machines. There are also shipyards and automobile-assembly plants in the state. Factories in the Newark area make suits, dresses, and other clothing.

The tourist industry. Many workers in New Jersey have jobs in hotels, restaurants, or other establishments that provide goods and services for tourists. In a single year, as many as sixteen million tourists may visit New Jersey.

293

Many of them are summer vacationers who are attracted by the sandy beaches and pleasant climate of the state's Atlantic coast. More than fifty resort cities and towns line this coast. Two famous resorts here are Atlantic City and Asbury Park. Many vacationers also visit the lakes in the highlands of New Jersey. Tourists spend about two billion dollars in New Jersey every year.

Farming. New Jersey is one of the most important truck-farming states in the Northeast. Every year, millions of dollars' worth of tomatoes, potatoes, asparagus, and other vegetables are grown on truck farms in the southern part of the state. Because so many vegetables are grown in New Jersey, its nickname is the "Garden State." On pages 157 and 158, you can read about a New Jersey truck farm.

There are several reasons why truck farming is important in New Jersey.

Harvesting beans. Farmers in New Jersey produce large quantities of vegetables, milk, and eggs for the millions of customers in nearby cities.

Farmers here are close to many large markets for fresh vegetables. The millions of people who live in the urban areas of New York and Philadelphia buy huge quantities of fresh foods each day. Vegetables can be rushed from New Jersey's farms to these cities on the same day they are harvested. In addition, canning and freezing plants in New Jersey process large amounts of fresh vegetables. The sandy soil in southern New Jersey is well suited for growing vegetables, and the long growing season makes it possible to grow more than one crop on the same land each year.

Farms in New Jersey also produce other kinds of foods for people in nearby cities. In the northern part of the state, dairy farms supply millions of gallons of fresh milk each year. On poultry farms, farmers raise chickens mainly for their eggs. From orchards and berry farms come peaches, apples, blueberries, and strawberries. Cranberries are grown in bogs in the southern part of the state.

Near the large urban areas of New Jersey are many greenhouses and nurseries. They supply cut flowers, potted plants, and shrubs for the homes and gardens of city dwellers.

People and cities. New Jersey is the most densely populated state in our country. About nine out of every ten people here live in urban areas. Most of New Jersey's large cities and towns are located in the northeastern part of the state. This section of New Jersey is actually part of the New York Metropolitan Region. (See page 205.) Bridges and tunnels link New Jersey with New York City. More than 200,000 New

Newark, New Jersey's largest city, is located along the Passaic River, not far from the Atlantic Ocean. It is a busy industrial and port city. Factories here make electrical machinery and many other goods. The Newark metropolitan area includes several other large cities.

Jersey residents have jobs in New York. Each workday, these people travel by bus, train, or car to offices and factories there.

About one fourth of New Jersey's people were born in foreign countries or have one or both parents who were foreign born. During the late 1800's and early 1900's, thousands of immigrants entered our country through New York City's port. Many of these people were attracted to the growing industrial cities in nearby New Jersey. Large numbers of people from Italy, Germany, Poland, and other European countries settled in New Jersey and took jobs in factories here.

New Jersey's population is increasing rapidly. In recent years, many Ne-

gro workers have moved from southern states to cities in New Jersey. In addition, each year many people move from New York City to the less-crowded residential areas here. Large suburban districts have grown up around the cities in New Jersey. Many houses, apartment buildings, and shopping centers are built each year to meet the needs of New Jersey's increasing population.

Newark (population about 402,000) is New Jersey's largest city. It is located on the west bank of the Passaic River, where the river flows into Newark Bay.

More than one and one-half million people live in the Newark metropolitan area. Included in this area are some of New Jersey's other important cities,

295

such as Elizabeth and East Orange. There are also many small residential towns and villages in the Newark metropolitan area.

Newark is served by many of the Northeast's main transportation routes. This location has helped Newark to become an important industrial and port city. Much of the ocean freight shipped in and out of the Northeast passes through the city's port. Raw materials for factories in Newark are brought in by ship or by freight train.

Factories in the Newark metropolitan area produce a wide variety of manufactured goods. Electrical machinery, textiles, clothing, chemicals, paints, jewelry, and leather goods are made here. Also, many insurance companies have their headquarters in Newark.

Newark is made up of sprawling industrial sections, crowded business districts, and quiet residential areas. Near the waterfront are huge warehouses and factories. Farther inland, tall skyscrapers rise above the main business district. In the city's western outskirts, homes and parks border treelined streets.

Jersey City (population about 271,000) is the second largest city in New Jersey. It is located on the Hudson River, directly across from the section of New York City called Manhattan.

Jersey City is an important transportation center and transfer point for the Northeast. Freight trains bring

Jersey City lies across the Hudson River from New York City. Large quantities of goods enter and leave the United States through Jersey City's busy port. Industry is also important in this city. Factories here make such goods as chemicals and clothing.

Assembling an electron microscope in a Camden factory. Camden lies just across the Delaware River from Philadelphia, Pennsylvania. Camden's shipyards are among the largest in the world. In addition to ships, products manufactured here include chemicals, leather, and electronic equipment.

goods here from all parts of our country. At Jersey City, some of the freight cars are loaded onto ferries and carried to New York City, where their cargo is unloaded. Other freight cars remain in Jersey City. Their cargo is loaded onto oceangoing ships for export. In turn, large amounts of goods from all over the world are unloaded at Jersey City's port for shipment by rail to other parts of the United States.

Many of Jersey City's workers are employed in factories that make such products as chemicals, clothing, and electrical equipment. Some have jobs in meat-packing plants. Others work for publishing companies.

Paterson (population about 150,000) is New Jersey's third largest city. It is located on the Passaic River, about twelve miles north of Newark. This location was selected by the city's founders because falls in the Passaic River could furnish waterpower to run machines in mills and factories.

More than one million people live in the Paterson metropolitan area. This area includes the cities of Passaic and Clifton, and also many smaller towns and residential communities. Many people who live in this part of New Jersey work in New York City.

The weaving and dyeing of silk textiles has been an important industry in

Paterson since the mid-1800's. Other products made here include chemicals, clothing, machinery, and plastics.

Camden (population about 118,000) is located on the Delaware River directly across from Philadelphia, Pennsylvania. It is actually a part of the Philadelphia metropolitan area. Many people who work in Philadelphia make their homes in or near Camden. Two bridges connect these cities.

The shipyards that line Camden's waterfront are among the largest in the world. Tankers, ocean liners, and freighters are among the many kinds of ships built here. Other important products manufactured in Camden include chemicals, leather, and electronic equipment. Food-processing plants here make soups and other products from vegetables grown on nearby truck farms. Camden is also an important shipping center for fresh vegetables.

Trenton (population about 102,000) is the capital of New Jersey. This city is located on the Delaware River, in the west central part of the state.

Factories in Trenton make rubber goods, cigars, and pottery products such as dishes and tiles. Some of the finest chinaware made in our country comes from Trenton. Steel cables made in factories here support many of the large bridges in our country, such as the Brooklyn Bridge in New York and the Golden Gate Bridge in California.

Learn About New Jersey With Maps
Study the map on page 289, and then answer the following questions:
1. What is the capital of New Jersey?
2. What river flows along the state's western border?
3. Name the cities in New Jersey that have populations of 100,000 or more.
4. What body of water borders most of New Jersey on the east?
5. Name the states that border New Jersey.

Questions To Guide Your Reading
1. In what main land regions of our country does New Jersey lie?
2. Why is New Jersey well suited to truck farming?
3. List three advantages that New Jersey offers for industry.
4. What part of New Jersey is the most densely populated?

Learn About New Jersey's History
Do some reading about the history of New Jersey and then write a report about it to share with your class. Your report should answer the following questions:

1. What groups of people first lived in the area that is now New Jersey?
2. Name some of the early explorers of this area.
3. Where and by whom were early settlements made in this area?
4. What important events took place here during the Revolutionary War?
5. When did New Jersey become a state?
6. What are some of the important developments that have taken place since statehood?

For help in locating information and writing your report, refer to the suggestions on pages 345-349.

Share Ideas in a Discussion
As a class, discuss the following question:
    In what ways is New Jersey important to the rest of our country?
Prepare for your discussion by reading and taking notes. Look for information about farming, natural resources, industry, and recreation facilities in New Jersey. The suggestions on page 351 will help you to have a successful discussion.

24 New York

Facts About New York		
	Number or Value	**Rank**
Area (square miles)	49,576	30
Population	18,078,000	2
Capital—Albany		
Admission Date:		
July 26, 1788		11
Colleges and Universities	214	1
Farm Products	$ 1,041,992,000	14
Dairy products	557,058,000	2
Vegetables	114,327,000	6
Poultry and eggs	90,751,000	14
Fish	$ 12,711,000	12
Timber Harvested (cubic feet)	153,287,000	23
Minerals	$ 299,636,000	19
Stone	63,510,000	4
Sand and gravel	45,812,000	5
Salt	42,488,000	5
Manufactures	$24,588,259,000	1
Printing and publishing	3,192,027,000	1
Nonelectrical machinery	2,695,362,000	4
Apparel and related products	2,586,075,000	1

LAND

The land in New York differs greatly from place to place. In this state are forested mountains, fertile lowlands, and many rivers and lakes. Most of New York lies in the Appalachian Highlands region of our country. (See map on page 27.) Less than one fourth of the state is made up of lowlands. However, most of the people of New York live in the lowland areas.

The lowlands. There are three main lowland areas in New York. These are the Erie-Ontario Lowland, the Hudson-Mohawk Lowland, and the Coastal Plain.

The Erie-Ontario Lowland. In the western part of New York State, fertile plains extend along the shores of Lake

The Erie-Ontario Lowland, near Syracuse. The fertile plains that make up this lowland extend along the shores of Lake Erie and Lake Ontario. Some of New York's great manufacturing cities, such as Syracuse, Buffalo, and Rochester, are located on this lowland.

Erie and Lake Ontario. (See map on opposite page.) The plain bordering Lake Ontario is about thirty miles wide. The Lake Erie plain is much narrower. Most of the Erie-Ontario Lowland is flat or gently rolling. In many places, there are orchards, vineyards, or truck farms. Some of New York's great manufacturing cities, such as Buffalo, Rochester, and Syracuse, are located on the Erie-Ontario Lowland.

At the western end of the Lake Ontario plain in New York is the Niagara River. This river flows from Lake Erie into Lake Ontario, and forms part of the border between the United States and Canada. At one point, the river plunges over a steep cliff, forming beautiful Niagara Falls. These falls attract more than three million tourists each year. Giant hydroelectric plants use water from the Niagara River to produce electric power for homes and factories in both the United States and Canada.

A gently rolling plain extends northeastward from Lake Ontario along the St. Lawrence River. (See map on opposite page.) This part of New York is becoming more important. A large hydroelectric power project on the St. Lawrence River, near the village of Massena, was completed in 1962. Low-cost hydroelectric power produced here is attracting new industry to the area.

The Hudson-Mohawk Lowland. The valleys of the Hudson and Mohawk rivers form another important lowland in New York. The Hudson River begins in the Adirondack Mountains, in the northeastern part of the state. It flows southward for more than three hundred miles and empties into the Atlantic Ocean at New York City. (See map on oppo-

300

site page.) The Mohawk River is the largest tributary* of the Hudson. It flows southeastward from the central part of the state and joins the Hudson near the city of Albany. The Hudson-Mohawk Lowland is a natural passageway through the Appalachian Highlands.

The Hudson-Mohawk Lowland has helped New York to grow into a great state. Early pioneers used the valleys of the Hudson and the Mohawk to travel westward. In 1825, the Erie Canal was opened. This canal connected the Hudson River with Lake Erie. After the canal was completed, farmers in the Midwest were able to ship their crops to cities along the Atlantic coast. Barges going westward through the canal carried goods manufactured in the factories of the Northeast. Towns that were situated along the canal began to prosper. Between 1820 and 1840, New York City, at the mouth of the Hudson River, more than doubled in population.

The Coastal Plain. Another major lowland area in New York is Long Island, which is part of the Coastal Plain region of our country. This large, fish-shaped island extends eastward into the Atlantic Ocean for a distance of about 120 miles. (See map on opposite page.) It is larger than the entire state of Rhode Island. The land on Long Island is generally low and level, and its soil is sandy.

Long Island is one of the most densely populated parts of the Northeast. More than seven million people live here. The western end of the island is part of New York City, and the rest is included in the New York Metropolitan Region. (See page 205.) The eastern part of Long Island is an important farming area.

*See Glossary

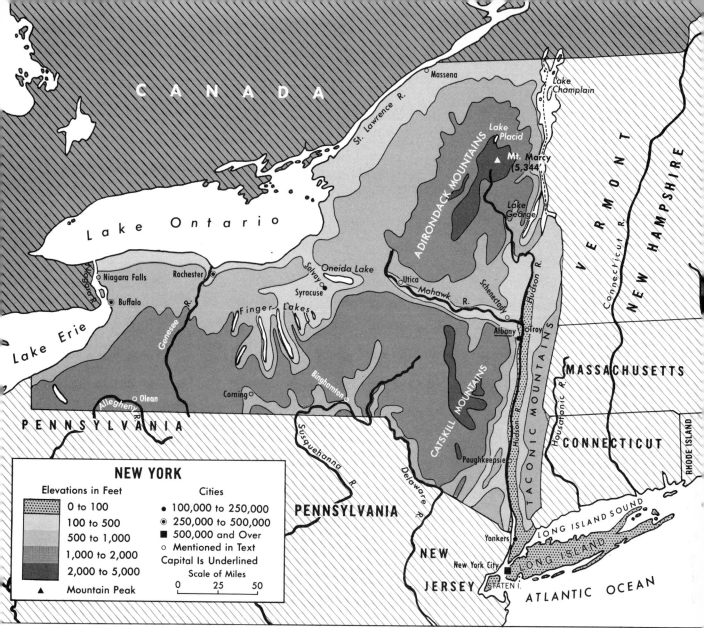

The following labels appear on the map:

CANADA

St. Lawrence R.

Massena

Lake Champlain

Lake Ontario

ADIRONDACK MOUNTAINS

Lake Placid

▲ Mt. Marcy (5,344')

Lake George

Niagara Falls

Rochester ◎

Oneida Lake

Solvay

Syracuse

Buffalo

Utica

Mohawk R.

Schenectady

Hudson R.

VERMONT

NEW HAMPSHIRE

Niagara R.

Genesee R.

Finger Lakes

Albany Troy

Connecticut R.

Lake Erie

Binghamton

Corning

Olean

Allegheny R.

PENNSYLVANIA

Susquehanna R.

CATSKILL MOUNTAINS

TACONIC MOUNTAINS

Housatonic R.

MASSACHUSETTS

CONNECTICUT

Delaware R.

Poughkeepsie

PENNSYLVANIA

RHODE ISLAND

NEW JERSEY

Yonkers

New York City

STATEN I.

LONG ISLAND SOUND

LONG ISLAND

ATLANTIC OCEAN

NEW YORK

Elevations in Feet
- 0 to 100
- 100 to 500
- 500 to 1,000
- 1,000 to 2,000
- 2,000 to 5,000
- ▲ Mountain Peak

Cities
- ● 100,000 to 250,000
- ◎ 250,000 to 500,000
- ■ 500,000 and Over
- ○ Mentioned in Text

Capital Is Underlined

Scale of Miles
0   25   50

New York is the largest state in the Northeast. Most of the state lies in the Appalachian Highlands region of our country. The Hudson-Mohawk Lowland forms a natural passageway through the highlands. Another important lowland area is Long Island, which lies in the Coastal Plain region.

The highlands. Most of New York State lies in the Appalachian Highlands region of our country. In New York, the two largest sections of the Appalachian Highlands are the Appalachian Plateau and the Adirondack Mountains. (See map on page 27.)

The Appalachian Plateau. Most of southern New York lies in the Appalachian Plateau. This area includes the Catskill Mountains and other highlands that extend westward from the Catskills almost to Lake Erie. (See map above.) There is very little level land in this part of the state. Through the centuries, rivers and streams have cut deep valleys through the plateau, leaving the land hilly and mountainous.

The rolling, wooded Catskill Mountains are the highest part of New York's Appalachian Plateau section. These mountains lie in the southeastern part of the state, west of the Hudson River. Many of the peaks are between three

In the Catskill Mountains. These rolling, wooded mountains, located only a short distance from New York City, are a popular resort area.

and four thousand feet above sea level. The Catskills are noted for their beauty. Because they are located only a short distance from New York City, they are a popular resort area. The Catskills are important for another reason. Here, rivers have been dammed to create large reservoirs.* (See page 132.)

West of the Catskills, the Appalachian Plateau is made up of ridges and rounded hills. In summer, thousands of dairy cattle graze on grassy slopes here. More milk is produced on farms in the Appalachian Plateau than in any other part of New York.

The Adirondack Mountains. The Adirondacks make up about one fourth of the land in New York. These forest-covered mountains are located in the northeastern part of the state. The highest mountain in New York is in the

Adirondacks. This is Mt. Marcy, which rises 5,344 feet above sea level. Although few people live in the Adirondacks, the rugged beauty of these mountains attracts large numbers of vacationers each year.

New York's lakes. In addition to the two Great Lakes that border New York, many other lakes lie in or border this state. Most of them were formed by glaciers. (See page 38.) The largest lake is Lake Champlain. It forms part of the boundary between New York and Vermont and extends into Canada. A section of the New York State Barge Canal connects this lake with the Hudson River. (See map on page 181.) Goods and passengers can travel by road or railroad through the Hudson-Champlain Valley. This is the best route to Canada from New York City.

Other lakes in New York include Oneida Lake, Lake George, Lake Placid, and the Finger Lakes. All of these are popular resort areas. The Finger Lakes get their name from their long, narrow shape. As the map on page 301 shows, these lakes look like the fingers of a hand.

CLIMATE

In New York State, summers are usually warm and humid, and winters are cold. Spring and autumn days are generally mild and pleasant. However, the climate varies considerably from one part of the state to another. Lowland areas are warmer in summer and milder in winter than the highlands. In some mountainous parts of the state, winters are often bitterly cold, and snow may stay on the ground until late spring.

The Erie-Ontario Lowland. On the plains along Lake Erie and Lake Ontario, the

302

climate is milder and the growing season is longer than in the highlands nearby. (See map on page 46.) The climate here is very favorable for growing apples, peaches, pears, and other fruits. In the spring, cool winds blow eastward over the Great Lakes and keep the fruit trees from blossoming until the danger of frost is over. In autumn, warm winds blowing over the lakes bring mild weather to the Erie-Ontario Lowland and help to protect the fruit from early frost.

Other lowland areas. In parts of Long Island and the lower Hudson Valley, summers are often hot and humid. During the summer, moist tropical air from the Gulf of Mexico moves northward over the eastern part of our country. It frequently reaches New York. In July and August, daytime temperatures in New York City sometimes are above ninety degrees for weeks at a time. The city's pavements and buildings reflect the heat, and the humid air makes both days and nights uncomfortable. Many New Yorkers flock to beaches on Long Island, where cooling breezes from the Atlantic Ocean bring some relief from the heat.

Winters are milder on Long Island and in the lower Hudson Valley than in other parts of the state. Cold winds from Canada bring snow and freezing temperatures throughout New York. However, the southeastern part of the state receives less snow than most other areas. It is partly sheltered from the cold winds by the highlands. The average annual snowfall in New York City is only about thirty inches.

The highlands. Winters in the highlands of New York are cold and snowy.

Snowfall is heavier on the western slopes of the Adirondack Mountains than anywhere else in the United States east of the Rocky Mountains. During the winter, winds from the west sweep over the Great Lakes and take up much moisture. When the winds reach the mountains, they rise and become cooler. Their moisture falls in the form of snow. An average of about twelve feet of snow falls each year in the Adirondacks. The part of the Appalachian Plateau that lies near Lake Erie also receives heavy snowfall.

Summers are pleasantly mild in the highlands of New York. The weather seldom becomes hot and humid, as it does in New York City. Many people visit the Catskill and Adirondack mountains in the summer to enjoy the refreshing mountain air.

Skiers enjoying a winter picnic in the Adirondack Mountains. In the highlands of New York, winters are cold and snowy. Summers here are pleasantly mild.

NATURAL RESOURCES

New York has a number of important natural resources. These include mineral resources, water, fisheries, and forests.

New York is one of our country's leading salt-producing states. There are extensive deposits of salt in the central and western parts of the state. Only a small part of the salt mined in New York is made into the salt we use to season our food. Most of it is used in the production of valuable chemicals. Some salt is fed to livestock. During the winter, salt is spread over roads and railroad tracks to help melt ice and snow.

New York also produces other important minerals. Large quantities of stone, sand, and gravel are taken from pits here. These are used in making a variety of materials, such as cement, brick, and glass. New York is a leading producer of cement. Iron ore is mined in the Adirondack Mountains. In the southwestern part of the state, oil and natural gas have been produced for many years. New York ranks first among our states in the production of emery, talc, and garnet.

The water from New York's rivers and lakes is one of the state's most important resources. Huge hydroelectric plants along the Niagara River and

A hydroelectric plant along the Niagara River. Waterpower is one of New York's most important natural resources. Huge hydroelectric plants along the Niagara and St. Lawrence rivers supply electric power to communities in New York and in other states of the Northeast.

the St. Lawrence River supply electric power to many communities in New York and in other states of the Northeast.

Fresh water is needed by the millions of people in New York for drinking, washing, cooking, and many other uses. New York City receives its water from reservoirs that are many miles away. During some years, New York City, like other parts of the Northeast, has suffered from a shortage of usable water. (See Chapter 8.)

Fishermen in New York take oysters, clams, cod, flounder, and other fish from the waters of the Atlantic Ocean and Long Island Sound. (See map on page 301.) Much of their catch is delivered to the Fulton Fish Market in New York City. This is the largest wholesale fish market in the Northeast.

Forests cover nearly half the land in New York. Millions of dollars' worth of timber is harvested from the Adirondacks and other forested areas each year. Much of this wood is used to make pulp and paper. Some is used by New York's furniture industry.

INDUSTRY

New York is our country's leading manufacturing state. Factories in New York produce about twenty-five billion dollars' worth of goods each year. (See table on page 299.) More than half of this amount is produced in the New York City metropolitan* area.

Printing and publishing. If you were to examine the books and magazines in your home, you would probably find that many of them were published* in New York City. Most of the nation's large publishing firms have their offices

A printer locks up a form on a color press. Many of the books and magazines produced in our country are printed or published in New York City. New York is our country's leading manufacturing state.

here. Three fourths of our country's books and more than one half of its leading magazines are published in this city.

Most publishers do not print their own books and magazines. They pay printing companies to do this work. There are more than 2,300 printing plants in the New York City metropolitan area.

Clothing. New York State leads the nation in the manufacture of clothing. A small, crowded section of New York City is known as the "garment district." Here almost 224,000 workers make ladies' dresses, coats, and other garments. New York City produces about one half of the women's clothing sold in our country. Nearly all of the nation's fur garments are also made here. New York City and Rochester are leading producers of men's clothing. Department stores all over the nation send clothing buyers to New York City. These buyers examine the latest fashions and select the styles of clothing that they think will sell well in their stores.

Machinery. New York is one of our country's leading producers of machinery. Electrical equipment is manufactured in cities throughout the state. The General Electric Company's plants in Schenectady are among the largest factories in the world producing electrical machinery. More than two and one-half billion dollars' worth of non-electrical machinery is also produced in New York factories every year. Typewriters and other office machines are made at Poughkeepsie and Binghamton. Factories at Buffalo and Olean manufacture pumps and diesel engines. Syracuse produces dry-cleaning and air-conditioning equipment. New York City is one of our nation's leading producers of printing presses and other types of printing machinery.

Food processing. To feed the millions of people who live in New York State, factories must process huge quantities of food. Dairy plants are located in or near most cities. In cities on the fertile Erie-Ontario Lowland, fruits and vegetables are frozen or canned, and grapes are made into wine. Bakeries, breweries, and plants that make soft drinks employ many workers.

Some factories in New York process farm products that are received from other states or from abroad. Wheat is transported from the central part of the United States and Canada by way of the Great Lakes to Buffalo. Here the wheat

Assembling turbines at Schenectady. Factories in New York produce about twenty-five billion dollars' worth of goods each year. In addition to the manufacture of machinery, important industries in this state include printing and publishing and the manufacture of clothing.

is ground into flour in giant mills. Ships carrying raw* sugar from islands in the West Indies dock at Brooklyn, in New York City. The raw sugar is unloaded from the ships into refineries located right at the water's edge. Here it is processed and packed into boxes and bags for sale.

Other industries. New York ranks fourth among our states in the production of transportation equipment. There are large plants in the Buffalo area that produce automobile and aircraft parts. Airplanes are also made on Long Island. Plants in Schenectady manufacture railroad locomotives.

Only New Jersey and Texas produce more chemicals and chemical products than New York. Factories at the small town of Solvay, near Syracuse, manufacture many different chemicals from salt that is mined nearby. In New York City, many firms make drugs, beauty preparations, and household cleansers that are sold in drugstores and supermarkets throughout the nation.

New York is a leading manufacturer of other important goods. It ranks first in the nation in the manufacture of paper products and photographic equipment. Only Massachusetts makes more shoes and other leather goods. New York ranks third among our states in the production of furniture. Glassware made at Corning is famous throughout our country.

FARMING

New York is the most important farming state in the Northeast. Farmers here sell more than one billion dollars' worth of products each year. The chief foods produced on New York's farms are milk, vegetables, eggs, meat, and fruit. Enormous quantities of these food items are needed each day by the many people who live in the New York City metropolitan area and other densely populated parts of the state.

Dairy farming on the Appalachian Plateau. Farmers in New York State receive more money from the sale of dairy products than from all other farm products combined. Most of the dairy farms are in the Appalachian Plateau section of the state. Here, most of the land is too hilly for raising crops. However, the grassy slopes provide excellent summer pastures for dairy cows. Many dairy farmers grow hay to feed their livestock during the cold winter months.

The most important dairy product in New York is milk. New York produces more milk than any other state except Wisconsin. Each day, fresh milk from dairy farms is rushed to dairy plants in the cities. Here it is pasteurized* and put in containers for delivery to customers.

Truck farming and poultry raising on Long Island. There are many truck farms in the eastern part of Long Island. Farmers here raise potatoes, cabbages, lima beans, and other vegetables. These crops grow well in the sandy soil of Long Island. Also, this part of the state has a long growing season. (See map on page 46.) Farmers can plant more than one crop of vegetables on the same land each year. They ship most of their vegetables to markets in New York City.

Poultry and eggs are also leading farm products of Long Island. Farmers here ship millions of dollars' worth of eggs, chickens, and turkeys to market each year. Large duck farms in the eastern part of Long Island produce about

A vineyard near the Finger Lakes. New York is the most important farming state in the Northeast. Among the leading farm products are grapes and other fruits, milk, vegetables, and poultry and eggs.

half of the ducks raised in the United States each year.

Fruit farming on the Erie-Ontario Lowland. New York is one of our country's leading fruit-growing states. The climate of the Erie-Ontario Lowland is well suited to growing fruit. Orchards and vineyards here produce apples, grapes, peaches, and many other fruits. Grapes are also grown in vineyards near the Finger Lakes in central New York. (See map on page 301.) New York produces more grapes than any state except California, and more apples than any state except Washington.

PEOPLE AND CITIES

More than eighteen million people live in New York State. This is nearly one out of every ten Americans. Only California has a larger population.

Many of the people who live in New York State were born in foreign coun-tries or have at least one parent who came to this country as an immigrant. This is especially true in New York City. Large numbers of immigrants enter the United States through the port here. Many of them remain in New York City or move to other cities in the state. As a result, people from almost every country in the world may be found in New York. Among New Yorkers of foreign descent, the largest groups are Italians, Germans, Russians, Poles, and Irish.

In recent years, large numbers of Negroes and Puerto Ricans have come to New York City. Most of these people have come in search of better working and living conditions. Many of them, however, lack the education or the training needed to obtain good jobs. It is difficult for them to find work, and they are often forced to live in crowded slums.

People of many different religions make up the population of New York. Roman Catholics are the largest religious group. There are more Catholics in New York than in any other state in our nation. People of almost every Protestant denomination also make their homes in New York. In New York City, about one fourth of the population is Jewish.

The people of New York live mainly in urban areas. More than one half of the state's residents make their homes in the New York City metropolitan area. New York City is described in Chapter 13. Many other people live in cities on the Erie-Ontario Lowland or in the Hudson-Mohawk Valley. The largest of these cities are Buffalo, Rochester, Syracuse, and Albany.

Buffalo (population about 482,000) is the second largest city in New York State. It is located at the eastern end of Lake Erie, at the entrance to the Niagara River. (See map on page 301.) The Buffalo metropolitan area includes the city of Niagara Falls and several other cities and villages in a two-county area. More than 1,300,000 people live in this area.

At the start of the nineteenth century, Buffalo was only a small village. With the completion of the Erie Canal in 1825, the city grew rapidly. Farm products and raw materials from the Midwest were shipped over the Great Lakes to Buffalo. Here they were transferred to canal barges for shipment to cities on the Atlantic coast. Manufactured goods from northeastern factories were sent to the Midwest by way of Buffalo. Many settlers traveling westward also passed through this city. Buffalo became an important transfer* point.

Improvements in transportation helped industry to develop in Buffalo. During the 1870's, a railroad was built connecting this city with the coalfields of Pennsylvania. This made it possible for mining companies to send coal by rail to Buffalo. At about this time, shipyards began to build large freighters for use on the Great Lakes. These new ships were able to carry heavy cargoes of iron ore to Buffalo from mines near Lake Superior. Factories in Buffalo used the coal and iron ore in steelmaking. Steel was used by other factories to make many products.

Buffalo, the second largest city in New York, lies at the eastern end of Lake Erie. Buffalo is the world's leading flour-milling city. Wheat and other grains are brought here by lake freighters. Oceangoing ships, canal barges, and trains also load and unload large amounts of goods here.

Near the end of the 1800's, the first hydroelectric plant in the world was built at nearby Niagara Falls. This plant supplied low-cost electric power, which helped industry in Buffalo to expand further.

Today, Buffalo and its neighboring cities and towns make up one of our country's great manufacturing areas. Along the shores of Lake Erie, giant steel mills light the night sky with their glow. Long lake freighters unload wheat and other kinds of grain at elevators on Buffalo's waterfront. This grain comes from farms in the central part of the United States and Canada. In Buffalo it is ground into flour or used in making breakfast cereals and livestock feed. Most of these products are shipped to other cities in the Northeast. Buffalo is the world's leading flour-milling city. The largest cereal-packing plant in our country is located here. In Buffalo and nearby cities, there are plants that manufacture automobile and aircraft parts, chemicals, and many other products.

Buffalo is an important transportation center. Ships, canal barges, trains, and trucks carry goods to and from the city. When the St. Lawrence Seaway* opened in 1959, Buffalo became a world port. It is the first major American port reached by ships entering the United States through the Seaway. Ships from many foreign countries are loaded and unloaded at Buffalo.

Rochester (population about 292,000) is the third largest city in New York State. It is located on the Lake Ontario plain about seventy miles northeast of Buffalo. (See map on page 301.) The city extends along both banks of the Genesee River. To the north is Lake Ontario. The New York State Barge Canal passes through the southern part of the city.

Rochester began as a small flour-milling community in the early 1800's. Wheat grown on the fertile Lake Ontario plain was brought to mills at Rochester to be ground into flour. These mills used waterpower from falls in the Genesee River. After the Erie Canal was opened, Rochester grew rapidly. Millers were now able to ship flour cheaply to buyers in cities along the Atlantic coast. During the middle of the 1800's, Rochester was the leading flour-milling city in the United States. Today, however, most of our country's wheat is grown in the Midwest and the Great Plains. The Lake Ontario plain is no longer a major wheat-producing area. All the flour mills in Rochester have been closed.

Other industries have taken the place of flour milling in Rochester. This city is our country's leading producer of cameras, film, optical* goods, thermometers, and dental equipment. Men's suits and coats are made in large factories here. Processing plants freeze and can fruits and vegetables that are grown on the fertile farmlands nearby.

Some of Rochester's industries are the result of inventions made by men who lived here. The most famous of these inventors was George Eastman. In 1880, he founded a small company to manufacture film and cameras. He invented several improved types of photographic equipment, and his company grew rapidly. Today, the Eastman Kodak Company is the largest producer of cameras and film in the world.

Although Rochester contains much industry, it does not have the appearance of many manufacturing cities. Its factories are widely scattered, and most of them are clean and modern. Rochester's many parks and fine residential areas help make it an attractive city.

Syracuse (population about 207,000) is located in the central part of New York State, about midway between Buffalo and Albany. (See map on page 301.)

The first permanent settlement on the site of present-day Syracuse was made shortly after the American Revolution. The early settlers found valuable deposits of salt nearby. They began to process the salt and ship it to cities on the Atlantic coast. After the Erie Canal was built across New York State, the salt industry in Syracuse grew rapidly. Until after the Civil War, Syracuse supplied most of the salt used in the United States. Today, salt from nearby mines is used as a raw material by chemical plants in the Syracuse area.

Syracuse's location has helped to attract many other industries to the city. The leading industry here is the manufacture of electronic* equipment. Factories here also make washing machines, typewriters, air conditioners, drycleaning equipment, and many other kinds of machines. Food processing is also an important industry in Syracuse.

Albany (population about 122,000) is the capital of New York State. It lies on the west bank of the Hudson River,

Albany, the capital of New York State, lies on the west bank of the Hudson River. In 1624, a group of Dutch colonists built a fort here. Today, Albany is an important transfer point for goods being shipped by railroad or canal barge.

311

about 140 miles north of New York City. Albany is located on the Hudson-Mohawk Lowland. The Mohawk River flows into the Hudson only a short distance from the city. (See map on page 301.)

Albany was one of the first permanent European settlements in our country. In 1624, a group of Dutch colonists built a fort on the site of present-day Albany. They called it Fort Orange. A small settlement grew up around the fort and soon became an important fur-trading center. When the English took over Dutch possessions in the New World, they named this settlement Albany.

After the American Revolution, Albany became a busy gateway to the West. Settlers assembled here with their oxcarts and wagon trains before starting the long trip westward. In the first half of the 1800's, roads and railroads were built that connected Albany with New York City and with the western settlements. The Erie Canal joined the Hudson River at a point near Albany. A steady stream of people and goods passed through Albany, and the city grew rapidly. Today, Albany is an important transfer point. Oceangoing freighters can sail up the Hudson River and dock here. Goods brought up the Hudson to Albany are transferred to trains or canal barges for shipment westward. Large quantities of grain, lumber, and petroleum pass through the city's port.

Albany is the center of a metropolitan area that has a population of more than 690,000. This area includes the cities of Schenectady and Troy, as well as several smaller communities. Because Albany is the state capital, many of the people who live here work in government offices. Factories in the area also employ large numbers of people. Plants in Schenectady produce heavy electrical equipment and locomotives. Troy is noted for factories that make men's shirts and other clothing.

Learn About New York With Maps

Study the map of New York on page 301 and then answer the following questions:
1. What is the capital of New York State?
2. What large bodies of water border New York State on the west?
3. What large body of water borders New York State on the southeast?
4. What large city is located at the mouth of the Hudson River?

Develop Important Understandings

1. How has the Hudson-Mohawk Lowland helped New York become a great state?
2. How were most of New York's lakes formed?
3. Why is the Erie-Ontario Lowland well suited for raising fruit?
4. How does New York State rank among all the states of our country in manufacturing?
5. Why are there people of many different nationalities in New York State?
6. List some of the reasons why Buffalo has become an important city.

Share an Imaginary Adventure

Choose one of the following scenic spots in New York State for an imaginary vacation trip.

The Catskill Mountains
Niagara Falls
The Adirondack Mountains

Write a story about your trip to share with your class. The suggestions on pages 347-349 will help you find the information you need.

25 Pennsylvania

Facts About Pennsylvania		
	Number or Value	Rank
Area (square miles)	45,333	33
Population	11,728,000	3
Capital—Harrisburg		
Admission Date:		
December 12, 1787		2
Colleges and Universities	143	3
Farm Products	$ 932,848,000	18
Dairy products	407,664,000	5
Poultry and eggs	139,055,000	8
Cattle and calves	104,820,000	30
Fish	$ 63,000	40
Timber Harvested (cubic feet)	188,728,000	20
Minerals	$ 904,044,000	6
Coal	506,227,000	2
Cement	131,882,000	2
Stone	108,151,000	1
Manufactures	$18,752,302,000	5
Primary metal products	3,758,875,000	1
Electrical machinery	1,856,971,000	5
Nonelectrical machinery	1,832,812,000	5

Land. In Pennsylvania, the land varies from forested mountain ridges to gently rolling hills and flat plains. As the map on page 27 shows, almost all of the state lies in the Appalachian Highlands region of our country. The only areas outside of this region are two lowlands. One of these lies along Lake Erie, and the other is along the Delaware River.

The highlands. Three main sections of the Appalachian Highlands extend through Pennsylvania. These are the Appalachian Plateau, the Appalachian Ridges and Valleys, and the Piedmont Plateau. In addition, the Blue Ridge occupies a small part of southern Pennsylvania. (See page 34.)

The Susquehanna Valley, in the Appalachian Plateau. This plateau, which covers most of northern and western Pennsylvania, consists mainly of forest-covered hills and mountains and narrow valleys. In some river valleys, however, there are areas of fairly level land.

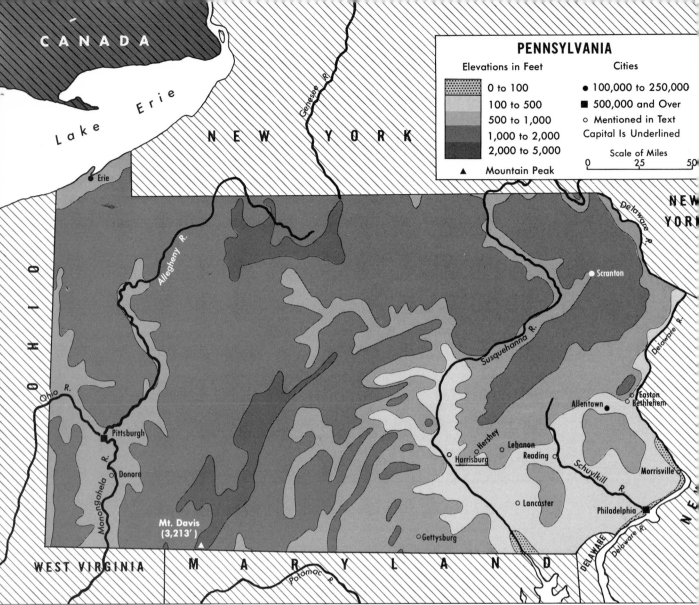

PENNSYLVANIA

Elevations in Feet

	0 to 100
	100 to 500
	500 to 1,000
	1,000 to 2,000
	2,000 to 5,000
▲	Mountain Peak

Cities

● 100,000 to 250,000
■ 500,000 and Over
○ Mentioned in Text
Capital Is Underlined

Scale of Miles
0   25   50

Pennsylvania is the second largest state in the Northeast. Almost all of the state lies in the Appalachian Highlands region of our country. The only areas outside of this region are two lowlands. One of these lies along Lake Erie, and the other is along the Delaware River.

The Appalachian Plateau includes most of western and northern Pennsylvania. This section of the state consists mainly of forest-covered hills and mountains and steep-sided, narrow valleys. Mount Davis, the highest point in the state, is located here. It rises more than three thousand feet above sea level. Except in some river valleys, the land of the Appalachian Plateau is generally too rugged for raising crops. Beneath the ground, however, are valuable deposits of coal and limestone.

The great manufacturing city of Pittsburgh is located on the Appalachian Plateau, in southwestern Pennsylvania.

Tourists visit the Appalachian Plateau at all times of the year. They come to admire the area's natural beauty and to enjoy such sports as hiking, fishing, and skiing. The Pocono Mountains, in the eastern part of the plateau, are especially noted for their many summer resorts.

South and east of the Appalachian Plateau is the Appalachian Ridges and

Valleys section of Pennsylvania. Many of the ridges here are steep and forest covered. The most important part of this section is the broad Great Valley. (See page 34.) This valley is a fertile farming area, known especially for its fine orchards of apple and peach trees. Many cities and towns are located in the Great Valley of Pennsylvania. Among them is Harrisburg, the state capital.

The Piedmont Plateau section of Pennsylvania lies southeast of the Appalachian Ridges and Valleys. This gently rolling plateau slopes downward to the Coastal Plain. Some of the most fertile farmland in our country is found on the Piedmont of Pennsylvania.

The lowlands. In southeastern Pennsylvania, along the Delaware River, is a narrow lowland area. This is part of the Coastal Plain region of our country. (See map on page 27.) The land here is level or gently rolling. Philadelphia, the state's largest city, is located on Pennsylvania's Coastal Plain, along the Fall Line. (See page 35.)

In northwestern Pennsylvania, another narrow strip of lowland extends along Lake Erie. This is an important fruit-growing area. The port city of Erie is on the Lake Erie Lowland.

Climate. The climate in Pennsylvania varies considerably from place to place. Generally, the climate is warmer in the lowlands than in the highlands. Much of Pennsylvania receives more than forty inches of rainfall each year.

In the highlands of northern and western Pennsylvania, winters are usually cold and snowy. Some areas here receive as much as seven feet of snow each winter. In summer, days are warm and nights are cool. The refreshing summer weather attracts thousands of vacationers to mountain resorts.

In southeastern Pennsylvania, winter weather is generally mild. Snowfall here is light, and January temperatures are usually above freezing. Summer weather is often hot and humid. Daytime temperatures here often rise above ninety degrees.

The growing season in Pennsylvania ranges from four to seven months. (See map on page 46.) It is longest in the southeastern part of the state, where crops can be grown outdoors for six to seven months. The long growing season helps to make this part of Pennsylvania an important farming area.

Natural resources. Pennsylvania ranks sixth in the nation in the value of mineral production. Coal is by far the state's most important mineral resource. (See table on page 313.) The production of coal brings more money to Pennsylvania than to any other state in our country except West Virginia. In western Pennsylvania are vast deposits of high-grade soft coal, called bituminous coal. Hard coal, or anthracite, is mined in eastern Pennsylvania. Some of the coal produced in the state is shipped to other parts of our country and abroad. However, much of it is used within Pennsylvania.

Bituminous coal has helped to make Pennsylvania a leading manufacturing state. As page 133 explains, this mineral has many uses. Large quantities of bituminous coal are used in Pennsylvania's steel mills to make coke.* Coal gas and coal tar are used as raw materials in the manufacture of many valuable chemical products. In addition, about nine tenths of Pennsylvania's electricity

*See Glossary

is produced in steam power plants that burn coal.

Pennsylvania produces much less anthracite today than it did fifty years ago. In the past, this type of coal was often used to heat homes. Today, however, gas or oil is used in most homes in the United States.

There are deposits of limestone in many parts of Pennsylvania. This mineral is used in the production of iron and steel. (See feature on page 145.)

Limestone is also the most important raw material used in making cement. Pennsylvania produces more cement than any other state except California.

Pennsylvania also produces other important minerals. In the northwestern part of the state are deposits of petroleum and natural gas. Large quantities of clay, slate, sand, and gravel are also found in this state.

Forests cover about half of Pennsylvania. Logs from these forests are cut

A push-button miner in Pennsylvania. This state ranks second in the nation in coal production.

From an electronic control booth (1) at the base of this push-button miner, one man directs a boring instrument (2) into a coal deposit deep underground. As the machine drills its way into the coal, it unwinds a long chain of portable conveyors from the storage ramp (3). These carry the coal back to the surface, where other conveyors deposit it in large piles. Machinery such as this makes mining safer and less expensive.

Molten iron is poured into a furnace in a steel plant near Pittsburgh. For more than a century, Pennsylvania has led the nation in the production of iron and steel. Factories in the state use steel to make machinery, hardware, and many other products. Steel produced in Pennsylvania is also shipped to other states and countries.

into lumber, which is used in manufacturing furniture and in constructing homes and other buildings. Pulp and paper are other forest products of Pennsylvania.

Water is one of Pennsylvania's most valuable resources. Some of the state's rivers, such as the Delaware and the Ohio, serve as important transportation routes. In addition, millions of gallons of water are used each day by steel mills and other factories in the state.

Industry. Pennsylvania is one of our country's leading manufacturing states. It ranks fifth in the nation in the value of manufactured products.

Iron and steel. The manufacture of iron and steel is Pennsylvania's leading industry. For more than one hundred years, this state has ranked first in the United States in the production of these metals. Today, about one fourth of our country's iron and steel comes from Pennsylvania.

Most of Pennsylvania's iron and steel is produced in and near Pittsburgh. Iron ore, coal, and limestone — the main raw materials needed by the iron and steel industry — can be brought here at low cost. Iron ore mined near Lake Superior can be shipped cheaply on the Great Lakes to ports along Lake Erie. From there, the ore goes a short distance by railroad to the Pittsburgh area. Not far from Pittsburgh are deposits of coal and limestone. Barges on the Ohio

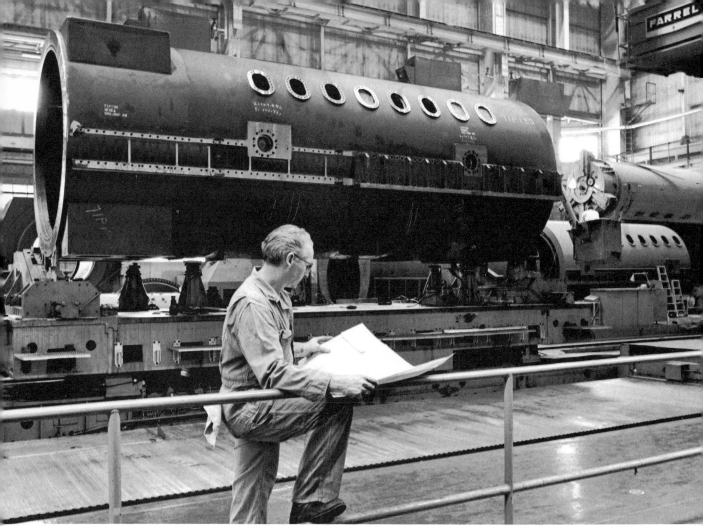

A huge generator under construction. Each year, Pennsylvania produces more than three and one-half billion dollars' worth of machinery, ranging from generators to toasters. Clothing, candy, and many other products are also made here. This is one of the nation's leading manufacturing states.

and Monongahela rivers carry cargoes of these minerals to the steel mills.

There are also many steel plants in eastern Pennsylvania. Among the steel-producing cities here are Bethlehem, Lebanon, and Morrisville. On pages 143-147, you can read about a steel plant in eastern Pennsylvania.

Steel from mills in Pennsylvania is shipped to many other states and to foreign countries. Factories in Michigan and Ohio use millions of tons of sheet steel each year to manufacture automobile bodies. Oil companies in Texas, Louisiana, and other oil-producing states use steel pipe to drill oil wells and build pipelines.

Many companies that manufacture machinery or other products requiring large quantities of steel have built factories near steel mills in Pennsylvania. Steel can be delivered to these factories at low cost.

Machinery. Factories in Pennsylvania manufacture more than three and one-half billion dollars' worth of machinery each year. Plants in Pittsburgh produce large cranes and other equipment needed in the area's huge steel mills. In several cities there are factories that make machine* tools. Looms, knitting machines, and other types of textile machinery are made in factories in or near Philadelphia.

Pennsylvania is one of the Northeast's leading producers of electrical machinery. Electrical machinery manufactured here ranges from huge motors and generators to refrigerators, toasters, and other household appliances. In Philadelphia are factories that make radios, television sets, and other types of electronic* equipment.

Other metal products. Factories in Pennsylvania make a variety of other metal goods. Aluminum products are made in Pittsburgh, Philadelphia, and other cities. Brass and bronze products are made in Pittsburgh, and factories in Reading make cutlery and hardware.

Food processing. Pennsylvania ranks fourth in our country in the manufacture of food products. Dairy plants in many parts of the state pasteurize and bottle fresh milk. Some of these dairies also process milk to make butter, cheese, and ice cream. Factories near fertile farming areas in southeastern Pennsylvania can and freeze large quantities of vegetables. On the Lake Erie Lowland and in the Great Valley are large plants that process fruits. Soft drink plants, breweries, and distilleries also employ many workers. Candy, cocoa, and other chocolate products are made in the small town of Hershey.

Clothing and textiles. Factories in Pennsylvania manufacture more than one billion dollars' worth of clothing and textiles each year. Almost half of this amount is produced in the Philadelphia metropolitan* area. Factories here make all types of clothing and textiles, including suits and coats, hosiery, carpets, and wool fabrics. More clothing is produced in Pennsylvania than in any other state except New York.

Other industries. Pennsylvania has several other important industries. Each year, factories here make more than one billion dollars' worth of chemicals and chemical products. Locomotives built near Philadelphia are used by railroads in many foreign countries as well as throughout the United States. Sand and natural gas from deposits near Pittsburgh are used in manufacturing plate glass and glass containers.

Farming. The best farmland in Pennsylvania is in the southeastern part of the state. Here the land is level or gently rolling, and the soil is fertile. Lancaster County, which is located here, is noted for its prosperous farms. (See pages 168 and 169.) The Great Valley is another productive farming area. In the rugged highlands of northern and western Pennsylvania, it is difficult to grow crops. Here, most farmers raise dairy cattle or other livestock.

Farmland in southeastern Pennsylvania. This is the most fertile farming area in the state. Corn and hay grown here are fed to livestock. Dairying is the main type of farming in Pennsylvania.

Farmers in Pennsylvania earn about three times as much money from the sale of livestock products as they do from the sale of crops. Milk is the state's leading farm product. Dairy farms in southeastern Pennsylvania help provide fresh milk for the millions of people living in Philadelphia, New York, and other large cities. There are also many dairy farms in the northern and western parts of the state. Since there are few cities here, large quantities of fresh milk are not needed. Much of the milk produced in northern and western Pennsylvania is made into butter and cheese.

There are thousands of poultry farms in Pennsylvania. More eggs are pro-duced here than in any other state in the Northeast. Farmers in Lancaster County raise millions of broiler chickens each year.

Pennsylvania farmers also raise beef cattle, hogs, and sheep. Beef cattle and sheep graze on green hillside pastures in western Pennsylvania. In the south-eastern part of the state are many feed-lots.* Here, cattle brought in from Vir-ginia, West Virginia, and other states are fed grains and other foods to fatten them for market. Hogs are also raised in southeastern Pennsylvania.

Pennsylvania ranks fifth among all the states in the sale of greenhouse and nursery products. Nurserymen raise trees, shrubs, and flowers for lawns and

A Pennsylvania nursery. Greenhouses and nurseries are located in or near large cities in Pennsylvania. Here, people buy trees, shrubs, and flowers for their lawns and gardens. Pennsylvania ranks fifth in the nation in the sale of greenhouse and nursery products.

Harvesting peaches. There are many orchards of apple and peach trees in the Great Valley of Pennsylvania. Another important fruit-growing area in this state is the Lake Erie Lowland. Here, grapes and cherries are the leading fruit crops.

gardens. Most of the greenhouses and nurseries are located in or near large cities.

Farmers in Pennsylvania grow a wide variety of other crops. Truck farms near large cities produce tomatoes, beans, cabbages, and other vegetables. Potatoes are the state's leading vegetable crop. They are grown in many areas. In Lancaster County, tobacco is an important crop. This tobacco is used mainly in making cigars. More than half of our nation's mushroom crop is grown in southeastern Pennsylvania. Mushrooms, which grow best in dark places, are raised here in large windowless sheds.

There are two important fruit-growing areas in Pennsylvania. The Great Valley section of the state is noted for its fine apple and peach orchards. On the Lake Erie Lowland, grapes and cherries are the leading fruit crops.

People and cities. More than eleven million people live in Pennsylvania. California and New York are the only states that have larger populations. About seven out of every ten people in Pennsylvania live in cities and towns. The state's largest cities are Philadelphia and Pittsburgh. Nearly two thirds of Pennsylvania's people live in the Philadelphia and Pittsburgh metropolitan areas.

Philadelphia (population about 2,050,-000) is the largest city in Pennsylvania and the fourth largest in our country. It is located in the southeastern part of the state, along the Delaware and Schuylkill rivers. (See map on page 314.) The Delaware links the city with the Atlantic Ocean, about one hundred miles to the south. Nearly five million people live in the Philadelphia metropolitan area. Some of the cities and towns that make up this huge urban area are located across the Delaware River, in the state of New Jersey.

Philadelphia was founded by William Penn in 1682. It quickly grew from a small settlement into a busy trading port. Sailing ships brought cargoes of sugar and molasses from the West Indies in exchange for lumber, grain, and other products. Shipbuilding became the city's most important industry. By the mid-1700's, Philadelphia was the largest city in the colonies. In the 1800's, many mills and factories were built in and near Philadelphia. Thousands of immigrants from Ireland, Germany, Poland, and other European countries came to work in these plants.

Today, factories in the Philadelphia metropolitan area produce a wide variety of goods. Among these are iron and steel, machinery, textiles, clothing, and food products. Along the Delaware River are many plants that manufacture basic* chemicals and such chemical products

Philadelphia is the largest city in Pennsylvania and the fourth largest in the nation. It is an important industrial city and seaport. Oceangoing ships reach Philadelphia by sailing up the Delaware River from the Atlantic Ocean.

Elfreth's Alley, in Philadelphia. The houses along this narrow street look much as they did two hundred years ago. Each year, more than two million tourists come to Philadelphia to see such historic places as Independence Hall, where the Declaration of Independence was signed.

as drugs and plastics. The printing and publishing industry is also important in Philadelphia.

Philadelphia is one of our country's busiest ports. Docks and wharves line the Delaware River for many miles. Crude oil, iron ore, and other raw materials are Philadelphia's leading imports. Exports include chemicals, gasoline, fuel oil, and other manufactured products.

In recent years, the people of Philadelphia have been rebuilding many sections of their city. Slums have been cleared away, and modern buildings rise in their place. Many homes and other buildings dating back to colonial times have been restored, so that some streets look much as they did two hundred years ago.

Each year, more than two million tourists come to Philadelphia to see such historic places as Independence Hall, where the Declaration of Independence and the Constitution were signed. In one of the city's many beautiful parks is the Philadelphia Museum of Art, which is noted for its collection of American and European paintings.

Pittsburgh (population about 546,-000) is Pennsylvania's second largest city. It is located in the southwestern part of the state, at the point where the Allegheny and Monongahela rivers join to form the Ohio. (See map on page 314.)

Pittsburgh began as a settlement which grew up around a British fort shortly before the Revolutionary War. After the war, this settlement became an important transfer point for people moving westward. Here, pioneer families exchanged their wagons for flatboats. Then they floated down the Ohio River on their way to the fertile farmlands of the Midwest. Factories and shops in Pittsburgh provided pioneers with cooking utensils, farm implements, and other supplies.

In the 1800's, Pittsburgh grew into a large industrial city. Until the Civil War, manufacturing iron and iron products was the city's most important industry. During the war, the steel industry began to develop here. By 1900, Pittsburgh had become our nation's leading iron- and steel-producing city.

Today, the manufacture of iron and steel is still Pittsburgh's leading industry. At night, flames from blast furnaces in the Pittsburgh area can be seen for many miles. Many other products are also manufactured here. Among these are machinery, glass, and chemicals.

Pittsburgh is an attractive, modern city. This has not always been true, however. At one time, the smoke from steel mills and other factories made Pittsburgh so dirty that it was known as the "Smoky City." In the 1940's, a smoke-control program was started, and

Pittsburgh's "Golden Triangle" lies at the point where the Allegheny and Monongahela rivers join to form the Ohio. Pittsburgh is the nation's leading iron- and steel-producing city. Raw materials for this industry are transported cheaply to Pittsburgh by water and by rail.

today Pittsburgh residents are proud of their clean city. Pittsburgh has become even more pleasant as a result of an urban-renewal program. Many changes have been made in the part of the city that lies at the point where the Allegheny and Monongahela rivers join. This area is called the "Golden Triangle." Here gleaming modern buildings, rising above green, spacious parks, have replaced run-down business places.

Erie (population about 142,000), Pennsylvania's third largest city, is located on Lake Erie. (See map on page 314.) It is an important transfer point for iron ore, coal, and other raw materials. Erie's leading industry is the manufacture of machinery, such as machine tools, construction machinery, and refrigeration equipment.

Harrisburg (population about 80,000) is the capital of Pennsylvania. It is located on the Susquehanna River, in the south central part of the state. Many people here work in government offices. Steelmaking and textile manufacturing are the city's main industries.

Other cities. There are several other large cities in Pennsylvania. Scranton, in the northeastern part of the state, was once an important anthracite-mining city. In recent years, many new factories have been opened here. (See page 134.) Among the products manufactured in Scranton are textiles, clothing, and steel. Allentown, Bethlehem, and Easton are the central cities of a large metropolitan area in the Lehigh River Valley. This area is noted for the production of cement and steel.

Develop Important Understandings

1. In what main land region of our country does most of Pennsylvania lie?
2. List two facts that help to explain why southeastern Pennsylvania is well suited to farming.
3. What are the main uses of the coal and limestone produced in Pennsylvania?
4. Why is the Pittsburgh area well suited for making iron and steel?
5. How has Philadelphia's location helped it to become an important city?
6. Name two important events in our country's history that took place in Independence Hall.
7. How has the appearance of Pittsburgh changed in the last twenty-five years?

Learn by Making Comparisons

How does the state in which you live compare with Pennsylvania? To find out, do some research and make a chart that shows your findings. Some of the things you might compare are:

a. area
b. population
c. climate
d. main industries

You may think of other things you want to compare. If so, add them to your chart. The suggestions on pages 347-349 will help you locate information for this project. When you have finished your chart, display it in your classroom.

Explore an Interesting Topic

Listed below are some interesting topics that will help you learn more about Pennsylvania. Choose one of these and prepare a report about it to share with your class. You will find the suggestions on pages 345-349 helpful in locating and organizing information.

The Life and Work of William Penn
Philadelphia — City of Brotherly Love
Our Country's First Oil Well

You may either write your report or give it orally.

26 Rhode Island

Facts About Rhode Island		
	Number or Value	Rank
Area (square miles)	1,214	50
Population	914,000	39
Capital—Providence		
Admission Date:		
May 29, 1790		13
Colleges and Universities	14	40
Farm Products	$ 20,278,000	49
Dairy products	5,202,000	49
Greenhouse and nursery products	4,899,000	31
Vegetables	4,121,000	43
Fish	$ 5,764,000	17
Timber Harvested (cubic feet)	2,042,000	48
Minerals	$ 4,222,000	49
Sand and gravel	2,546,000	48
Stone	Not available	
Manufactures	$1,354,881,000	33
Miscellaneous manufacturing	237,655,000	8
Textile mill products	183,366,000	11
Nonelectrical machinery	169,927,000	21

Land. Rhode Island is the smallest state in the United States. It would fit into Alaska, our largest state, almost five hundred times. Despite Rhode Island's small size, nearly one million people live here. It is one of the most densely populated states in our country.

Rhode Island is made up of lowlands and highlands. More than half the state lies in the lowlands. Highlands make up most of western Rhode Island.

The lowlands. Rhode Island's lowlands include the land bordered by the Atlantic Ocean and by Narragansett Bay, which is an arm of the Atlantic. A number of islands in the bay, as well as Block Island in the Atlantic Ocean, are also part of the lowlands. (See map on opposite page.) The largest island

Aquidneck Island lies in Narragansett Bay, a long arm of the Atlantic Ocean. This island is part of the state's coastal lowlands. These lowlands are generally flat and sandy. Most of the state's cities are located in these lowland areas.

in Narragansett Bay is Rhode Island, for which the state was named. This island is also known as Aquidneck.

The coastal lowlands of Rhode Island are generally flat and sandy. Most of the land here is less than one hundred feet above sea level. Many wide, sandy beaches extend along the shores of the bay and the ocean. However, in some places, rocky cliffs rise above the sea. Farther inland, the land is higher and gently rolling.

Most of Rhode Island's cities are located in the lowlands. Providence, which lies at the head of Narragansett Bay, is the capital of the state. It is the central city of a large metropolitan* area.

The highlands. The highlands of Rhode Island are made up of rough hills covered by forests of oak, cedar, and maple trees. Most of the hills do not rise very high above sea level, however. The highest point in Rhode Island is Jerimoth Hill, which has an elevation of 812 feet. (See map on this page.)

Climate. Rhode Island's climate is generally milder than that of most other New England states. Summers are seldom very hot, and winters are not extremely cold. The climate is influenced by the Atlantic Ocean and by Narragansett Bay. Breezes blowing from these bodies of water in summertime cool the land. In the winter, winds are warmed when they pass over the water. (See pages 44 and 45.) These winds keep the land temperatures from dropping very low.

Winters in Rhode Island are usually not severe. The average temperature in January is about thirty degrees. During most winters, the snowfall is

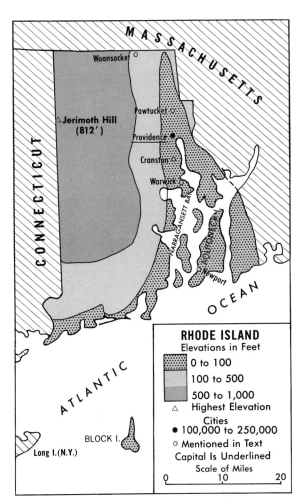

Rhode Island is the nation's smallest state. Although much of western Rhode Island is hilly, the state's highest point is only about eight hundred feet in elevation.

only about thirty inches. Snow seldom stays on the ground for more than a few days at a time.

Spring brings slowly rising temperatures to Rhode Island. The growing season for most of the state begins in early May and lasts until mid-October.

Summer is a pleasant season in Rhode Island. The average temperature in July is only about seventy degrees. Thousands of tourists visit Narragansett Bay in summer to enjoy the mild weather.

Autumn is a season of sunny, clear days and cool nights. In the forests,

*See Glossary

A fisherman unloading his catch. Fisheries are among Rhode Island's most valuable natural resources. From Narragansett Bay, Rhode Island fishermen take many tons of shellfish, such as clams and scallops. They catch cod, mackerel, and other fish in the Atlantic Ocean.

leaves turn from green to shades of red and gold. Shorter days and longer nights are a reminder that winter is near.

Natural resources. Rhode Island is not rich in natural resources. It has only small amounts of minerals, and its forests provide little timber.

Fisheries are among Rhode Island's most valuable natural resources. Each year, many tons of shellfish are caught in Narragansett Bay. Fishermen using traps* and nets bring in large catches of clams, scallops, and lobsters. In the Atlantic Ocean, Rhode Island fishermen catch cod, mackerel, and other kinds of fish.

Sand and gravel are Rhode Island's leading mineral resources. These materials are used in road building. There

are granite quarries in the southwestern part of the state. Granite is used mainly for monuments and other stone products.

Industry. About four out of every ten workers in Rhode Island are employed in industry. This is a higher proportion than that of most other states in our country. Since Rhode Island produces few of the raw materials needed by industry, it may seem surprising that so many workers are engaged in manufacturing.

There are several reasons why industry is important in Rhode Island. Waterpower gave factory owners in this state an early start. Several rivers begin in the highlands of Rhode Island and flow swiftly across the state into

Narragansett Bay. In these rivers are many waterfalls. During Rhode Island's early history, these waterfalls provided power for factories. The first textile mill in the United States was opened at Pawtucket on the Blackstone River in 1790. (See page 92.) As the years passed, many more factories were built along rivers in Rhode Island. Workers in these factories developed important manufacturing skills. Today, Rhode Island's main advantages for industry are its many highly skilled workers and its nearness to large markets.

About one sixth of Rhode Island's industrial workers earn their living in textile mills. There are about three hundred textile mills in the state. Some of these mills spin wool and cotton fibers into yarn.* Others weave yarn into woolen or cotton cloth. Fabrics made of synthetic fibers, such as rayon and nylon, are also produced in Rhode Island. Most of the state's textile mills are located in the cities of Providence, Woonsocket, and Pawtucket.

Although textile manufacturing is a leading industry in Rhode Island, there are fewer textile mills here today than there were in the past. Beginning in the 1920's, many owners of cotton textile mills moved their businesses from Rhode Island to cotton-producing states in the South. They were attracted not only by the nearness of raw materials but also by cheap hydroelectric power, low taxes, and low labor costs. The closing of textile mills in Rhode Island left many workers without jobs.

In recent years, new industries have been attracted to Rhode Island. Today, many factories here manufacture rubber and plastic products, electronic*

equipment, or metal products. Many persons who once worked in textile mills are now employed in plants that produce such items as golf balls, television tubes, or hand tools.

For many years, Rhode Island has been a leader in the production of jewelry and silverware. Fine jewelry and costume jewelry are both made in this state. Fine jewelry is made from expensive metals, such as gold and silver. Costume jewelry is made from less expensive metals, which are covered with a very thin coating of silver or gold. Factories in Rhode Island produce much of the silverware that is used in our country. One of the world's leading silverware manufacturers is located in Providence.

Farming. Only about one out of every one hundred workers in Rhode Island earns his living by farming. This is

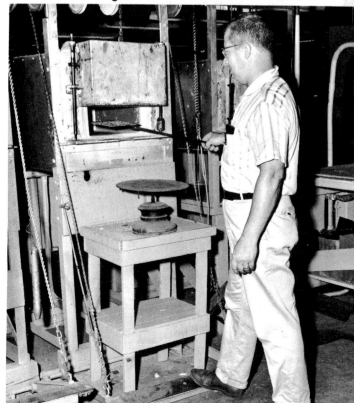

Making jewelry. Textiles, jewelry, and silverware have long been important products of Rhode Island. Today, factories here also make such articles as golf balls and television tubes.

partly because the state has little productive farmland. Cities and towns occupy much of Rhode Island's most level, fertile land. In the highlands, the available land is generally too hilly and the soil too stony for growing crops. The state's best farmland is on the narrow lowland along Narragansett Bay and on some of the islands in the bay.

Milk is Rhode Island's most important farm product. Herds of dairy cattle graze on green pastures in the highlands. However, not enough milk is produced in Rhode Island to meet the needs of the people in the state. Therefore, milk must be brought in from nearby states.

There are poultry farms throughout Rhode Island. Many farmers raise a type of chicken called the Rhode Island Red. This breed, which is noted for the high-quality eggs it produces, was developed in the state in 1854. Today, Rhode Island Reds are raised by farmers in many parts of the world.

A variety of crops are raised in Rhode Island. Potatoes are the state's most important vegetable crop. Truck farms also supply nearby cities with cabbages, tomatoes, and other fresh vegetables. Flowers, shrubs, and other special crops are raised in greenhouses and nurseries.

Cities. Most of Rhode Island's people live in the Providence metropolitan area. This area includes Providence and a number of smaller cities nearby, such as Pawtucket, Warwick, Cranston, and Woonsocket.

Providence, Rhode Island's capital and largest city, lies along a fine natural harbor at the head of Narragansett Bay. Nearly one third of the workers in Providence are employed in industry. They make textiles, jewelry, and many other products.

Providence (population about 187,000) is Rhode Island's capital and largest city. It was founded by Roger Williams in 1636. (See page 65.) The city is located along a fine natural harbor at the head of Narragansett Bay. It has been a leading port city since colonial times. Most ships that dock at Providence bring raw materials for the city's industries. Oil is the chief cargo. This fuel is used to produce electric power for homes and factories.

Providence is also an important manufacturing city. Factories here make all the products described earlier in this chapter, as well as many others. Nearly one third of the workers in Providence are employed in manufacturing. Many others work in banks, stores, or state government offices.

Newport (population about 36,000) is a famous resort city located on Aquidneck Island. In the summertime, cool ocean breezes make Newport's weather very pleasant. During the late 1800's, some of America's wealthiest people built large summer homes in Newport. Today, thousands of people come to the Newport area each year to spend their vacations. They are attracted by the pleasant weather, the sandy beaches, and the sparkling green waters of Narragansett Bay. During the summer months, the bay is dotted with sailboats and powerboats. Many vacationers enjoy fishing for tuna, swordfish, and bluefish.

Besides being a popular summer resort, Newport is an important naval base. It is the home of the Cruiser-Destroyer Force of the United States Atlantic Fleet. The United States Naval War College is also located at Newport.

At the Naval Destroyer School in Newport, students learn how a ship's boiler works. Newport, which is located on Aquidneck Island, is a popular resort city and the site of an important naval base.

Reading for a Purpose
1. How does Rhode Island compare in size with other states of our country?
2. What areas are included in the lowlands of Rhode Island?
3. How do the Atlantic Ocean and Narragansett Bay affect Rhode Island's climate?
4. Name some of the different kinds of fish brought to port by fishermen in Rhode Island.
5. List facts that help to explain why industry is important in Rhode Island.
6. Why is so little land in Rhode Island used for farming?
7. In what metropolitan area do most of Rhode Island's people live?
8. Why does Newport attract so many visitors each year?

27 Vermont

Facts About Vermont		
	Number or Value	Rank
Area (square miles)	9,609	43
Population	425,000	48
Capital—Montpelier		
Admission Date:		
March 4, 1791		14
Colleges and Universities	18	36
Farm Products	$141,243,000	44
Dairy products	110,069,000	15
Cattle and calves	11,904,000	42
Poultry and eggs	4,454,000	46
Timber Harvested (cubic feet)	49,454,000	34
Minerals	$ 28,715,000	44
Stone	21,401,000	23
Sand and gravel	2,806,000	47
Asbestos	Not available	
Manufactures	$514,191,000	41
Nonelectrical machinery	105,684,000	29
Electrical machinery	101,633,000	26
Paper and allied products	34,984,000	32

Land. Vermont is a small state in the northwestern part of New England. It is the only New England state that does not have a coastline on the Atlantic Ocean. However, it is bounded in two places by water. Lake Champlain extends more than halfway along Vermont's western border. The Connecticut River forms the eastern boundary of the state.

Rolling hills and low mountains make up most of the land in Vermont. The state's only large lowland area lies along Lake Champlain.

Highlands. Vermont is nicknamed the "Green Mountain State." It gets this name from a mountain range that extends from north to south through the state. (See map on opposite page.)

The Green Mountains extend from north to south through Vermont. Mount Mansfield, the highest peak in the state, is located here. Nearly all of Vermont is hilly or mountainous.

The gently rounded peaks in the Green Mountains are covered with dense forests. Mount Mansfield, the highest peak in Vermont, is in this range. It rises almost 4,400 feet above sea level.

To the east of the Green Mountains, most of the land in Vermont is hilly or gently rolling. The Granite Hills extend from the middle of the state northward to Canada. In these hills are large deposits of granite. Several low peaks in the northeastern corner of Vermont are part of the White Mountains, which extend into New Hampshire and Maine. Along the Connecticut River is a narrow lowland, with fertile soil.

West of the Green Mountains are both highlands and lowlands. The Taconic Mountains, in the southwestern part of the state, resemble the Green Mountains in appearance. However, they are not as high.

Lowlands. North of the Taconics is a broad lowland called the Champlain Valley, which extends all the way into Canada. In the Champlain Valley are the largest stretches of low, level land in Vermont. In summertime, herds of dairy cattle graze on rich, green pastures in the Champlain Valley. Apple orchards and fields of corn and hay dot the countryside. Burlington, the largest city in Vermont, is located in the Champlain Valley.

Climate. In Vermont, winters are cold and snowy. The temperature seldom rises above freezing for weeks at a time. The first snowfall comes in November or December, and snow stays on the ground until April. In the Green Mountains, the average yearly snowfall is about ten feet. Here, the deep snow and cold, clear winter days are

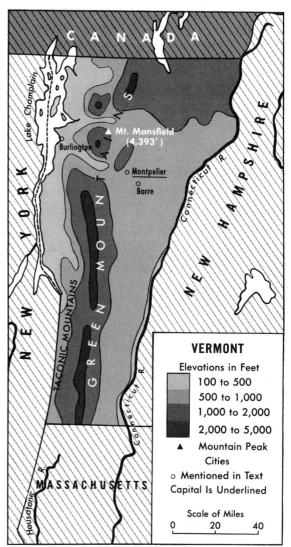

Vermont is the only New England state without an Atlantic coastline. The state's largest lowland lies along Lake Champlain.

excellent for skiing and other winter sports. Lowland areas receive about half as much snow as the mountains.

Summers in Vermont are mild and short. Daytime temperatures are seldom hot, although they are warm enough for outdoor sports. Nights are pleasantly cool. In summer, people from large northeastern cities come to the Green Mountains to escape the hot weather at home.

Most parts of Vermont have a growing season less than five months long.

In the Green Mountains, the frost-free period lasts for less than four months. Farmers here must grow hay and other crops that do not take long to ripen. Along Lake Champlain, the growing season is about six months long. Warm winds from the lake help to prevent early frosts in autumn.

Natural resources. The most important minerals found in Vermont are three kinds of stone. These are granite, marble, and slate.

Near the city of Barre are the largest granite quarries in the United States. Granite is a very hard stone that lasts through all kinds of weather. For this reason, it is widely used in making monuments and tombstones. In the past, granite was also used in constructing many public buildings. Today, however, most large buildings are made of steel and concrete.

Granite quarries near Barre are the largest in the United States. Vermont also produces much fine marble. Products made of granite and marble are sold throughout our country.

Vermont produces more marble than any other state. There are many large marble quarries on the western slopes of the Green Mountains. The marble quarried here is very beautiful, and it can be cut and polished easily. It is used for statues, monuments, and public buildings. The Jefferson Memorial and the Supreme Court Building in Washington, D.C., are both made of fine, white Vermont marble.

In the Taconic Mountains are large deposits of slate. Much of the slate mined here is used as roofing material for houses. Slate is also used in making blackboards, electrical devices, and other items.

Forests cover about three fifths of Vermont. The pines, spruces, firs, and hemlocks that grow on many mountainsides remain green even during winter. Hardwoods such as maples, birches, and beeches grow mainly in the lowlands. In the autumn, they add splashes of bright red and yellow to the countryside. Many trees are harvested each year for lumber and for wood pulp, which is used in making paper.

Two of the most famous products of Vermont are maple syrup and maple sugar. These delicious foods are made from the sap of the sugar maple tree. In early spring, when the sap begins to flow, farmers bore holes in the trunks of their sugar maples. Some farmers insert a spout in each hole and hang a bucket below the spout to catch the sap as it drips from the tree. On other farms, the sap is allowed to flow through long plastic tubes into a storage tank. After the sap has been collected, it is poured into a large machine called an evaporator. This

Making maple candy from soft maple sugar. Vermont is famous for the products of its sugar maple trees. Farmers collect sap from these trees and use it to make syrup and sugar. Much of our country's supply of these delicious products comes from Vermont.

machine boils away most of the liquid, leaving maple syrup. If the syrup is boiled for a longer time, it becomes maple sugar. Vermont maple syrup and maple sugar are shipped to grocery stores throughout the United States.

Waterpower is another important resource in Vermont. Hydroelectric plants produce most of the electricity used in this state. The largest plants are along the Connecticut River, but there are many smaller plants on swift streams that flow down from the Green Mountains.

Industry. There are fewer factories in Vermont than there are in the other New England states. This is partly be-

cause Vermont does not have a coast-line on the Atlantic Ocean. In the past, it was difficult to bring in raw materials for manufacturing. It was also difficult to ship manufactured goods to other places. Many of Vermont's factories were small, employing fewer than twenty workers. They generally used raw materials produced within the state, such as wood, stone, and milk.

Today, a number of fine highways connect Vermont with other states. Goods can easily be shipped to and from Vermont by truck. In recent years, many new factories have been built in the state. Some of these plants are very large, employing hundreds of workers.

More people in Vermont now earn their living from manufacturing than from any other kind of work.

The leading industry in Vermont is the manufacture of nonelectrical machinery. This industry requires much skill and precision. Vermont workers have long been noted for their craftsmanship. In the southeastern part of the state are several large factories that make machine tools. Several plants in the state specialize in making scales for almost every purpose, from weighing eggs to weighing airplanes.

The manufacture of electrical equipment is also important in Vermont. In the Burlington area, tiny electronic circuits for computers are produced. Electrical wire and cable also are made in this area. In other parts of the state, electrical equipment such as aircraft instruments is produced.

The forests of Vermont provide raw materials for several industries. Factories throughout the state manufacture paper and paper products. Many workers are employed in these factories. Others work in sawmills or in plants that make such items as furniture and wooden toys.

Food processing is another important industry in Vermont. Dairies, cheese factories, and ice cream plants process much of the milk produced on Vermont farms. Mills and factories here use grain in making products such as flour and livestock feed.

Stone products are also manufactured in this state. Huge blocks of granite and marble are taken from quarries in Vermont and transported to nearby mills. Here, they are carved into various shapes and polished. Monuments and tombstones of Vermont marble and granite are sold throughout the United States.

Farming. One out of every ten workers in Vermont earns his living by farming. The state's most important farming area is the lowland along Lake Champlain.

Milk is by far the leading farm product of Vermont. About three fourths of all the money earned by farmers in this state comes from the sale of milk. Vermont is one of the most important dairying states in the Northeast.

There are several reasons why dairy farming is so important in Vermont. In many parts of the state, the land is too rugged or the climate is too cool for growing most crops. However, dairy cows can be raised on hillside pastures. Also, they give more milk where summers are cool. During the summertime, there is enough rainfall in Vermont to provide plenty of drinking water for cattle and to produce large crops of grass and hay.

Dairy cows grazing. In Vermont, farming is an important occupation. One tenth of the state's workers earn their living in this way.

Another reason why dairy farming is so important in Vermont is the large market for fresh milk in northeastern cities. Most of the milk produced in the Champlain Valley is shipped by truck to New York City and Boston. There it is bottled for delivery to stores and homes. Not all of the milk produced in Vermont is sold fresh, however. Large amounts are made into cheese and other food products.

Only a few other farm products besides milk are important in Vermont. Some farmers raise beef cattle or poultry. There are apple orchards in the Champlain Valley, where the climate is milder than in the rest of the state. Potatoes, which do not need a long growing season, are raised in many areas.

The tourist industry. Many people in Vermont earn their living by providing food, lodging, or other services for tourists. About five million people visit this state each year. During the summertime, Vermont's cool weather and beautiful scenery attract many people. In Vermont there are more than sixty state parks and forests, as well as Green Mountains National Forest. Vacationers can hike along mountain trails or go swimming, fishing, and boating in the many lakes and streams. In the winter, resorts in the Green Mountains are crowded with skiers from all over the world.

People and cities. Fewer people live in Vermont than in any other state of the Northeast. Burlington, the state's largest city, has a population of about 40,000. Only about 9,000 people live in Montpelier, the state capital. Most people in Vermont live on farms or in small towns.

Because most towns in Vermont are small, nearly everyone can take an active part in local government. In the small towns of Vermont, citizens gather at the town hall once a year to elect officials and to decide on matters of importance to everyone, such as taxes and local laws. All citizens who are old enough to vote can take part in the town meeting. In the past, town meetings were common throughout New England. Today, however, many communities are so large that it would be impossible for all citizens to discuss every law before it could be passed. Town meetings are usually held only in places with a small population.

Burlington (population about 40,000) is located on the shores of Lake Champlain, in northwestern Vermont. It is a busy lake port and manufacturing city. Factories here produce many kinds of goods, including lumber, food products, and electrical equipment. The University of Vermont is located in Burlington.

Learn About Vermont With Maps
Study the map on page 333, and then answer the following questions:
1. What is the capital of Vermont?
2. What body of water forms much of the western border of the state?
3. What mountain range is located in central Vermont?
4. What country borders Vermont on the north?

Questions To Guide Your Reading
1. Where is Vermont's largest lowland area located?
2. Why is there a long growing season near Lake Champlain?
3. How is maple sugar made?
4. Why is dairy farming important in Vermont?

337

28 West Virginia

Facts About West Virginia		
	Number or Value	Rank
Area (square miles)	24,181	41
Population	1,802,000	33
Capital—Charleston		
Admission Date:		
June 20, 1863		35
Colleges and Universities	22	33
Farm Products	$ 100,265,000	46
Poultry and eggs	23,438,000	35
Cattle and calves	22,722,000	40
Dairy products	21,429,000	42
Timber Harvested (cubic feet)	163,737,000	22
Minerals	$ 917,708,000	5
Coal	775,720,000	1
Natural gas	62,086,000	7
Stone	16,789,000	27
Manufactures	$2,146,937,000	27
Chemicals and allied products	856,973,000	10
Primary metal industries	441,614,000	14
Stone, clay, and glass products	229,397,000	11

Land. West Virginia extends farther west than any other state in the Northeast. Until 1861, it was the western part of the state of Virginia. (See page 109.)

West Virginia has been nicknamed the "Mountain State." The state's average elevation is about 1,500 feet above sea level — higher than that of any other state east of the Mississippi River. West Virginia is also known as the "Panhandle State." One panhandle extends eastward between Maryland and Virginia. The other extends northward between Ohio and Pennsylvania. (See map on opposite page.)

All of West Virginia lies in the Appalachian Highlands region of our country. Two main sections of this region

The Appalachian Ridges and Valleys extends through the eastern part of West Virginia. Here, parallel ridges are separated by narrow valleys. Forests cover much of this mountainous land. Some valleys and hillsides, however, are used for farming.

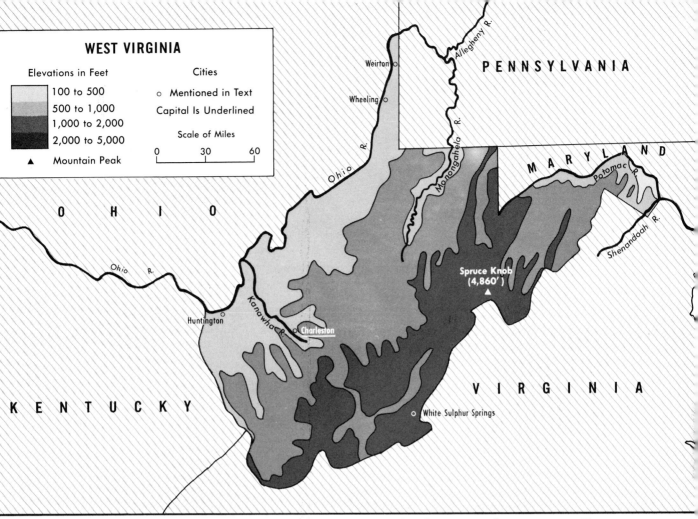

West Virginia lies entirely within the Appalachian Highlands region of our country. The state may be divided into two sections — the Appalachian Plateau and the Appalachian Ridges and Valleys. The Appalachian Plateau covers about three fourths of West Virginia.

extend through the state. These are the Appalachian Plateau and the Appalachian Ridges and Valleys.

The Appalachian Plateau. About three fourths of West Virginia lies in the Appalachian Plateau. Most of this section is made up of rugged mountains, steep-sided hills, and narrow river valleys. Along the eastern border of the plateau, many peaks rise more than four thousand feet above sea level.

Most parts of the Appalachian Plateau are thinly populated, mainly because the land here is so rugged. During the early years of our country, the mountains served as a barrier to pioneers moving westward. For many years,

large areas remained unsettled. Most of the early settlements were established in the Ohio and Kanawha river valleys. Today, West Virginia's largest cities are located in these valleys.

The Appalachian Ridges and Valleys. East of the Appalachian Plateau is the Appalachian Ridges and Valleys section of West Virginia. Here, the land is made up of nearly parallel ridges separated by narrow valleys. Spruce Knob, the highest point in the state, is located in this section. (See map above.) In the southeastern part of the state is White Sulphur Springs. This popular mountain resort attracts thousands of vacationers each year.

Mining coal with an auger. This machine drills into coal deposits and pulls out the coal it has cut. More bituminous coal is mined in West Virginia than in any other state. This type of coal provides coke, which is used in manufacturing steel.

The Appalachian Ridges and Valleys section of West Virginia includes the state's eastern panhandle. The tip of this panhandle lies in the valley of the Shenandoah River. This fertile valley is an important fruit-growing area.

Climate. In most of West Virginia, summers are warm and winters are moderately cold. Throughout the year, however, the weather is usually cooler in the mountains than in the valleys. On summer days when the weather is mild and refreshing in the mountains, it is often hot and humid at lower elevations. Winters are generally more severe in the high mountains than in other parts of the state. As much as one hundred inches of snow may fall in some mountainous areas in a single winter.

The southwestern part of the state, on the other hand, usually receives less than twenty inches of snow each year.

Nearly all of West Virginia receives more than forty inches of rainfall each year. Some mountainous areas receive as much as sixty inches, mainly as a result of orographic rainfall. (See page 51.) The growing season lasts for five months or more except in the highest mountains.

Natural resources. West Virginia is rich in mineral resources. Deposits of bituminous coal lie under more than half of the state. These deposits are part of the great Appalachian Highlands coalfield. (See feature on page 135.) More coal is mined in West Virginia than in any other state in our country.

Large quantities of coal are used by industries in West Virginia. Mills along the Ohio River use this mineral in the manufacture of iron and steel. In plants in the western part of the state, coal is used in making a variety of chemicals and chemical products. In addition, most of the state's electricity is produced in steam power plants that burn coal.

Millions of tons of bituminous coal are shipped each year from West Virginia to other states. Barges carry coal down the Monongahela River from mines in the northern part of the state to steel mills in or near Pittsburgh, Pennsylvania. Large quantities of coal are also transported on the Ohio River to factories in the Midwest. Some of West Virginia's coal is hauled in railroad cars to port cities in Virginia. There it is loaded on freighters and shipped to coastal cities in the Northeast as well as to foreign countries.

In recent years, coal miners in West Virginia have been faced with serious problems. Machines are now used to do most jobs that miners once performed by hand. As a result, many miners are now unemployed. (See page 343.)

Natural gas is another important mineral resource in West Virginia. There are hundreds of gas wells in the Appalachian Plateau. Gas produced here is piped to factories and homes throughout the state. In addition, natural gas produced in Texas and other states is carried by pipeline to West Virginia, where it is stored in empty gas wells. It is distributed to other states in the Northeast as it is needed.

West Virginia also produces a number of other minerals. Rich deposits of limestone are located in the eastern part of the state. Large amounts of limestone quarried in West Virginia are used here in the production of cement. Sand and gravel are dredged from the state's rivers and streams. These minerals are mixed with cement to make concrete. High-quality sand is dug from sand pits or ground from sandstone. This sand is used as a raw material in glass factories in West Virginia. In the western part of the state are deposits of salt and petroleum.

Industry. The manufacture of chemicals and chemical products is West Virginia's leading industry. Most of the chemical plants are located along the Ohio and Kanawha rivers. These plants are close to supplies of coal, salt, natural gas, and petroleum, which are used in making chemicals. Most of West Virginia's chemical plants manufacture basic* chemicals, such as sulfuric

*See Glossary

Making a beautiful glass vase. Glassmaking is one of West Virginia's chief industries. The most important products manufactured in this state are chemicals and steel.

acid and soda ash. Plants here also make antifreeze, plastics, nylon, and many other chemical products.

West Virginia's bituminous coal deposits have helped to make the manufacture of iron and steel a leading industry of this state. Iron ore mined near Lake Superior is brought here by railroad from ports along Lake Erie. Large steel mills line the Ohio River in and near the West Virginia cities of Weirton and Wheeling. River barges bring cargoes of coal to these mills. Mills in the Weirton and Wheeling areas manufacture steel, tinplate,* and many other products.

Many different clay and glass products are manufactured in West Virginia. Factories in Charleston, Huntington, and other cities produce such items as plate glass, fine glassware, and glass containers. In the northern panhandle

are extensive clay deposits. Clay is used in making chinaware, bricks, tiles, and other products.

A wide variety of other goods are produced in West Virginia. Workers in processing plants make butter and other dairy products, baked goods, or beverages. In Charleston and other cities, hand tools, cutlery, and other metal products are manufactured.

Farming. Few areas in West Virginia are well suited to farming. This is mainly because the land is too rugged. To earn an adequate living, people who live on farms often hold jobs in mines, mills, or factories.

About three fourths of the money earned by farmers in West Virginia comes from the sale of livestock products. Cattle, poultry, and sheep can be raised on land that is unsuitable for growing crops. There are poultry and dairy farms in nearly all parts of West Virginia. Some farmers in the eastern part of the state raise turkeys or broiler chickens for sale in the large cities of the Northeast.

Herds of beef cattle graze on hilly pastures in many parts of West Virginia. Some farmers raise Angus and Hereford cattle, which are especially valued for their fine beef. Most of the beef cattle raised in West Virginia are shipped to feedlots in surrounding states to be fattened for market.

Apples are West Virginia's most valuable crop. Apple orchards cover large areas of land in the Shenandoah Valley. Some of the apples are processed in West Virginia to make cider and other products.

People and cities. Fewer people live in West Virginia today than in 1960.

Beef cattle graze on hilly land in many parts of West Virginia. Raising livestock is an important type of farming in this state.

342

Charleston is West Virginia's capital and largest city. It is located on the Kanawha River, in the western part of the state. Charleston's location on the Kanawha and its nearness to supplies of raw materials have made it an important trading and manufacturing city.

This is one of the few states in our country in which the population is decreasing. Many people have been leaving West Virginia because of the lack of job opportunities. Thousands of former coal miners who were unable to find new jobs have left the state in order to seek work elsewhere. Many miners who remained at home are still unemployed, and they and their families are living in poverty. Since unemployed people are unable to purchase many products or services, business has been declining. As a result, many other people have become discouraged about business conditions in West Virginia and have moved out of the state.

In an attempt to provide more employment opportunities, manufacturers have brought several new industries into West Virginia in recent years. However, many West Virginians remain unemployed because they lack the education and skills needed to hold jobs in modern industry. Government programs are now under way to help train these people so they will be able to support their families and have a better way of life. Today, the people of West Virginia are hopeful that their state will soon recover from the decline of the past years.

Almost two thirds of the people in West Virginia live in rural areas. Only

343

three cities have populations of more than fifty thousand. These are Charleston, Huntington, and Wheeling.

Charleston (population about 86,000) is West Virginia's capital. It is also the largest city in the state. It is located on the banks of the Kanawha River, in the western part of the state. (See map on page 339.) Charleston began as a settlement around an army fort, in the late 1700's. This fort was built to protect settlers in the Kanawha Valley from Indian attacks.

Charleston's location on the Kanawha River and its nearness to supplies of coal, natural gas, salt, and other raw materials helped the city to grow. Today, it is an important trading and transportation center for a large area. Large plants along the Kanawha near Charleston manufacture basic chemicals and chemical products. Glassware, machinery, and hand tools are among the goods manufactured in factories in the city.

Huntington and Wheeling. Two of West Virginia's largest cities, Huntington and Wheeling, are located on the Ohio River. Both are important industrial cities and transportation centers.

Huntington (population about 81,000) is West Virginia's second largest city. It began as a railroad terminus* in 1871. Today, railroads employ thousands of the city's workers. Many of these people work in shops where railroad equipment is repaired. Factories in Huntington produce chemicals, glass, and many other products.

Wheeling (population about 50,000) is located in the northern panhandle. It was founded in 1769, and is one of West Virginia's oldest cities. Since the early 1800's, Wheeling has been a leading port city on the Ohio River. Today, the manufacture of iron and steel is the city's most important industry. Other products manufactured in the Wheeling area include glass, pottery, and textiles.

Questions To Help You Learn
1. Why has West Virginia been nicknamed the "Mountain State"?
2. West Virginia was once part of another state. Name that state.
3. How does West Virginia rank among all the states in the production of coal?
4. List some of the ways in which the coal mined in West Virginia is used.
5. What is the leading industry in West Virginia? Name some of the products of this industry.
6. How are iron ore and coal transported to iron and steel mills in West Virginia?
7. State the main reason why few areas in the state are well suited to farming.
8. Why has West Virginia's population been decreasing in recent years?

Explore the Problems of Appalachia
West Virginia lies in an area of our country called Appalachia, where more than one million families are living in poverty. Do research about Appalachia and then make an oral report to your class about your findings. The following questions will help you carry on your research.
1. What other states lie partly in Appalachia?
2. What are some of the problems that face the people living in Appalachia?
3. What is being done to solve these problems?
4. What more do you think could be done? You will find the suggestions on pages 345-349 helpful in finding the information you need and in organizing it into a report.

Reading with understanding is a skill that will help you to have a more satisfying life.

Learning Social Studies Skills

What is a skill? A skill is something that you have learned to do well. To learn some skills, such as swimming, you must train the muscles of your arms and legs. To learn others, such as typing, you must train your fingers. Still other skills require you to train your mind. For example, reading with understanding is a skill that requires much mental training. The skills that you use in the social studies are largely mental skills.

Why are skills important? Mastering different skills will help you to have a more satisfying life. You will be healthier and enjoy your leisure time more if you develop skills needed to take part in various sports. By developing artistic skills, you will be able to express your feelings more fully. It is even more important for you to develop skills of the mind. These skills are the tools that you will use in obtaining and using the knowledge you need to live successfully in today's world.

To develop a skill, you must practice it correctly. If you ask a fine athlete or musician how he gained his skill, he will say, "Through practice." To develop skills of the mind, you must practice also. Remember, however, that a person cannot become a good ballplayer if he keeps throwing the ball incorrectly. The same thing is true of mental skills. To master them, you must practice them correctly.

The following pages contain suggestions about how to perform correctly several important skills needed in the social studies. Study these skills carefully, and use them.

MAKING REPORTS

There are many occasions when you need to share information or ideas with others. Sometimes you will need to do this in writing. Other times you will need to do it orally. One of the best ways to develop your writing and speaking skills is by making oral and written reports. The success of your report will depend on how well you have organized your material. It will also depend on your skill in presenting it. Here are some guidelines that will help you in preparing a good report.

Decide upon a goal. Have your purpose clearly in mind. Are you mainly interested in communicating information? Do you want to give your own viewpoint on a subject, or are you trying to persuade other people to agree with you?

Find the information you need. Be sure to use more than one source. If you are not sure how to locate information about your topic, read the suggestions on pages 347-349.

Take good notes. To remember what you have read, you must take notes. Before you begin taking notes, however, you will need to make a list of the questions you want your report to answer. As you do research, write down the facts that answer these questions. You may find some interesting and important facts that do not answer any of your questions. If you feel that they might be useful in your report, write them down, too. Your notes should be brief and in your own words except when you want to use exact quotations. When you use a quotation, be sure to put quotation marks around it.

You will be able to make the best use of your notes if you write them on file cards. Use a separate card for each statement or group of statements that answers one of your questions. To remember where your information came from, write on each card the title, author, and date of the source. When you have finished taking notes, group the cards according to the questions they answer. This will help you arrange your material in logical order.

Make an outline. After you have reviewed your notes, make an outline. This is a general plan that shows the order and the relationship of the ideas you want to include in your report. The first step in making an outline is to pick out the main ideas. These will be the main headings in your outline. (See sample outline below.) Next, list under each of these headings the ideas and facts that support or explain it. These related ideas are called subheadings. As you arrange your information, ask yourself the following questions.

a. Is there one main idea that I must put first because everything else depends on it?

b. Have I arranged my facts in such a way as to show relationships among them?

c. Are there some ideas that will be clearer if they are discussed after other ideas have been explained?

d. Have I included enough facts so that I can complete my outline with a summary statement or a logical conclusion?

When you have completed your first outline, you may find that some parts of it are skimpy. If so, you may wish to do more research. When you are satisfied that you have enough information, make your final outline. Remember that this outline will serve as the basis of your finished report.

Example of an outline. The author of this feature prepared the following outline before writing "Making Reports."

I.   Introduction
II. Deciding upon a goal
III. Finding information
IV. Taking notes
   A. List main ideas to be researched
   B. Write on file cards facts that support or explain these ideas
   C. Group cards according to main ideas
V.   Making an outline
   A. Purpose of an outline
   B. Guidelines for arranging information
   C. Sample outline of this section
VI. Preparing a written report
VII. Presenting an oral report

Special guidelines for a written report. Using your outline as a guide, write your report. Your report is more likely to be interesting and clear if you follow these rules:

Create word pictures that your readers can see in their minds. Before you begin to write, imagine that you are going to make a movie of the subject you plan to write about. What scenes would you like to show on the screen? Next, think of the words that will create these same pictures in your readers' minds.

Group your sentences into good paragraphs. It is usually best to begin a paragraph with a topic sentence that says to the reader, "This is what you will learn about in this paragraph." The other sentences in the paragraph should help to support or explain the topic sentence.

A sample paragraph. Below is a sample paragraph from *The Northeast*. The topic sentence has been underlined. Notice how clear it is and how well the other sentences support it. Also notice how many pictures the paragraph puts in your mind.

One of the most interesting sights in this part of the Northeast is beautiful Niagara Falls. These falls are located on the Niagara River, which forms part of the border between the United States and Canada. The Niagara River flows northward from Lake Erie to Lake Ontario. Lake Erie is much higher than Lake Ontario. About midway between these two lakes, the river plunges over a steep cliff, forming Niagara Falls. Each year, thousands of tourists come to see these famous falls. Waterpower from the falls is used to produce electricity for factories and homes in both the United States and Canada.

Other guidelines. There are two other things to remember in writing a good report. First, use the dictionary to find the spelling of words you are doubtful about. Second, make a list of the sources of information you used, and include it at the beginning or end of your report. This list is called a bibliography.

Special guidelines for an oral report. When you are going to give a report orally, you will also want to organize your information in a logical order by making an outline. Prepare notes to guide you during your talk. These notes should be complete enough to help you remember all the points you want to make. You may even write out certain portions of your report that you prefer to read.

When you present your report, speak directly to your audience. Pronounce your words correctly and distinctly. Remember to speak slowly enough for your listeners to follow what you are saying, and use a tone of voice that will hold their interest. Stand up straight, but try not to be too stiff. Remember, the only way to improve your speaking skills is to practice them correctly.

HOW TO FIND INFORMATION YOU NEED

Each day of your life you seek information. Sometimes you want to know certain facts just because you are curious. Most of the time, however, you want information for some special purpose. If your hobby is baseball, for example, you may want to know how to figure batting averages. If you collect stamps, you need to know how to identify the countries they come from. As a student in today's world, you need information for many purposes. As an adult, you will need even more knowledge in order to live successfully in tomorrow's world.

You may wonder how you can possibly learn all the facts you are going to need during your lifetime. The answer is that you can't. Therefore, knowing how to find information when you need it is of vital importance to you. On the following pages are suggestions for locating good sources of information and for using these sources to find the facts that you need.

Books are an important source of information.

Written Sources of Information

1. <u>Books</u>. You may be able to find the information you need in books that you have at home or in your classroom. To see if a textbook or other nonfiction book has the information you need, look at the table of contents and the index.

Sometimes, you will need to go to your school or community library to locate books that contain the information you want. To make the best use of a library, you should learn to use the card catalog. This is a file that contains information about the books in the library. Each nonfiction book has at least three cards, filed in alphabetical order. One is for the title, one is for the author, and one is for the subject of the book. Each card gives the book's special number. This number will help you to find the book, since all the nonfiction books in the library are arranged on the shelves in numerical order. If you cannot find a book you want, the librarian will be glad to help you.

2. <u>Reference volumes</u>. You will find much useful information in special books known as reference volumes. These include dictionaries, encyclopedias, atlases, and other special books. Some companies publish a book each year with statistics and general information about the events of the preceding year. Such books are usually called yearbooks, annuals, or almanacs.

3. <u>Newspapers and magazines</u>. These are important sources of up-to-date information. Sometimes you will want to look for information in papers or magazines that you do not have at home. You can usually find the ones you want at the library.

The *Readers' Guide to Periodical Literature,* which is available in most libraries, will direct you to magazine articles about the subject you are investigating. This is a series of volumes that list articles by title, author, and subject. In the front of each volume is an explanation of the abbreviations used to indicate the different magazines and their dates.

4. <u>Booklets, pamphlets, and bulletins</u>. Many materials of this type are available from local and state governments, as well as from our federal government. Chambers of commerce, travel bureaus, trade organizations, private companies, and embassies of foreign countries publish materials that contain a wealth of information.

Many booklets and bulletins give accurate information. You should remember, however, that some of them are intended to promote certain products or ideas. Information obtained from such sources should be checked carefully.

Reading for Information

The following suggestions will help you to save time and effort when you are looking for information in books and other written materials.

1. <u>Use the table of contents and the index</u>. The table of contents appears at the beginning of the book and generally is a list of the chapters in the book. By looking at this list, you can usually tell

whether the book has the type of information you need.

The index is a more detailed list of the topics that are discussed in the book. It will help you locate the pages on which specific facts are discussed. In most books, the index is at the back. Encyclopedias often include the index in a separate volume, however.

At the beginning of an index, you will usually find an explanation that makes it easier to use. For example, the explanation at the beginning of the Index for *The Northeast* tells you that *p* means picture, *m* means map, and *t* means table.

The topics, or entries, in the index are arranged in alphabetical order. To locate all the information you need, you may have to look under more than one entry. For example, to find out what pages in *The Northeast* discuss climate, look up the entry for climate, and also see if climate is listed under the entries for the individual states in the Northeast.

2. Skim the written material to see if it contains the information you need. Before you begin reading a chapter or a page, skim it to see if it has the information you need. In this way you will not run the risk of wasting time reading something that is of little or no value to you. When you skim, you look mainly for topic headings, topic sentences, and key words. For example, imagine you are looking for the answer to the question: "What are the people in the Northeast doing to conserve their forest resources?" You might look for a topic heading that says "Forests." When you find this topic heading, you might look for the key words "conserving forests."

3. Read carefully when you think you have located the information you need. When you think you have found the page that contains the information you are looking for, read it carefully. Does it really tell you what you want to know? If not, you will need to look further.

Other Ways of Obtaining Information

1. Direct experience. What you observe or experience for yourself may be a good source of information if you have observed carefully and remembered accurately. First-hand information can often be obtained by visiting places in your community or nearby, such as museums, factories, or government offices.

2. Radio and television. Use the listings in your local newspaper to find programs about the subjects in which you are interested.

3. Movies, filmstrips, recordings, and slides. Materials on a great variety of subjects are available. They can be obtained from schools, libraries, museums, and private companies.

4. Resource people. Sometimes, you will be able to obtain information by interviewing a person who has special knowledge. On occasion, you may wish to invite someone to speak to your class and answer questions.

EVALUATING INFORMATION

During your lifetime, you will constantly need to evaluate what you see, hear, and read. Information is not true or significant simply because it is presented on television or is written in a book, magazine, or newspaper. The following suggestions will help you in evaluating information.

Learn to tell the difference between primary and secondary sources of information. A primary source of information is a first-hand record. For example, a photograph taken of an event while it is happening is a primary source. So is the report you write about a field trip you take. Original documents, such as the Constitution of the United States, are primary sources, also.

A secondary source is a secondhand report. For example, if you write a report about what someone else told you he saw, your report will be a secondary source of information. Another example of a secondary source is a history book.

Advanced scholars like to use primary sources whenever possible. However, these sources are often difficult to obtain. Most students in elementary and high school use secondary sources. You should always be aware that you are using secondhand information when you use a secondary source.

Find out who said it and when it was said. The next step in evaluating information is to ask, "Who said it?" Was he a scholar with special training in the subject about which he wrote? Was he a newsman with a reputation for careful reporting of the facts?

Another question you should ask is, "When was it said?" Changes take place rapidly in our world, and the information you are using may be out of date. For example, many nations in Africa have won independence in recent years, so a political map of this continent that is five years old is no longer accurate.

Find out if it is mainly fact or opinion. The next step in evaluating information is to decide whether it is based on facts or whether it mainly consists of unsupported opinions. You can do this best if you are aware of these three types of statements:

1. Statements of fact that can be checked. For example, "Voters in the United States choose their representatives by secret ballot," is a statement of fact that can be checked by observing how voting is carried on in different parts of our country.

2. Inferences, or conclusions that are based on facts. The statement, "The people of the United States live in a democracy," is an inference. This inference is based on the fact that the citizens choose their representatives by secret ballot, and on other facts that can be proved. It is important to remember that inferences can be false or only partly true.

3. Value judgments, or opinions. The statement, "It is wrong for people to be forced to live in poverty," is a value judgment. Since a value judgment is an opinion, you need to examine it very critically. On what facts and inferences is it based? For example, what facts and conclusions do you think form the basis of the opinion: "It is wrong for people to be forced to live in poverty"? Do you agree with these conclusions? A reliable writer or reporter is careful to let his reader know which statements in his writing are his own opinions. He also tries to base his opinions as much as possible on facts that can be proved.

Find out why it was said. The next step in evaluating information is to find out the purpose for which it was prepared. Many books and articles are prepared in an honest effort to give you accurate information. For example, a scientist writing about a new scientific discovery will usually try to report his findings as accurately as possible, and he will be careful to distinguish between what he has actually observed and the conclusions he has drawn from these facts.

Some information, however, is prepared mainly to persuade people to believe or act a certain way. Information of this kind is called propaganda.

Some propaganda is used to promote causes that are generally considered good. A United States Army recruiting poster with a big picture of Uncle Sam and the words, "Uncle Sam needs *you*," is an example of this type of propaganda.

Propaganda is also used to make people support causes they would not agree with if they knew more about them. This kind of propaganda may consist of information that is true, partly true, or false. Even when it is true, however, the information may be presented in such a way as to mislead you.

Propaganda generally appeals to people's emotions rather than to their reasoning ability. For this reason, you should learn to identify information that is propaganda. Then you can think about it calmly and clearly, and evaluate it intelligently.

Seven Propaganda Tricks

People who use propaganda have learned many ways of presenting information to influence you in the direction they wish. Seven propaganda tricks to watch for are listed below.

Name Calling. Giving a label that is disliked or feared, such as "un-American," to an organization, a person, or an idea. This trick often persuades people to reject something they know nothing about.

Glittering Generalities. Trying to win support by using fine-sounding phrases, such as "the best deal in town" or "the American way." These phrases have no clear meaning when you stop and think about them.

Transfer. Connecting a person, product, or idea with something that people already feel strongly about. For example, displaying a picture of a church next to a speaker to give the impression that he is honest and trustworthy.

Testimonial. Getting well-known persons or organizations to announce in public their support of a person, product, or idea.

Plain Folks. Trying to win support by giving the impression of being just an ordinary person who can be trusted. For example, a political candidate may try to win people's confidence by giving the impression that he is a good father who loves children and dogs.

Card Stacking. Giving the wrong impression by giving only part of the facts about a person, product, or idea. For example, giving favorable facts and leaving out unfavorable ones.

Bandwagon. Trying to win support by saying that "everybody knows that" or "everyone is doing this."

HOLDING A GROUP DISCUSSION

One of the important ways in which you learn is by exchanging ideas with other people. You do this frequently in informal conversation. You are likely to learn more, however, when you take part in the special kind of group conversation that we call a discussion. A discussion is more orderly than a conversation, and it usually has a definite, serious purpose. This purpose may be the sharing of information or the solving of a problem. In order to reach its goal, the discussion group must arrive at a conclusion or make a decision of some kind.

A discussion is more likely to be successful when those who take part in it observe the following guidelines:

1. Be prepared. Think about the topic to be discussed ahead of time. Prepare for the discussion by reading and taking notes. You may also want to make an outline of the ideas you want to share with the group.

2. Take part. Contribute to the discussion; express your ideas clearly and concisely. Be sure that the statements you make and the questions you ask deal with the topic being discussed. This will help the discussion move along toward a successful conclusion.

3. Listen and think. Listen thoughtfully to others. Encourage all of the members of the discussion group to express their ideas. Do not make up your mind about a question or a problem until all of the facts have been given. Be ready to help the group summarize the information presented during the discussion.

4. Be courteous. When you speak, address the entire group. Ask and answer questions politely. When you disagree with someone, point out your reasons calmly and in a friendly way.

WORKING WITH OTHERS

In school and throughout life, you will find that there are many projects that can be done better by a group than by one person working alone. Some of these projects would take too long to finish if they were done by a single individual. Others have different parts that can be done best by people with different talents.

Before your group begins a project, you should decide several matters. First, determine exactly what you are trying to accomplish. Second, decide what part of the project each person should do. Third, schedule when the project is to be completed.

The group will do a better job and reach its goals more quickly if each person follows these suggestions:

1. Do your part. Remember that the success of your project depends on every member of the group. Be willing to do your share of the work and to accept your share of the responsibility.

2. Follow the rules. Help the group decide on sensible rules, and then follow them. When a difference of opinion cannot be settled by discussion, make a decision by majority vote.

3. Share your ideas. Be willing to share your ideas and talents with the group. When you submit an idea for discussion, be prepared to see it criticized or even rejected. At the same time, have the courage to stick up for a principle or a belief that is really important to you.

4. Respect others. Remember that every person is an individual with different beliefs and talents. Give the other members of the group a chance to be heard, and be ready to appreciate the work and ideas they contribute.

5. Be friendly, thoughtful, helpful, and cheerful. Try to express your opinions seriously and sincerely without hurting others or losing their respect. Listen politely to the ideas of others.

6. Learn from your mistakes. Look for ways in which you can be a better group member the next time you work with others on a project.

BUILDING YOUR VOCABULARY

When you do research in many different types of reading materials, you are likely to find several words you have never seen before. If you skip over these words, the chances are that you will not fully understand what you are reading. The following suggestions will help you to discover the meanings of new words and build your vocabulary.

1. See how the word is used in the sentence. When you come to a new word, don't stop reading. Read on beyond the new word to see if you can discover any clues to what its meaning might be. Trying to figure out the meaning of a word from the way it is used may not give you the exact definition. However, it will give you a general idea of what the word means.

2. Sound out the word. Break the word up into syllables, and try to pronounce it. When you say the word aloud, you may find that you know it after all but have simply never seen it in print.

3. Look in the dictionary. When you think you have figured out what a word means and how it is pronounced, check with the dictionary. Have you pronounced it correctly? Did you decide upon the right definition? Remember, most words have several meanings. Do you know which meaning should be used?

4. Make a list of the new words you learn. In your own words, write a definition of each word you include in your list. Review this list from time to time.

A good vocabulary is a useful skill.

Learning Map Skills

The earth is a sphere. Our earth is round like a ball. We call any object with this shape a sphere. The earth is, of course, a very large sphere. Its diameter* is about 8,000 miles. Its circumference* is about 25,000 miles. The earth is not quite a perfect sphere, however, for it is slightly flattened at the North and South poles.

Globes and maps. The globe in your classroom is also a sphere. It is a model of the earth. The surface of the globe shows the shapes of the landmasses and bodies of water on the earth. By looking at the globe, you can see exactly where the continents, islands, and oceans are located. Globes are made with the North Pole at the top, but they are usually tilted to represent the way that the earth is tilted. Maps are flat drawings that represent part or all of the earth's surface.

*See Glossary

Scale. Globes and maps give information about distance. When you use them, you need to know how many miles on the earth are represented by a given distance on the globe or map. This relationship is called the scale. The scale of a globe or map may be expressed in several different ways.

On most maps, the scale is shown by a small drawing. For example:

Scale of Miles
0   200   400

Sometimes, the scale is expressed in this way: 1 inch = 400 miles.

Scale is often shown in another way, especially on globes and large maps. For example: 1:10,000,000. These numbers mean that any given distance on the globe or map represents a distance on the earth that is ten million times as large. When the scale is shown in this way, you may use any kind of measuring unit you wish. If you choose the inch, then one inch on the globe or map equals ten million inches on the earth, or about 158 miles. You might, however, prefer to use the centimeter,* another measuring unit. In that case, one centimeter on the globe or map would represent ten million centimeters on the earth, or 100 kilometers.

Long Island is a different size on each of the four maps below. This is because one inch on each of these maps represents a different distance on the earth. In other words, the scale of each of these maps is different.

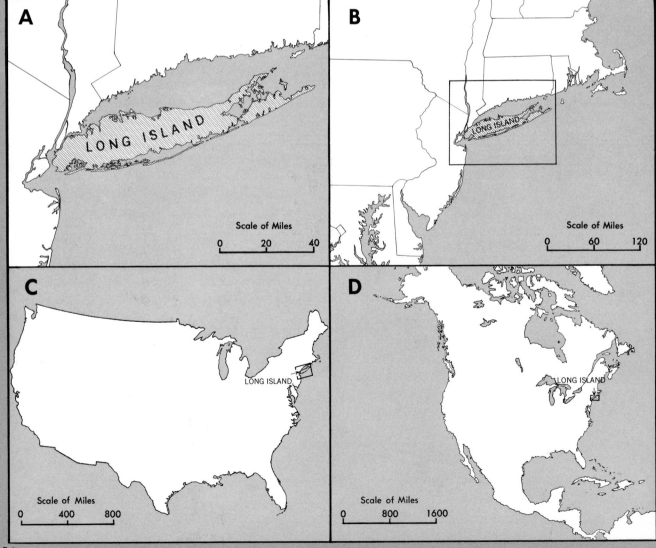

354

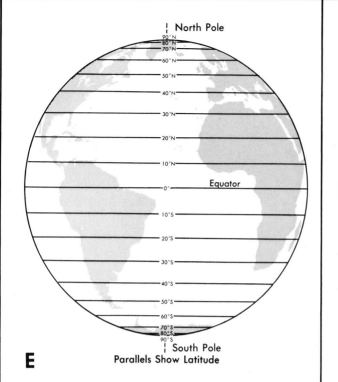

North Pole

Equator

South Pole

E Parallels Show Latitude

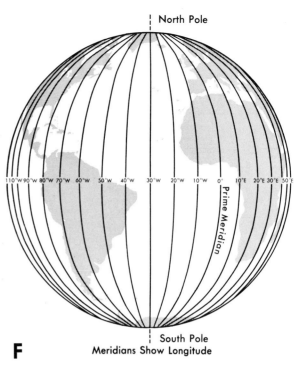

North Pole

Prime Meridian

South Pole

F Meridians Show Longitude

Locating places on the earth. Map makers, travelers, and other curious people have always wanted to know just where certain places are located. Over the years, a very accurate way of giving such information has been worked out. This system is used all over the world.

In order to work out a system for locating anything, you need starting points and a measuring unit. The North and South poles and the equator are the starting points for the system we use to locate places on the earth. The measuring unit for our system is called the degree (°).

Parallels show latitude. When we want to locate a place on the earth, we first find out how far it is north or south of the equator. This distance measured in degrees is called north or south latitude. The equator represents zero latitude. The North Pole is located at 90 degrees north latitude, and the South Pole is at 90 degrees south latitude.

All points on the earth that have the same latitude are the same distance from the equator. A line connecting such points is called a parallel. This is because it is parallel to the equator. (See illustration E, above.)

Meridians show longitude. After we know the latitude of a place, we need to know its location in an east-west direction. This is called its longitude. The lines that show longitude are called meridians. They are drawn so as to connect the North and South poles. (See illustration F, above.) Longitude is measured from the meridian that passes through Greenwich, England. This line of zero longitude is called the prime meridian. Distance east or west of this meridian measured in degrees is called east or west longitude.

Locating places on a globe. The location of a certain place might be given to you like this: 30°N 90°W. This means that this place is located 30 degrees north of the equator, and 90 degrees west of the prime meridian. See if you can find this place on the globe in your classroom. It is helpful to remember that parallels and meridians are drawn every ten or fifteen degrees on most globes.

The round earth on a flat map. An important fact about a sphere is that you cannot flatten out its surface perfectly. To prove this, you might perform an experiment. Cut an orange in half and scrape away the fruit.

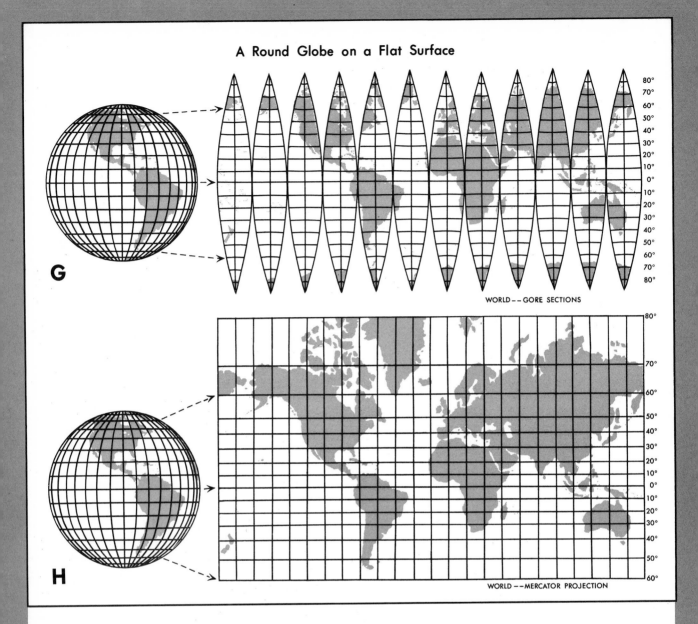

G

WORLD – – GORE SECTIONS

80°
70°
60°
50°
40°
30°
20°
10°
0°
10°
20°
30°
40°
50°
60°
70°
80°

H

WORLD – – MERCATOR PROJECTION

You will not be able to press either piece of orange peel flat without crushing it. If you cut one piece in half, however, you can press these smaller pieces nearly flat. Next, cut one of these pieces of peel into three sections, or gores, shaped like those in illustration G, above. You will be able to press these small sections quite flat.

A map like the one shown in illustration G can be made by cutting the surface of a globe into twelve pieces shaped like the smallest sections of your orange peel. Such a map would be fairly accurate. However, an "orange-peel" map is not an easy map to use, because the continents and oceans are split apart.

A flat map can never show the earth's surface as truthfully as a globe can. On globes, shape, size, distance, and direction are all accurate. Although a single flat map of the world cannot be drawn to show all four of these things correctly, flat maps can be made that show some of these things accurately. The various ways of drawing maps of the world to show different things correctly are called map projections.

The Mercator* projection. Illustration H, above, shows a world map called a Mercator projection. When you compare this map with a globe, you can see that continents, islands, and oceans have almost the right shape. On this kind of map, however, North America seems larger than Africa, which is not true. On Mercator maps, lands far from the equator appear larger than they are.

Because they show true directions, Mercator maps are especially useful to navigators. For instance, the city of Lisbon, Portugal, lies almost exactly east of Baltimore, Maryland. A Mercator map shows that a ship could reach Lisbon by sailing from Baltimore straight east across the Atlantic Ocean.

The shortest route. Strangely enough, the best way to reach Lisbon from Baltimore is not by traveling straight east. There is a shorter route. In order to understand why this is so, you might like to perform the following experiment.

On your classroom globe, locate Lisbon and Baltimore. Both cities lie just south of the 40th parallel. Take a piece of string and connect the two cities. Let the string follow the true east-west direction of the 40th parallel. Now, draw the string tight. Notice that it passes far to the north of the 40th parallel. The path of the tightened string is the shortest route between Baltimore and Lisbon. The shortest route between any two points on the earth is called the great* circle route.

The gnomonic (nō mon′ ik) projection. Using a globe and a piece of string is not a very handy or accurate way of finding great circle routes. Instead, sailors and fliers use a special kind of map called the gnomonic projection. (See illustration I, below.) On this kind of map, the great circle route between any two places can be found simply by drawing a straight line between them.

Equal-area projections. Mercator and gnomonic maps are both very useful, but they do not show true areas. They cannot be used when you want to compare areas in different parts of the world. This is because sections of these maps that are the same size do not always represent the same amounts of the earth's surface.

Maps that do show true areas are called equal-area projections. If one square* inch of such a map represents a certain number of square miles on the earth's surface, then every other square inch of the map will represent an equal number of square miles on the earth. In order to draw an equal-area map of the world on a flat surface, the shapes of the landmasses and bodies of water must be distorted. (See illustration J, below.) To avoid this, some equal-area maps are broken, or interrupted. The breaks are arranged to fall at places that are not important. (See illustration K, below.)

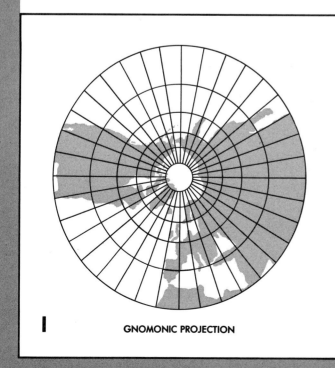

I GNOMONIC PROJECTION

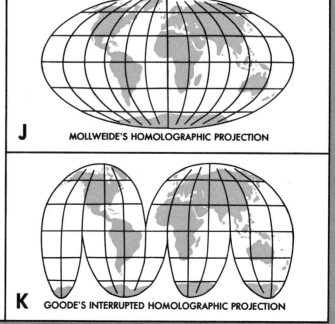

J MOLLWEIDE'S HOMOLOGRAPHIC PROJECTION

K GOODE'S INTERRUPTED HOMOLOGRAPHIC PROJECTION

SPECIAL-PURPOSE MAPS

Maps that show part of the earth. For some purposes, we prefer maps that do not show the entire surface of the earth. A map of a very small area can be drawn more accurately than a map of a large area. It can also include more details.

Illustration L, below, shows a photograph and a map of the same small part of the earth. The drawings on the map that show the shape and location of things on the earth are called symbols. The small drawing that shows directions is called a compass* rose.

Maps for special purposes. Maps can show the location of many different kinds of things. For instance, a map can show what minerals are found in certain places, or what crops are grown. A small chart that lists the symbols and their meanings is usually included on a map. This is called the legend, or key. (See map N, below.)

Symbols on some geography maps stand for the amounts of things in different places. For instance, map M, below, gives information about the number of people in the western part of the United States. The key tells the meaning of the symbols, which in this case are dots and circles.

On different maps, the same symbol may stand for different things and amounts. For example, each dot on map M stands for 10,000 persons. On other maps, a dot might represent 5,000 sheep or 1,000 bushels of wheat.

There are other ways of giving information about quantity. For example, various designs or patterns may be used on a rainfall map to indicate the areas that receive different amounts of rain each year.

L

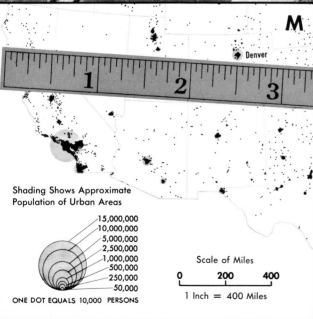

M

Shading Shows Approximate Population of Urban Areas

15,000,000
10,000,000
5,000,000
2,500,000
1,000,000
500,000
250,000
50,000

ONE DOT EQUALS 10,000 PERSONS

Scale of Miles

0   200   400

1 Inch = 400 Miles

N

WATERWAYS IN CHINA
Miles
0   250   500   750
——— Rivers
ᴡᴡᴡᴡ Grand Canal
• Main Seaports

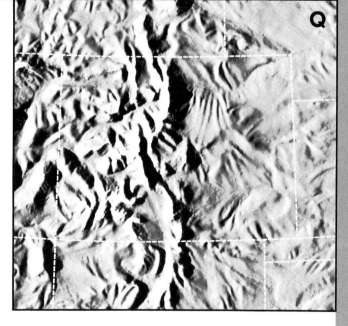

RELIEF MAPS

Some globes and maps show the roughness of the earth's surface. From a jet plane, you can see that the earth's surface is irregular. You can see mountains and valleys, hills and plains. For some purposes, globes and maps that show these things are needed. They are called relief globes and maps.

Since globes are three-dimensional models of the earth, you may wonder why most globes do not show the roughness of the earth's surface. The reason for this is that the highest mountain on the earth is not very large when it is compared with the earth's diameter. Even a very large globe would be almost perfectly smooth.

In order to make a relief globe or map, you must use a different scale for the height of the land. For example, you might start with a large flat map. One inch on your flat map represents a distance of one hundred miles on the earth. Now you are going to make a model of a mountain on your map. On the earth, this mountain is two miles high. If you let one inch represent a height of two miles on the earth, your mountain should rise one inch above the flat surface of

your map. Other mountains and hills should be modeled on this same scale.

By photographing relief globes and maps, flat maps can be made that show the earth much as it looks from an airplane. Maps O and P, at the top of this page, are photographs of a relief globe. Map Q is a photograph of a relief map.

Topographic maps. Another kind of map that shows the roughness of the earth's surface is called a topographic, or contour, map. On this kind of map, lines are drawn to show

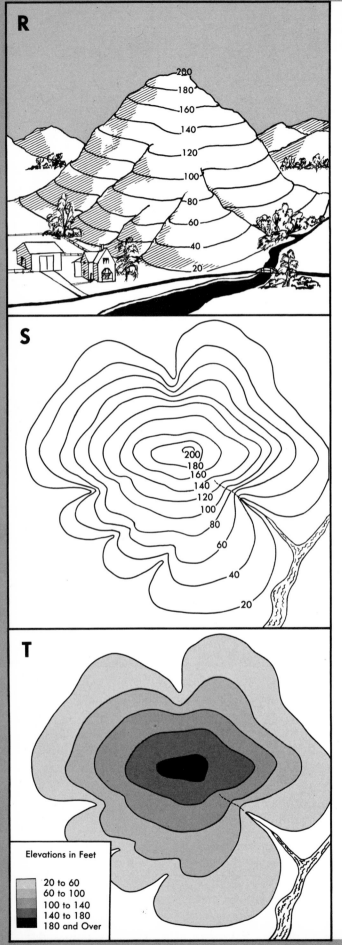

different heights of the earth's surface. These are called contour lines. The illustrations on this page help to explain how topographic maps are made.

Illustration R is a drawing of a hill. Around the bottom of the hill is our first contour line. This line connects all the points at the base of the hill that are exactly twenty feet above sea level. Higher up the hill, another contour line is drawn, connecting all the points that are exactly forty feet above sea level. A line is also drawn at a height of sixty feet. Other lines are drawn every twenty feet until the top of the hill is reached. Since the hill is shaped somewhat like a cone, each contour line is shorter than the one just below it.

Illustration S shows how the contour lines in the drawing of the hill (R) can be used to make a topographic map. This map gives us a great deal of information about the hill. Since each line is labeled with the height it represents, you can tell how high the different parts of the hill are. It is important to remember that land does not really rise in layers, as you might think when you look at a topographic map. Wherever the contour lines are far apart, you can be sure that the land slopes gently. Where they are close together, the slope is steep. With practice, you can picture the land in your mind as you look at such a map. Topographic maps are especially useful to men who design such things as roads and buildings.

On a topographic map, the spaces between the contour lines may be filled in with different shades of gray. If a different shade of gray were used for each different height of land shown in map S, there would be ten shades. It would be very hard for you to tell these different shades of gray apart. Therefore on map T, at left, black and four shades of gray were used to show differences in height of forty feet. The key box shows the height of the land represented by the different shades. On some topographic maps, colors are used to represent different heights of land.

GLOSSARY
Complete Pronunciation Key

The pronunciation of each word is shown just after the word, in this way: **equator** (i kwā′tər). The letters and signs used are pronounced as in the words below. The mark ′ is placed after a syllable with a primary or strong accent, as in the example above. The mark ′ after a syllable shows a secondary or lighter accent, as in **Hiawatha** (hī′ə woth′ə).

a	hat, cap	j	jam, enjoy	u	cup, butter
ā	age, face	k	kind, seek	u̇	full, put
ã	care, air	l	land, coal	ü	rule, move
ä	father, far	m	me, am	ū	use, music
b	bad, rob	n	no, in		
ch	child, much	ng	long, bring		
d	did, red	o	hot, rock	v	very, save
		ō	open, go	w	will, woman
		ô	order, all	y	young, yet
e	let, best	oi	oil, voice	z	zero, breeze
ē	equal, see	ou	house, out	zh	measure, seizure
ėr	term, learn	p	paper, cup		
f	fat, if	r	run, try	ə	represents:
g	go, bag	s	say, yes	a	in about
h	he, how	sh	she, rush	e	in taken
		t	tell, it	i	in pencil
i	it, pin	th	thin, both	o	in lemon
ī	ice, five	ŦH	then, smooth	u	in circus

abstract. As applied to the arts, refers to painting or sculpture that does not represent persons or objects directly. Instead, it represents the artist's ideas, emotions, or impressions about a subject.

acre. A unit of area. A football field covers about one and one-third acres.

alewife. A fish of the herring family that is abundant along the Atlantic coast. Alewives may be pickled or canned for food, or made into products such as oil and fertilizer.

alfalfa. A plant with clover-like leaves, and long roots that grow deep in the soil. Hay made from alfalfa is used as food for farm animals.

amendment. A change in, or an addition to, a constitution or a law.

annex. To make one territory part of another.

anthracite (an′thrə sīt). A high-quality coal. It is hard, black, and shiny, and burns with little smoke. (See page 135.)

Appalachian (ap′ə lā′chən) **Highlands.** A geographical region of eastern North America. In the United States, this region extends from central Alabama and Georgia northeastward to Canada. (See map, page 27.)

Appalachian (ap′ə lā′chən) **Mountains.** A name often used to refer to mountainous sections of the Appalachian Highlands. (Compare maps, pages 19 and 27.)

Appalachian (ap′ə lā′chən) **Plateau.** The westernmost section of the Appalachian Highlands region. (See map, page 27.)

Appalachian (ap′ə lā′chən) **Ridges and Valleys.** A section of the Appalachian Highlands region that extends from central Alabama into eastern New York. (See map, page 27.)

aqueduct (ak′wə dukt). A man-made canal, tunnel, or large pipe through which water travels to the place where it is to be used.

atmosphere (at′mə sfir). The name given to the layer of air that surrounds the earth.

361

atomic energy. Energy that is stored in atoms. All matter is made up of atoms, which are much too small to be seen. When atoms are split or combined in certain ways, great amounts of energy are released. This energy can be used for many purposes, including the production of electricity.

ballet (bal′ā). A special kind of dance performed by a group of dancers on a stage. The movements of the dance usually tell a story.

basalt. A hard, dark-colored rock. It is used for road making and as a building stone.

basic chemicals. Common chemicals that are produced in large quantities for use in industry.(See **chemicals.**)Sulfuric acid and ammonia are examples of basic chemicals.

bearings. Objects such as metal balls and rollers that enable one part of a machine or a mechanical device to slide smoothly over or around another part. Ball bearings are used in roller-skate wheels, for example.

bifocal lens. A special lens with two parts, used for eyeglasses. The upper part is used for looking at distant objects, and the lower part is used for looking at nearby objects.

Bill of Rights. In the United States, refers to the first ten amendments to the Constitution. These amendments guarantee certain basic rights to the people of our country.

bituminous (bə tü′mə nəs) **coal.** Another name for high-grade soft coal, the most plentiful and important type of coal. It is used as a fuel, especially for the production of electric power. Large amounts of high-quality bituminous coal are made into coke. See **coke.**

blast furnace. A cylinder-shaped furnace in which iron is made from iron ore. It is called a blast furnace because a strong blast of air is blown into the bottom of the furnace. The air, which rises through a mixture of iron ore, coke, and limestone, makes the coke burn at the high temperature needed for producing iron. A modern blast furnace may be as high as a fifteen-story building.

blight. Any disease or injury that causes plants to wither and die.

Blue Ridge. A section of the Appalachian Highlands region that extends from northern Georgia into Pennsylvania. (See map, page 27.) The Blue Ridge is a chain of forested mountain ranges.

bog. An area of soft, wet, spongy ground.

bond. A certificate issued as a promise that money loaned to an organization such as a business or government will be paid back. For example, a school district may issue bonds in order to raise money for a new school building. People buy the bonds as an investment, knowing they will later get back the money they invested plus an additional amount in return for the use of their money.

Cabot (kab′ət), **John,** 1450-1498. An Italian seaman who made two voyages to North America for the English. (See center map, page 61.)

capital. In economics, refers to wealth that is used to produce more wealth. Money, factory buildings, and machines are important forms of capital.

capitol. A building in which a lawmaking body meets. When spelled with a capital *C,* this word refers to the place in Washington, D.C., where Congress meets.

carbon. A common substance found in nature in many different forms. A diamond is pure carbon as is graphite, the black writing material in your pencil. Anthracite, a high-quality coal, is composed almost entirely of carbon. In combination with other substances, carbon is found in all living things, in many kinds of rock, and in petroleum.

case study. A special study made of a situation or problem. A case study serves as an example that can be used in considering other similar situations or problems.

centimeter. A unit for measuring length. It is equal to slightly less than half an inch. The centimeter is a unit in the metric system of measurement. The metric system is used in most countries and by scientists throughout the world. In this system, 100 centimeters equal one meter, and 1000 meters equal one kilometer. A meter is about 39 inches in length, and a kilometer is equal to about two thirds of a mile.

central city. The main city, or one of the main cities, of a metropolitan area. See **metropolitan area.**

century. Any period of one hundred years, but especially one of the hundred-year periods of time before (B.C.) or after (A.D.) the birth of Christ. The first century A.D. extended from the year 1 through the year 100, and the second century lasted from 101 through 200. The twentieth century began in 1901.

charcoal. A dark, lightweight substance usually made by partly burning wood in an airtight oven. Charcoal is used mainly as a fuel or as a filtering material.

chemicals. Substances that are used in or obtained from chemical processes. These are processes that produce new materials by changing the composition of the original substances. Many chemicals are complicated substances with strange-sounding names. Others, such as salt, soda, and ammonia, are simple and familiar household items.

circumference (sər kum′fər əns). The distance around an object or a geometric figure, especially a circle or a sphere.

Civil War, 1861-1865. The war that resulted when a group of states in the South broke away from the Union and formed a separate nation known as the Confederacy. The war began on April 12, 1861, when Confederate soldiers fired on Union troops stationed at Fort Sumter, in South Carolina. After four years of fighting, the Union forces won the war. (See Chapter 6.)

climate. The average weather conditions of a given place over a period of many years. A description of climate includes such things as wind, sunshine, temperature, the amount of moisture in the air, and the amount of rain, hail, and snow that falls.

clover. Any one of a number of plants of the pea family. Several kinds of clover are grown as food for livestock.

coal gas. A gas manufactured from coal for use as a fuel.

Coastal Plain. A large region of the United States that borders the Atlantic Ocean and the Gulf of Mexico. (See map, page 27.) The land in this region is level or gently rolling.

coke. A fuel made by roasting coal in special airtight ovens. It is one of the three main raw materials used in the production of iron. (See feature, page 145.) Coke, together with iron ore and limestone, is loaded into the blast furnace. The coke serves as a fuel, burning at a very high temperature, to melt the other materials. The burning coke also provides gases that react with the molten ore to separate the iron from waste materials.

colony. A settlement or territory outside the country that controls it.

commercial. Refers to something that is done for profit.

commute. To travel back and forth regularly, especially between a home in the suburbs and a place of work in the city.

compass rose. A small drawing included on a map to show directions. A compass rose is often used as a decoration. Here are three examples of compass roses:

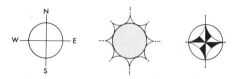

computer. An automatic machine that solves complicated mathematical problems very rapidly, usually by means of electronic devices.

condense. To change from a gas to a liquid. For example, when steam is cooled it condenses into water.

Confederacy (kən fed′ər ə si). Common name for the Confederate States of America. This was a nation made up of eleven states that withdrew from and fought against the Union in the Civil War. The Confederacy included Texas and all of the states that now make up the South except Kentucky. See **South.**

Confederate (kən fed′ər it). Of or relating to the Confederacy. See **Confederacy.**

Congress. The lawmaking, or legislative, branch of the United States government. It consists of the Senate and the House of Representatives.

PRONUNCIATION KEY: hat, āge, cãre, fär; let, ēqual, tėrm; it, īce; hot, ōpen, ôrder; oil, out; cup, put, rüle, ūse; child; long; thin; ᵺen; zh, measure; ə represents a in about, e in taken, i in pencil, o in lemon, u in circus. For the complete key, see page 361.

constitution (kon'stə tü'shən). A system of basic principles or rules that provides the basis for a government. When spelled with a capital *C*, this word means the document that outlines the basic principles of the government of the United States.

contagious diseases. Diseases that are spread by contact. The common cold and measles are contagious diseases.

contemporary. Refers to events or people of the present time.

conterminous (kən tėr'mə nəs) **United States.** The forty-eight states of the United States that are enclosed by an unbroken boundary. The word conterminous means "having the same boundary."

continent. One of the main landmasses on the earth. There are six continents—Eurasia, Africa, North America, South America, Australia, and Antarctica. Some people consider Eurasia to be two continents—Europe and Asia.

Continental Army. The army of the thirteen colonies in North America that became the United States.

Continental armies. The armies that made up the Continental Army. See **Continental Army.**

Continental Congress. Either of two Continental Congresses, which were meetings of representatives from the British colonies that joined together to form the United States. The First Continental Congress met in September and October of 1774 and asked for fair treatment of the colonies by Great Britain. The Second Continental Congress first met in May, 1775, and united the colonies for the struggle against Great Britain. In 1776, Congress declared that the colonies were independent of Great Britain. The Second Continental Congress served as the government until 1781, when a new form of government was established.

corporation. A business firm that consists of a group of persons authorized by law to act as a unit. A corporation may buy and sell property or carry on other business.

county. In most states of our country, the largest division established for local government. Exceptions are Alaska, which is divided into boroughs, and Louisiana, which is divided into parishes.

The powers of county governments differ from state to state, but most counties have a court, a sheriff, and committees or boards that control such matters as roads, airports, welfare, and schools.

crude oil. Petroleum as it comes from the ground, before it has been refined.

cultivate. To break up the soil around the roots of growing plants, mainly for the purpose of killing weeds. Also, to prepare and use land for growing crops.

cultural. Refers to the development and expression of artistic and other mental abilities.

Cumberland Road. See **National Road.**

cutlery. Implements for eating. Also, cutting tools such as knives and scissors.

Declaration of Independence. A document adopted on July 4, 1776, in which representatives of thirteen British colonies in North America declared their independence from Great Britain, and stated their reasons for taking this action. These colonies became our first thirteen states.

degree. A unit of measurement. Any circle may be divided into 360 equal parts, which are called degrees.

Delmarva Peninsula. A peninsula along the Atlantic coast of the United States, about 180 miles long and 70 miles across at its widest part. It is bordered by Chesapeake Bay on the west, and by the Delaware River, Delaware Bay, and the Atlantic Ocean on the east. Most of the state of Delaware and parts of Maryland and Virginia lie on this peninsula.

democracy. A political system in which people govern themselves, or a country with such a system of government. In successful democracies, the people generally share the following five beliefs: 1. Every person is important. 2. People have the right to govern themselves. 3. Decisions should be made by majority vote. 4. All people have certain natural rights. 5. Laws should apply equally to all citizens of a country.

density of population. The average number of people per square mile, or some other unit of area, in a given place. Density of population may be figured by dividing the total number of people in an area by the area's total number of square miles or other units.

depression. In economics, a period of decreased business activity and widespread unemployment.

diameter. The length of a straight line that extends from one side of an object to the other. This line must pass through the exact center of the object.

dictatorship. A government that is run by a single leader or by a small group of leaders who are not responsible to the people.

discrimination. The act of withholding rights or freedoms from people because they belong to minority groups. (See page 215.)

displaced person. A person who has been forced to leave his own country because of war or because of his political beliefs.

distill. To cause a substance to give off vapor by heating it, and then to condense the vapor. The product or products that result may be entirely different from the original substance. Often, however, the product is a purer form of the original substance. For example, pure water can be obtained by distilling seawater.

distillery. A plant where alcoholic beverages such as whiskey are made. Also, any place where distilling is carried on. See **distill.**

drift mine. A type of mine in which a tunnel is dug horizontally into the side of a hill.

Eastern Orthodox (ôr'thə doks). Refers to one of the three main branches of Christianity. (See **Roman Catholic** and **Protestant.**) This branch of Christianity consists of a loosely connected group of independent churches located mainly in western Asia and eastern Europe. Eastern Orthodox also refers to members of these churches.

electronic (i lek'tron'ik). Refers to certain devices, such as vacuum tubes and transistors, or to products that make use of such devices. Radios, television sets, computers, and X-ray machines are examples of electronic products.

emery. A dark-colored, grainy rock that contains several hard minerals. Crushed or powdered emery is used for grinding and polishing such materials as glass, gemstones, and metals.

England. A division of the United Kingdom. England occupies most of southern Great Britain. See **Great Britain** and **United Kingdom.**

equator (i kwā'tər). An imaginary line around the middle of the earth, halfway between the North and South poles. It divides the earth into two equal parts—the Northern Hemisphere and the Southern Hemisphere.

equinox (ē'kwə noks). Either of two times of the year when the sun shines directly on the equator. These occur about March 21 and September 22. At these two times, day and night are of equal length everywhere on earth.

Erie Canal. A canal in New York that connected the Hudson River, near Albany, with the port city of Buffalo, on Lake Erie. It was completed in 1825. In the early 1900's, the Erie Canal became part of the New York State Barge Canal. See **New York State Barge Canal.**

erosion. The process by which the rock and soil of the earth's surface are worn away or dissolved by the forces of nature. Erosion includes wearing away by the action of rainfall, running water, ice, wind, and waves. Erosion may benefit man, as when soil is formed from rocks, or it may be harmful, as when fertile soil is washed away.

essay. A literary composition that usually expresses the author's personal ideas.

Eurasia (yu̇ rā'zha). The largest continent on the earth. It is sometimes considered to be two separate continents—Europe and Asia.

Europe. The western part of Eurasia. Europe, which is sometimes considered to be a separate continent, extends generally westward from the Ural Mountains in the Soviet Union to the Atlantic Ocean.

evaporate (i vap'ə rāt). To change from a liquid to a gas or vapor.

Fall Line. The border between the Piedmont Plateau and the Coastal Plain. (See page 35.)

PRONUNCIATION KEY: hat, āge, cãre, fär; let, ēqual, tėrm; it, īce; hot, ōpen, ôrder; oil, out; cup, pu̇t, rüle, ūse; child; long; thin; ᴛʜen; zh, measure; ə represents a in about, e in taken, i in pencil, o in lemon, u in circus. For the complete key, see page 361.

365

famine (fam'ən). A severe shortage of food.

Farewell Address. A message to the American people, published by George Washington in September, 1796, a few months before the end of his last term as president. In his address, he warned of the problems faced by the young nation.

federal. Refers to the national government of the United States, as opposed to a state or local government.

feedlots. Places where cattle are kept while being fattened for market.

fertilizer. A substance that is added to soil to make it produce larger yields or better-quality crops. Manure and lime are examples of fertilizers.

fiction. Novels, short stories, and other prose writings that tell about imaginary people or events.

finance (fə nans'). Matters that concern money and credit.

First Continental Congress. See **Continental Congress.**

flounder. Any one of a group of important food fishes that have flat bodies and both eyes on one side.

forge. A furnace, or a workshop together with its furnace, where iron is made. Also, a shop where iron is heated and then hammered into different shapes.

French and Indian War, 1754-1763. A war in North America in which the French and their Indian allies fought the British. The war was fought mainly over conflicting claims to land that lay between the British settlements and the Mississippi River. The British won the war and gained most of the French possessions in North America. (See maps, page 75.)

French Revolution. The period of violence and disorder in France from 1789 to 1799, during which the people overthrew the king. Although the people gained control of the country, the republic they established did not last. However, even under Napoleon Bonaparte, who ruled France as a dictator from 1799 until 1815, the French people had more equality of opportunity than they had ever known before.

garnet. A hard, glassy mineral that occurs in several varieties. Crushed garnet is used for grinding and polishing. A dark-red, transparent variety of garnet is used as a gem.

generator. A machine that changes mechanical energy into electrical energy. In an automobile, a small generator uses mechanical force from the drive shaft to produce the electricity needed to run the lights and starter. In large power plants, huge generators produce electricity from mechanical force provided by engines called turbines. (See page 131.)

glacier (glā'shər). A mass of slowly moving ice. (See page 38.)

Great Britain. The largest island of the British Isles, a group of islands off the western coast of Europe. Great Britain includes three divisions of the United Kingdom — England, Scotland, and Wales. At one time these areas had separate rulers. However, Wales has been joined to England since the sixteenth century, and Scotland and England were officially united in 1707. Today, the name Great Britain is often used to mean the United Kingdom. See **United Kingdom.**

great circle. Any imaginary circle around the earth that divides its surface exactly in half. The equator, for example, is a great circle. The shortest route between any two points on the earth always lies on the great circle that passes through them.

Great Lakes. Five huge lakes in the central part of North America. These are Lakes Superior, Michigan, Huron, Erie, and Ontario. (See map, page 19.)

Great Lakes–St. Lawrence Waterway. A great inland waterway that consists of the St. Lawrence River, the five Great Lakes, and the canals, straits, and rivers that connect them. Cargo ships can sail on this waterway from the Atlantic Ocean to the western end of Lake Superior, a distance of about 2,300 miles. The system of canals, dams, and locks on the St. Lawrence between Lake Ontario and the city of Montreal, Canada, is known as the St. Lawrence Seaway.

Great Valley. A long chain of valleys in the eastern part of the United States. The Great Valley forms a large part of the Appalachian Ridges and Valleys section of the Appalachian Highlands.

gristmill. A mill for grinding grain.

growing season. The period of time when crops can be grown outdoors without danger of being killed by frost.

Gulf of Mexico. An arm of the Atlantic Ocean that extends along part of the southeastern coast of North America. (See map, page 20.)

gypsum. A chalky mineral used in making cement and plaster and as a fertilizer.

halibut. A large, flat fish that is used for food.

harbor. A sheltered area of deep water where ships may dock or anchor.

Harvard University. A leading American university, located in Cambridge, Massachusetts. Harvard, which was founded in 1636 by the Puritans, is the oldest institution of higher learning in the United States.

Hawaiians. The brown-skinned people who first inhabited the Hawaiian Islands, or their descendants.

Hiawatha (hī′ə woth′ə). A Mohawk Indian chief who, according to tradition, encouraged peace among the Iroquois and helped found the League of the Five Nations. Hiawatha is famous as the hero of a long poem called *The Song of Hiawatha,* by Henry Wadsworth Longfellow. This poem is based on Indian legends about various heroes, including the real Hiawatha.

Huguenots (hū′gə nots). The name given in the sixteenth and seventeenth centuries to the Protestants in France. The Huguenots were often persecuted by French Roman Catholics. Thousands of Huguenots were imprisoned or killed, and many fled to other countries.

humid (hū′mid). Moist. When used in connection with weather or climate, refers to air that contains a large amount of moisture.

hydroelectric (hī′drō i lek′trik). Refers to hydroelectricity. See **hydroelectricity.**

hydroelectricity (hī′drō i lek′tris′ə ti). Electricity produced by waterpower. The force of rushing water is used to run machines called generators, which produce electricity. (See page 131.)

immigrant. A person of foreign nationality who enters a country to make it his permanent home.

immigration. Entering a foreign country or region with the purpose of living there permanently. Also, the movement of immigrants into a country. See **immigrant.**

import (im pôrt′). To bring goods into a country or region from another country or region, especially for the purpose of selling them. These goods are called imports (im′pôrts).

impressment. The act of seizing men by force to serve in an army or navy.

inalienable (in āl′yə nə bəl) **rights.** Those natural rights that a person cannot give up or transfer to the government. In a democracy, the government respects and protects the inalienable rights of the people. Our Declaration of Independence states that among our inalienable rights are "Life, Liberty, and the pursuit of Happiness."

industrialized. Refers to a country or region where industry is highly developed.

interstate commerce. Trade or transportation that crosses one or more of the state borders in the United States. The Constitution gives Congress the power to regulate trade, or commerce, among the states. Congress does not, however, generally have any control over commerce within each state. Congress controls interstate commerce through various agencies such as the Interstate Commerce Commission. Through these agencies, Congress is able to regulate rates, trade practices, and employment policies of companies engaged in interstate commerce.

invest. To use money for the purpose of bringing a profit.

Iroquois (ir′ə kwoi). A group of Indian tribes that were loosely united in a league for both defense and offense. These were the Seneca, Cayuga, Onondaga, Oneida, and Mohawk tribes, and later also the Tuscarora. (See page 57.)

PRONUNCIATION KEY: hat, āge, cāre, fär; let, ēqual, tėrm; it, īce; hot, ōpen, ôrder; oil, out; cup, put, rüle, ūse; child; long; thin; ᴛʜen; zh, measure; ə represents a in about, e in taken, i in pencil, o in lemon, u in circus. For the complete key, see page 361.

irrigate. To supply land with water by artificial rather than natural means. Ditches, canals, pipelines, and sprinklers are common means of irrigation.

Islam (is'ləm). One of the world's major religions. Islam was founded by an Arabian prophet named Mohammed, who was born in A.D. 570. According to this faith, which was derived from Judaism, there is only one God, called Allah, and Mohammed is his prophet. Followers of Islam are called Moslems. See **Judaism**.

Jew. A person who follows the religion of Judaism. Also, someone descended from a people who lived in Palestine from the sixth century B.C. until the first century A.D. See **Judaism**.

Judaism (jü'di iz əm). One of the world's major religions. It is based on the teachings of the Old Testament, and on the Talmud, which is an interpretation of these teachings. Followers of Judaism are called Jews. The main beliefs of Judaism are that there is only one God, and that the Jews are God's chosen people. Two other major world religions, Christianity and Islam, are derived from Judaism.

kerosene (ker'ə sēn). An oily liquid generally obtained from petroleum. Much of the kerosene now being produced is mixed with gasoline and used as fuel for jet-aircraft engines. In many areas where there is no electricity, kerosene is still used as a fuel for lamps and stoves. It is also used in the manufacture of liquids for killing insects.

kilometer. A unit of measurement equal to about two thirds of a mile. See **centimeter**.

limestone. A common rock that occurs in various colors. Since limestone is easily cut into blocks, it is often used as a building stone. The better grades, which are usually white, tan, or light gray in color, are used for this purpose. Large amounts of limestone are made into cement. Limestone is also used in the production of iron and steel.

livestock. Farm animals, such as cattle, hogs, sheep, horses, and poultry.

loam. A fertile, crumbly soil that is a mixture of clay, sand, and humus. Humus is decayed animal and vegetable matter.

loamy. See **loam**.

lock. A section of a canal or river that is used to raise or lower ships from one water level to another. Gates at each end permit ships to enter or leave the lock. When a ship is in the lock, the gates are closed. The water level in the lock is raised or lowered to the level of the part of the canal or river toward which the ship is bound. Then the gates in front of the ship are opened, and the ship passes out of the lock.

Long Island. A large island in the Atlantic Ocean that extends about 120 miles eastward from New York Bay. (See map, page 301.) Much of New York City is located on this island.

Long Island Sound. An inlet of the Atlantic Ocean that lies between Connecticut, on the north, and Long Island, on the south. (See map, page 301.)

loom. A frame or machine for weaving two or more sets of threads into cloth.

lubricants (lü'brə kənts). Substances, such as oil and grease, that are used to reduce the amount of heat and wear produced when two solid objects rub together. For example, certain parts of lawnmowers and sewing machines must be coated with oil as a lubricant so they will work easily.

lubricate (lü'brə kāt). To apply a lubricant to something, such as a machine, to make it run smoothly. See **lubricants**.

machine tools. Power-driven machines that cut, grind, or bore holes through metal to produce parts needed in making other machines.

majority (mə jôr'ə ti) **vote.** The voting procedure in which the larger part of the total votes cast determines a decision or choice. Usually, any number over half is considered a majority.

Manhattan. One of the five boroughs into which New York City is divided. The Borough of Manhattan consists mainly of an island, also called Manhattan, that lies at the mouth of the Hudson River. (See bottom map, page 205.) It also includes several very small islands nearby.

Mann, Horace, 1796-1859. A Massachusetts-born lawyer, politician, and educator who made important contributions to our American system of public education. As a leader in his state legislature, Horace Mann helped Massachusetts to establish the first state board of education in our country. Mann then accepted a position as secretary of the new board. Many of the improvements he made in the Massachusetts school system influenced educators in other parts of the United States. For example, Mann established the first state teacher-training school in our country. Soon, other states established similar schools. Mann later served in the United States House of Representatives. At the time of his death, he was president of Antioch College, in Yellow Springs, Ohio.

Megalopolis (meg′ ə lop′ə lis). A densely populated area that lies along the Atlantic Coast between northern Virginia and southern New Hampshire. (See map, page 197.)

menhaden (men hā′dən). The most abundant fish along the Atlantic coast of the United States. Menhaden are chiefly used to make fertilizer, livestock feed, and oil.

Mercator (mer kā′tər) **projection.** One of many possible arrangements of meridians and parallels on which a map of the world may be drawn. It was devised by Gerhardus Mercator, a Flemish geographer who lived from 1512 to 1594. On a Mercator map, all meridians are drawn straight up and down, with north at the top. The parallels are drawn straight across, but increasingly farther apart toward the poles. If you will compare the first section, or gore, of the "orange-peel" map on page 356 with the section of the Mercator map directly below it, you will see how the Mercator map straightens out the meridians. Because the earth features have been stretched in an east-west direction, except at the equator, they appear wider in the Mercator section than they do in the "orange-peel" section. To make up for this east-west stretching, earth features on the Mercator map are also stretched in a north-south direction. Therefore, on Mercator maps the shapes of landmasses and bodies of water are fairly accurate, but their sizes are not.

metropolitan (met′rə pol′ə tən) **area.** A densely populated area that includes at least one large central city. In addition to the central city, a metropolitan area usually includes several neighboring towns and settled sections. For example, the New York metropolitan area includes New York City, the rest of Long Island, and two counties north of New York City.

Middle Atlantic states. One of the two groups of states into which the Northeast may be divided. The Middle Atlantic states are New York, Pennsylvania, New Jersey, Delaware, Maryland, and West Virginia.

middle latitudes. Regions of the earth that lie generally between the 30 and 60 degree parallels of latitude in both the Northern and Southern hemispheres.

Midwest. A part of the United States. The Midwest includes the states of Illinois, Indiana, Iowa, Michigan, Minnesota, Missouri, Ohio, and Wisconsin. (See map, page 21.)

migration. The movement of people out of one region or country and into another, with the intention of making it their permanent home.

mineral. Any of various substances found in the earth that have a definite chemical composition. Diamonds and coal are examples of minerals.

missile. A self-propelled weapon, such as a bomb or a rocket. Missiles are guided by electronic devices. See **electronic.**

monadnock (mə nad′nok). An isolated mountain that remains after the surrounding mountainous area has been worn down by wind and rainfall. (See page 282.)

monarch (mon′ərk). A king, queen, emperor, or other ruler who usually inherits his position.

nationality. A large group of people with the same background and history. Usually, the members of a nationality speak the same language and live in the same geographical area. Examples of nationalities are the English, the French, and the Dutch.

national origin. Generally refers to the country where a person was born, or where his parents or grandparents were born.

National Road. For many years, the main American road leading westward from the Atlantic coast. The first section of this road, which was begun in 1811 and completed in 1818, connected Cumberland, in western Maryland, with Wheeling, in what is now West Virginia. This section was known as the Cumberland Road. Later, the road was extended westward to Vandalia, in south central Illinois. It was then known as the National Road.

natural gas. A gas found in layers of sand or rock beneath the surface of the earth. Natural gas is used as a fuel and as a raw material for the manufacture of many chemicals.

natural resources. The things in nature that are useful to man. Natural resources include soil, water, minerals, forests, air, and sunshine.

Nazi (nät′si). Refers to the National Socialist Party. This anti-democratic political party controlled Germany from 1933 to 1945, with Adolf Hitler as leader of the party and dictator of the country. Under the Nazis, who believed Germans were superior to other people, Germany attempted to gain control of much of the world.

New England. One of the two groups of states into which the Northeast may be divided. New England is made up of Maine, New Hampshire, Vermont, Massachusetts, Connecticut, and Rhode Island.

Newfoundland. A large island that lies off the Atlantic coast of North America, opposite the mouth of the St. Lawrence River. The island forms part of the Canadian province of Newfoundland.

newsprint. An inexpensive, coarse paper made mostly from wood pulp. It is mainly used for newspapers.

New York Bay. An arm of the Atlantic Ocean, at the mouth of the Hudson River. (See map, page 205.)

New York Metropolitan Region. A heavily populated district that includes New York City and a number of nearby cities and towns. Most of the New York Metropolitan Region is in New York State, but parts of it lie in New Jersey and Connecticut. (See page 205.)

New York State Barge Canal. A system of canals that enables boats to travel between the Hudson River and Lake Erie. The main part of this system is an improvement of the old Erie Canal. (See **Erie Canal.**) Branch canals connect the Erie Canal with Lake Ontario, Lake Champlain, and several other lakes. (See map, page 181.)

noble. A person who is entitled to hold high rank or title, usually by reason of his birth into a specially favored social class.

nonmetallic minerals. Minerals that are useful to man for purposes other than the production of metals. Examples of nonmetallic minerals that are important in industry are sulfur, salt, graphite, and limestone.

North. In American history, refers to the states and territories that supported the Union during the Civil War period. See **Civil War.**

Northern Hemisphere (hem′ə sfir). The half of the earth that is north of the equator. See **equator.**

Nova Scotia (nō′və skō′shə). A province in eastern Canada. It is made up of Cape Breton Island and a peninsula that extends into the Atlantic Ocean.

novel. A long story, usually telling about imaginary characters and events.

nuclear (nü′kli ər). Refers to the production or use of atomic energy. See **atomic energy.**

nursery. A place where young trees, plants, and shrubs are raised, either for later transplanting or for sale.

open-hearth furnace. A huge, oven-like furnace in which steel is made. In an open-hearth furnace, the raw materials are exposed directly to the flames that melt them.

opera. A musical play that is entirely or mostly sung by the actors, accompanied by orchestra music. Operas usually have elaborate scenery and costumes.

optical. Relating to the eyes. Also, refers to goods used for aiding eyesight or for examining the eyes. Eyeglasses and telescopes are examples of optical goods.

orbit. The path followed by one object as it revolves around another. For example, the path followed by the earth as it moves around the sun is its orbit.

ore. Rock or other material that contains enough of some valuable substance, such as a metal, to make it worth mining.

orographic (ôr′ə graf′ik). Refers to rainfall produced when warm air rises to cross over a mountain range. (See pages 50 and 51.)

oxygen (ok′sə jən). A colorless, odorless, tasteless gas that makes up about one fifth of the earth's atmosphere. In combination with other substances, oxygen is found in all plants and animals, in water, and in many kinds of rock.

Panama Canal. An artificial waterway built across the Isthmus of Panama to connect the Atlantic Ocean with the Pacific Ocean. It was completed in 1914.

panhandle. A relatively narrow strip of territory that extends into another area.

parallel. Any imaginary circle drawn east and west around the earth, connecting all points of the same latitude. Also, such a line drawn on a map or globe. Lines of latitude are called parallels because they are always parallel to the equator. (See page 355.)

Parliament (pär′lə mənt). Britain's highest lawmaking body.

pasteurize (pas′chə rīz). To heat a liquid such as milk to a high temperature and then chill it rapidly. This process kills harmful germs.

patented. Refers to an invention that has received an official government grant, called a patent. A patent guarantees that no one except the owner can make or sell the invention for a certain number of years.

pelt. The skin of an animal that has wool, hair, or fur. Usually means the skin as it is taken from the animal, before it is cleaned and ready to be used.

peninsula (pə nin′sə lə). An area of land that is almost surrounded by water and is connected to a larger body of land.

per capita income. A country's per capita income is the total income of all the people divided by the number of people in the country.

persecute. To do harm to certain persons or cause them to suffer, usually because of their beliefs.

petrochemicals (pet′rō kem′ə kəlz). Chemicals obtained from petroleum or natural gas. Petrochemicals are used in making hundreds of products, such as paint, fertilizer, and synthetic rubber.

petroleum. A thick, oily liquid obtained from the earth. Used to make gasoline, kerosene, asphalt, and many other products. Petroleum is usually dark brown or greenish black in color.

Piedmont (pēd′mont) **Plateau.** A section of the Appalachian Highlands that extends from New York into Alabama. (See map, page 27.) Land in the Piedmont is gently rolling.

pipeline. A line of pipes connected to form one long, continuous pipe. Used for transporting water, oil, gas, and other substances. Many pipelines are more than 1,000 miles long. Pumps and other devices on the pipeline control the flow of the gas or liquid passing through it.

plantation. A large farm, usually located in regions with a warm climate, where crops such as cotton or tobacco are grown. Generally, the work on a plantation is done by large numbers of laborers who live there.

plateau (pla tō′). A large, generally level area of high land.

pollute. To make something dirty or impure.

Poor Richard's Almanac. An almanac published by Benjamin Franklin each year for twenty-five years. These books, which Franklin wrote under the pen name of Richard Saunders, contained recipes, poems, and information about such things as weather and tides. Many of Franklin's clever sayings first appeared in *Poor Richard's Almanac.*

pope. The head of the Roman Catholic Church. See **Roman Catholic.**

population density. See **density of population.**

prejudice. An opinion or attitude that is formed before all of the facts are known. The dislike of an individual just because he happens to belong to a minority group is a common kind of prejudice.

process. To treat foods or other substances in some special way to make them more useful. For example, corn is said to be processed when it is canned, frozen, or made into products such as flour and cereal.

PRONUNCIATION KEY: hat, āge, cāre, fär; let, ēqual, tėrm; it, īce; hot, ōpen, ôrder; oil, out; cup, put, rüle, ūse; child; long; thin; ᴛʜen; zh, measure; ə represents a in about, e in taken, i in pencil, o in lemon, u in circus. For the complete key, see page 361.

371

Proclamation of 1763. An order by the British King that prohibited the American colonists from settling west of the Appalachian Mountains.

proprietor (prə prī′ə tər). The owner of a business. In American history, a person granted ownership and control of a colony by the British government.

prose. All writing that is not poetry.

Protestant. Refers to one of the three main branches of Christianity. (See **Roman Catholic** and **Eastern Orthodox**.) Also, a member of any one of the many different Protestant groups, such as the Methodist, Baptist, or Presbyterian denominations. The oldest Protestant churches date from the early sixteenth century.

prune. To cut off dead or useless parts of a tree, bush, or other plant. Usually, a plant is pruned to give it a better shape or to aid its growth.

publish. To issue a book, pamphlet, magazine, newspaper, or other material in printed form.

Puerto Rico (pwer′tō rē′kō). An island about one thousand miles southeast of Florida. Since 1952, Puerto Rico has been a self-governing commonwealth associated with the United States.

pulp. A soft, damp material usually made from wood or rags. It consists of many tiny threads, or fibers. Pulp is used in making paper and other products.

pulpwood. Wood that is used to make pulp. Trees commonly cut for pulpwood include pine, hemlock, spruce, and aspen.

Quaker. A member of a Christian group called the Society of Friends. Quakers have no uniform creed. In general, however, they believe in living and dressing simply, and they refuse to take any active part in war.

quarry. An open pit in the earth from which stone is taken.

quota. When referring to immigration, quota means the number of immigrants who are legally allowed to enter one country from another country during a given period of time.

radar (rā′där). An electronic system used mainly for determining the location and speed of a moving object such as an airplane.

ratify. Give official approval.

raw materials. Substances that can be manufactured into useful products. For example, flax is the raw material used to make linen cloth.

raw sugar. A form of sugar obtained by processing the juice squeezed from sugarcane. It is yellowish brown in color because the sugar crystals are covered with a thin film of molasses. Raw sugar is refined to produce the white sugar sold in stores.

rayon. Refers to man-made fibers produced by treating cellulose with chemicals. Cellulose is the material that forms the woody part of plants. Rayon also refers to cloth made from rayon fibers.

refine. To separate a useful substance from worthless materials or impurities.

refinery. A place where something is refined. Usually, the building and equipment used for refining metals, sugar, or petroleum. In a zinc refinery, for example, zinc is separated from waste materials in the zinc ore and purified. In a petroleum refinery, crude oil is separated into gasoline, kerosene, and other useful products.

refugee (ref′yə jē′). A person who flees to a foreign country to escape persecution or other danger.

repeal. To abolish, or do away with.

reservation. An area of land owned by the government and set aside for some special use. Especially, such an area set aside for use by Indians.

reservoir (rez′ər vwär). A lake, either natural or man-made, that stores large quantities of water until it is needed. The water may be used in homes, in manufacturing, or for irrigating dry land.

retail (rē′tāl). Refers to stores that sell goods directly to the person who will use the product. Grocery stores and department stores are examples of retail stores.

Revolutionary War, 1775-1783. The war in which thirteen British colonies in America won their independence from Great Britain. (See Chapter 5.)

Roman Catholic. Refers to a church which is one of the three main branches of Christianity, or to members of this church. (See **Eastern Orthodox** and **Protestant**.) The pope is the head of the

Roman Catholic Church, which has its headquarters, called the Vatican, in Rome.

St. Lawrence River. A river about 750 miles long that flows northeastward from Lake Ontario to the Gulf of St. Lawrence, a bay of the Atlantic Ocean. The St. Lawrence is the main outlet of the Great Lakes. See **Great Lakes–St. Lawrence Waterway.**

St. Lawrence Seaway. See **Great Lakes–St. Lawrence Waterway.**

sardine. A small, saltwater fish related to the herring. Young sardines are preserved in oil, canned, and sold as food. Tiny herring and other small fish are sometimes prepared in the same way and sold as sardines.

satellite. A body in space that revolves around a larger body. For example, the moon is a satellite of our planet, earth. The word satellite is also used for any man-made object that is sent into orbit around the earth or some other heavenly body.

scallop (skol′əp). Any of several clamlike shellfish. The muscle that opens and closes the scallop's shell is used for food.

scrap. Metal that is thrown away. Steel scrap is generally used to replace part of the iron ore needed to make steel. Each ton of steel scrap used saves two tons of iron ore.

secede (si sēd′). To withdraw from an organization, or to declare oneself no longer part of it.

secondary school. Any school above the elementary level but below the college level. A high school.

Second Continental Congress. See **Continental Congress.**

second growth. Refers to a forest that has grown naturally after the original forest was cut down or burned.

seed potatoes. Potatoes that are grown for sale as seed. Seed potatoes may be planted whole, or they may be cut into small sections for planting. Each section must contain at least one bud, called an eye, in order to produce a potato plant.

segregation. The separation of a minority group from other people, either by law or by custom. In the United States, for example, many Negroes attend schools where there are few, if any, white children. Although segregation in schools has been ruled unconstitutional, many all-Negro schools remain because they are located in neighborhoods where there are no white people. This is known as *de facto* segregation.

shad. Any of several important food fishes of Europe and North America, related to the herring.

shellfish. Any animal, such as a shrimp or an oyster, that lives in water and is covered by a shell or a bony skeleton. Shellfish do not have backbones, gills, or fins.

silage (sī′lij). Livestock feed consisting of chopped cornstalks or other green fodder that has been stored in an airtight structure called a silo. Silos, which are usually cylinder-shaped, may be built of various materials such as wood, metal, or concrete blocks. In the silo, part of the green material ferments. This helps to preserve the silage as a feed for cattle and other animals in wintertime.

slate. A dark-colored rock, usually bluish gray, that splits easily into thin layers. Slate is used to make shingles, blackboards, and other items.

slum. A crowded section of a town or city, where the houses and other buildings are old, dirty, and run-down, and most of the people are very poor.

smelt. To separate the metal from the other materials in ore by melting the ore in a special furnace.

smelter. A place where smelting is done. Also, a furnace in which ore is smelted. See **smelt.**

smuggle. To take goods out of a country or into a country without paying required taxes.

PRONUNCIATION KEY: hat, āge, cāre, fär; let, ēqual, tèrm; it, īce; hot, ōpen, ôrder; oil, out; cup, pu̇t, rüle, ūse; child; long; thin; ᴛʜen; zh, measure; ə represents a in about, e in taken, i in pencil, o in lemon, u in circus. For the complete key, see page 361.

soda ash. An important basic chemical used in the manufacture of products such as soap, glass, and paper. It is also used in the manufacture of various chemicals and chemical products. Soda ash is commonly made from salt by a rather complicated method called the Solvay process.

solstice (sol'stis). Either of two times of the year when the direct rays of the sun are farthest from the equator. This occurs about June 21, when the sun shines directly on the Tropic of Cancer, and about December 22, when the sun shines directly on the Tropic of Capricorn. See **Tropic of Cancer** and **Tropic of Capricorn.**

sound. A passage of water that separates an island from the mainland, or that connects two larger bodies of water. A sound may also be an arm or inlet of the ocean.

South. A region of the United States, which includes Alabama, Arkansas, Florida, Georgia, Kentucky, Louisiana, Mississippi, North Carolina, South Carolina, Tennessee, and Virginia. "South" also refers to the states that opposed the Union in the Civil War. See **Civil War.**

Southern Hemisphere (hem'ə sfir). The half of the earth that is south of the equator. See **equator.**

soybean. A bushy plant of the pea family. It has hairy stems, leaves, and pods. Soybeans are raised as a farm crop in many parts of our country. The beans and oil pressed from the beans are used to make foods, paint, and many other products. The green plants are sometimes used as feed for livestock. They may also be plowed into a field to enrich the soil.

spacecraft. A vehicle designed to fly beyond the earth's atmosphere.

square inch. A unit for measuring area, equal to the area of a square that measures one inch on each side.

square mile. A unit for measuring area, equal to the area of a square that measures one mile on each side. One square mile contains 640 acres. See **acre.**

standard of living. The average level of conditions in a community or a country, or the level of conditions that people consider necessary for a happy, satisfying life. Among the factors considered in determining standard of living are the general living and working conditions of the people, and the amount and kind of things they possess. In countries with a high standard of living, many different goods and services are generally considered to be necessities. In countries with a low standard of living, many of these same items are luxuries enjoyed by only a few people.

steel. A strong, hard metal that consists mainly of iron, mixed with a small amount of carbon. Different kinds of steel contain different amounts of carbon, but always less than 2 percent. Special steels also contain other substances. For example, stainless steel may contain as much as 18 percent of the metal chromium and 8 percent nickel.

stock. The total capital of a corporation. (See **capital.**) The stock of a company is usually divided into small portions called shares. To invest money in such a business, a person may buy one or more shares. He thus owns part of the business. When a person buys shares of stock in various companies, he is said to buy stocks.

stock exchange. A place where stocks and bonds are bought and sold. Also, an association of dealers in stocks and bonds.

suburb. An outer part of a city, or a smaller community near a city.

suburban. Refers to suburbs. See **suburb.**

sulfuric (sul fyūr'ik) **acid.** A heavy, colorless, oily liquid that is widely used in manufacturing. Sulfuric acid is a strong acid that eats away many materials. It is used in refining petroleum and in making fertilizer, chemicals, steel, explosives, and plastics.

Supreme Court. The highest court in the United States.

surveyor. A person who determines the exact size and location of a piece of land.

suspension bridge. A bridge hung from large cables. The cables are fastened to high towers on each side of the water or gap to be bridged.

synthetic (sin thet'ik). Refers to certain man-made substances, such as plastics and nylon, developed to replace similar natural materials.

talc. A soft, nonmetallic mineral that may be white, gray, or greenish in color. Talc has a soapy or greasy feel. It is used in the manufacture of products such as paint, paper, soap, and talcum powder.

tannery. A place where animal hides or skins are treated to make leather.

tariff. A duty, or tax, that must be paid on articles brought into or taken out of a country.

telegraph. Refers to an electrical system for communicating over long distances by wire. Telegraph messages, called telegrams, are transmitted by means of coded signals.

tenement. An apartment building occupied by many families. Usually, a tenement is in a run-down condition and is occupied by families that do not have much money.

terminus. The end of a transportation route.

textile. Refers to woven cloth or the yarn used to weave cloth.

three-dimensional (də men'shə nəl). Having length, width, and height.

thresh. Separate the grain from the husks and stems of the plant.

tidal flat. A low, flat, coastal area that is underwater during periods of high tide.

tinplate. Thin sheets of steel that have been coated with tin.

toll. A tax or fee charged for a privilege such as the use of a highway or bridge.

topographic (top'ə graf'ik). Refers to the physical features of an area, such as lakes, rivers, and hills. A topographic map shows the elevation of these features and their location in relation to each other.

topsoil. The top layer of soil on the earth's surface. It is seldom much more than one foot deep. Normally, topsoil is more fertile than the soil beneath it, because it contains a larger amount of decayed plant material.

traitor. A person who betrays his country.

transfer point. A place where connections can be made between transportation routes of various kinds.

trap. A device for catching wild animals or fish.

treaty. An agreement, usually written, between two or more independent governments.

tributary (trib'yə ter'i). A stream or river that flows into a larger stream or a lake.

tropical. Refers to the tropics, which is the part of the earth that lies between the Tropic of Cancer and the Tropic of Capricorn. (See top chart, page 42.) The weather in the tropics is generally hot all year round.

Tropic of Cancer. An imaginary line around the earth, about 1,600 miles north of the equator. (See top chart, page 42.)

Tropic of Capricorn. An imaginary line around the earth, about 1,600 miles south of the equator. (See top chart, page 42.)

truck farm. A farm on which vegetables are raised to be sold. One meaning of the word "truck" is to trade things. Formerly, vegetables often were traded for other products.

trust company. A bank or other company that has the legal authority to take care of money and property for other people.

tugboat. A small boat with a powerful engine. Tugboats are used to tow huge ocean liners safely into port.

turnpike. A highway for the use of which a fee, or toll, is charged. Early in our country's history, certain roads were blocked by long poles placed at various points where a toll had to be paid. On these poles were sharp points called pikes. When a traveler paid his toll, the pole at that point was turned aside so he could pass. Because these poles were called turnpikes, toll roads also came to be known as turnpikes.

unconstitutional (un'kon stə tü'shə nəl). Contrary to a constitution. Especially, contrary to the Constitution of the United States.

Union. The United States. When used in referring to the Civil War period, means the states that did not secede.

United Kingdom. Short name for the United Kingdom of Great Britain and Northern Ireland. A country in western Europe made up of England, Scotland, Wales, and Northern Ireland. See **Great Britain.**

United Nations. An organization formed in 1945 to work for world peace. More than 125 nations are members. Agencies related to the United Nations work to solve problems in such fields as health, agriculture, and labor.

urban. Refers to cities or other heavily populated areas as opposed to small towns or rural areas.

urban renewal. The improvement of a city or other urban area by clearing away slums and replacing them with modern buildings, playgrounds, or parks.

vegetation. Any plant life, such as trees, grass, shrubs, and flowers.

Verrazano (ver ə zän′ō), **Giovanni da,** 1485?-?1528. An Italian navigator who explored for the French. In 1524 he explored part of the eastern coast of North America.

vineyard (vin′yərd). A place where grapevines have been planted.

Wall Street. A short, narrow street in New York City, on or near which many banks and other financial institutions are located. It is the headquarters of much of the nation's business activity. In the 1600's, the Dutch of New Amsterdam built a wall at this place to protect their town from attack. The wall is gone, but the street is still called Wall Street.

weather. The condition of the atmosphere at a given time and place. A description of weather includes such things as wind, sunshine, temperature, and moisture. The average weather conditions of a particular place over a long period of time make up its climate. See **climate.**

West Indies. A group of islands located between North America and South America. (See top map, page 61.) Cuba is the largest island in the West Indies.

whiting. A silver-colored food fish caught along the Atlantic coast of the United States, from Maine to Virginia.

Whitney, Eli, 1765-1825. An American inventor and manufacturer. Whitney is perhaps best known for his invention of the cotton gin, a machine for cleaning the seeds from cotton fibers. Whitney also developed tools and machines that could be used to produce parts for guns. (See pages 92 and 93.)

wholesale. Refers to companies that sell large quantities of goods to smaller companies and stores for resale. For example, a wholesale drug company in New York would buy a large quantity of drugs direct from the manufacturer. The wholesale company would then package the drugs and sell them to drugstores throughout the country. See **retail.**

wigwam. The kind of house built by some of the Indians who originally lived in the eastern part of the United States. Wigwams were usually dome-shaped. They were made by covering a framework of poles with bark, hides, or mats made of rushes.

wood pulp. See **pulp.**

World War I, 1914-1918. The first war in history which involved nearly every part of the world. (See page 120.)

World War II, 1939-1945. The second war in history which involved nearly every part of the world. (See page 124.)

writ. During the colonial period of American history, a legal document in the form of a letter, issued in the name of the English king.

yarn. A thread or a strand of twisted threads used in weaving cloth. Knitted materials are also made from yarn.

yield. Amount produced. In farming, yield is often expressed as the average number of bushels of a crop produced per acre of land.

zinc. A silvery, bluish white metal that has great commercial importance. Zinc resists rust and is used chiefly as a protective coating over other metals, especially iron and steel.

INDEX

Explanation of abbreviations used in this Index:
p — pictures   *m* — maps   *t* — tables

PRONUNCIATION KEY: hat, āge, cãre, fär; let, ēqual, tėrm; it, īce; hot, ōpen, ôrder; oil, out; cup, pùt, rüle, ūse; child; long; thin; ᴛнen; zh, measure; ə represents a in about, e in taken, i in pencil, o in lemon, u in circus. For the complete key, see page 361.

PRONUNCIATION KEY: hat, āge, cãre, fär; let, ēqual, tėrm; it, īce; hot, ōpen, ôrder; oil, out; cup, pùt, rüle, ūse; child; long; thin; ŦHen; zh, measure; ə represents a in about, e in taken, i in pencil, o in lemon, u in circus. For the complete key, see page 361.

Hitler, Adolf, 124
Holyoke, Massachusetts, 272, 276; *m* 272
Homer, Winslow, 230
Hooker, Thomas, 65-66; *p* 65
Housatonic River, 235; *m* 181
Howe, Elias, 103
Howells, William Dean, 230
Hudson, Henry, 66
Hudson-Mohawk Lowland, 198, 206, 300, 312
Hudson River, 32, 99, 132, 182, 203, 209, 288, 289, 300, 312; *m* 301
Huntington, West Virginia, 342, 344; *m* 339
hydroelectricity, 26, 149, 258, 274, 284, 300, 304-305, 335; *p* 131, 304

immigrants, 103, 105, 117-119, 186-189, 192-193, 194, 200-201, 206, 240, 261, 278, 280, 287, 295, 308, 322; *p* 118, 188, 189, 192; *chart* 187
Indians, *see* history
Industrial Revolution, 88, 89, 90-91, 112, 125; *m* 91
industry, 22-23, 143-156, 203, 206, 207, 208; *p* 143, 145-150, 153-155; *m* 151
  after the Civil War, 112-115
  capital for, 144, 148, 362
  chemical, 154-155, 246-247, 266, 292, 307, 319, 322-323, 341-342; *p* 154, 246, 291
  clay and glass, 307, 342; *p* 341
  clothing, 103, 155, 206, 247, 275, 276, 305-306, 319; *p* 155, 206, 276
  development of, 88, 90-91, 92-93, 96, 103, 105
  electrical machinery, 152, 239, 275, 286, 292-293, 306, 319, 336; *p* 275, 285
  electronic equipment, 153, 239, 275, 285-286, 319, 329, 336; *p* 297
  fishing, 140-142, 258-259, 265, 273-274, 290-291, 328; *p* 258, 259, 265, 328; *chart* 142
  food processing, 156, 208, 247, 258-259, 266, 274, 275, 291, 293, 306-307, 319, 336, 342; *p* 259, 292
  furniture, 305, 307
  in colonial times, 70
  iron and steel, 103, 112-113, 120, 128, 135, 143-147, 152, 266, 317-318, 342; *p* 111, 113, 127, 143, 145, 146, 266, 317
  leather, 156, 247, 276, 285, 307

machinery, 152-153, 238, 274-275, 306, 318-319, 336; *p* 153, 275, 306, 318
  metal, 152-154, 247, 275, 293, 319, 329, 342
  oil refining, 114, 120, 136, 154, 293
  photographic equipment, 307, 310
  printing and publishing, 206, 207, 276, 287, 297, 305, 323; *p* 305
  pulp and paper, 138, 258, 286, 305, 307, 336; *p* 284
  textile, 88, 92, 103, 122, 155, 199, 247, 259, 275-276, 285, 297-298, 319, 329; *p* 90, 92, 276
  tourist, 286, 293-294, 337
  transportation equipment, 153-154, 238, 247, 259, 266-267, 293, 298, 307, 319; *p* 147, 238
Inness, George, 230
Intolerable Acts, 78
inventions, 90, 100, 102-103, 112, 114-115, 120-121, 125, 310
Irving, Washington, 228; *p* 228

James, Henry, 230
Jamestown, Virginia, 62
Jay, John, 227
Jefferson, Thomas, 80, 84; *p* 80, 84
Jefferson Memorial, 251, 334; *m* 252
Jerimoth Hill, 327; *m* 327
Jersey City, New Jersey, 296-297; *p* 296; *m* 289
John F. Kennedy International Airport, 204, 208; *p* 179; *m* 205

Kanawha River, 339, 341, 344; *m* 339
Kelly, William, 112
Kennebec River, 256, 260, 261; *m* 256
Kennedy, John F., 194, 232, 253
Key, Francis Scott, 95; *p* 97
Kittery, Maine, 259; *m* 256

La Guardia Airport, 208; *m* 205
Lake Candlewood, 235; *p* 235; *m* 236
Lake Champlain, 95, 302, 332; *p* 96; *m* 333
Lake Erie, 31-32, 33, 182, 300, 309, 310, 325; *m* 101, 181

Lake Erie Lowland, 315, 319, 321
Lake Ontario, 31-32, 300, 310; *m* 181
Lake Superior, 317; *m* 19
Lake Winnipesaukee, 282; *m* 282
Lancaster, Pennsylvania, 99; *m* 101
Lancaster County, Pennsylvania, 168-170, 319, 320, 321; *p* 168
Lancaster Turnpike, 99; *p* 98; *m* 101
land, 24-39; *p* 24, 28-30, 32-34, 36-38; *m* 25, 27, 35, 38
  Fall Line, 34, 35; *m* 35
  highlands, 33-34, 36-37, 39
  lowlands, 25-26, 28-33
  See also names of states
Lebanon, Pennsylvania, 318; *m* 314
Lehigh River Valley, 325
Lexington, Massachusetts, 79, 80, 81; *p* 79; *m* 81, 272
Lincoln, Abraham, 108, 110; *p* 108, 109
Lincoln Memorial, 251; *m* 252
literature, *see* arts
Longfellow, Henry Wadsworth, 229
Long Island, 30, 164, 165, 208, 300, 303, 307-308, 368; *m* 301
Long Island Sound, 30, 234, 236, 242, 305, 368; *m* 236, 301
Louisiana Purchase, 104; *m* 104
Lowell, Massachusetts, 199; *m* 272

MacDowell, Edward, 230
Madison, James, 227
Maine, 255-261; *p* 255, 257-261; *m* 233, 256
  admission date, *t* 255
  area, *t* 255
  capital, 261; *m* 256
  cities, 261; *m* 256
  climate, 257-258
  colleges and universities, *t* 255
  farming, 259-260; *p* 47
  farm products, 260; *p* 47; *t* 255
  fisheries, 258-259; *p* 258; *t* 255; *chart* 142
  forest products, 258; *p* 257
  forests, 255-256, 258; *p* 255
  history, 66
  industry, 258-259; *p* 257, 259; *t* 255
  land, 255-257; *p* 255; *m* 256

PRONUNCIATION KEY: hat, āge, cāre, fär; let, ēqual, tėrm; it, īce; hot, ōpen, ôrder; oil, out; cup, pùt, rüle, ūse; child; long; thin; ŦHen; zh, measure; ə represents a in about, e in taken, i in pencil, o in lemon, u in circus. For the complete key, see page 361.

PRONUNCIATION KEY: hat, āge, cãre, fär; let, ēqual, tėrm; it, īce; hot, ōpen, ôrder; oil, out; cup, pút, rüle, ūse; child; long; thin; ŧHen; zh, measure; ə represents a in about, e in taken, i in pencil, o in lemon, u in circus. For the complete key, see page 361.

PRONUNCIATION KEY: hat, āge, cãre, fär; let, ēqual, tèrm; it, īce; hot, ōpen, ôrder; oil, out; cup, pùt, rüle, ūse; child; long; thin; ᴛʜen; zh, measure; ə represents a in about, e in taken, i in pencil, o in lemon, u in circus. For the complete key, see page 361.